OSF®DCE
Application Development Reference
Volume 2

Revision 1.1

Open Software Foundation

For book and bookstore information

http://www.prenhall.com

 Prentice Hall PTR, Upper Saddle River, New Jersey 07458

This book was formatted with troff

 Published by Prentice Hall P T R
A Division of Simon & Schuster
Upper Saddle River, New Jersey 07458

Printed in the United States of America
10   9   8   7   6   5   4   3   2

ISBN   0-13-241464-3

Prentice-Hall International (UK) Limited, *London*
Prentice-Hall of Australia Pty. Limited, *Sydney*
Prentice-Hall Canada Inc., *Toronto*
Prentice-Hall Hispanoamericana, S.A., *Mexico*
Prentice-Hall of India Private Limited, *New Delhi*
Prentice-Hall of Japan, Inc., *Tokyo*
Simon & Schuster Asia Pte. Ltd., *Singapore*
Editora Prentice-Hall do Brasil, Ltda., *Rio de Janeiro*

Contents

Preface

The *OSF DCE Application Development Reference* provides complete and detailed reference information to help application programmers use the correct syntax for Distributed Computing Environment (DCE) calls when writing UNIX applications for a distributed computing environment. It is divided into Volumes 1 and 2; this is Volume 2.

Audience

This document is written for application programmers who want to write Distributed Computing Environment applications for a UNIX environment.

Applicability

This is Revision 1.1 of this document. It applies to the OSF® DCE Version 1.1 offering and related updates. See your software license for details.

Purpose

The purpose of this document is to assist application programmers when writing UNIX applications for a distributed computing environment. After reading this manual, application programmers should be able to use the correct syntax for DCE calls.

Document Usage

The two volumes of this document are organized into six chapters.

- For DCE Routines, see Volume 1, Chapter 1.
- For DCE Remote Procedure Call, see Volume 1, Chapter 2.
- For DCE Directory Service, see Volume 1, Chapter 3.
- For DCE Threads, see Volume 2, Chapter 1.
- For DCE Distributed Time Service, see Volume 2, Chapter 2.
- For DCE Security Service, see Volume 2, Chapter 3.

Related Documents

For additional information about the Distributed Computing Environment, refer to the following documents:

- *Introduction to OSF DCE*
- *OSF DCE Command Reference*
- *OSF DCE Administration Guide—Introduction*
- *OSF DCE Administration Guide—Core Components*
- *OSF DCE DFS Administration Guide and Reference*
- *OSF DCE GDS Administration Guide and Reference*
- *OSF DCE Application Development Guide—Introduction and Style Guide*
- *OSF DCE Application Development Guide—Core Components*
- *OSF DCE Application Development Guide—Directory Services*
- *OSF DCE Problem Determination Guide*
- *OSF DCE Porting and Testing Guide*

Typographic and Keying Conventions

This document uses the following typographic conventions:

Bold	**Bold** words or characters represent system elements that you must use literally, such as commands, options, and pathnames.
Italic	*Italic* words or characters represent variable values that you must supply.
`Constant width`	Examples and information that the system displays appear in `constant width` typeface.
[]	Brackets enclose optional items in format and syntax descriptions.

{ }	Braces enclose a list from which you must choose an item in format and syntax descriptions.
|	A vertical bar separates items in a list of choices.
< >	Angle brackets enclose the name of a key on the keyboard.
...	Horizontal ellipsis points indicate that you can repeat the preceding item one or more times.

This document uses the following keying conventions:

<Ctrl-*x*> or ^*x*	The notation **<Ctrl-*x*>** or ^*x* followed by the name of a key indicates a control character sequence. For example, **<Ctrl-c>** means that you hold down the control key while pressing **<c>**.
<Return>	The notation **<Return>** refers to the key on your terminal or workstation that is labeled with the word Return or Enter, or with a left arrow.

Pathnames of Directories and Files in DCE Documentation

For a list of the pathnames for directories and files referred to in this document, see the *OSF DCE Administration Guide—Introduction* and the *OSF DCE Porting and Testing Guide*.

Problem Reporting

If you have any problems with the software or documentation, please contact your software vendor's customer service department.

Chapter 1

DCE Threads

thr_intro

Purpose   Introduction to DCE Threads

Description

DCE Threads is a set of routines that you can call to create a multithreaded program. Multithreading is used to improve the performance of a program. Routines implemented by DCE Threads that are not specified by Draft 4 of the POSIX 1003.4a standard are indicated by an **_np** suffix on the name. These routines are new primitives.

The threads routines sort alphabetically in the reference pages; however, the tables in this introduction list the routines in the following functional groups:

- Threads routines

- Routines that implicitly initialize threads package

- Attributes object routines

- Mutex routines

- Condition variable routines

- Thread-specific data routines

- Threads cancellation routines

- Threads priority and scheduling routines

- Cleanup routines

- The **atfork( )** routine

- Signal handling routines

Threads Routines	
Routine	**Description**
pthread_create( )	Creates a thread
pthread_delay_np( )	Causes a thread to wait for a period of time
pthread_detach( )	Marks a thread for deletion
pthread_equal( )	Compares one thread identifier to another thread identifier
pthread_exit( )	Terminates the calling thread
pthread_join( )	Causes the calling thread to wait for the termination of a specified thread
pthread_once( )	Calls an initialization routine to be executed only once
pthread_self( )	Obtains the identifier of the current thread
pthread_yield( )	Notifies the scheduler that the current thread will release its processor to other threads of the same or higher priority

The following DCE Threads routines will, when called, implicitly perform any necessary initialization of the threads package. Thus any application using DCE Threads should call one of the following routines before calling any other threads routines, in order to ensure that the package is properly initialized.

Routines that Implicitly Perform Threads Initialization	
Routine	**Description**
pthread_attr_create( )	Creates a thread attributes object
pthread_create( )	Creates a thread
pthread_self( )	Obtains the identifier of the current thread
pthread_setprio( )	Changes the scheduling priority attribute
pthread_getprio( )	Obtains the scheduling priority attribute
pthread_setscheduler( )	Changes the scheduling policy attribute
pthread_getscheduler( )	Obtains the scheduling policy attribute
pthread_once( )	Calls an initialization routine to be executed only once
pthread_keycreate( )	Generates a unique thread-specific data key value
pthread_mutexattr_create( )	Creates a mutex attributes object
pthread_mutex_init( )	Creates a mutex
pthread_condattr_create( )	Creates a condition variable attributes object
pthread_cond_init( )	Creates a condition variable
pthread_testcancel( )	Requests delivery of a pending cancel
pthread_setcancel( )	Enables or disables the current thread's general cancelability
pthread_setasynccancel( )	Enables or disables the current thread's asynchronous cancelability
pthread_delay_np( )	Causes a thread to wait for a period of time

Attributes Object Routines	
Routine	**Description**
pthread_attr_create( )	Creates a thread attributes object
pthread_attr_delete( )	Deletes a thread attributes object
pthread_attr_getinheritsched( )	Obtains the inherit scheduling attribute
pthread_attr_getprio( )	Obtains the scheduling priority attribute
pthread_attr_getsched( )	Obtains the scheduling policy attribute
pthread_attr_getstacksize( )	Obtains the stacksize attribute
pthread_attr_setinheritsched( )	Changes the inherit scheduling attribute
pthread_attr_setprio( )	Changes the scheduling priority attribute
pthread_attr_setsched( )	Changes the scheduling policy attribute
pthread_attr_setstacksize( )	Changes the stacksize attribute
pthread_condattr_create( )	Creates a condition variable attributes object
pthread_condattr_delete( )	Deletes a condition variable attributes object
pthread_mutexattr_create( )	Creates a mutex attributes object
pthread_mutexattr_delete( )	Deletes a mutex attributes object
pthread_mutexattr_getkind_np( )	Obtains the mutex type attribute
pthread_mutexattr_setkind_np( )	Changes the mutex type attribute

Mutex Routines	
Routine	**Description**
pthread_lock_global_np( )	Locks a global mutex
pthread_mutex_destroy( )	Deletes a mutex
pthread_mutex_init( )	Creates a mutex
pthread_mutex_lock( )	Locks a mutex and waits if the mutex is already locked
pthread_mutex_trylock( )	Locks a mutex and returns if the mutex is already locked
pthread_mutex_unlock( )	Unlocks a mutex
pthread_unlock_global_np( )	Unlocks a global mutex

Condition Variable Routines	
Routine	**Description**
pthread_cond_broadcast( )	Wakes all threads waiting on a condition variable
pthread_cond_destroy( )	Deletes a condition variable
pthread_cond_init( )	Creates a condition variable
pthread_cond_signal( )	Wakes one thread waiting on a condition variable
pthread_cond_timedwait( )	Causes a thread to wait for a specified period of time for a condition variable to be signaled or broadcast
pthread_cond_wait( )	Causes a thread to wait for a condition variable to be signaled or broadcast
pthread_get_expiration_np( )	Obtains a value representing a desired expiration time

Thread-Specific Data	
Routine	**Description**
pthread_getspecific( )	Obtains the thread-specific data associated with the specified key
pthread_keycreate( )	Generates a unique thread-specific data key value
pthread_setspecific( )	Sets the thread-specific data associated with the specified key

Threads Cancellation Routines	
Routine	**Description**
pthread_cancel( )	Allows a thread to request termination
pthread_setasynccancel( )	Enables or disables the current thread's asynchronous cancelability
pthread_setcancel( )	Enables or disables the current thread's general cancelability
pthread_signal_to_cancel_np( )	Cancels a thread if a signal is received by the process
pthread_testcancel( )	Requests delivery of a pending cancel

Threads Priority and Scheduling Routines	
Routine	**Description**
pthread_getprio( )	Obtains the current priority of a thread
pthread_getscheduler( )	Obtains the current scheduling policy of a thread
pthread_setprio( )	Changes the current priority of a thread
pthread_setscheduler( )	Changes the current scheduling policy and priority of a thread

Cleanup Routines	
Routine	**Description**
pthread_cleanup_pop( )	Removes a cleanup handler from the stack
pthread_cleanup_push( )	Establishes a cleanup handler

The atfork( ) Routine	
Routine	**Description**
atfork( )	Arranges for fork cleanup handling

Signal Handling Routines	
Routine	**Description**
sigaction( )	Specifies action to take on receipt of signal
sigpending( )	Examines pending signals
sigprocmask( )	Sets the current signal mask
sigwait( )	Causes thread to wait for asynchronous signal

threads data types

Purpose   Data types used by DCE Threads

Description

The DCE Threads data types can be divided into two broad categories: primitive system and application level.

Primitive System Data Types

The first category consists of types that represent structures used by (and internal to) DCE Threads. These types are defined as being primitive system data types.

- **pthread_attr_t**

- **pthread_cond_t**

- **pthread_condattr_t**

- **pthread_key_t**

- **pthread_mutex_t**

- **pthread_mutexattr_t**

- **pthread_once_t**

- **pthread_t**

Although applications must know about these types, passing them in and receiving them from various DCE Threads routines, the structures themselves are opaque: they cannot be directly modified by applications, and they can be manipulated only (and only in some cases) through specific DCE Threads routines. (The **pthread_key_t** type is somewhat different from the others in this list, in that it is essentially a handle to a thread-private block of memory requested by a call to **pthread_keycreate( )**.)

Application Level Data Types

The second category of DCE Threads data consists of types used to describe objects that originate in the application:

- **pthread_addr_t**

- **pthread_destructor_t**

- **pthread_initroutine_t**

- **pthread_startroutine_t**

- **sigset_t**

All of the above types, with the exception of the last, are various kinds of memory addresses that must be passed by callers of certain DCE Threads routines. These types are extensions to POSIX. They permit DCE Threads to be used on platforms that are not fully ANSI C compliant. While being extensions to permit the use of compilers that are not ANSI C compatible, they are fully portable data types.

The last data type, **sigset_t**, exhibits properties of both primitive system and application level data types. While objects of this type originate in the application, the data type is opaque. A set of functions is provided to manipulate objects of this type.

For further information, see the following descriptions, listed in sorted order.

DATA TYPE DESCRIPTIONS

Following are individual descriptions of each of the DCE Threads data types. The descriptions include the routines where the data type is modified, such as, created, changed or deleted/destroyed, but not the routines referencing or using them that do not change them.

- **pthread_addr_t**

  A miscellaneous data type representing an address value that must be passed by the caller of various threads routines. Usually the **pthread_addr_t** value is the address of an area which contains various parameters to be made accessible to an implicitly called routine. For example, when the **pthread_create()** routine is called, one of the parameters passed is a **pthread_addr_t** value that contains an address which will be passed to the *start_routine* which the thread is being created to execute; presumably the routine will extract necessary parameters from the area referenced by this address.

- **pthread_attr_t**

  Threads attribute object, used to specify the attributes of a thread when it is created by a call to **pthread_create()**. The object is created by a call to **pthread_attr_create()**, then modified as desired by calls to

  — **pthread_attr_setinheritsched()**

  — **pthread_attr_setprio()**

— **pthread_attr_setsched( )**

— **pthread_attr_setstacksize( )**

(Note that there are **_get** versions of these four calls, which can be used to retrieve the respective values.)

- **pthread_cond_t**

  Data type representing a threads condition variable. The variable is created by a call to **pthread_cond_init( )**, and destroyed by a call to **pthread_-cond_destroy( )**.

- **pthread_condattr_t**

  Data type representing a threads condition variable attributes object. Created by a call to **pthread_condattr_create( )**. The range of possible modifications to a condition variable attributes object is not great: creation (via **pthread_condattr_create( )**) and deletion (via **pthread_condattr_-delete( )**) are all. The object is created with default values.

- **pthread_destructor_t**

  Data type, passed in a call to **pthread_keycreate( )**, representing the address of a procedure to be called to destroy a data value associated with a unique thread-specific data key value when the thread terminates.

- **pthread_initroutine_t**

  Data type representing the address of a procedure that performs a one-time initialization for a thread. It is passed in a call to **pthread_once( )**. The **pthread_once( )** routine, when called, executes the initialization routine. The specified routine is *guaranteed to be executed only once*, even though the **pthread_once( )** call occurs in multithreaded code.

- **pthread_key_t**

  Data type representing a thread-specific data key, created by a call to **pthread_keycreate( )**. The key is an address of memory. Associating a static block of memory with a specific thread in this way is an alternative to using stack memory for the thread. The key is destroyed by the application-supplied procedure specified by the routine specified using the **pthread_destructor_t** data type in the call to **pthread_keycreate( )**.

- **pthread_mutex_t**

  Data type representing a mutex object. It is created by a call to **pthread_mutex_init( )** and destroyed by a call to **pthread_mutex_- destroy( )**. Care should be taken not to attempt to destroy a locked object.

- **pthread_mutexattr_t**

  Data type representing an attributes object which defines the characteristics of a mutex. Created by a call to **pthread_mutexattr_create( )**; modified by calls to **pthread_mutexattr_setkind_np( )** (which allows you to specify fast, recursive, or nonrecursive mutexes); passed to **pthread_mutex_init( )** to create the mutex with the specified atttributes. The only other modification allowed is to destroy the mutex attributes object, with **pthread_mutexattr_delete( )**.

- **pthread_once_t**

  A data structure that defines the characteristics of the one-time initialization routine executed by calling **pthread_once( )**. The structure is opaque to the application, and cannot be modified by it, but it must be explicitly declared by the client code, and initialized by a call to **pthread_once_init( )**. The **pthread_once_t** type must not be an array.

- **pthread_startroutine_t**

  Data type representing the address of the application routine or other routine, whatever it is, that a new thread is created to execute as its start routine.

- **pthread_t**

  Data type representing a thread handle, created by a call to **pthread_create( )**. The thread handle is used thenceforth to identify the thread to calls such as **pthread_cancel( )**, **pthread_detach( )**, **pthread_equal( )** (to which two handles are passed for comparison).

- **sigset_t**

  Data type representing a set of signals. It is always an integral or structure type. If a structure, it is intended to be a simple structure, such as, a set of arrays as opposed to a set of pointers. It is opaque in that a set of functions called the **sigsetops** primitives is provided to manipulate signal sets. They operate on signal set data objects addressable by the application, not on any objects known to the system.

The primitives are **sigemptyset( )** and **sigfillset( )** which initialize the set as either empty or full, **sigaddset( )** and **sigdelset( )** which add or delete signals from the set, and **sigismember( )** which permits the application to check if a object (signal) of type **sigset_t** is a mcmbcr of the signal set. Applications must call at least one of the initialization primitives at least once for each object of type **sigset_t** prior to any other use of that object (signal set).

The object, or objects, represented by this data type when used by **sigaction( )** is (are) used in conjunction with a **sigaction** structure by the **sigaction** function to describe an action to be taken with (a) specified **sigset_t**-type object(s).

atfork

Purpose   Arranges for fork cleanup handling

Synopsis   **#include <pthread.h>**

void atfork
        void (**user_state,
        void (**pre_fork*)( ),
        void (**parent_fork*)( ),
        void (**child_fork*)( ));

Parameters

user_state   Pointer to the user state that is passed to each routine.

pre_fork   Routine to be called before performing the fork.

parent_fork   Routine to be called in the parent after the fork.

child_fork   Routine to be called in the child after the fork.

Description

The **atfork( )** routine allows you to register three routines to be executed at different times relative to a fork. The different times and/or places are as follows:

- Just prior to the fork in the parent process.

- Just after the fork in the parent process.

- Just after the fork in the created (child) process.

Use these routines to clean up just prior to **fork( )**, to set up after **fork( )**, and to perform locking relative to **fork( )**. You are allowed to provide one parameter to be used in conjunction with all the routines. This parameter must be *user_state*.

Return Values

The **atfork( )** routine does not return a value. Instead, an exception is raised if there is insufficient table space to record the handler addresses.

Related Information

Functions: **fork(2)**.

exceptions

Purpose   Exception handling in DCE Threads

Description

DCE Threads provides the following two ways to obtain information about the status of a threads routine:

- The routine returns a status value to the thread.

- The routine raises an exception.

Before you write a multithreaded program, you must choose only one of the preceding two methods of receiving status. These two methods cannot be used together in the same code module.

The POSIX P1003.4a (pthreads) draft standard specifies that errors be reported to the thread by setting the external variable **errno** to an error code and returning a function value of -1. The threads reference pages document this status value-returning interface. However, an alternative to status values is provided by DCE Threads in the exception-returning interface.

Access to exceptions from the C language is defined by the macros in the **exc_handling.h** file. The **exc_handling.h** header file is included automatically when you include **pthread_exc.h.**

To use the exception-returning interface, replace **#include <pthread.h>** with the following include statement:

#include <dce/pthread_exc.h>

The following example shows the syntax for handling exceptions:

```
TRY
    try_block
[CATCH (exception_name)
    handler_block]...
[CATCH_ALL
    handler_block]
ENDTRY
```

pthread_attr_create

Purpose   Creates a thread attributes object

Synopsis   **#include <pthread.h>**

    int pthread_attr_create(
        pthread_attr_t *_attr_**);**

Parameters

    attr   Thread attributes object created.

Description

The **pthread_attr_create( )** routine creates a thread attributes object that is used to specify the attributes of threads when they are created. The attributes object created by this routine is used in calls to **pthread_create( )**.

The individual attributes (internal fields) of the attributes object are set to default values. (The default values of each attribute are discussed in the descriptions of the following services.) Use the following routines to change the individual attributes:

- **pthread_attr_setinheritsched( )**
- **pthread_attr_setprio( )**
- **pthread_attr_setsched( )**
- **pthread_attr_setstacksize( )**

When an attributes object is used to create a thread, the values of the individual attributes determine the characteristics of the new thread. Attributes objects perform in a manner similar to additional parameters. Changing individual attributes does not affect any threads that were previously created using the attributes object.

pthread_attr_create(3thr)

Return Values

If the function fails, -1 is returned and **errno** may be set to one of the following values:

Return	Error	Description
-1	[ENOMEM]	Insufficient memory exists to create the thread attributes object.
-1	[EINVAL]	The value specified by *attr* is invalid.

Related Information

Functions: **pthread_attr_delete(3thr)**, **pthread_attr_setinheritsched(3thr)**, **pthread_attr_setprio(3thr)**, **pthread_attr_setsched(3thr)**, **pthread_attr_setstacksize(3thr)**, **pthread_create(3thr)**.

pthread_attr_delete

Purpose   Deletes a thread attributes object

Synopsis   #include <pthread.h>

int pthread_attr_delete(
        pthread_attr_t *attr);

Parameters

attr   Thread attributes object deleted.

Description

The **pthread_attr_delete( )** routine deletes a thread attributes object and gives permission to reclaim storage for the thread attributes object. Threads that were created using this thread attributes object are not affected by the deletion of the thread attributes object.

The results of calling this routine are unpredictable if the value specified by the attr parameter refers to a thread attributes object that does not exist.

Return Values

If the function fails, **errno** may be set to one of the following values:

Return	Error	Description
0		Successful completion.
-1	**[EINVAL]**	The value specified by attr is invalid.

Related Information

Functions: **pthread_attr_create(3thr)**.

pthread_attr_getinheritsched

Purpose   Obtains the inherit scheduling attribute

Synopsis   **#include <pthread.h>**

int pthread_attr_getinheritsched(
        pthread_attr_t *attr*);

Parameters

attr   Thread attributes object whose inherit scheduling attribute is obtained.

Description

The **pthread_attr_getinheritsched( )** routine obtains the value of the inherit scheduling attribute in the specified thread attributes object. The inherit scheduling attribute specifies whether threads created using the attributes object inherit the scheduling attributes of the creating thread, or use the scheduling attributes stored in the attributes object that is passed to **pthread_create( )**.

The default value of the inherit scheduling attribute is **PTHREAD_INHERIT_-SCHED**.

Return Values

On successful completion, this routine returns the inherit scheduling attribute value.

If the function fails, **errno** may be set to one of the following values:

Return	Error	Description
Inherit scheduling attribute		Successful completion.
-1	**[EINVAL]**	The value specified by *attr* is invalid.

Related Information

Functions: **pthread_attr_create(3thr)**, **pthread_attr_setinheritsched(3thr)**, **pthread_create(3thr)**.

pthread_attr_getprio

Purpose   Obtains the scheduling priority attribute

Synopsis   **#include <pthread.h>**

int pthread_attr_getprio(
            pthread_attr_t *attr***);**

Parameters

attr   Thread attributes object whose priority attribute is obtained.

Description

The **pthread_attr_getprio( )** routine obtains the value of the scheduling priority of threads created using the thread attributes object specified by the *attr* parameter.

Return Values

On successful completion, this routine returns the scheduling priority attribute value.

If the function fails, **errno** may be set to one of the following values:

Return	Error	Description
Scheduling priority attribute		Successful completion.
-1	**[EINVAL]**	The value specified by *attr* is invalid.

Related Information

Functions: **pthread_attr_create(3thr)**, **pthread_attr_setprio(3thr)**, **pthread_create(3thr)**.

pthread_attr_getsched

Purpose   Obtains the value of the scheduling policy attribute

Synopsis   **#include <pthread.h>**

int pthread_attr_getsched(
         pthread_attr_t *attr*)**;**

Parameters

   attr   Thread attributes object whose scheduling policy attribute is
                obtained.

Description

   The **pthread_attr_getsched( )** routine obtains the scheduling policy of threads
   created using the thread attributes object specified by the *attr* parameter. The
   default value of the scheduling attribute is **SCHED_OTHER**.

Return Values

   On successful completion, this routine returns the value of the scheduling policy
   attribute.

   If the function fails, **errno** may be set to one of the following values:

Return	Error	Description
Scheduling policy attribute		Successful completion.
-1	**[EINVAL]**	The value specified by *attr* is invalid.

Related Information

   Functions: **pthread_attr_create(3thr)**, **pthread_attr_setsched(3thr)**,
   pthread_create(3thr).

pthread_attr_getstacksize

Purpose   Obtains the value of the stacksize attribute

Synopsis   #include <pthread.h>

long pthread_attr_getstacksize(
        pthread_attr_t *attr*);

Parameters

attr   Thread attributes object whose stacksize attribute is obtained.

Description

The **pthread_attr_getstacksize( )** routine obtains the minimum size (in bytes) of
the stack for a thread created using the thread attributes object specified by the *attr*
parameter.

Return Values

On successful completion, this routine returns the stacksize attribute value.

If the function fails, **errno** may be set to one of the following values:

Return	Error	Description
Stacksize attribute		Successful completion.
-1	[**EINVAL**]	The value specified by *attr* is invalid.

Related Information

Functions: **pthread_attr_create(3thr)**, **pthread_attr_setstacksize(3thr)**,
pthread_create(3thr).

pthread_attr_setinheritsched

Purpose   Changes the inherit scheduling attribute

Synopsis   **#include <pthread.h>**

int pthread_attr_setinheritsched(
        pthread_attr_t *attr*,
        int *inherit*)**;**

Parameters

    attr   Thread attributes object to be modified.

    inherit   New value for the inherit scheduling attribute. Valid values are as
                follows:

        PTHREAD_INHERIT_SCHED
                        This is the default value. The created thread inherits
                        the current priority and scheduling policy of the
                        thread calling **pthread_create( )**.

        PTHREAD_DEFAULT_SCHED
                        The created thread starts execution with the priority
                        and scheduling policy stored in the thread attributes
                        object.

Description

    The **pthread_attr_setinheritsched( )** routine changes the inherit scheduling
    attribute of thread creation. The inherit scheduling attribute specifies whether
    threads created using the specified thread attributes object inherit the scheduling
    attributes of the creating thread, or use the scheduling attributes stored in the thread
    attributes object that is passed to **pthread_create( )**.

    The first thread in an application that is not created by an explicit call to
    pthread_create( ) has a scheduling policy of **SCHED_OTHER**. (See the
    pthread_attr_setprio( ) and **pthread_attr_setsched( )** routines for more
    information on valid priority values and valid scheduling policy values,
    respectively.)

Inheriting scheduling attributes (instead of using the scheduling attributes stored in the attributes object) is useful when a thread is creating several helper threads—threads that are intended to work closely with the creating thread to cooperatively solve the same problem. For example, inherited scheduling attributes ensure that helper threads created in a sort routine execute with the same priority as the calling thread.

Return Values

If the function fails, -1 is returned, and **errno** may be set to one of the following values:

Return	Error	Description
-1	**[EINVAL]**	The value specified by *attr* is invalid.
-1	**[EINVAL]**	The value specified by *inherit* is invalid.

Related Information

Functions: **pthread_attr_create(3thr)**, **pthread_attr_getinheritsched(3thr)**, **pthread_attr_setprio(3thr)**, **pthread_attr_setsched(3thr)**, **pthread_create(3thr)**.

pthread_attr_setprio

Purpose   Changes the scheduling priority attribute of thread creation

Synopsis   **#include <pthread.h>**

int pthread_attr_setprio(
        pthread_attr_t **attr***,**
        int *priority***);**

Parameters

attr   Thread attributes object modified.

priority   New value for the priority attribute. The priority attribute depends
                on scheduling policy. Valid values fall within one of the following
                ranges:

- **PRI_OTHER_MIN** <= *priority* <= **PRI_OTHER_MAX**
  (use with the **SCHED_OTHER** policy)

- **PRI_FIFO_MIN** <= *priority* <= **PRI_FIFO_MAX**
  (use with the **SCHED_FIFO** policy)

- **PRI_RR_MIN** <= *priority* <= **PRI_RR_MAX**
  (use with the **SCHED_RR** policy)

- **PRI_FG_MIN_NP** <= *priority* <= **PRI_FG_MAX_NP**
  (use with the **SCHED_FG_NP** policy)

- **PRI_BG_MIN_NP** <= *priority* <= **PRI_BG_MAX_NP**
  (use with the **SCHED_BG_NP** policy)

The default priority is the midpoint between **PRI_OTHER_MIN** and
PRI_OTHER_MAX. To specify a minimum or maximum priority, use the
appropriate symbol; for example, **PRI_FIFO_MIN** or **PRI_FIFO_MAX**. To
specify a value between the minimum and maximum, use an appropriate arithmetic
expression. For example, to specify a priority midway between the minimum and
maximum for the Round Robin scheduling policy, specify the following concept
using your programming language's syntax:

```
pri_rr_mid = (PRI_RR_MIN + PRI_RR_MAX + 1)/2
```

If your expression results in a value outside the range of minimum to maximum, an
error results when you attempt to use it.

Description

The **pthread_attr_setprio( )** routine sets the execution priority of threads that are created using the attributes object specified by the *attr* parameter.

By default, a created thread inherits the priority of the thread calling **pthread_create( )**. To specify a priority using this routine, scheduling inheritance must be disabled at the time the thread is created. Before calling this routine and **pthread_create( )**, call **pthread_attr_setinheritsched( )** and specify the value **PTHREAD_DEFAULT_SCHED** for the *inherit* parameter.

An application specifies priority only to express the urgency of executing the thread relative to other threads. Priority is not used to control mutual exclusion when accessing shared data.

Return Values

If the function fails, **errno** may be set to one of the following values:

Return	Error	Description
0		Successful completion.
-1	**[EINVAL]**	The value specified by *attr* is invalid.
-1	**[ERANGE]**	One or more parameters supplied have an invalid value.

Related Information

Functions: **pthread_attr_create(3thr)**, **pthread_attr_getprio(3thr)**, **pthread_attr_setinheritsched(3thr)**, **pthread_create(3thr)**.

pthread_attr_setsched

Purpose   Changes the scheduling policy attribute of thread creation

Synopsis   #include <pthread.h>

int pthread_attr_setsched(
          pthread_attr_t *attr
          int *scheduler);

Parameters

attr   Thread attributes object modified.

scheduler   New value for the scheduling policy attribute. Valid values are as follows:

SCHED_FIFO
                (First In, First Out) The highest-priority thread runs until it blocks. If there is more than one thread with the same priority, and that priority is the highest among other threads, the first thread to begin running continues until it blocks.

SCHED_RR   (Round Robin) The highest-priority thread runs until it blocks; however, threads of equal priority, if that priority is the highest among other threads, are timesliced. Timeslicing is a process in which threads alternate using available processors.

SCHED_OTHER
                (Default)   All   threads   are   timesliced. **SCHED_OTHER** ensures that all threads, regardless of priority, receive some scheduling so that no thread is completely denied execution time. (However, **SCHED_OTHER** threads can be denied execution time by **SCHED_FIFO** or **SCHED_RR** threads.)

SCHED_FG_NP
                (Foreground) Same as **SCHED_OTHER**. Threads are timesliced and priorities can be modified dynamically by the scheduler to ensure fairness.

SCHED_BG_NP

> (Background) Ensures that all threads, regardless of priority, receive some scheduling. However, **SCHED_BG NP** can be denied execution by **SCHED_FIFO** or **SCHED_RR** threads.

Description

The **pthread_attr_setsched( )** routine sets the scheduling policy of a thread that is created using the attributes object specified by the *attr* parameter. The default value of the scheduling attribute is **SCHED_OTHER**.

Return Values

If the function fails, **errno** may be set to one of the following values:

Return	Error	Description
0		Successful completion.
-1	[EINVAL]	The value specified by *attr* is invalid.
-1	[EINVAL]	The value specified by *scheduler* is invalid.
-1	[EPERM]	The caller does not have the appropriate privileges to set the scheduling policy attribute in the specified threads attribute object.

Related Information

Functions: **pthread_attr_create(3thr), pthread_attr_getsched(3thr), pthread_attr_setinheritsched(3thr), pthread_create(3thr)**.

pthread_attr_setstacksize

Purpose   Changes the stacksize attribute of thread creation

Synopsis   **#include <pthread.h>**

                  int pthread_attr_setstacksize(
                              pthread_attr_t **attr*,
                              long *stacksize*);

Parameters

    attr   Thread attributes object modified.

    stacksize   New value for the stacksize attribute. The *stacksize* parameter specifies the minimum size (in bytes) of the stack needed for a thread.

Description

The **pthread_attr_setstacksize( )** routine sets the minimum size (in bytes) of the stack needed for a thread created using the attributes object specified by the *attr* parameter. Use this routine to adjust the size of the writable area of the stack. The default value of the stacksize attribute is machine specific.

A thread's stack is fixed at the time of thread creation. Only the main or initial thread can dynamically extend its stack.

Most compilers do not check for stack overflow. Ensure that your thread stack is large enough for anything that you call from the thread.

Return Values

If the function fails, **errno** may be set to one of the following values:

Return	Error	Description
0		Successful completion.
-1	**[EINVAL]**	The value specified by *attr* is invalid.
-1	**[EINVAL]**	The value specified by *stacksize* is invalid.

Related Information

Functions: **pthread_attr_create(3thr)**, **pthread_attr_getstacksize(3thr)**, **pthread_create(3thr)**.

pthread_cancel

Purpose   Allows a thread to request that it or another thread terminate execution

Synopsis   #include <pthread.h>

int pthread_cancel(
        pthread_t *thread*);

Parameters

thread   Thread that receives a cancel request.

Description

The **pthread_cancel( )** routine sends a cancel to the specified thread. A cancel is a mechanism by which a calling thread informs either itself or the called thread to terminate as quickly as possible. Issuing a cancel does not guarantee that the canceled thread receives or handles the cancel. The canceled thread can delay processing the cancel after receiving it. For instance, if a cancel arrives during an important operation, the canceled thread can continue if what it is doing cannot be interrupted at the point where the cancel is requested.

Because of communications delays, the calling thread can only rely on the fact that a cancel eventually becomes pending in the designated thread (provided that the thread does not terminate beforehand). Furthermore, the calling thread has no guarantee that a pending cancel is to be delivered because delivery is controlled by the designated thread.

Termination processing when a cancel is delivered to a thread is similar to **pthread_exit( )**. Outstanding cleanup routines are executed in the context of the target thread, and a status of -1 is made available to any threads joining with the target thread.

This routine is preferred in implementing Ada's **abort** statement and any other language (or software-defined construct) for requesting thread cancellation.

The results of this routine are unpredictable if the value specified in *thread* refers to a thread that does not currently exist.

pthread_cancel(3thr)

Return Values

If the function fails, **errno** may be set to one of the following values:

Return	Error	Description
0		Successful completion.
-1	[**EINVAL**]	The specified thread is invalid.
-1	[**ERSCH**]	The specified thread does not refer to a currently existing thread.

Related Information

Functions: **pthread_exit(3thr)**, **pthread_join(3thr)**, **pthread_setasynccancel(3thr)**, **pthread_setcancel(3thr)**, **pthread_testcancel(3thr)**.

pthread_cleanup_pop

Purpose   Removes the cleanup handler at the top of the cleanup stack and optionally executes it

Synopsis   **#include <pthread.h>**

void pthread_cleanup_pop(
        int *execute***);**

Parameters

> *execute*   Integer that specifies whether the cleanup routine that is popped should be executed or just discarded. If the value is nonzero, the cleanup routine is executed.

Description

> The **pthread_cleanup_pop( )** routine removes the routine specified in **pthread_cleanup_push( )** from the top of the calling thread's cleanup stack and executes it if the value specified in *execute* is nonzero.

> This routine and **pthread_cleanup_push( )** are implemented as macros and must be displayed as statements and in pairs within the same lexical scope. You can think of the **pthread_cleanup_push( )** macro as expanding to a string whose first character is a { (left brace) and **pthread_cleanup_pop** as expanding to a string containing the corresponding } (right brace).

Return Values

> This routine must be used as a statement.

Related Information

> Functions: **pthread_cleanup_push(3thr)**.

pthread_cleanup_push

Purpose   Establishes a cleanup handler

Synopsis   **#include <pthread.h>**

void pthread_cleanup_push(
        void *routine*,
        pthread_addr_t *arg*);

Parameters

routine   Routine executed as the cleanup handler.

arg   Parameter executed with the cleanup routine.

Description

The **pthread_cleanup_push( )** routine pushes the specified routine onto the calling thread's cleanup stack. The cleanup routine is popped from the stack and executed with the *arg* parameter when any of the following actions occur:

- The thread calls **pthread_exit( )**.

- The thread is canceled.

- The thread calls **pthread_cleanup_pop( )** and specifies a nonzero value for the *execute* parameter.

This routine and **pthread_cleanup_pop( )** are implemented as macros and must be displayed as statements and in pairs within the same lexical scope. You can think of the **pthread_cleanup_push( )** macro as expanding to a string whose first character is a **{** (left brace) and **pthread_cleanup_pop( )** as expanding to a string containing the corresponding **}** (right brace).

Return Values

This routine must be used as a statement.

Related Information

Functions: **pthread_cancel(3thr)**, **pthread_cleanup_pop(3thr)**, **pthread_exit(3thr)**, **pthread_testcancel(3thr)**.

pthread_cond_broadcast

Purpose   Wakes all threads that are waiting on a condition variable

Synopsis   #include <pthread.h>

int pthread_cond_broadcast(
        pthread_cond_t *cond);

Parameters

cond   Condition variable broadcast.

Description

The **pthread_cond_broadcast( )** routine wakes all threads waiting on a condition
variable. Calling this routine implies that data guarded by the associated mutex has
changed so that it might be possible for one or more waiting threads to proceed. If
any one waiting thread might be able to proceed, call **pthread_cond_signal( )**.

Call this routine when the associated mutex is either locked or unlocked.

Return Values

If the function fails, **errno** may be set to one of the following values:

Return	Error	Description
0		Successful completion.
-1	**[EINVAL]**	The value specified by *cond* is invalid.

Related Information

Functions: **pthread_cond_destroy(3thr)**, **pthread_cond_init(3thr)**,
pthread_cond_signal(3thr), **pthread_cond_timedwait(3thr)**,
pthread_cond_wait(3thr).

pthread_cond_destroy

Purpose Deletes a condition variable

Synopsis #include <pthread.h>

int pthread_cond_destroy(
        pthread_cond_t *cond);

Parameters

cond   Condition variable deleted.

Description

The **pthread_cond_destroy( )** routine deletes a condition variable. Call this routine when a condition variable is no longer referenced. The effect of calling this routine is to give permission to reclaim storage for the condition variable.

The results of this routine are unpredictable if the condition variable specified in cond does not exist.

The results of this routine are also unpredictable if there are threads waiting for the specified condition variable to be signaled or broadcast when it is deleted.

Return Values

If the function fails, **errno** may be set to one of the following values:

Return	Error	Description
0		Successful completion.
-1	**[EINVAL]**	The value specified by cond is invalid.
-1	**[EBUSY]**	A thread is currently executing a **pthread_cond_timedwait( )** routine or **pthread_cond_wait( )** on the condition variable specified in cond.

Related Information

Functions: **pthread_cond_broadcast(3thr)**, **pthread_cond_init(3thr)**, **pthread_cond_signal(3thr)**, **pthread_cond_timedwait(3thr)**, **pthread_cond_wait(3thr)**.

pthread_cond_init

Purpose   Creates a condition variable

Synopsis   **#include <pthread.h>**

int pthread_cond_init(
        pthread_cond_t *_cond_,
        pthread_condattr_t _attr_**);**

Parameters

cond   Condition variable that is created.

attr   Condition variable attributes object that defines the characteristics of the condition variable created. If you specify **pthread_-condattr_default**, default attributes are used.

Description

The **pthread_cond_init( )** routine creates and initializes a condition variable. A condition variable is a synchronization object used in conjunction with a mutex. A mutex controls access to shared data; a condition variable allows threads to wait for that data to enter a defined state. The state is defined by a Boolean expression called a predicate.

A condition variable is signaled or broadcast to indicate that a predicate might have become true. The broadcast operation indicates that all waiting threads need to resume and reevaluate the predicate. The signal operation is used when any one waiting thread can continue.

If a thread that holds a mutex determines that the shared data is not in the correct state for it to proceed (the associated predicate is not true), it waits on a condition variable associated with the desired state. Waiting on the condition variable automatically releases the mutex so that other threads can modify or examine the shared data. When a thread modifies the state of the shared data so that a predicate might be true, it signals or broadcasts on the appropriate condition variable so that threads waiting for that predicate can continue.

It is important that all threads waiting on a particular condition variable at any time hold the *same* mutex. If they do not, the behavior of the wait operation is unpredictable (an implementation can use the mutex to control internal access to the condition variable object). However, it is legal for a client to store condition variables and mutexes and later reuse them in different combinations. The client must ensure that no threads use the condition variable with the old mutex. At any time, an arbitrary number of condition variables can be associated with a single mutex, each representing a different predicate of the shared data protected by that mutex.

Condition variables are not owned by a particular thread. Any associated storage is not automatically deallocated when the creating thread terminates.

Return Values

If the function fails, **errno** may be set to one of the following values:

Return	Error	Description
0		Successful completion.
-1	[EAGAIN]	The system lacks the necessary resources to initialize another condition variable.
-1	[EINVAL]	Invalid attributes object.
-1	[ENOMEM]	Insufficient memory exists to initialize the condition variable.

Related Information

Functions: **pthread_cond_broadcast(3thr)**, **pthread_cond_destroy(3thr)**, **pthread_cond_signal(3thr)**, **pthread_cond_timedwait(3thr)**, **pthread_cond_wait(3thr)**.

pthread_cond_signal

Purpose   Wakes one thread that is waiting on a condition variable

Synopsis   **#include <pthread.h>**

int pthread_cond_signal(
         pthread_cond_t **cond**);**

Parameters

cond   Condition variable signaled.

Description

The **pthread_cond_signal( )** routine wakes one thread waiting on a condition variable. Calling this routine implies that data guarded by the associated mutex has changed so that it is possible for a single waiting thread to proceed. Call this routine when any thread waiting on the specified condition variable might find its predicate true, but only one thread needs to proceed.

The scheduling policy determines which thread is awakened. For policies **SCHED_FIFO** and **SCHED_RR** a blocked thread is chosen in priority order.

Call this routine when the associated mutex is either locked or unlocked.

Return Values

If the function fails, **errno** may be set to one of the following values:

Return	Error	Description
0		Successful completion.
-1	[**EINVAL**]	The value specified by *cond* is invalid.

Related Information

Functions: **pthread_cond_broadcast(3thr)**, **pthread_cond_destroy(3thr)**, **pthread_cond_init(3thr)**, **pthread_cond_timedwait(3thr)**, **pthread_cond_wait(3thr)**.

pthread_cond_timedwait

Purpose   Causes a thread to wait for a condition variable to be signaled or broadcast

Synopsis   #include <pthread.h>

int pthread_cond_timedwait(
        pthread_cond_t *cond,
        pthread_mutex_t *mutex,
        struct timespec *abstime);

Parameters

cond   Condition variable waited on.

mutex   Mutex associated with the condition variable specified in cond.

abstime   Absolute time at which the wait expires, if the condition has not been signaled or broadcast. (See the **pthread_get_expiration_np( )** routine, which you can use to obtain a value for this parameter.)

Description

The **pthread_cond_timedwait( )** routine causes a thread to wait until one of the following occurs:

- The specified condition variable is signaled or broadcast.

- The current system clock time is greater than or equal to the time specified by the abstime parameter.

This routine is identical to **pthread_cond_wait( )** except that this routine can return before a condition variable is signaled or broadcast—specifically, when a specified time expires.

If the current time equals or exceeds the expiration time, this routine returns immediately, without causing the current thread to wait.

Call this routine after you lock the mutex specified in mutex. The results of this routine are unpredictable if this routine is called without first locking the mutex.

Return Values

If the function fails, **errno** may be set to one of the following values:

Return	Error	Description
0		Successful completion.
-1	[**EINVAL**]	The value specified by *cond*, *mutex*, or *abstime* is invalid.
-1	[**EAGAIN**]	The time specified by *abstime* expired.
-1	[**EDEADLK**]	A deadlock condition is detected.

Related Information

Functions: **pthread_cond_broadcast(3thr)**, **pthread_cond_destroy(3thr)**, **pthread_cond_init(3thr)**, **pthread_cond_signal(3thr)**, **pthread_cond_wait(3thr)**, **pthread_get_expiration_np(3thr)**.

pthread_cond_wait

Purpose   Causes a thread to wait for a condition variable to be signaled or broadcast

Synopsis   **#include <pthread.h>**

int pthread_cond_wait(
       pthread_cond_t *_cond_**,**
       pthread_mutex_t *_mutex_**);**

Parameters

cond   Condition variable waited on.

mutex   Mutex associated with the condition variable specified in _cond_.

Description

The **pthread_cond_wait( )** routine causes a thread to wait for a condition variable to be signaled or broadcast. Each condition corresponds to one or more predicates based on shared data. The calling thread waits for the data to reach a particular state (for the predicate to become true).

Call this routine after you have locked the mutex specified in _mutex_. The results of this routine are unpredictable if this routine is called without first locking the mutex.

This routine automatically releases the mutex and causes the calling thread to wait on the condition. If the wait is satisfied as a result of some thread calling **pthread_cond_signal( )** or **pthread_cond_broadcast( )**, the mutex is reacquired and the routine returns.

A thread that changes the state of storage protected by the mutex in such a way that a predicate associated with a condition variable might now be true must call either **pthread_cond_signal( )** or **pthread_cond_broadcast( )** for that condition variable. If neither call is made, any thread waiting on the condition variable continues to wait.

This routine might (with low probability) return when the condition variable has not been signaled or broadcast. When a spurious wakeup occurs, the mutex is reacquired before the routine returns. (To handle this type of situation, enclose this routine in a loop that checks the predicate.)

pthread_cond_wait(3thr)

Return Values

If the function fails, **errno** may be set to one of the following values:

Return	Error	Description
0		Successful completion.
-1	[EINVAL]	The value specified by *cond* or *mutex* is invalid.
-1	[EDEADLK]	A deadlock condition is detected.

Related Information

Functions: **pthread_cond_broadcast(3thr), pthread_cond_destroy(3thr), pthread_cond_init(3thr), pthread_cond_signal(3thr), pthread_cond_timedwait(3thr)**.

pthread_condattr_create

Purpose   Creates a condition variable attributes object

Synopsis   **#include <pthread.h>**

int pthread_condattr_create(
        pthread_condattr_t **attr***);**

Parameters

attr   Condition variable attributes object that is created.

Description

The **pthread_condattr_create**( ) routine creates a condition variable attributes object that is used to specify the attributes of condition variables when they are created. The condition variable attributes object is initialized with the default value for all of the attributes defined by a given implementation.

When a condition variable attributes object is used to create a condition variable, the values of the individual attributes determine the characteristics of the new object. Attributes objects act like additional parameters to object creation. Changing individual attributes does not affect objects that were previously created using the attributes object.

Return Values

The created condition variable attributes object is returned to the *attr* parameter.

If the function fails, **errno** may be set to one of the following values:

Return	Error	Description
0		Successful completion.
-1	[EINVAL]	The value specified by *attr* is invalid.
-1	[ENOMEM]	Insufficient memory exists to create the condition variable attributes object.

Related Information

Functions: **pthread_cond_init(3thr)**, **pthread_condattr_delete(3thr)**.

pthread_condattr_delete

Purpose   Deletes a condition variable attributes object

Synopsis   #include <pthread.h>

        int pthread_condattr_delete(
                pthread_condattr_t *_attr_**);**

Parameters

      attr   Condition variable attributes object deleted.

Description

The **pthread_condattr_delete( )** routine deletes a condition variable attributes object. Call this routine when a condition variable attributes object created by **pthread_condattr_create( )** is no longer referenced.

This routine gives permission to reclaim storage for the condition variable attributes object. Condition variables that are created using this attributes object are not affected by the deletion of the condition variable attributes object.

The results of calling this routine are unpredictable if the handle specified by the _attr_ parameter refers to an attributes object that does not exist.

Return Values

If the function fails, **errno** may be set to one of the following values:

Return	Error	Description
0		Successful completion.
-1	[**EINVAL**]	The value specified by _attr_ is invalid.

Related Information

Functions: **pthread_condattr_create(3thr)**.

pthread_create

Purpose   Creates a thread object and thread

Synopsis   **#include <pthread.h>**

int pthread_create(
      pthread_t *___thread___,
      pthread_attr_t _attr_,
      pthread_startroutine_t _start_routine_,
      pthread_addr_t _arg_);

Parameters

thread   Handle to the thread object created.

attr   Thread attributes object that defines the characteristics of the thread being created. If you specify **pthread_attr_default**, default attributes are used.

_start_routine_ Function executed as the new thread's start routine.

arg   Address value copied and passed to the thread's start routine.

Description

The **pthread_create( )** routine creates a thread object and a thread. A _thread_ is a single, sequential flow of control within a program. It is the active execution of a designated routine, including any nested routine invocations. A thread object defines and controls the executing thread.

Creating a Thread

Calling this routine sets into motion the following actions:

- An internal thread object is created to describe the thread.

- The associated executable thread is created with attributes specified by the _attr_ parameter (or with default attributes if **pthread_attr_default** is specified).

- The _thread_ parameter receives the new thread.

- The _start_routine_ function is called. This may occur before this routine returns successfully.

Thread Execution

The thread is created in the ready state and therefore might immediately begin executing the function specified by the *start_routine* parameter. The newly created thread begins running before **pthread_create( )** completes if the new thread follows the **SCHED_RR** or **SCHED_FIFO** scheduling policy or has a priority higher than the creating thread, or both. Otherwise, the new thread begins running at its turn, which with sufficient processors might also be before **pthread_create( )** returns.

The *start_routine* parameter is passed a copy of the *arg* parameter. The value of the *arg* parameter is unspecified.

The thread object exists until the **pthread_detach( )** routine is called or the thread terminates, whichever occurs last.

The synchronization between the caller of **pthread_create( )** and the newly created thread is through the use of the **pthread_join( )** routine (or any other mutexes or condition variables they agree to use).

Terminating a Thread

A thread terminates when one of the following events occurs:

- The thread returns from its start routine.

- The thread exits (within a routine) as the result of calling the **pthread_exit( )** routine.

- The thread is canceled.

When a Thread Terminates

The following actions are performed when a thread terminates:

- If the thread terminates by returning from its start routine or calling **pthread_exit( )**, the return value is copied into the thread object. If the start routine returns normally and the start routine is a procedure that does not return a value, then the result obtained by **pthread_join( )** is unpredictable. If the thread has been cancelled, a return value of -1 is copied into the thread object. The return value can be retrieved by other threads by calling the **pthread_join( )** routine.

- A destructor for each thread-specific data point is removed from the list of destructors for this thread and then is called. This step destroys all the thread-specific data associated with the current thread.

- Each cleanup handler that has been declared by **pthread_cleanup_push( )** and not yet removed by **pthread_cleanup_pop( )** is called. The most recently pushed handler is called first.

- A flag is set in the thread object indicating that the thread has terminated. This flag must be set in order for callers of **pthread_join( )** to return from the call.

- A broadcast is made so that all threads currently waiting in a call to **pthread_join( )** can return from the call.

- The thread object is marked to indicate that it is no longer needed by the thread itself. A check is made to determine if the thread object is no longer needed by other threads; that is, if **pthread_detach( )** has been called. If that routine is called, then the thread object is deallocated.

Return Values

Upon successful completion, this routine stores the identifier of the created thread at *thread* and returns 0. Otherwise, a value of -1 is returned and no thread is created, the contents of *thread* are undefined, and **errno** may be set to one of the following values:

Return	Error	Description
0		Successful completion.
-1	[**EAGAIN**]	The system lacks the necessary resources to create another thread.
-1	[**ENOMEM**]	Insufficient memory exists to create the thread object. This is not a temporary condition.

Related Information

Functions: **pthread_attr_create(3thr)**, **pthread_cancel(3thr)**, **pthread_detach(3thr)**, **pthread_exit(3thr)**, **pthread_join(3thr)**.

pthread_delay_np

Purpose   Causes a thread to wait for a specified period

Synopsis   **#include <pthread.h>**

int pthread_delay_np(
        struct timespec **interval*);

Parameters

interval   Number of seconds and nanoseconds that the calling thread waits before continuing execution. The value specified must be greater than or equal to 0 (zero).

Description

The **pthread_delay_np( )** routine causes a thread to delay execution for a specified period of elapsed wall clock time. The period of time the thread waits is at least as long as the number of seconds and nanoseconds specified in the *interval* parameter.

Specifying an interval of 0 (zero) seconds and 0 (zero) nanoseconds is allowed and can result in the thread giving up the processor or delivering a pending cancel.

The **struct timespec** structure contains two fields, as follows:

- The **tv_sec** field is an integer number of seconds.

- The **tv_nsec** field is an integer number of nanoseconds.

This routine is a new primitive.

Return Values

If the function fails, **errno** may be set to one of the following values:

Return	Error	Description
0		Successful completion.
-1	**[EINVAL]**	The value specified by *interval* is invalid.

Related Information

Functions: **pthread_yield(3thr)**.

pthread_detach

Purpose   Marks a thread object for deletion

Synopsis   **#include <pthread.h>**

int pthread_detach(
        pthread_t **thread***);**

Parameters

thread   Thread object marked for deletion.

Description

The **pthread_detach( )** routine indicates that storage for the specified thread is reclaimed when the thread terminates. This includes storage for the *thread* parameter's return value. If *thread* has not terminated when this routine is called, this routine does not cause it to terminate.

Call this routine when a thread object is no longer referenced. Additionally, call this routine for every thread that is created to ensure that storage for thread objects does not accumulate.

You cannot join with a thread after the thread has been detached.

The results of this routine are unpredictable if the value of *thread* refers to a thread object that does not exist.

Return Values

If the function fails, **errno** may be set to one of the following values:

Return	Error	Description
0		Successful completion.
-1	[EINVAL]	The value specified by *thread* is invalid.
-1	[ESRCH]	The value specified by *thread* does not refer to an existing thread.

pthread_detach(3thr)

Related Information

Functions: **pthread_cancel(3thr)**, **pthread_create(3thr)**, **pthread_exit(3thr)**, **pthread_join(3thr)**.

pthread_equal

Purpose   Compares one thread identifier to another thread identifier.

Synopsis   **#include <pthread.h>**

boolean32 pthread_equal(
pthread_t *thread1*,
pthread_t *thread2*);

Parameters

thread1   The first thread identifier to be compared.

thread2   The second thread identifier to be compared.

Description

This routine compares one thread identifier to another thread identifier. (This routine does not check whether the objects that correspond to the identifiers currently exist.) If the identifiers have values indicating that they designate the same object, 1 (true) is returned. If the values do not designate the same object, 0 (false) is returned.

This routine is implemented as a C macro.

Return Values

Possible return values are as follows:

Return	Error	Description
0		Values of thread1 and thread2 do not designate the same object.
1		Values of thread1 and thread2 designate the same object.

Related Information

Functions: **pthread_create(3thr)**

pthread_exit

Purpose   Terminates the calling thread

Synopsis   **#include <pthread.h>**

void pthread_exit(
            pthread_addr_t *status***);**

Parameters

status   Address value copied and returned to the caller of **pthread_join( )**.

Description

The **pthread_exit( )** routine terminates the calling thread and makes a status value available to any thread that calls **pthread_join( )** and specifies the terminating thread.

An implicit call to **pthread_exit( )** is issued when a thread returns from the start routine that was used to create it. The function's return value serves as the thread's exit status. If the return value is -1, an error exit is forced for the thread instead of a normal exit. The process exits when the last running thread calls **pthread_exit( )**, with an undefined exit status.

Restrictions

The **pthread_exit( )** routine does not work in the main (initial) thread because DCE Threads relies on information at the base of thread stacks; this information does not exist in the main thread.

Return Values

No value is returned.

Related Information

Functions: **pthread_create(3thr)**, **pthread_detach(3thr)**, **pthread_join(3thr)**.

pthread_get_expiration_np

Purpose   Obtains a value representing a desired expiration time

Synopsis   **#include <pthread.h>**

int pthread_get_expiration_np(
        struct timespec *delta,
        struct timespec *abstime);

Parameters

delta   Number of seconds and nanoseconds to add to the current system
               time. The result is the time when a timed wait expires.

abstime   Value representing the expiration time.

Description

The **pthread_get_expiration_np( )** routine adds a specified interval to the current
absolute system time and returns a new absolute time. This new absolute time is
used as the expiration time in a call to **pthread_cond_timedwait( )**. This routine
is a new primitive.

The **struct timespec** structure contains two fields, as follows:

- The **tv_sec** field is an integer number of seconds.

- The **tv_nsec** field is an integer number of nanoseconds.

Return Values

If the function fails, **errno** may be set to one of the following values:

Return	Error	Description
0		Successful completion.
-1	**[EINVAL]**	The value specified by *delta* is invalid.

Related Information

Functions: **pthread_cond_timedwait(3thr)**.

pthread_getprio

Purpose   Obtains the current priority of a thread

Synopsis   **#include <pthread.h>**

int pthread_getprio(
         pthread_t *thread***);**

Parameters

  thread   Thread whose priority is obtained.

Description

The **pthread_getprio( )** routine obtains the current priority of a thread. The current priority is different from the initial priority of the thread if the **pthread_setprio( )** routine is called.

The exact effect of different priority values depends upon the scheduling policy assigned to the thread.

Return Values

The current priority value of the thread specified in *thread* is returned. (See the **pthread_setprio( )** reference page for valid values.)

If the function fails, **errno** may be set to one of the following values:

Return	Error	Description
Priority value		Successful completion.
-1	[EINVAL]	The value specified by *thread* is invalid.
-1	[ESRCH]	The value specified by *thread* does not refer to an existing thread.

Related Information

Functions: **pthread_attr_setprio(3thr), pthread_setprio(3thr), pthread_setscheduler(3thr)**.

pthread_getscheduler

Purpose   Obtains the current scheduling policy of a thread

Synopsis   #include <pthread.h>

int pthread_getscheduler(
        pthread_t *thread*);

Parameters

thread   Thread whose scheduling policy is obtained.

Description

The **pthread_getscheduler**( ) routine obtains the current scheduling policy of a thread. The current scheduling policy of a thread is different from the initial scheduling policy if the **pthread_setscheduler**( ) routine is called.

Return Values

The current scheduling policy value of the thread specified in *thread* is returned. (See the **pthread_setscheduler**( ) reference page for valid values.)

If the function fails, **errno** may be set to one of the following values:

Return	Error	Description
Current scheduling policy		Successful completion.
-1	[**EINVAL**]	The value specified by *thread* is invalid.
-1	[**ESRCH**]	The value specified by *thread* does not refer to an existing thread.

Related Information

Functions: **pthread_attr_setscheduler(3thr)**, **pthread_setscheduler(3thr)**.

pthread_getspecific

Purpose   Obtains the thread-specific data associated with the specified key

Synopsis   **#include <pthread.h>**

int pthread_getspecific(
        pthread_key_t *key*,
        pthread_addr_t *value);

Parameters

key   Context key value that identifies the data value obtained. This key
            value must be obtained from **pthread_keycreate( )**.

value   Address of the current thread-specific data value associated with the
            specified key.

Description

The **pthread_getspecific( )** routine obtains the thread-specific data associated with
the specified key for the current thread.

Return Values

If the function fails, **errno** may be set to one of the following values:

Return	Error	Description
0		Successful completion.
-1	[**EINVAL**]	The key value is invalid.

Related Information

Functions: **pthread_keycreate(3thr)**, **pthread_setspecific(3thr)**.

pthread_join

Purpose   Causes the calling thread to wait for the termination of a specified thread

Synopsis   **#include <pthread.h>**

int pthread_join(
        pthread_t *thread*,
        pthread_addr_t *status);

Parameters

thread   Thread whose termination is awaited by the caller of this routine.

status   Status value of the terminating thread when that thread calls **pthread_exit( )**.

Description

The **pthread_join( )** routine causes the calling thread to wait for the termination of a specified thread. A call to this routine returns after the specified thread has terminated.

Any number of threads can call this routine. All threads are awakened when the specified thread terminates.

If the current thread calls this routine to join with itself, an error is returned.

The results of this routine are unpredictable if the value for *thread* refers to a thread object that no longer exists.

Return Values

If the thread terminates normally, the exit status is the value that is is optionally returned from the thread's start routine.

If the function fails, **errno** may be set to one of the following values:

Return	Error	Description
0		Successful completion.
-1	[EINVAL]	The value specified by *thread* is invalid.
-1	[ESRCH]	The value specified by *thread* does not refer to a currently existing thread.
-1	[EDEADLK]	A deadlock is detected.

Related Information

Functions: **pthread_create(3thr)**, **pthread_detach(3thr)**, **pthread_exit(3thr)**.

pthread_keycreate

Purpose   Generates a unique thread-specific data key value

Synopsis   **#include <pthread.h>**

int pthread_keycreate(
        pthread_key_t **key*,
        void (**destructor*) (**void** **value*));

Parameters

    key   Value of the new thread-specific data key.

    destructor   Procedure to be called to destroy a data value associated with the created key when the thread terminates.

Description

The **pthread_keycreate( )** routine generates a unique thread-specific data key value. This key value identifies a thread-specific data value, which is an address of memory generated by the client containing arbitrary data of any size.

Thread-specific data allows client software to associate information with the current thread.

For example, thread-specific data can be used by a language runtime library that needs to associate a language-specific thread-private data structure with an individual thread. The thread-specific data routines also provide a portable means of implementing the class of storage called thread-private static, which is needed to support parallel decomposition in the FORTRAN language.

This routine generates and returns a new key value. Each call to this routine within a process returns a key value that is unique within an application invocation. Calls to **pthread_keycreate( )** must occur in initialization code guaranteed to execute only once in each process. The **pthread_once( )** routine provides a way of specifying such code.

When multiple facilities share access to thread-specific data, the facilities must agree on the key value that is associated with the context. The key value must be created only once and needs to be stored in a location known to each facility. (It may be desirable to encapsulate the creation of a key, and the setting and getting of context values for that key, within a special facility created for that purpose.)

When a thread terminates, thread-specific data is automatically destroyed. For each thread-specific data currently associated with the thread, the *destructor* routine associated with the key value of that context is called. The order in which per-thread context destructors are called at thread termination is undefined.

Return Values

If the function fails, **errno** may be set to one of the following values:

Return	Error	Description
0		Successful completion.
-1	**[EINVAL]**	The value specified by *key* is invalid.
-1	**[EAGAIN]**	An attempt was made to allocate a key when the key namespace is exhausted. This is not a temporary condition.
-1	**[ENOMEM]**	Insufficient memory exists to create the key.

Related Information

Functions: **pthread_getspecific(3thr)**, **pthread_setspecific(3thr)**.

pthread_lock_global_np

Purpose   Locks the global mutex

Synopsis   **#include <pthread.h>**

void pthread_lock_global_np( );

Description

The **pthread_lock_global_np( )** routine locks the global mutex. If the global mutex is currently held by another thread when a thread calls this routine, the thread waits for the global mutex to become available.

The thread that has locked the global mutex becomes its current owner and remains the owner until the same thread has unlocked it. This routine returns with the global mutex in the locked state and with the current thread as the global mutex's current owner.

Use the global mutex when calling a library package that is not designed to run in a multithreaded environment. (Unless the documentation for a library function specifically states that it is compatible with multithreading, assume that it is not compatible; in other words, assume it is nonreentrant.)

The global mutex is one lock. Any code that calls any function that is not known to be reentrant uses the same lock. This prevents dependencies among threads calling library functions and those functions calling other functions, and so on.

The global mutex is a recursive mutex. A thread that has locked the global mutex can relock it without deadlocking. (The locking thread must call **pthread_-unlock_global_np( )** as many times as it called this routine to allow another thread to lock the global mutex.)

This routine is a new primitive.

Return Values

No value is returned.

Related Information

Functions: **pthread_mutex_lock(3thr)**, **pthread_mutex_unlock(3thr)**, **pthread_mutexattr_setkind_np(3thr)**, **pthread_unlock_global_np(3thr)**.

pthread_mutex_destroy

Purpose   Deletes a mutex

Synopsis   **#include <pthread.h>**

int pthread_mutex_destroy(
        pthread_mutex_t **mutex***);**

Parameters

    mutex   Mutex to be deleted.

Description

The **pthread_mutex_destroy( )** routine deletes a mutex and must be called when a mutex object is no longer referenced. The effect of calling this routine is to reclaim storage for the mutex object.

It is illegal to delete a mutex that has a current owner (in other words, is locked).

The results of this routine are unpredictable if the mutex object specified in the *mutex* parameter does not currently exist.

Return Values

If the function fails, **errno** may be set to one of the following values:

Return	Error	Description
0		Successful completion.
-1	**[EBUSY]**	An attempt was made to destroy a mutex that is locked.
-1	**[EINVAL]**	The value specified by *mutex* is invalid.

Related Information

Functions: **pthread_mutex_init(3thr)**, **pthread_mutex_lock(3thr)**, **pthread_mutex_trylock(3thr)**, **pthread_mutex_unlock(3thr)**.

pthread_mutex_init

Purpose Creates a mutex

Synopsis #include <pthread.h>

int pthread_mutex_init(
       pthread_mutex_t *mutex,
       pthread_mutexattr_t attr);

Parameters

mutex   Mutex that is created.

attr   Attributes object that defines the characteristics of the created
            mutex. If you specify **pthread_mutexattr_default**, default
            attributes are used.

Description

The **pthread_mutex_init()** routine creates a mutex and initializes it to the
unlocked state. If the thread that called this routine terminates, the created mutex
is not automatically deallocated, because it is considered shared among multiple
threads.

Return Values

If an error condition occurs, this routine returns -1, the mutex is not initialized, the
contents of mutex are undefined, and **errno** may be set to one of the following
values:

Return	Error	Description
0		Successful completion.
-1	**[EAGAIN]**	The system lacks the necessary resources to initialize another mutex.
-1	**[EINVAL]**	The value specified by attr is invalid.
-1	**[ENOMEM]**	Insufficient memory exists to initialize the mutex.

Related Information

Functions: **pthread_mutex_lock(3thr), pthread_mutex_trylock(3thr), pthread_mutex_unlock(3thr), pthread_mutexattr_create(3thr), pthread_mutexattr_getkind_np(3thr), pthread_mutexattr_setkind_np(3thr).**

pthread_mutex_lock

Purpose   Locks an unlocked mutex

Synopsis   **#include <pthread.h>**

int pthread_mutex_lock(
        pthread_mutex_t *mutex**);**

Parameters

  mutex   Mutex that is locked.

Description

The **pthread_mutex_lock( )** routine locks a mutex. If the mutex is locked when a thread calls this routine, the thread waits for the mutex to become available.

The thread that has locked a mutex becomes its current owner and remains the owner until the same thread has unlocked it. This routine returns with the mutex in the locked state and with the current thread as the mutex's current owner.

If you specified a fast mutex in a call to **pthread_mutexattr_setkind_np( )**, a deadlock can result if the current owner of a mutex calls this routine in an attempt to lock the mutex a second time. If you specified a recursive mutex in a call to **pthread_mutexattr_setkind_np( )**, the current owner of a mutex can relock the same mutex without blocking. If you specify a nonrecursive mutex in a call to **pthread_mutexattr_setkind_np( )**, an error is returned and the thread does not block if the current owner of a mutex calls this routine in an attempt to lock the mutex a second time.

The preemption of a lower-priority thread that locks a mutex possibly results in the indefinite blocking of higher-priority threads waiting for the same mutex. The execution of the waiting higher-priority threads is blocked for as long as there is a sufficient number of runnable threads of any priority between the lower-priority and higher-priority values. Priority inversion occurs when any resource is shared between threads with different priorities.

Return Values

If the function fails, **errno** may be set to one of the following values:

Return	Error	Description
0		Successful completion.
-1	[**EINVAL**]	The value specified by *mutex* is invalid.
-1	[**EDEADLK**]	A deadlock condition is detected.

Related Information

Functions: **pthread_mutex_destroy(3thr)**, **pthread_mutex_init(3thr)**,
pthread_mutex_trylock(3thr), **pthread_mutex_unlock(3thr)**,
pthread_mutexattr_setkind_np(3thr).

pthread_mutex_trylock

Purpose   Locks a mutex

Synopsis   **#include <pthread.h>**

int pthread_mutex_trylock(
        pthread_mutex_t **mutex***);**

Parameters

mutex   Mutex that is locked.

Description

The **pthread_mutex_trylock( )** routine locks a mutex. If the specified mutex is locked when a thread calls this routine, the calling thread does not wait for the mutex to become available.

When a thread calls this routine, an attempt is made to lock the mutex immediately. If the mutex is successfully locked, 1 is returned and the current thread is then the mutex's current owner.

If the mutex is locked by another thread when this routine is called, 0 (zero) is returned and the thread does not wait to acquire the lock. If a fast mutex is owned by the current thread, 0 is returned. If a recursive mutex is owned by the current thread, 1 is returned and the mutex is relocked. (To unlock a recursive mutex, each call to **pthread_mutex_trylock( )** must be matched by a call to the **pthread_-mutex_unlock( )** routine.)

Return Values

If the function fails, **errno** may be set to one of the following values:

Return	Error	Description
1		Successful completion.
0		The mutex is locked; therefore, it was not acquired.
-1	**[EINVAL]**	The value specified by *mutex* is invalid.

pthread_mutex_trylock(3thr)

Related Information

Functions: **pthread_mutex_destroy(3thr)**, **pthread_mutex_init(3thr)**,
pthread_mutex_lock(3thr), **pthread_mutex_unlock(3thr)**,
pthread_mutexattr_setkind_np(3thr).

pthread_mutex_unlock

Purpose   Unlocks a mutex

Synopsis   #include <pthread.h>

int pthread_mutex_unlock(
    pthread_mutex_t *mutex);

Parameters

mutex   Mutex that is unlocked.

Description

The **pthread_mutex_unlock( )** routine unlocks a mutex. If no threads are waiting for the mutex, the mutex unlocks with no current owner. If one or more threads are waiting to lock the specified mutex, this routine causes one thread to return from its call to **pthread_mutex_lock( )**. The scheduling policy is used to determine which thread acquires the mutex. For the **SCHED_FIFO** and **SCHED_RR** policies, a blocked thread is chosen in priority order.

The results of calling this routine are unpredictable if the mutex specified in *mutex* is unlocked. The results of calling this routine are also unpredictable if the mutex specified in *mutex* is currently owned by a thread other than the calling thread.

Return Values

If the function fails, **errno** may be set to one of the following values:

Return	Error	Description
0		Successful completion.
-1	**[EINVAL]**	The value specified by *mutex* is invalid.

Related Information

Functions: **pthread_mutex_destroy(3thr)**, **pthread_mutex_init(3thr)**, **pthread_mutex_lock(3thr)**, **pthread_mutex_trylock(3thr)**, **pthread_unlock_global_np(3thr)**, **pthread_mutexattr_setkind_np(3thr)**.

pthread_mutexattr_create

Purpose   Creates a mutex attributes object

Synopsis   #include <pthread.h>

int pthread_mutexattr_create(
        pthread_mutexattr_t *attr);

Parameters

attr   Mutex attributes object created.

Description

The **pthread_mutexattr_create( )** routine creates a mutex attributes object used to specify the attributes of mutexes when they are created. The mutex attributes object is initialized with the default value for all of the attributes defined by a given implementation.

When a mutex attributes object is used to create a mutex, the values of the individual attributes determine the characteristics of the new object. Attributes objects act like additional parameters to object creation. Changing individual attributes does not affect any objects that were previously created using the attributes object.

Return Values

The created mutex attributes object is returned to the *attr* parameter.

If the function fails, **errno** may be set to one of the following values:

Return	Error	Description
0		Successful completion.
-1	[EINVAL]	The value specified by *attr* is invalid.
-1	[ENOMEM]	Insufficient memory exists to create the mutex attributes object.

Related Information

Functions: **pthread_create(3thr), pthread_mutex_init(3thr), pthread_mutexattr_delete(3thr), pthread_mutexattr_getkind_np(3thr), pthread_mutexattr_setkind_np(3thr)**.

pthread_mutexattr_delete

Purpose   Deletes a mutex attributes object

Synopsis   #include <pthread.h>

int pthread_mutexattr_delete(
        pthread_mutexattr_t *attr);

Parameters

attr   Mutex attributes object deleted.

Description

The **pthread_mutexattr_delete**( ) routine deletes a mutex attributes object. Call this routine when a mutex attributes object is no longer referenced by the **pthread_mutexattr_create**( ) routine.

This routine gives permission to reclaim storage for the mutex attributes object. Mutexes that were created using this attributes object are not affected by the deletion of the mutex attributes object.

The results of calling this routine are unpredictable if the attributes object specified in the *attr* parameter does not exist.

Return Values

If the function fails, **errno** may be set to one of the following values:

Return	Error	Description
0		Successful completion.
-1	[**EINVAL**]	The value specified by *attr* is invalid.

Related Information

Functions: **pthread_mutexattr_create(3thr)**.

pthread_mutexattr_getkind_np

Purpose   Obtains the mutex type attribute used when a mutex is created

Synopsis   #include <pthread.h>

int pthread_mutexattr_getkind_np(
        pthread_mutexattr_t *attr*);

Parameters

attr   Mutex attributes object whose mutex type is obtained.

Description

The **pthread_mutexattr_getkind_np( )** routine obtains the mutex type attribute
that is used when a mutex is created. See the **pthread_mutexattr_setkind_np( )**
reference page for information about mutex type attributes.

This routine is a new primitive.

Return Values

If the function fails, **errno** may be set to one of the following values:

Return	Error	Description
Mutex type attribute		Successful completion.
-1	[EINVAL]	The value specified by *attr* is invalid.

Related Information

Functions: **pthread_mutex_init(3thr)**, **pthread_mutexattr_create(3thr)**,
pthread_mutexattr_setkind_np(3thr).

pthread_mutexattr_setkind_np

Purpose   Specifies the mutex type attribute

Synopsis   **#include <pthread.h>**

int pthread_mutexattr_setkind_np(
   pthread_mutexattr_t *attr,
   int *kind***);**

Parameters

attr   Mutex attributes object modified.

kind   New value for the mutex type attribute. The *kind* parameter
                specifies the type of mutex that is created. Valid values are
                MUTEX_FAST_NP (default), **MUTEX_RECURSIVE_NP**, and
                MUTEX_NONRECURSIVE_NP.

Description

The **pthread_mutexattr_setkind_np( )** routine sets the mutex type attribute that is
used when a mutex is created.

A fast mutex is locked and unlocked in the fastest manner possible. A fast mutex
can only be locked (obtained) once. All subsequent calls to **pthread_mutex_-
lock( )** cause the calling thread to block until the mutex is freed by the thread that
owns it. If the thread that owns the mutex attempts to lock it again, the thread
waits for itself to release the mutex (causing a deadlock).

A recursive mutex can be locked more than once by the same thread without
causing that thread to deadlock. In other words, a single thread can make
consecutive calls to **pthread_mutex_lock( )** without blocking. The thread must
then call **pthread_mutex_unlock( )** the same number of times as it called
pthread_mutex_lock( ) before another thread can lock the mutex.

A nonrecursive mutex is locked only once by a thread, like a fast mutex. If the
thread tries to lock the mutex again without first unlocking it, the thread receives
an error. Thus, nonrecursive mutexes are more informative than fast mutexes
because fast mutexes block in such a case, leaving it up to you to determine why
the thread no longer executes. Also, if someone other than the owner tries to
unlock a nonrecursive mutex, an error is returned.

pthread_mutexattr_setkind_np(3thr)

Never use a recursive mutex with condition variables because the implicit unlock performed for a **pthread_cond_wait( )** or **pthread_cond_timedwait( )** might not actually release the mutex. In that case, no other thread can satisfy the condition of the predicate.

This routine is a new primitive.

Return Values

If the function fails, **errno** may be set to one of the following values:

Return	Error	Description
0		Successful completion.
-1	[EINVAL]	The value specified by *attr* is invalid.
-1	[EPERM]	The caller does not have the appropriate privileges.
-1	[ERANGE]	One or more parameters supplied have an invalid value.

Related Information

Functions: **pthread_mutex_init(3thr)**, **pthread_mutexattr_create(3thr)**, **pthread_mutexattr_getkind_np(3thr)**.

pthread_once

Purpose   Calls an initialization routine executed by one thread, a single time

Synopsis   **#include <pthread.h>**

int pthread_once(
         pthread_once_t ***once_block****,**
         pthread_initroutine_t *init_routine*);

Parameters

once_block   Address of a record that defines the one-time initialization code. Each one-time initialization routine must have its own unique **pthread_once_t** data structure.

init_routine   Address of a procedure that performs the initialization. This routine is called only once, regardless of the number of times it and its associated *once_block* are passed to **pthread_once( )**.

Description

The **pthread_once( )** routine calls an initialization routine executed by one thread, a single time. This routine allows you to create your own initialization code that is guaranteed to be run only once, even if called simultaneously by multiple threads or multiple times in the same thread.

For example, a mutex or a thread-specfic data key must be created exactly once. Calling **pthread_once( )** prevents the code that creates a mutex or thread-specific data from being called by multiple threads. Without this routine, the execution must be serialized so that only one thread performs the initialization. Other threads that reach the same point in the code are delayed until the first thread is finished.

This routine initializes the control record if it has not been initialized and then determines if the client one-time initialization routine has executed once. If it has not executed, this routine calls the initialization routine specified in *init_routine*. If the client one-time initialization code has executed once, this routine returns.

The **pthread_once_t** data structure is a record that allows client initialization operations to guarantee mutual exclusion of access to the initialization routine, and that each initialization routine is executed exactly once.

The client code must declare a variable of type **pthread_once_t** to use the client initialization operations. This variable must be initialized using the **pthread_once_init** macro, as follows:

```
static pthread_once_t myOnceBlock = pthread_once_init;
```

Return Values

If the function fails, **errno** may be set to one of the following values:

Return	Error	Description
-1	[EINVAL]	The value specified by a parameter is invalid.
0		Successful completion.

pthread_self

Purpose   Obtains the identifier of the current thread

Synopsis   **#include <pthread.h>**

pthread_t pthread_self( );

Description

The **pthread_self( )** routine allows a thread to obtain its own identifier. For example, this identifier allows a thread to set its own priority.

This value becomes meaningless when the thread object is deleted; that is, when the thread terminates its execution and **pthread_detach( )** is called.

Return Values

Returns the identifier of the calling thread to **pthread_t**.

Related Information

Functions: **pthread_create(3thr)**, **pthread_setprio(3thr)**, **pthread_setscheduler(3thr)**.

pthread_setasynccancel

Purpose   Enables or disables the current thread's asynchronous cancelability

Synopsis   **#include <pthread.h>**

int pthread_setasynccancel(
          int *state***);**

Parameters

state   State of asynchronous cancelability set for the calling thread. On
               return, receives the prior state of asynchronous cancelability. Valid
               values are as follows:

               CANCEL_ON
                         Asynchronous cancelability is enabled.

               CANCEL_OFF
                         Asynchronous cancelability is disabled.

Description

The **pthread_setasynccancel( )** routine enables or disables the current thread's
asynchronous cancelability and returns the previous asynchronous cancelability
state.

When general cancelability is set to **CANCEL_OFF**, a cancel cannot be delivered
to the thread, even if a cancelable routine is called or asynchronous cancelability is
enabled. When general cancelability is set to **CANCEL_ON**, cancelability
depends on the state of the thread's asynchronous cancelability.

When general cancelability is set to **CANCEL_ON** and asynchronous
cancelability is set to **CANCEL_OFF**, the thread can only receive a cancel at
specific cancellation points (for example, condition waits, thread joins, and calls to
the **pthread_testcancel( )** routine). If both general cancelability and asynchronous
cancelability are set to **CANCEL_ON**, the thread can be canceled at any point in
its execution.

When a thread is created, the default asynchronous cancelability state is
CANCEL_OFF.

If you call this routine to enable asynchronous cancels, call it in a region of code where asynchronous delivery of cancels is disabled by a previous call to this routine. Do not call threads routines in regions of code where asynchronous delivery of cancels is enabled. The previous state of asynchronous delivery can be restored later by another call to this routine.

Return Values

On successful completion, the previous state of asynchronous cancelability is returned. If the function fails, -1 is returned. Following are the possible return values and the possible corresponding values (if any) for **errno**:

Return	Error	Description
CANCEL_ON		Asynchronous cancelability was on.
CANCEL_OFF		Asynchronous cancelability was off.
-1	[EINVAL]	The specified state is not **CANCEL_ON** or **CANCEL_OFF**.

Related Information

Functions: **pthread_cancel(3thr)**, **pthread_setcancel(3thr)**, **pthread_testcancel(3thr)**.

pthread_setcancel

Purpose   Enables or disables the current thread's general cancelability

Synopsis   **#include <pthread.h>**

int pthread_setcancel(
        int *state***);**

Parameters

state   State of general cancelability set for the calling thread. On return, receives the prior state of general cancelability. Valid values are as follows:

CANCEL_ON
                General cancelability is enabled.

CANCEL_OFF
                General cancelability is disabled.

Description

The **pthread_setcancel( )** routine enables or disables the current thread's general cancelability and returns the previous general cancelability state.

When general cancelability is set to **CANCEL_OFF**, a cancel cannot be delivered to the thread, even if a cancelable routine is called or asynchronous cancelability is enabled.

When a thread is created, the default general cancelability state is **CANCEL_ON**.

Possible Dangers of Disabling Cancelability

The most important use of cancels is to ensure that indefinite wait operations are terminated. For example, a thread waiting on some network connection, which may take days to respond (or may never respond), is normally made cancelable.

However, when cancelability is disabled, no routine is cancelable. Waits must be completed normally before a cancel can be delivered. As a result, the program stops working and the user is unable to cancel the operation.

When disabling cancelability, be sure that no long waits can occur or that it is necessary for other reasons to defer cancels around that particular region of code.

Return Values

On successful completion, the previous state of general cancelability is returned. If the function fails, -1 is returned. Following are the possible return values and the possible corresponding values (if any) for **errno**:

Return	Error	Description
CANCEL_ON		Asynchronous cancelability was on.
CANCEL_OFF		Asynchronous cancelability was off.
-1	**[EINVAL]**	The specified state is not **CANCEL_ON** or **CANCEL_OFF**.

Related Information

Functions: **pthread_cancel(3thr)**, **pthread_setasynccancel(3thr)**, **pthread_testcancel(3thr)**.

pthread_setprio

Purpose   Changes the current priority of a thread

Synopsis   **#include <pthread.h>**

int pthread_setprio(
        pthread_t *thread*,
        int *priority*)**;**

Parameters

thread   Thread whose priority is changed.

priority   New priority value of the thread specified in *thread*. The priority
                value depends on scheduling policy. Valid values fall within one of
                the following ranges:

- **PRI_OTHER_MIN <=** *priority* **<= PRI_OTHER_MAX**

- **PRI_FIFO_MIN <=** *priority* **<= PRI_FIFO_MAX**

- **PRI_RR_MIN <=** *priority* **<= PRI_RR_MAX**

- **PRI_FG_MIN_NP <=** *priority* **<= PRI_FG_MAX_NP**

- **PRI_BG_MIN_NP <=** *priority* **<= PRI_BG_MAX_NP**

If you create a new thread without specifying a threads attributes object that
contains a changed priority attribute, the default priority of the newly created
thread is the midpoint between **PRI_OTHER_MIN** and **PRI_OTHER_MAX** (the
midpoint between the minimum and the maximum for the **SCHED_OTHER**
policy).

When you call this routine to specify a minimum or maximum priority, use the
appropriate symbol; for example, **PRI_FIFO_MIN** or **PRI_FIFO_MAX**. To
specify a value between the minimum and maximum, use an appropriate arithmetic
expression. For example, to specify a priority midway between the minimum and
maximum for the Round Robin scheduling policy, specify the following concept
using your programming language's syntax:

```
pri_rr_mid = (PRI_RR_MIN + PRI_RR_MAX + 1)/2
```

If your expression results in a value outside the range of minimum to maximum, an
error results when you use it.

Description

The **pthread_setprio( )** routine changes the current priority of a thread. A thread can change its own priority using the identifier returned by **pthread_self( )**.

Changing the priority of a thread can cause it to start executing or be preempted by another thread. The effect of setting different priority values depends on the scheduling priority assigned to the thread. The initial scheduling priority is set by calling the **pthread_attr_setprio( )** routine.

Note that **pthread_attr_setprio( )** sets the priority attribute that is used to establish the priority of a new thread when it is created. However, **pthread_setprio( )** changes the priority of an existing thread.

Return Values

If successful, this routine returns the previous priority. If the function fails, **errno** may be set to one of the following values:

Return	Error	Description
Previous priority		Successful completion.
-1	[EINVAL]	The value specified by *thread* is invalid.
-1	[ENOTSUP]	An attempt is made to set the policy to an unsupported value.
-1	[ESRCH]	The value specified by *thread* does not refer to an existing thread.
-1	[EPERM]	The caller does not have the appropriate privileges to set the priority of the specified thread.

Related Information

Functions: **pthread_attr_setprio(3thr)**, **pthread_attr_setsched(3thr)**, **pthread_create(3thr)**, **pthread_self(3thr)**, **pthread_setscheduler(3thr)**.

pthread_setscheduler

Purpose   Changes the current scheduling policy and priority of a thread

Synopsis   **#include <pthread.h>**

int pthread_setscheduler(
    pthread_t *thread,*
    int *scheduler,*
    int *priority*)**;**

Parameters

thread   Thread whose scheduling policy is to be changed.

scheduler   New scheduling policy value for the thread specified in *thread.*
                Valid values are as follows:

SCHED_FIFO
        (First In, First Out) The highest-priority thread runs
        until it blocks. If there is more than one thread with
        the same priority, and that priority is the highest
        among other threads, the first thread to begin running
        continues until it blocks.

SCHED_RR   (Round Robin) The highest-priority thread runs until
        it blocks; however, threads of equal priority, if that
        priority is the highest among other threads, are
        timesliced. Timeslicing is a process in which threads
        alternate using available processors.

SCHED_OTHER
        (Default)   All   threads   are   timesliced.
        SCHED_OTHER ensures that all threads, regardless
        of priority, receive some scheduling, and thus no
        thread is   completely   denied   execution   time.
        (However, **SCHED_OTHER** threads can be denied
        execution time by **SCHED_FIFO** or **SCHED_RR**
        threads.)

SCHED_FG_NP

(Foreground) Same as **SCHED_OTHER**. Threads are timesliced and priorities can be modified dynamically by the scheduler to ensure fairness.

SCHED_BG_NP

(Background) Like **SCHED_OTHER**, ensures that all threads, regardless of priority, receive some scheduling. However, **SCHED_BG_NP** can be denied execution by any of the other scheduling policies.

priority   New priority value of the thread specified in *thread*. The priority attribute depends on scheduling policy. Valid values fall within one of the following ranges:

- **PRI_OTHER_MIN** <= *priority* <= **PRI_OTHER_MAX**

- **PRI_FIFO_MIN** <= *priority* <= **PRI_FIFO_MAX**

- **PRI_RR_MIN** <= *priority* <= **PRI_RR_MAX**

- **PRI_FG_MIN_NP** <= *priority* <= **PRI_FG_MAX_NP**

- **PRI_BG_MIN_NP** <= *priority* <= **PRI_BG_MAX_NP**

If you create a new thread without specifying a threads attributes object that contains a changed priority attribute, the default priority of the newly created thread is the midpoint between **PRI_OTHER_MIN** and **PRI_OTHER_MAX** (the midpoint between the minimum and the maximum for the **SCHED_OTHER** policy).

When you call this routine to specify a minimum or maximum priority, use the appropriate symbol; for example, **PRI_FIFO_MIN** or **PRI_FIFO_MAX**. To specify a value between the minimum and maximum, use an appropriate arithmetic expression. For example, to specify a priority midway between the minimum and maximum for the Round Robin scheduling policy, specify the following concept using your programming language's syntax:

```
pri_rr_mid = (PRI_RR_MIN + PRI_RR_MAX)/2
```

If your expression results in a value outside the range of minimum to maximum, an error results when you use it.

pthread_setscheduler(3thr)

Description

The **pthread_setscheduler( )** routine changes the current scheduling policy and priority of a thread. Call this routine to change both the priority and scheduling policy of a thread at the same time. To change only the priority, call the **pthread_setprio( )** routine.

A thread changes its own scheduling policy and priority by using the identifier returned by **pthread_self( )**. Changing the scheduling policy or priority, or both, of a thread can cause it to start executing or to be preempted by another thread.

This routine differs from **pthread_attr_setprio( )** and **pthread_attr_setsched( )** because those routines set the priority and scheduling policy attributes that are used to establish the priority and scheduling policy of a new thread when it is created. This routine, however, changes the priority and scheduling policy of an existing thread.

Return Values

If successful, the previous scheduling policy value is returned. If the function fails, **errno** may be set to one of the following values:

Return	Error	Description
Previous policy		Successful completion.
-1	**[EINVAL]**	The value specified by *thread* is invalid.
-1	**[ENOTSUP]**	An attempt is made to set the policy to an unsupported value.
-1	**[ESRCH]**	The value specified by *thread* does not refer to an existing thread.
-1	**[EPERM]**	The caller does not have the appropriate privileges to set the scheduling policy of the specified thread.

Related Information

Functions: **pthread_attr_setprio(3thr), pthread_attr_setsched(3thr), pthread_create(3thr), pthread_self(3thr), pthread_setprio(3thr)**.

pthread_setspecific

Purpose   Sets the thread-specific data associated with the specified key for the current thread

Synopsis   **#include <pthread.h>**

int pthread_setspecific(
        pthread_key_t *key*,
        pthread_addr_t *value*);

Parameters

key   Context key value that uniquely identifies the context value specified in *value*. This key value must have been obtained from **pthread_keycreate( )**.

value   Address containing data to be associated with the specified key for the current thread; this is the thread-specific data.

Description

The **pthread_setspecific( )** routine sets the thread-specific data associated with the specified key for the current thread. If a value has already been defined for the key in this thread, the new value is substituted for it.

Different threads can bind different values to the same key. These values are typically pointers to blocks of dynamically allocated memory that are reserved for use by the calling thread.

Return Values

If the function fails, -1 is returned, and **errno** may be set to the following value:

Return	Error	Description
-1	**[EINVAL]**	The key value is invalid.

Related Information

Functions: **pthread_getspecific(3thr)**, **pthread_keycreate(3thr)**.

pthread_signal_to_cancel_np

Purpose   Cancels the specified thread

Synopsis   #include <pthread.h>

int pthread_signal_to_cancel_np(
        sigset_t *sigset,
        pthread_t *thread);

Parameters

sigset   Signal mask containing a list of signals that, when received by the process, cancels the specified thread.

thread   Thread canceled if a valid signal is received by the process.

Description

The **pthread_signal_to_cancel_np( )** routine requests that the specified thread be canceled if one of the signals specified in the signal mask is received by the process. The set of legal signals is the same as that for the **sigwait( )** service. The sigset parameter is not validated. If it is invalid, this routine will return successfully but neither the specified thread nor the previously specified thread will be canceled if a signal occurs.

Note that the address of the specified thread is saved in a per-process global variable. Therefore, any subsequent call to this routine by your application or any library function will supercede the thread specified in the previous call, and that thread will not be canceled if one of the signals specified for it is delivered to the process. In other words, take care when you call this routine; if another thread calls it after you do, the expected result of this routine will not occur.

Return Values

If the function fails, **errno** may be set to one of the following values:

Return	Error	Description
0		Successful completion.
-1	[**EINVAL**]	The value specified by *thread* is invalid.

Related Information

Functions: **pthread_cancel(3thr)**.

pthread_testcancel

Purpose   Requests delivery of a pending cancel to the current thread

Synopsis   #include <pthread.h>

void pthread_testcancel( );

Description

The **pthread_testcancel( )** routine requests delivery of a pending cancel to the
current thread. The cancel is delivered only if a cancel is pending for the current
thread and general cancel delivery is not currently disabled. (A thread disables
delivery of cancels to itself by calling the **pthread_setcancel( )** routine.)

This routine, when called within very long loops, ensures that a pending cancel is
noticed within a reasonable amount of time.

Return Values

No value is returned.

Related Information

Functions: **pthread_cancel(3thr), pthread_setasynccancel(3thr),
pthread_setcancel(3thr).**

pthread_unlock_global_np

Purpose   Unlocks a global mutex

Synopsis   **#include <pthread.h>**

void pthread_unlock_global_np( );

Description

The **pthread_unlock_global_np( )** routine unlocks the global mutex when each call to **pthread_lock_global_np( )** is matched by a call to this routine. For example, if you called **pthread_lock_global_np( )** three times, **pthread_unlock_global_np( )** unlocks the global mutex when you call it the third time. If no threads are waiting for the global mutex, it becomes unlocked with no current owner. If one or more threads are waiting to lock the global mutex, one thread returns from its call to **pthread_lock_global_np( )**. The scheduling policy is used to determine which thread acquires the global mutex. For the policies **SCHED_FIFO** and **SCHED_RR**, a blocked thread is chosen in priority order.

The results of calling this routine are unpredictable if the global mutex is already unlocked. The results of calling this routine are also unpredictable if the global mutex is owned by a thread other than the calling thread.

This routine is a new primitive.

Return Values

No value is returned.

Related Information

Functions: **pthread_lock_global_np(3thr)**, **pthread_mutex_lock(3thr)**, **pthread_mutex_unlock(3thr)**, **pthread_mutexattr_setkind_np(3thr)**.

pthread_yield

Purpose   Notifies the scheduler that the current thread is willing to release its processor

Synopsis   #include <pthread.h>

void pthread_yield( );

Description

The **pthread_yield( )** routine notifies the scheduler that the current thread is willing to release its processor to other threads of the same priority. (A thread releases its processor to a thread of a higher priority without calling this routine.)

If the current thread's scheduling policy (as specified in a call to the **pthread_attr_setsched( )** or **pthread_setscheduler( )** routine) is **SCHED_FIFO** or **SCHED_RR**, this routine yields the processor to other threads of the same or a higher priority. If no threads of the same priority are ready to execute, the thread continues.

This routine allows knowledge of the details of an application to be used to increase fairness. It increases fairness of access to the processor by removing the current thread from the processor. It also increases fairness of access to shared resources by removing the current thread from the processor as soon as it is finished with the resource.

Call this routine when a thread is executing code that denies access to other threads on a uniprocessor if the scheduling policy is **SCHED_FIFO**.

Use **pthread_yield( )** carefully because misuse causes unnecessary context switching, which increases overhead without increasing fairness. For example, it is counterproductive for a thread to yield while it has a needed resource locked.

Return Values

No value is returned.

Related Information

Functions: **pthread_attr_setsched(3thr)**, **pthread_setscheduler(3thr)**.

sigaction

Purpose   Examines and changes synchronous signal actions (POSIX software signal facilities)

Synopsis   **#include <signal.h>**

struct sigaction {
    void (*sa_handler) ( );
    sigset_t *sa_mask***;**
    int *sa_flags***;**
};

int sigaction(*sig, act, oact***)**
int *sig***;**
const struct sigaction **act***;**
struct sigaction **oact***;**

Parameters

sig   Synchronous signal to examine or change.

act   Points to a **sigaction** structure that describes the action to be taken upon receipt of the signal indicated by the value of the *act* parameter.

oact   Points to a **sigaction** structure in which the signal action data in effect at the time of the **sigaction( )** function call is returned.

Description

The **sigaction** POSIX service allows for per-thread handlers to be installed for catching synchronous signals. It is called in a multithreaded process to establish thread specific actions for such signals. This call is the POSIX equivalent of the **sigaction( )** system call with the following exceptions or modifications:

- The **sigaction( )** routine only modifies behavior for individual threads.

- The **sigaction( )** routine only works for synchronous signals. Attempting to set a signal action for an asynchronous signal is an error. This is true even in a single-threaded process.

Any multithreaded application using DCE Threads will need to use the **sigwait( )** function for dealing with asynchronous signals. The **sigwait( )** function can be used to synchronously wait for delivery of asynchronously generated signals.

- The **SA_RESTART** flag is always set by the underlying system in POSIX mode so that interrupted system calls will fail with return value of -1 and the **EINTR** error in *errno* instead of getting restarted.

  The system's **SA_RESTART** flag has the opposite meaning of the **SA_-RESTART** flag in the *sa_flags* field and is always set in the underlying system call resulting from **sigaction( )** regardless of whether **SA_-RESTART** was indicated in *sa_flags*.

- The signal mask is manipulated using the POSIX § 3.3.3 **sigsetops( )** functions. They are **sigemptyset( )**, **sigfillset( )**, **sigaddset( )**, **sigdelset( )**, and **sigismember( )**.

The **sigaction( )** function can be used to inquire about the current handling of a given signal by specifying a null pointer for *act*, since the action is unchanged unless this parameter is not a null pointer. In order for the signal action in effect at the time of the **sigaction( )** call to be returned, the *oact* parameter must not be a null pointer.

Return Values

Possible return values are as follows:

Return	Error	Description
0		Successful completion.
-1	[EFAULT]	Either *act* or *oact* points to memory which is not a valid part of the process address space. A new signal handler is not installed.
-1	[EINVAL]	The value specified by *sig* is invalid. A new signal handler is not installed.
-1	[EINVAL]	An attempt is made to ignore or supply a handler for **SIGKILL** or **SIGSTOP**. A new signal handler is not installed.

Related Information

Functions: **setjmp(3)**, **siginterrupt(3)**, **sigpending(3thr)**, **sigprocmask(3thr)**, **sigsetops(3)**, **sigsuspend(3)**, **sigvec(2)**, **tty(4)**.

sigppending

Purpose   Examines pending signals (POSIX software signal facilities)

Synopsis   **#include <signal.h>**

    int sigpending(sigset_t **set*);

Parameters

set   Points to a location in which the signals that are blocked from delivery and pending at the time of the **sigpending( )** function call are returned.

Description

The **sigpending( )** function stores the set of signals that are blocked from delivery and pending for the calling process in the space pointed to by the argument *set*.

The **sigpending( )** function may be called by any thread in a multithreaded process to determine which signals are in the pending set for that thread. Since DCE Threads supports the **{_POSIX_THREADS_PER_PROCESS_SIGNALS_1}** option, signals pending upon the thread are those that are pending upon the process.

Return Values

Possible return values are as follows:

Return	Error	Description
0		Successful completion.
-1	**[EFAULT]**	The *set* argument points to memory that is not a valid part of the process address space.

Related Information

Functions: **sigprocmask(3thr), sigsetops(3).**

sigprocmask

Purpose   Examines and changes blocked signals (POSIX software signal facilities)

Synopsis   **#include <signal.h>**

int sigprocmask(int *how*, **const sigset_t** *set, **sigset_t** *oset)**;**

Parameters

how	The manner in which the values in *set* are changed as defined by one of the described argument values.
set	A set of signals that will be used to change the current thread's signal mask according to the value in the *how* parameter.
oset	Points to a location in which the signal mask in effect at the time of the **sigprocmask( )** function call is returned.

Description

The **sigprocmask( )** function is used to examine or change (or both) the signal mask of the calling process. If the value of the argument *set* is not NULL, it points to a set of signals to be used to change the currently blocked set according to the *how* parameter as follows:

SIG_BLOCK
The resulting signal set is the union of the current set and the signal set pointed to by the argument *set*.

SIG_UNBLOCK
The resulting signal set is the intersection of the current set and the and the complement of the signal set pointed to by the argument *set*.

SIG_SETMASK
The resulting signal set is the signal set pointed to by the argument *set*.

If the argument *oset* is not NULL, the previous mask is stored in the space pointed to by *oset*.

sigprocmask(3thr)

The **sigprocmask( )** function can be used to inquire about the currently blocked signals by specifying a null pointer for *set*, since the value of the argument *how* is not significant and the signal mask of the process is unchanged unless this parameter is not a null pointer. In order for the signal mask in effect at the time of the **sigprocmask( )** call to be returned, the *oset* argument must not be a null pointer.

If there are any pending unblocked signals after the call to the **sigprocmask( )** function, at least one of those signals shall be delivered before the **sigprocmask( )** function returns. As a system restriction, the SIGKILL and SIGSTOP signals cannot be blocked.

If the **sigprocmask( )** function fails, the signal mask of the process is not changed by this function call.

Return Values

Possible return values are as follows:

Return	Error	Description
0		Successful completion.
-1	[EINVAL]	The value specified by the *how* parameter is not equal to one of the defined values. The signal mask of the process remains unchanged.

Related Information

Functions: **sigaction(3thr)**, **sigpending(3thr)**, **sigsetops(3)**, **sigsuspend(3)**.

sigwait

Purpose   Causes a thread to wait for an asynchronous signal

Synopsis   **#include <pthread.h>**

int sigwait(
    sigset_t *_set_);

Parameters

    set   Set of pending signals upon which the calling thread will wait.

Description

This routine causes a thread to wait for an asynchronous signal. It atomically chooses a pending signal from *set*, atomically clears it from the system's set of pending signals and returns that signal number. If no signal in *set* is pending at the time of the call, the thread is blocked until one or more signals becomes pending. The signals defined by *set* may be unblocked during the call to this routine and will be blocked when the thread returns from the call unless some other thread is currently waiting for one of those signals.

A thread must block the signals it waits for using **sigprocmask**() prior to calling this function.

If more than one thread is using this routine to wait for the same signal, only one of these threads will return from this routine with the signal number.

A call to **sigwait**() is a cancellation point.

Return Values

Possible return values are as follows:

Return	Error	Description
Signal number		Successful completion.
-1	[**EINVAL**]	One or more of the values specified by *set* is invalid.
-1	[**EINVAL**]	One or more of the values specified by *set* is not blocked.
-1	[**EINVAL**]	There are no values specified in *set*.

Related Information

Functions: **pause(3)**, **pthread_cancel(3thr)**, **pthread_setasynccancel(3thr)**, **sigpending(3)**, **sigprocmask(3)**, **sigsetops(3)**.

Chapter 2

DCE Distributed Time Service

dts_intro

Purpose   Introduction to DCE Distributed Time Service (DTS)

Description

The DCE Distributed Time Service programming routines can obtain timestamps that are based on Coordinated Universal Time (UTC), translate between different timestamp formats, and perform calculations on timestamps. Applications can call the DTS routines from server or clerk systems and use the timestamps that DTS supplies to determine event sequencing, duration, and scheduling.

The DTS routines can perform the following basic functions:

- Retrieve the current (UTC-based) time from DTS.

- Convert binary timestamps expressed in the **utc** time structure to or from **tm** structure components.

- Convert the binary timestamps expressed in the **utc** time structure to or from **timespec** structure components.

- Convert the binary timestamps expressed in the **utc** time structure to or from ASCII strings.

- Compare two binary time values.

- Calculate binary time values.

- Obtain time zone information.

DTS can convert between several types of binary time structures that are based on different calendars and time unit measurements. DTS uses UTC-based time structures, and can convert other types of time structures to its own presentation of UTC-based time.

Absolute time is an interval on a time scale; absolute time measurements are derived from system clocks or external time-providers. For DTS, absolute times reference the UTC standard and include the inaccuracy and other information. When you display an absolute time, DTS converts the time to ASCII text, as shown in the following display:

```
1992-11-21-13:30:25.785-04:00I000.082
```

Relative time is a discrete time interval that is often added to or subtracted from an absolute time. A TDF associated with an absolute time is one example of a relative time. Note that a relative time does not use the calendar date fields, since these fields concern absolute time.

UTC is the international time standard that DTS uses. The zero hour of UTC is based on the zero hour of Greenwich Mean Time (GMT). The documentation consistently refers to the time zone of the Greenwich Meridian as GMT. However, this time zone is also sometimes referred to as UTC.

The Time Differential Factor (TDF) is the difference between UTC and the time in a particular time zone.

The user's environment determines the time zone rule (details are system dependent). For example, on OSF/1 systems, the user selects a time zone by specifying the **TZ** environment variable. (The reference information for the **localtime( )** system call, which is described in the **ctime(3)** reference page, provides additional information.)

If the user's environment does not specify a time zone rule, the system's rule is used (details of the rule are system dependent). For example, on OSF/1 systems, the rule in **/etc/zoneinfo/localtime** applies.

The *OSF DCE Application Development Guide* provides additional information about UTC and GMT, TDF and time zones, and relative and absolute times.

Unless otherwise specified, the default input and output parameters are as follows:

- If NULL is specified for a *utc* input parameter, the current time is used.

- If NULL is specified for any output parameter, no result is returned.

The following illustration categorizes the DTS portable interface routines by function.

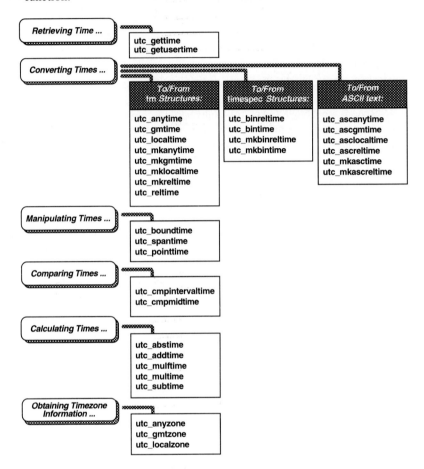

An alphabetical listing of the DTS portable interface routines and a brief description of each one follows:

utc_abstime( )

Computes the absolute value of a relative binary timestamp.

utc_addtime( )

Computes the sum of two binary timestamps; the timestamps can be two relative times or a relative time and an absolute time.

utc_anytime( )

Converts a binary timestamp to a **tm** structure by using the TDF information contained in the timestamp to determine the TDF returned with the **tm** structure.

utc_anyzone( )

Gets the time zone label and offset from GMT by using the TDF contained in the *utc* input parameter.

utc_ascanytime( )

Converts a binary timestamp to an ASCII string that represents an arbitrary time zone.

utc_ascgmtime( )

Converts a binary timestamp to an ASCII string that expresses a GMT time.

utc_asclocaltime( )

Converts a binary timestamp to an ASCII string that represents a local time.

utc_ascreltime( )

Converts a relative binary timestamp to an ASCII string that represents the time.

utc_binreltime( )

Converts a relative binary timestamp to two **timespec** structures that express relative time and inaccuracy.

utc_bintime( )

Converts a binary timestamp to a **timespec** structure.

utc_boundtime( )

Given two UTC times, one before and one after an event, returns a single UTC time whose inaccuracy includes the event.

utc_cmpintervaltime( )

Compares two binary timestamps or two relative binary timestamps.

utc_cmpmidtime( )

Compares two binary timestamps or two relative binary timestamps, ignoring inaccuracies.

utc_gettime( )

Returns the current system time and inaccuracy as a binary timestamp.

utc_getusertime( )
> Returns the time and process-specific TDF, rather than the system-specific TDF.

utc_gmtime( )
> Converts a binary timestamp to a **tm** structure that expresses GMT or the equivalent UTC.

utc_gmtzone( )
> Gets the time zone label for GMT.

utc_localtime( )
> Converts a binary timestamp to a **tm** structure that expresses local time.

utc_localzone( )
> Gets the local time zone label and offset from GMT, given **utc**.

utc_mkanytime( )
> Converts a **tm** structure and TDF (expressing the time in an arbitrary time zone) to a binary timestamp.

utc_mkascreltime( )
> Converts a NULL-terminated character string that represents a relative timestamp to a binary timestamp.

utc_mkasctime( )
> Converts a NULL-terminated character string that represents an absolute timestamp to a binary timestamp.

utc_mkbinreltime( )
> Converts a **timespec** structure expressing a relative time to a binary timestamp.

utc_mkbintime( )
> Converts a **timespec** structure to a binary timestamp.

utc_mkgmtime( )
> Converts a **tm** structure that expresses GMT or UTC to a binary timestamp.

utc_mklocaltime( )
> Converts a **tm** structure that expresses local time to a binary timestamp.

utc_mkreltime( )
> Converts a **tm** structure that expresses relative time to a relative binary timestamp.

utc_mulftime( )

Multiplies a relative binary timestamp by a floating-point value.

utc_multime( )

Multiplies a relative binary timestamp by an integer factor.

utc_pointtime( )

Converts a binary timestamp to three binary timestamps that represent the earliest, most likely, and latest time.

utc_reltime( )

Converts a relative binary timestamp to a **tm** structure.

utc_spantime( )

Given two (possibly unordered) binary timestamps, returns a single UTC time interval whose inaccuracy spans the two input binary timestamps.

utc_subtime( )

Computes the difference between two binary timestamps that express either an absolute time and a relative time, two relative times, or two absolute times.

Related Information

Books: *OSF DCE Application Development Guide—Core Components*.

utc_abstime

Purpose   Computes the absolute value of a relative binary timestamp

Synopsis   **#include <dce/utc.h>**

int utc_abstime(
     utc_t* *result*,
     utc_t *utc)**;**

Parameters

Input

utc   Relative binary timestamp. Use NULL if you want this routine to
             use the current time for this parameter.

Output

result   Absolute value of the input relative binary timestamp.

Description

The **utc_abstime( )** routine computes the absolute value of a relative binary
timestamp. The input timestamp represents a relative (delta) time.

Return Values

0   Indicates that the routine executed successfully.

-1   Indicates an invalid time parameter or invalid results.

Examples   The following example scales a relative time, computes its absolute value, and
prints the result.

```
utc_t      relutc, scaledutc;
char       timstr[UTC_MAX_STR_LEN];

/*
 *   Make sure relative timestamp represents a positive interval...
 */
```

```
utc_abstime(&relutc,              /* Out: Abs-value of rel time  */
            &relutc);             /* In:  Relative time to scale */

/*
 *    Scale it by a factor of 17...
 */

utc_multime(&scaledutc,           /* Out: Scaled relative time   */
            &relutc,              /* In:  Relative time to scale */
            17L);                 /* In:  Scale factor           */

utc_ascreltime(timstr,            /* Out: ASCII relative time    */
            UTC_MAX_STR_LEN,      /* In:  Length of input string */
            &scaledutc);          /* In:  Relative time to       */
                                  /*      convert                */

printf("%s\n",timstr);

/*
 *    Scale it by a factor of 17.65...
 */

utc_mulftime(&scaledutc,          /* Out: Scaled relative time   */
            &relutc,              /* In:  Relative time to scale */
            17.65);               /* In:  Scale factor           */

utc_ascreltime(timstr,            /* Out: ASCII relative time    */
            UTC_MAX_STR_LEN,      /* In:  Length of input string */
            &scaledutc);          /* In:  Relative time to       */
                                  /*      convert                */

printf("%s\n",timstr);
```

utc_addtime

Purpose   Computes the sum of two binary timestamps

Synopsis   **#include <dce/utc.h>**

  int utc_addtime(
      utc_t* *result,*
      utc_t **utc1,*
      utc_t **utc2);*

Parameters

Input

  utc1   Binary timestamp or relative binary timestamp. Use NULL if you want this routine to use the current time for this parameter.

  utc2   Binary timestamp or relative binary timestamp. Use NULL if you want this routine to use the current time for this parameter.

Output

  result   Resulting binary timestamp or relative binary timestamp, depending upon the operation performed:

  - *relative time+relative time=relative time*

  - *absolute time+relative time=absolute time*

  - *relative time+absolute time=absolute time*

  - *absolute time+absolute time* is undefined. (See the note later in this reference page.)

Description

The **utc_addtime( )** routine adds two binary timestamps, producing a third binary timestamp whose inaccuracy is the sum of the two input inaccuracies. One or both of the input timestamps typically represents a relative (delta) time. The TDF in the first input timestamp is copied to the output. The timestamps can be two relative times or a relative time and an absolute time.

Notes   Although no error is returned, the combination *absolute time+absolute time* should *not* be used.

Return Values

0   Indicates that the routine executed successfully.

-1   Indicates an invalid time parameter or invalid results.

Examples   The following example shows how to compute a timestamp that represents a time at least 5 seconds in the future.

```
utc_t               now, future, fivesec;
reltimespec_t       tfivesec;
timespec_t          tzero;

/*  Construct a timestamp that represents 5 seconds...
 */
tfivesec.tv_sec = 5;
tfivesec.tv_nsec = 0;
tzero.tv_sec = 0;
tzero.tv_nsec = 0;
utc_mkbinreltime(&fivesec,       /* Out: 5 secs in binary timestamp   */
                 &tfivesec,      /* In:  5 secs in timespec           */
                 &tzero);        /* In:  0 secs inaccuracy in timespec */

/*  Get the maximum possible current time...
 *  (The NULL input parameter is used to specify the current time.)
 */
utc_pointtime((utc_t *)0,        /* Out: Earliest possible current time */
              (utc_t *)0,        /* Out: Midpoint of current time       */
              &now,              /* Out: Latest possible current time   */
              (utc_t *)0);       /* In:  Use current time               */

/*  Add 5 seconds to get future timestamp...
 */
utc_addtime(&future,             /* Out: Future binary timestamp        */
            &now,                /* In:  Latest possible time now       */
            &fivesec);           /* In:  5 secs                         */
```

Related Information

Functions: **utc_subtime(3dts)**.

utc_anytime

Purpose   Converts a binary timestamp to a **tm** structure

Synopsis   **#include <dce/utc.h>**

        int utc_anytime(
                struct tm *_timetm,_
                long *_tns,_
                struct tm *_inacctm,_
                long *_ins,_
                long *_tdf,_
                utc_t *_utc_**);**

Parameters

Input

    utc   Binary timestamp. Use NULL if you want this routine to use the current time for this parameter.

Output

    timetm   Time component of the binary timestamp expressed in the timestamp's local time.

    tns   Nanoseconds since the time component of the binary timestamp.

    inacctm   Seconds of the inaccuracy component of the binary timestamp. If the inaccuracy is finite, then **tm_mday** returns a value of -1 and **tm_mon** and **tm_year** return values of 0 (zero). The field **tm_yday** contains the inaccuracy in days. If the inaccuracy is unspecified, all **tm** structure fields return values of -1.

    ins   Nanoseconds of the inaccuracy component of the binary timestamp.

    tdf   TDF component of the binary timestamp in units of seconds east of GMT.

Description

The **utc_anytime( )** routine converts a binary timestamp to a **tm** structure by using the TDF information contained in the timestamp to determine the TDF returned with the **tm** structure. The TDF information contained in the timestamp is returned with the time and inaccuracy components; the TDF component determines the offset from GMT and the local time value of the **tm** structure. Additional returns include nanoseconds since time and nanoseconds of inaccuracy.

Return Values

0   Indicates that the routine executed successfully.

-1   Indicates an invalid time argument or invalid results.

Examples

The following example converts a timestamp by using the TDF information in the timestamp, and then prints the result.

```
utc_t              evnt;
struct tm          tmevnt;
timespec_t         tevnt, ievnt;
char               tznam[80];


/*   Assume evnt contains the timestamp to convert...
 *
 *   Get time as a tm structure, using the time zone information in
 *   the timestamp...
 */
utc_anytime(&tmevnt,           /* Out: tm struct of time of evnt    */
            (long *)0,         /* Out: nanosec of time of evnt      */
            (struct tm *)0,    /* Out: tm struct of inacc of evnt   */
            (long *)0,         /* Out: nanosec of inacc of evnt     */
            (int *)0,          /* Out: tdf of evnt                  */
            &evnt);            /* In:  binary timestamp of evnt     */

/*   Get the time and inaccuracy as timespec structures...
 */
utc_bintime(&tevnt,            /* Out: timespec of time of evnt     */
            &ievnt,            /* Out: timespec of inacc of evnt    */
            (int *)0,          /* Out: tdf of evnt                  */
            &evnt);            /* In:  Binary timestamp of evnt     */

/*   Construct the time zone name from time zone information in the
 *   timestamp...
 */
```

utc_anytime(3dts)

```
utc_anyzone(tznam,         /* Out: Time zone name           */
            80,            /* In:  Size of time zone name   */
            (long *)0,     /* Out: tdf of event             */
            (long *)0,     /* Out: Daylight saving flag     */
            &evnt);        /* In:  Binary timestamp of evnt */

/*    Print timestamp in the format:
 *
 *          1991-03-05-21:27:50.023I0.140 (GMT-5:00)
 *          1992-04-02-12:37:24.003Iinf (GMT+7:00)
 */

printf("%d-%02d-%02d-%02d:%02d:%02d.%03d",
        tmevnt.tm_year+1900, tmevnt.tm_mon+1, tmevnt.tm_mday,
        tmevnt.tm_hour, tmevnt.tm_min, tmevnt.tm_sec,
        (tevnt.tv_nsec/1000000));

if ((long)ievnt.tv_sec == -1)
    printf("Iinf");
else
    printf("I%d.%03d", ievnt.tv_sec, (ievnt.tv_nsec/1000000));

printf(" (%s)\n", tznam);
```

Related Information

Functions: **utc_anyzone(3dts), utc_gettime(3dts), utc_getusertime(3dts), utc_gmtime(3dts), utc_localtime(3dts), utc_mkanytime(3dts).**

utc_anyzone

Purpose   Gets the time zone label and offset from GMT

Synopsis   **#include <dce/utc.h>**

int utc_anyzone(
            char **tzname,*
            size_t *tzlen,*
            long **tdf,*
            int **isdst,*
            const utc_t **utc);*

Parameters

Input

    tzlen   Length of the *tzname* buffer.

    utc   Binary timestamp. Use NULL if you want this routine to use the
                current time for this parameter.

Output

    tzname   Character string that is long enough to hold the time zone label.

    tdf   Long word with differential in seconds east of GMT.

    isdst   Integer with a value of -1, indicating that no information is supplied
                as to whether it is standard time or daylight saving time. A value of
                -1 is always returned.

Description

The **utc_anyzone( )** routine gets the time zone label and offset from GMT by using
the TDF contained in the *utc* input parameter. The label returned is always of the
form GMT+*n* or GMT-*n* where *n* is the *tdf* expressed in *hours:minutes*. (The label
associated with an arbitrary time zone is not known; only the offset is known.)

utc_anyzone(3dts)

Notes　　All of the output parameters are optional. No value is returned and no error occurs if the pointer is NULL.

Return Values

0　　　　Indicates that the routine executed successfully.

-1　　　Indicates an invalid time argument or an insufficient buffer.

Examples　See the sample program in the **utc_anytime(3dts)** reference page.

Related Information

Functions: **utc_anytime(3dts)**, **utc_gmtzone(3dts)**, **utc_localzone(3dts)**.

utc_ascanytime

Purpose   Converts a binary timestamp to an ASCII string that represents an arbitrary time zone

Synopsis   **#include <dce/utc.h>**

int utc_ascanytime(
       char *cp,
       size_t *stringlen*,
       utc_t **utc***);**

Parameters

Input

stringlen	The length of the *cp* buffer.
utc	Binary timestamp. Use NULL if you want this routine to use the current time for this parameter.

Output

cp	ASCII string that represents the time.

Description

The **utc_ascanytime( )** routine converts a binary timestamp to an ASCII string that expresses a time. The TDF component in the timestamp determines the local time used in the conversion.

Return Values

0	Indicates that the routine executed successfully.
-1	Indicates an invalid time parameter or invalid results.

utc_ascanytime(3dts)

Examples   The following example converts a time to an ASCII string that expresses the time in the time zone where the timestamp was generated.

```
utc_t      evnt;
char       localTime[UTC_MAX_STR_LEN];

/*
 *  Assuming that evnt contains the timestamp to convert, convert
 *  the time to ASCII in the following format:
 *
 *          1991-04-01-12:27:38.37-8:00I2.00
 */

utc_ascanytime(localtime,           /* Out: Converted time     */
               UTC_MAX_STR_LEN,     /* In:  Length of string   */
               &evnt);              /* In:  Time to convert    */
```

Related Information

Functions: **utc_ascgmtime(3dts)**, **utc_asclocaltime(3dts)**.

utc_ascgmtime

Purpose   Converts a binary timestamp to an ASCII string that expresses a GMT time

Synopsis   **#include <dce/utc.h>**

int utc_ascgmtime(
          char *cp,
          size_t *stringlen,*
          utc_t **utc);*

Parameters

Input

stringlen	Length of the *cp* buffer.
utc	Binary timestamp.

Output

cp	ASCII string that represents the time.

Description

The **utc_ascgmtime( )** routine converts a binary timestamp to an ASCII string that expresses a time in GMT.

Return Values

0	Indicates that the routine executed successfully.
-1	Indicates an invalid time parameter or invalid results.

Examples The following example converts the current time to GMT format.

```
char    gmTime[UTC_MAX_STR_LEN];

/*   Convert the current time to ASCII in the following format:
 *          1991-04-01-12:27:38.37I2.00
 */
utc_ascgmtime(gmTime,              /* Out: Converted time      */
              UTC_MAX_STR_LEN,     /* In:  Length of string    */
              (utc_t*) NULL);      /* In:  Time to convert     */
                                   /* Default is current time  */
```

Related Information

Functions: **utc_ascanytime(3dts), utc_asclocaltime(3dts)**.

utc_asclocaltime

Purpose   Converts a binary timestamp to an ASCII string that represents a local time

Synopsis   **#include <dce/utc.h>**

int utc_asclocaltime(
        char *cp,
        size_t *stringlen,*
        utc_t *utc);

Parameters

Input

      stringlen   Length of the *cp* buffer.

      utc   Binary timestamp. Use NULL if you want this routine to use the current time for this parameter.

Output

      cp   ASCII string that represents the time.

Description

The **utc_asclocaltime( )** routine converts a binary timestamp to an ASCII string that expresses local time.

The user's environment determines the time zone rule (details are system dependent). For example, on OSF/1 systems, the user selects a time zone by specifying the **TZ** environment variable. (The reference information for the **localtime( )** system call, which is described in the **ctime(3)** reference page, provides additional information.)

If the user's environment does not specify a time zone rule, the system's rule is used (details of the rule are system dependent). For example, on OSF/1 systems, the rule in **/etc/zoneinfo/localtime** applies.

Return Values

0   Indicates that the routine executed successfully.

-1   Indicates an invalid time parameter or invalid results.

Examples   The following example converts the current time to local time.

```
char    localTime[UTC_MAX_STR_LEN];

/*  Convert the current time...
 */

utc_asclocaltime(localTime,      /* Out:  Converted time      */
                 UTC_MAX_STR_LEN,  /* In:   Length of string    */
                 (utc_t*) NULL);   /* In:   Time to convert     */
                                   /* Default is current time   */
```

Related Information

Functions: **utc_ascanytime(3dts)**, **utc_ascgmtime(3dts)**.

utc_ascreltime

Purpose   Converts a relative binary timestamp to an ASCII string that represents the time

Synopsis   **#include <dce/utc.h>**

int utc_ascreltime(
        char *cp,
        const size_t *stringlen*,
        utc_t *utc);

Parameters

Input

  utc   Relative binary timestamp.

  stringlen Length of the *cp* buffer.

Output

  cp   ASCII string that represents the time.

Description

The **utc_ascreltime( )** routine converts a relative binary timestamp to an ASCII string that represents the time.

Return Values

  0   Indicates that the routine executed successfully.

  -1   Indicates an invalid time parameter or invalid results.

Examples   See the sample program in the **utc_abstime(3dts)** reference page.

Related Information

Functions: **utc_mkascreltime(3dts)**.

utc_binreltime

Purpose   Converts a relative binary timestamp to two **timespec** structures that express relative time and inaccuracy

Synopsis   **#include <dce/utc.h>**

int utc_binreltime(
         reltimespec_t **timesp,*
         timespec_t **inaccsp,*
         utc_t **utc*);

Parameters

Input

        utc   Relative binary timestamp. Use NULL if you want this routine to use the current time for this parameter.

Output

        timesp   Time component of the relative binary timestamp, in the form of seconds and nanoseconds since the base time (1970-01-01:00:00:00.0+00:00I0).

        inaccsp   Inaccuracy component of the relative binary timestamp, in the form of seconds and nanoseconds.

Description

        The **utc_binreltime( )** routine converts a relative binary timestamp to two **timespec** structures that express relative time and inaccuracy. These **timespec** structures describe a time interval.

Return Values

        0   Indicates that the routine executed successfully.

        -1   Indicates an invalid time argument or invalid results.

Examples   The following example measures the duration of a process, then prints the resulting
relative time and inaccuracy.

```
utc_t              before, duration;
reltimespec_t      tduration;
timespec_t         iduration;

/*   Get the time before the start of the operation...
 */
utc_gettime(&before);             /* Out: Before binary timestamp    */

/*      ...Later...
 *      Subtract, getting the duration as a relative time.
 *
 *          NOTE: The NULL argument is used to obtain the current time.
 */

utc_subtime(&duration,            /* Out: Duration rel bin timestamp */
            (utc_t *)0,           /* In:  After binary timestamp     */
            &before);             /* In:  Before binary timestamp    */

/*   Convert the relative times to timespec structures...
 */

utc_binreltime(&tduration,        /* Out: Duration time timespec     */
               &iduration,        /* Out: Duration inacc timespec    */
               &duration);        /* In:  Duration rel bin timestamp */

/*   Print the duration...
 */
printf("%d.%04d", tduration.tv_sec, (tduration.tv_nsec/10000));

if ((long)iduration.tv_sec == -1)
    printf("Iinf\n");
else
    printf("I%d.%04d\n", iduration.tv_sec, (iduration.tv_nsec/100000));
```

Related Information

Functions: **utc_mkbinreltime(3dts)**.

utc_bintime

Purpose   Converts a binary timestamp to a **timespec** structure

Synopsis   **#include <dce/utc.h>**

int utc_bintime(
    timespec_t **timesp,*
    timespec_t **inaccsp,*
    long **tdf,*
    utc_t **utc***);**

Parameters

Input

  utc   Binary timestamp. Use NULL if you want this routine to use the current time for this parameter.

Output

  timesp   Time component of the binary timestamp, in the form of seconds and nanoseconds since the base time.

  inaccsp Inaccuracy component of the binary timestamp, in the form of seconds and nanoseconds.

  tdf   TDF component of the binary timestamp in the form of signed number of seconds east of GMT.

Description

The **utc_bintime( )** routine converts a binary timestamp to a **timespec** structure. The TDF information contained in the timestamp is returned.

Return Values

  0   Indicates that the routine executed successfully.

  -1   Indicates an invalid time argument or invalid results.

Examples   See the sample program in the **utc_anytime(3dts)** reference page.

Related Information

Functions: **utc_binreltime(3dts)**, **utc_mkbintime(3dts)**.

utc_boundtime

Purpose   Given two UTC times, one before and one after an event, returns a single UTC time whose inaccuracy includes the event

Synopsis   **#include <dce/utc.h>**

int utc_boundtime(
            utc_t **result**,
            utc_t **utc1**,
            utc_t **utc2**);

Parameters

Input

utc1   Before binary timestamp or relative binary timestamp. Use NULL if you want this routine to use the current time for this parameter.

utc2   After binary timestamp or relative binary timestamp. Use NULL if you want this routine to use the current time for this parameter.

Output

result   Spanning timestamp.

Description

Given two UTC times, the **utc_boundtime( )** routine returns a single UTC time whose inaccuracy bounds the two input times. This is useful for timestamping events: the routine gets the **utc** values before and after the event, then calls **utc_boundtime( )** to build a timestamp that includes the event.

Notes   The TDF in the output UTC value is copied from the utc2 input parameter. If one or both input values have unspecified inaccuracies, the returned time value also has an unspecified inaccuracy and is the average of the two input values.

Return Values

0   Indicates that the routine executed successfully.

-1   Indicates an invalid time parameter or invalid parameter order.

Examples   The following example records the time of an event and constructs a single timestamp, which includes the time of the event. Note that the **utc_getusertime( )** routine is called so the time zone information that is included in the timestamp references the user's environment rather than the system's default time zone.

The user's environment determines the time zone rule (details are system dependent). For example, on OSF/1 systems, the user selects a time zone by specifying the **TZ** environment variable. (The reference information for the **localtime( )** system call, which is described in the **ctime(3)** reference page, provides additional information.)

If the user's environment does not specify a time zone rule, the system's rule is used (details of the rule are system dependent). For example, on OSF/1 systems, the rule in **/etc/zoneinfo/localtime** applies.

```
utc_t                before, after, evnt;

/*  Get the time before the event...
 */
utc_getusertime(&before);        /* Out: Before binary timestamp    */

/*  Get the time after the event...
 */
utc_getusertime(&after);         /* Out: After binary timestamp     */

/*  Construct a single timestamp that describes the time of the
 *    event...
 */
utc_boundtime(&evnt,             /* Out: Timestamp that bounds event */
            &before,             /* In:  Before binary timestamp    */
            &after);             /* In:  After binary timestamp     */
```

Related Information

Functions: **utc_gettime(3dts)**, **utc_pointtime(3dts)**, **utc_spantime(3dts)**.

utc_cmpintervaltime

Purpose   Compares two binary timestamps or two relative binary timestamps

Synopsis   **#include <dce/utc.h>**

int utc_cmpintervaltime(
        enum utc_cmptype **relation*,
        utc_t **utc1*,
        utc_t **utc2*);

Parameters

Input

utc1   Binary timestamp or relative binary timestamp. Use NULL if you want this routine to use the current time for this parameter.

utc2   Binary timestamp or relative binary timestamp. Use NULL if you want this routine to use the current time for this parameter.

Output

relation   Receives the result of the comparison of *utc1*:*utc2* where the result is an enumerated type with one of the following values:

- **utc_equalTo**

- **utc_lessThan**

- **utc_greaterThan**

- **utc_indeterminate**

Description

The **utc_cmpintervaltime( )** routine compares two binary timestamps and returns a flag indicating that the first time is greater than, less than, equal to, or overlapping with the second time. Two times overlap if the intervals (*time − inaccuracy*, *time + inaccuracy*) of the two times intersect.

The input binary timestamps express two absolute or two relative times. Do *not* compare relative binary timestamps to absolute binary timestamps. If you do, no meaningful results and no errors are returned.

The following routine does a temporal ordering of the time intervals.

```
utc1 is utc_lessThan utc2 iff
        utc1.time + utc1.inacc < utc2.time - utc2.inacc

utc1 is utc_greaterThan utc2 iff
        utc1.time - utc1.inacc > utc2.time + utc2.inacc

utc1 utc_equalTo utc2 iff
        utc1.time == utc2.time and
        utc1.inacc == 0 and
        utc2.inacc == 0
```

utc1 is **utc_indeterminate** with respect to **utc2** if the intervals overlap.

Return Values

0   Indicates that the routine executed successfully.

-1   Indicates an invalid time argument.

Examples   The following example checks to see if the current time is definitely after 13:00 local time.

```
struct tm           tmtime, tmzero;
enum utc_cmptype    relation;
utc_t               testtime;

/*   Zero the tm structure for inaccuracy...
 */
memset(&tmzero, 0, sizeof(tmzero));

/*  Get the current time, mapped to a tm structure...
 *
 *          NOTE: The NULL argument is used to get the current time.
 */
utc_gmtime(&tmtime,          /* Out: Current GMT time in tm struct   */
           (long *)0,        /* Out: Nanoseconds of time             */
           (struct tm *)0,   /* Out: Current inaccuracy in tm struct */
           (long *)0,        /* Out: Nanoseconds of inaccuracy       */
           (utc_t *)0);      /* In:  Current timestamp               */

/*   Alter the tm structure to correspond to 13:00 local time        */
 */
```

```
            tmtime.tm_hour = 13;
            tmtime.tm_min = 0;
            tmtime.tm_sec = 0;

            /*  Convert to a binary timestamp...
             */
            utc_mkgmtime(&testtime,      /* Out: Binary timestamp of 13:00    */
                        &tmtime,         /* In:  1:00 PM in tm struct         */
                        0,               /* In:  Nanoseconds of time          */
                        &tmzero,         /* In:  Zero inaccuracy in tm struct */
                        0);              /* In:  Nanoseconds of inaccuracy    */

            /*   Compare to the current time. Note the use of the NULL argument */
             */
            utc_cmpintervaltime(&relation,    /* Out: Comparison relation      */
                                (utc_t *)0,   /* In:  Current timestamp        */
                                &testtime);   /* In:  13:00 PM timestamp       */

            /*   If it is not later - wait, print a message, etc.
             */

            if (relation != utc_greaterThan) {

            /*
             *     Note: It could be earlier than 13:00 local time or it could be
             *           indeterminate.  If indeterminate, for some applications
             *           it might be worth waiting.
             */
            }
```

Related Information

Functions: **utc_cmpmidtime(3dts)**.

utc_cmpmidtime

Purpose   Compares two binary timestamps or two relative binary timestamps, ignoring inaccuracies

Synopsis   **#include <dce/utc.h>**

int utc_cmpmidtime(
          enum utc_cmptype **relation,*
          utc_t **utc1,*
          utc_t **utc2***);**

Parameters

Input

utc1	Binary timestamp or relative binary timestamp. Use NULL if you want this routine to use the current time for this parameter.
utc2	Binary timestamp or relative binary timestamp. Use NULL if you want this routine to use the current time for this parameter.

Output

relation	Result of the comparison of *utc1:utc2* where the result is an enumerated type with one of the following values:

- **utc_equalTo**

- **utc_lessThan**

- **utc_greaterThan**

Description

The **utc_cmpmidtime( )** routine compares two binary timestamps and returns a flag indicating that the first timestamp is greater than, less than, or equal to the second timestamp. Inaccuracy information is ignored for this comparison; the input values are therefore equivalent to the midpoints of the time intervals described by the input binary timestamps.

The input binary timestamps express two absolute or two relative times. Do *not* compare relative binary timestamps to absolute binary timestamps. If you do, no meaningful results and no errors are returned.

The following routine does a lexical ordering on the time interval midpoints.

```
utc1 is utc_lessThan utc2 iff
        utc1.time < utc2.time


utc1 is utc_greaterThan utc2 iff
        utc1.time > utc2.time


utc1 is utc_equalTo utc2 iff
        utc1.time == utc2.time
```

Return Values

    0   Indicates that the routine executed successfully.

    -1   Indicates an invalid time argument.

Examples

The following example checks if the current time (ignoring inaccuracies) is after 13:00 local time.

```
struct tm           tmtime, tmzero;
enum utc_cmptype    relation;
utc_t               testtime;

/*   Zero the tm structure for inaccuracy...
 */
memset(&tmzero, 0, sizeof(tmzero));

/*   Get the current time, mapped to a tm structure...
 *
 *        NOTE:  The NULL argument is used to get the current time.
 */
utc_localtime(&tmtime,      /* Out: Current local time in tm struct */
        (long *)0,          /* Out: Nanoseconds of time             */
        (struct tm *)0,     /* Out: Current inacc in tm struct      */
        (long *)0,          /* Out: Nanoseconds of inaccuracy       */
        (utc_t *)0);        /* In:  Current timestamp               */
```

```
    /*   Alter the tm structure to correspond to 13:00 local time.
     */
tmtime.tm_hour = 13;
tmtime.tm_min = 0;
tmtime.tm_sec = 0;

    /*   Convert to a binary timestamp...
     */
utc_mklocaltime(&testtime,       /* Out: Binary timestamp of 13:00    */
                &tmtime,         /* In:  13:00 in tm struct           */
                0,               /* In:  Nanoseconds of time          */
                &tmzero,         /* In:  Zero inaccuracy in tm struct */
                0);              /* In:  Nanoseconds of inaccuracy    */

    /*   Compare to the current time.  Note the use of the NULL argument
     */
utc_cmpmidtime(&relation,        /* Out: Comparison relation          */
               (utc_t *)0,       /* In:  Current timestamp            */
               &testtime);       /* In:  13:00 local time timestamp   */

    /*   If the time is not later - wait, print a message, etc.
     */
if (relation != utc_greaterThan) {

    /*        It is not later then 13:00 local time.  Note that
     *        this depends on the setting of the user's environment.
     */
}
```

Related Information

Functions: **utc_cmpintervaltime(3dts)**.

utc_gettime

Purpose   Returns the current system time and inaccuracy as a binary timestamp

Synopsis   **#include <dce/utc.h>**

int utc_gettime(
                utc_t *utc);

Parameters

Input

None.

Output

utc   System time as a binary timestamp.

Description

The **utc_gettime( )** routine returns the current system time and inaccuracy in a binary timestamp. The routine takes the TDF from the operating system's kernel; the TDF is specified in a system-dependent manner.

Return Values

0   Indicates that the routine executed successfully.

-1   Generic error that indicates the time service cannot be accessed.

Examples   See the sample program in the **utc_binreltime(3dts)** reference page.

utc_getusertime

Purpose   Returns the time and process-specific TDF, rather than the system-specific TDF

Synopsis   **#include <dce/utc.h>**

int utc_getusertime(
      utc_t **utc***);**

Parameters

Input

None.

Output

utc   System time as a binary timestamp.

Description

The **utc_getusertime( )** routine returns the system time and inaccuracy in a binary timestamp. The routine takes the TDF from the user's environment, which determines the time zone rule (details are system dependent). For example, on OSF/1 systems, the user selects a time zone by specifying the **TZ** environment variable. (The reference information for the **localtime( )** system call, which is described in the **ctime(3)** reference page, provides additional information.)

If the user environment does not specify a TDF, the system's TDF is used. The system's time zone rule is applied (details of the rule are system dependent). For example, on OSF/1 systems, the rule in **/etc/zoneinfo/localtime** applies.

Return Values

0   Indicates that the routine executed successfully.

-1   Generic error that indicates the time service cannot be accessed.

utc_getusertime(3dts)

Examples See the sample program in the **utc_boundtime(3dts)** reference page.

Related Information

Functions: **utc_gettime(3dts)**.

utc_gmtime

Purpose   Converts a binary timestamp to a **tm** structure that expresses GMT or the equivalent UTC

Synopsis   **#include <dce/utc.h>**

int utc_gmtime(
   struct tm **timetm,*
   long **tns,*
   struct tm **inacctm,*
   long **ins,*
   utc_t **utc*);

Parameters

Input

  utc   Binary timestamp to be converted to **tm** structure components. Use NULL if you want this routine to use the current time for this parameter.

Output

  timetm Time component of the binary timestamp.

  tns   Nanoseconds since the time component of the binary timestamp.

  inacctm Seconds of the inaccuracy component of the binary timestamp. If the inaccuracy is finite, then **tm_mday** returns a value of -1 and **tm_mon** and **tm_year** return values of 0 (zero). The field **tm_yday** contains the inaccuracy in days. If the inaccuracy is unspecified, all **tm** structure fields return values of -1.

  ins   Nanoseconds of the inaccuracy component of the binary timestamp. If the inaccuracy is unspecified, *ins* returns a value of -1.

utc_gmtime(3dts)

Description

The **utc_gmtime( )** routine converts a binary timestamp to a **tm** structure that expresses GMT (or the equivalent UTC). Additional returns include nanoseconds since time and nanoseconds of inaccuracy.

Return Values

0   Indicates that the routine executed successfully.

-1   Indicates an invalid time argument or invalid results.

Examples   See the sample program in the **utc_cmpintervaltime(3dts)** reference page.

Related Information

Functions: **utc_anytime(3dts), utc_gmtzone(3dts), utc_localtime(3dts), utc_mkgmtime(3dts)**.

utc_gmtzone

Purpose   Gets the time zone label for GMT

Synopsis   **#include <dce/utc.h>**

> **int utc_gmtzone(**
> > **char *** *tzname*,
> > **size_t** *tzlen*,
> > **long ***tdf*,
> > **int ***isdst*,
> > **utc_t ***utc***);**

Parameters

Input

tzlen	Length of buffer *tzname*.
utc	Binary timestamp. This parameter is ignored.

Output

tzname	Character string long enough to hold the time zone label.
tdf	Long word with differential in seconds east of GMT. A value of 0 (zero) is always returned.
isdst	Integer with a value of 0 (zero), indicating that daylight saving time is not in effect. A value of 0 (zero) is always returned.

Description

The **utc_gmtzone( )** routine gets the time zone label and zero offset from GMT. Outputs are always *tdf*=**0** and *tzname*=**GMT**. This routine exists for symmetry with the **utc_anyzone( )** and the **utc_localzone( )** routines. Use NULL if you want this routine to use the current time for this parameter.

utc_gmtzone(3dts)

Notes   All of the output parameters are optional. No value is returned and no error occurs if the *tzname* pointer is NULL.

Return Values

0   Indicates that the routine executed successfully (always returned).

Examples   The following example prints out the current time in both local time and GMT time.

```
utc_t       now;
struct tm   tmlocal, tmgmt;
long        tzoffset;
int         tzdaylight;
char        tzlocal[80], tzgmt[80];

/* Get the current time once, so both conversions use the same
 *  time...
 */
utc_gettime(&now);

/* Convert to local time, using the process TZ environment
 *  variable...
 */
utc_localtime(&tmlocal,        /* Out: Local time tm structure       */
              (long *)0,        /* Out: Nanosec of time               */
              (struct tm *)0,   /* Out: Inaccuracy tm structure       */
              (long *)0,        /* Out: Nanosec of inaccuracy         */
              (int *)0,         /* Out: TDF of local time             */
              &now);            /* In:  Current timestamp (ignore)    */


/*   Get the local time zone name, offset from GMT, and current
 *   daylight savings flag...
 */
utc_localzone(tzlocal,         /* Out: Local time zone name          */
              80,               /* In:  Length of loc time zone name  */
              &tzoffset,        /* Out: Loc time zone offset in secs  */
              &tzdaylight,      /* Out: Local time zone daylight flag */
              &now);            /* In:  Current binary timestamp      */
```

```
/*   Convert to GMT...
 */

utc_gmtime(&tmgmt,              /* Out: GMT tm structure            */
          (long *)0,           /* Out: Nanoseconds of time         */
          (struct tm *)0,      /* Out: Inaccuracy tm structure     */
          (long *)0,           /* Out: Nanoseconds of inaccuracy   */
          &now);               /* In:  Current binary timestamp    */


/*   Get the GMT time zone name...
 */

utc_gmtzone(tzgmt,             /* Out: GMT time zone name          */
          80,                  /* In:  Size of GMT time zone name  */
          (long *)0,           /* Out: GMT time zone offset in secs */
          (int *)0,            /* Out: GMT time zone daylight flag */
          &now);               /* In:  Current binary timestamp    */
                               /*      (ignore)                    */


/*   Print out times and time zone information in the following
 *   format:
 *
 *        12:00:37 (EDT) = 16:00:37 (GMT)
 *        EDT is -240 minutes ahead of Greenwich Mean Time.
 *        Daylight savings time is in effect.
 */
printf("%d:%02d:%02d (%s) = %d:%02d:%02d (%s)\n",
      tmlocal.tm_hour, tmlocal.tm_min, tmlocal.tm_sec, tzlocal,
      tmgmt.tm_hour, tmgmt.tm_min, tmgmt.tm_sec, tzgmt);
printf("%s is %d minutes ahead of Greenwich Mean Time\n", tzlocal, tzoffset/60);
if (tzdaylight != 0)
    printf("Daylight savings time is in effect\n");
```

Related Information

Functions: **utc_anyzone(3dts)**, **utc_gmtime(3dts)**, **utc_localzone(3dts)**.

utc_localtime

Purpose   Converts a binary timestamp to a **tm** structure that expresses local time

Synopsis   #include <dce/utc.h>

int utc_localtime(
      struct tm *timetm,
      long *tns,
      struct tm *inacctm,
      long *ins,
      utc_t *utc);

Parameters

Input

    utc   Binary timestamp. Use NULL if you want this routine to use the current time for this parameter.

Output

    timetm   Time component of the binary timestamp, expressing local time.

    tns   Nanoseconds since the time component of the binary timestamp.

    inacctm   Seconds of the inaccuracy component of the binary timestamp. If the inaccuracy is finite, then **tm_mday** returns a value of -1 and **tm_mon** and **tm_year** return values of 0 (zero). The field **tm_yday** contains the inaccuracy in days. If the inaccuracy is unspecified, all **tm** structure fields return values of -1.

    ins   Nanoseconds of the inaccuracy component of the binary timestamp. If the inaccuracy is unspecified, *ins* returns a value of -1.

Description

The **utc_localtime( )** routine converts a binary timestamp to a **tm** structure that expresses local time.

The user's environment determines the time zone rule (details are system dependent). For example, on OSF/1 systems, the user selects a time zone by specifying the **TZ** environment variable. (The reference information for the **localtime**( ) system call, which is described in the **ctime(3)** reference page, provides additional information.)

If the user's environment does not specify a time zone rule, the system's rule is used (details of the rule are system dependent). For example, on OSF/1 systems, the rule in **/etc/zoneinfo/localtime** applies.

Additional returns include nanoseconds since time and nanoseconds of inaccuracy.

Return Values

0   Indicates that the routine executed successfully.

-1   Indicates an invalid time argument or invalid results.

Examples   See the sample program in the **utc_gmtzone(3dts)** reference page.

Related Information

Functions: **utc_anytime(3dts)**, **utc_gmtime(3dts)**, **utc_localzone(3dts)**, **utc_mklocaltime(3dts)**.

utc_localzone

Purpose   Gets the local time zone label and offset from GMT, given **utc**

Synopsis   **#include <dce/utc.h>**

        int utc_localzone(
                char **tzname,*
                size_t *tzlen,*
                long **tdf,*
                int **isdst,*
                utc_t **utc***);**

Parameters

Input

tzlen   Length of the *tzname* buffer.

utc   Binary timestamp. Use NULL if you want this routine to use the current time for this parameter.

Output

tzname   Character string long enough to hold the time zone label.

tdf   Long word with differential in seconds east of GMT.

isdst   Integer with a value of 0 (zero) if standard time is in effect or a value of 1 if daylight saving time is in effect.

Description

The **utc_localzone( )** routine gets the local time zone label and offset from GMT, given **utc**.

The user's environment determines the time zone rule (details are system dependent). For example, on OSF/1 systems, the user selects a time zone by specifying the **TZ** environment variable. (The reference information for the **localtime( )** system call, which is described in the **ctime(3)** reference page, provides additional information.)

If the user's environment does not specify a time zone rule, the system's rule is used (details of the rule are system dependent). For example, on OSF/1 systems, the rule in **/etc/zoneinfo/localtime** applies.

Notes

All of the output parameters are optional. No value is returned and no error occurs if the pointer is NULL.

Return Values

0   Indicates that the routine executed successfully.

-1   Indicates an invalid time argument or an insufficient buffer.

Examples

See the sample program in the **utc_gmtzone(3dts)** reference page.

Related Information

Functions: **utc_anyzone(3dts)**, **utc_gmtzone(3dts)**, **utc_localtime(3dts)**.

utc_mkanytime

Purpose   Converts a **tm** structure and TDF (expressing the time in an arbitrary time zone) to a binary timestamp

Synopsis   **#include <dce/utc.h>**

int utc_mkanytime(
        utc_t **utc,*
        struct tm **timetm,*
        long *tns,*
        struct tm **inacctm,*
        long *ins,*
        long *tdf***);**

Parameters

Input

timetm   A **tm** structure that expresses the local time; **tm_wday** and **tm_yday** are ignored on input; the value of **tm_isdt** should be -1.

tns   Nanoseconds since the time component.

inacctm   A **tm** structure that expresses days, hours, minutes, and seconds of inaccuracy. If a null pointer is passed, or if **tm_yday** is negative, the inaccuracy is considered to be unspecified; **tm_mday**, **tm_mon**, **tm_wday**, and **tm_isdst** are ignored on input.

ins   Nanoseconds of the inaccuracy component.

tdf   Time differential factor to use in conversion.

Output

utc   Resulting binary timestamp.

Description

The **utc_mkanytime( )** routine converts a **tm** structure and TDF (expressing the time in an arbitrary time zone) to a binary timestamp. Required inputs include nanoseconds since time and nanoseconds of inaccuracy.

Return Values

0	Indicates that the routine executed successfully.
-1	Indicates an invalid time argument or invalid results.

Examples The following example converts a string ISO format time in an arbitrary time zone to a binary timestamp. This may be part of an input timestamp routine, although a real implementation will include range checking.

```
utc_t        utc;
struct tm    tmtime, tminacc;
float        tsec, isec;
double       tmp;
long         tnsec, insec;
int          i, offset, tzhour, tzmin, year, mon;
char         *string;

/*  Try to convert the string...                              */

if(sscanf(string, "%d-%d-%d-%d:%d:%e+%d:%dI%e",
        &year, &mon, &tmtime.tm_mday, &tmtime.tm_hour,
        &tmtime.tm_min, &tsec, &tzhour, &tzmin, &isec) != 9) {

/*  Try again with a negative TDF...                          */

if (sscanf(string, "%d-%d-%d-%d:%d:%e-%d:%dI%e",
        &year, &mon, &tmtime.tm_mday, &tmtime.tm_hour,
        &tmtime.tm_min, &tsec, &tzhour, &tzmin, &isec) != 9) {

/*  ERROR                                                     */

    exit(1);
}
```

utc_mkanytime(3dts)

```
            /*  TDF is negative                                    */

                tzhour = -tzhour;
                tzmin = -tzmin;

            }

            /*  Fill in the fields...                              */

            tmtime.tm_year = year - 1900;
            tmtime.tm_mon = --mon;
            tmtime.tm_sec = tsec;
            tnsec = (modf(tsec, &tmp)*1.0E9);
            offset = tzhour*3600 + tzmin*60;
            tminacc.tm_sec = isec;
            insec = (modf(isec, &tmp)*1.0E9);

            /* Convert to a binary timestamp...                    */

            utc_mkanytime(&utc,       /* Out: Resultant binary timestamp    */
                        &tmtime,      /* In:  tm struct that represents input  */
                        tnsec,        /* In:  Nanoseconds from input        */
                        &tminacc,     /* In:  tm struct that represents inacc */
                        insec,        /* In:  Nanoseconds from input        */
                        offset);      /* In:  TDF from input                */
```

Related Information

Functions: **utc_anytime(3dts)**, **utc_anyzone(3dts)**.

utc_mkascreltime

Purpose   Converts a NULL-terminated character string that represents a relative timestamp to a binary timestamp

Synopsis   **#include <dce/utc.h>**

int utc_mkascreltime(
        utc_t *utc,
        char *string);

Parameters

Input

    string   A NULL-terminated string that expresses a relative timestamp in its ISO format.

Output

    utc   Resulting binary timestamp.

Description

The **utc_mkascreltime( )** routine converts a NULL-terminated string, which represents a relative timestamp, to a binary timestamp.

Notes   The ASCII string must be NULL-terminated.

Return Values

    0   Indicates that the routine executed successfully.

    -1   Indicates an invalid time parameter or invalid results.

utc_mkascreltime(3dts)

Examples The following example converts an ASCII relative time string to its binary equivalent.

```
utc_t      utc;
char       str[UTC_MAX_STR_LEN];

/*   Relative time of -333 days, 12 hours, 1 minute, 37.223 seconds
 *   Inaccuracy of 50.22 seconds in the format:   -333-12:01:37.223I50.22
 */
(void)strcpy((void *)str,
          "-333-12:01:37.223I50.22");

utc_mkascreltime(&utc,   /* Out: Binary utc              */
             str);   /* In:  String                  */
```

Related Information

Functions: **utc_ascreltime(3dts)**.

utc_mkasctime

Purpose   Converts a NULL-terminated character string that represents an absolute timestamp to a binary timestamp

Synopsis   **#include <dce/utc.h>**

int utc_mkasctime(
        utc_t **utc***,**
        char **string***);**

Parameters

Input

string   A NULL-terminated string that expresses an absolute time.

Output

utc   Resulting binary timestamp.

Description

The **utc_mkasctime( )** routine converts a NULL-terminated string that represents an absolute time to a binary timestamp.

Notes   The ASCII string must be NULL-terminated.

Return Values

0   Indicates that the routine executed successfully.

-1   Indicates an invalid time parameter or invalid results.

utc_mkasctime(3dts)

Examples The following example converts an ASCII time string to its binary equivalent.

```
utc_t      utc;
char       str[UTC_MAX_STR_LEN];

/*    July 4, 1776, 12:01:37.223 local time
 *    TDF of -5:00 hours
 *    Inaccuracy of 3600.32 seconds
 */
(void)strcpy((void *)str,
            "1776-07-04-12:01:37.223-5:00I3600.32");

utc_mkasctime(&utc,     /* Out: Binary utc        */
              str);     /* In:  String            */
```

Related Information

Functions: **utc_ascanytime(3dts)**, **utc_ascgmtime(3dts)**, **utc_asclocaltime(3dts)**.

utc_mkbinreltime

Purpose   Converts a **timespec** structure expressing a relative time to a binary timestamp

Synopsis   **#include <dce/utc.h>**

    int utc_mkbinreltime(
        utc_t **utc,*
        reltimespec_t **timesp,*
        timespec_t **inaccsp***);**

Parameters

Input

    timesp   A **reltimespec** structure that expresses a relative time.

    inaccsp   A **timespec** structure that expresses inaccuracy. If a null pointer is passed, or if **tv_sec** is set to a value of -1, the inaccuracy is considered to be unspecified.

Output

    utc   Resulting relative binary timestamp.

Description

The **utc_mkbinreltime( )** routine converts a **timespec** structure that expresses relative time to a binary timestamp.

Return Values

    0   Indicates that the routine executed successfully.

    -1   Indicates an invalid time argument or invalid results.

Examples   See the sample program in the **utc_addtime(3dts)** reference page.

Related Information

Functions: **utc_binreltime(3dts)**, **utc_mkbintime(3dts)**.

utc_mkbintime

Purpose   Converts a **timespec** structure to a binary timestamp

Synopsis   **#include <dce/utc.h>**

int utc_mkbintime(
      utc_t **utc***,**
      timespec_t **timesp***,**
      timespec_t **inaccsp***,**
      long *tdf***);**

Parameters

Input

    timesp   A **timespec** structure that expresses time since 1970-01-01:00:00:00.0+00:00I0.

    inaccsp   A **timespec** structure that expresses inaccuracy. If a null pointer is passed, or if **tv_sec** is set to a value of -1, the inaccuracy is considered to be unspecified.

    tdf   TDF component of the binary timestamp.

Output

    utc   Resulting binary timestamp.

Description

The **utc_mkbintime( )** routine converts a **timespec** structure time to a binary timestamp. The TDF input is used as the TDF of the binary timestamp.

Return Values

    0   Indicates that the routine executed successfully.

    -1   Indicates an invalid time argument or invalid results.

Examples   The following example obtains the current time from **time(3)**, converts it to a binary timestamp with an inaccuracy of 5.2 seconds, and specifies GMT.

```
timespec_t    ttime, tinacc;
utc_t         utc;

/*   Obtain the current time (without the inaccuracy)...
 */

ttime.tv_sec = time((time_t *)0);
ttime.tv_nsec = 0;

/*   Specify the inaccuracy...
 */

tinacc.tv_sec = 5;
tinacc.tv_nsec = 200000000;

/*   Convert to a binary timestamp...
 */

utc_mkbintime(&utc,         /* Out: Binary timestamp          */
              &ttime,       /* In:  Current time in timespec  */
              &tinacc,      /* In:  5.2 seconds in timespec   */
              0);           /* In:  TDF of GMT                */
```

Related Information

Functions: **utc_bintime(3dts)**, **utc_mkbinreltime(3dts)**.

utc_mkgmtime

Purpose   Converts a **tm** structure that expresses GMT or UTC to a binary timestamp

Synopsis   **#include <dce/utc.h>**

int utc_mkgmtime(
        utc_t **utc,*
        struct tm **timetm,*
        long *tns,*
        struct tm **inacctm,*
        long *ins*);

Parameters

Input

timetm	A **tm** structure that expresses GMT. On input, **tm_wday** and **tm_yday** are ignored; the value of **tm_isdt** should be -1.
tns	Nanoseconds since the time component.
inacctm	A **tm** structure that expresses days, hours, minutes, and seconds of inaccuracy. If a null pointer is passed, or if **tm_yday** is negative, the inaccuracy is considered to be unspecified. On input, **tm_mday**, **tm_mon**, **tm_wday**, and **tm_isdst** are ignored.
ins	Nanoseconds of the inaccuracy component.

Output

utc	Resulting binary timestamp.

Description

The **utc_mkgmtime( )** routine converts a **tm** structure that expresses GMT or UTC to a binary timestamp. Additional inputs include nanoseconds since the last second of time and nanoseconds of inaccuracy.

utc_mkgmtime(3dts)

Return Values

    0   Indicates that the routine executed successfully.

    -1   Indicates an invalid time argument or invalid results.

Examples   See the sample program in the **utc_cmpintervaltime(3dts)** reference page.

Related Information

Functions: **utc_gmtime(3dts)**.

utc_mklocaltime

Purpose   Converts a **tm** structure that expresses local time to a binary timestamp

Synopsis   **#include <dce/utc.h>**

   int utc_mklocaltime(
       utc_t *utc,
       struct tm *timetm,
       long *tns*,
       struct tm *inacctm,
       long *ins*);

Parameters

Input

   timetm   A **tm** structure that expresses the local time. On input, **tm_wday**
              and **tm_yday** are ignored; the value of **tm_isdst** should be -1.

   tns   Nanoseconds since the time component.

   inacctm   A **tm** structure that expresses days, hours, minutes, and seconds of
              inaccuracy. If a null pointer is passed, or if **tm_yday** is negative,
              the inaccuracy is considered to be unspecified. On input, **tm_mday**,
              tm_mon, **tm_wday**, and **tm_isdst** are ignored.

   ins   Nanoseconds of the inaccuracy component.

Output

   utc   Resulting binary timestamp.

Description

   The **utc_mklocaltime( )** routine converts a **tm** structure that expresses local time
   to a binary timestamp.

   The user's environment determines the time zone rule (details are system
   dependent). For example, on OSF/1 systems, the user selects a time zone by
   specifying the **TZ** environment variable. (The reference information for the
   localtime( ) system call, which is described in the **ctime(3)** reference page,
   provides additional information.)

utc_mklocaltime(3dts)

If the user's environment does not specify a time zone rule, the system's rule is used (details of the rule are system dependent). For example, on OSF/1 systems, the rule in **/etc/zoneinfo/localtime** applies.

Additional inputs include nanoseconds since the last second of time and nanoseconds of inaccuracy.

Return Values

0   Indicates that the routine executed successfully.

-1   Indicates an invalid time argument or invalid results.

Examples   See the sample program in the **utc_cmpmidtime(3dts)** reference page.

Related Information

Functions: **utc_localtime(3dts)**.

utc_mkreltime

Purpose   Converts a **tm** structure that expresses relative time to a relative binary timestamp

Synopsis   **#include <dce/utc.h>**

int utc_mkreltime(
    utc_t **utc,*
    struct tm **timetm,*
    long *tns,*
    struct tm **inacctm,*
    long *ins***);**

Parameters

Input

timetm	A **tm** structure that expresses a relative time. On input, **tm_wday** and **tm_yday** are ignored; the value of **tm_isdst** should be -1.
tns	Nanoseconds since the time component.
inacctm	A **tm** structure that expresses seconds of inaccuracy. If a null pointer is passed, or if **tm_yday** is negative, the inaccuracy is considered to be unspecified. On input, **tm_mday**, **tm_mon**, **tm_year**, **tm_wday**, **tm_isdst**, and **tm_zone** are ignored.
ins	Nanoseconds of the inaccuracy component.

Output

utc	Resulting relative binary timestamp.

Description

The **utc_mkreltime( )** routine converts a **tm** structure that expresses relative time to a relative binary timestamp. Additional inputs include nanoseconds since the last second of time and nanoseconds of inaccuracy.

Return Values

0   Indicates that the routine executed successfully.

-1   Indicates an invalid time argument or invalid results.

Examples   The following example converts the relative time **125-03:12:30.1I120.25** to a relative binary timestamp.

```
utc_t      utc;
struct tm  tmtime,tminacc;
long       tnsec,insec;

    /* Fill in the fields
     */
    memset((void *)&tmtime,0,sizeof(tmtime));
    tmtime.tm_mday = 125;
    tmtime.tm_hour = 3;
    tmtime.tm_min  = 12;
    tmtime.tm_sec  = 30;
    tnsec = 100000000;      /* .1 * 1.0E9 */

    memset((void *)&tminacc,0,sizeof(tminacc));
    tminacc.tm_sec = 120;
    tnsec = 250000000;      /* .25 * 1.0E9 */

/* Convert to a relative binary timestamp...
 */
utc_mkreltime(&utc,        /* Out: Resultant relative binary timestamp */
             &tmtime,      /* In:  tm struct that represents input      */
             tnsec,        /* In:  Nanoseconds from input               */
             &tminacc,     /* In:  tm struct that represents inacc      */
             insec);       /* In:  Nanoseconds from input               */
```

utc_mulftime

Purpose   Multiplies a relative binary timestamp by a floating-point value

Synopsis   **#include <dce/utc.h>**

int utc_mulftime(
        utc_t *result,
        utc_t *utc1,
        double *factor*);

Parameters

Input

utc1   Relative binary timestamp. Use NULL if you want this routine to use the current time for this parameter.

factor   Real scale factor (double-precision, floating-point value).

Output

result   Resulting relative binary timestamp.

Description

The **utc_mulftime( )** routine multiplies a relative binary timestamp by a floating-point value. Either or both may be negative; the resulting relative binary timestamp has the appropriate sign. The unsigned inaccuracy in the relative binary timestamp is also multiplied by the absolute value of the floating-point value.

Return Values

0   Indicates that the routine executed successfully.

-1   Indicates an invalid time argument or invalid results.

Examples   The following example scales a relative time by a floating-point factor and prints
the result.

```
utc_t        relutc, scaledutc;
struct tm    scaledreltm;
char         timstr[UTC_MAX_STR_LEN];

/*   Assume relutc contains the time to scale.
 */
utc_mulftime(&scaledutc,              /* Out: Scaled rel time     */
             &relutc,                 /* In:  Rel time to scale   */
             17.65);                  /* In:  Scale factor        */

utc_ascreltime(timstr,                /* Out: ASCII rel time      */
               UTC_MAX_STR_LEN,       /* In:  Input buffer length */
               &scaledutc);           /* In:  Rel time to convert */

printf("%s\n",timstr);

/*   Convert it to a tm structure and print it.
 */
utc_reltime(&scaledreltm,             /* Out: Scaled rel tm        */
            (long *)0,                /* Out: Scaled rel nano-sec  */
            (struct tm *)0,           /* Out: Scaled rel inacc tm  */
            (long *)0,                /* Out: Scd rel inacc nanos  */
            &scaledutc);              /* In:  Rel time to convert  */

printf("Approximately %d days, %d hours and %d minutes\n",
       scaledreltm.tm_yday, scaledreltm.tm_hour, scaledreltm.tm_min);
```

Related Information

Functions: **utc_multime(3dts)**.

utc_multime

Purpose   Multiplies a relative binary timestamp by an integer factor

Synopsis   **#include <dce/utc.h>**

int utc_multime(
         utc_t **result*,
         utc_t **utc1*,
         long *factor*);

Parameters

Input

> *utc1*   Relative binary timestamp.
>
> *factor*   Integer scale factor.

Output

> *result*   Resulting relative binary timestamp.

Description

The **utc_multime( )** routine multiplies a relative binary timestamp by an integer. Either or both may be negative; the resulting binary timestamp has the appropriate sign. The unsigned inaccuracy in the binary timestamp is also multiplied by the absolute value of the integer.

Return Values

> 0   Indicates that the routine executed successfully.
>
> -1   Indicates an invalid time argument or invalid results.

utc_multime(3dts)

Examples The following example scales a relative time by an integral value and prints the result.

```
utc_t        relutc, scaledutc;

char         timstr[UTC_MAX_STR_LEN];

/*   Assume relutc contains the time to scale.  Scale it by a factor
 *   of 17 ...
 */
utc_multime(&scaledutc,         /* Out: Scaled rel time     */
              &relutc,          /*  In: Rel time to scale   */
                 17L);          /*  In: Scale factor        */

utc_ascreltime(timstr,          /* Out: ASCII rel time      */
       UTC_MAX_STR_LEN,         /*  In: Input buffer length */
            &scakedutc);        /*  In: Rel time to convert */

printf("Scaled result is %s0, timstr);
```

Related Information

Functions: **utc_mulftime(3dts)**.

utc_pointtime

Purpose   Converts a binary timestamp to three binary timestamps that represent the earliest, most likely, and latest time

Synopsis   **#include <dce/utc.h>**

> **int utc_pointtime(**
> > **utc_t** **utclp,*
> > **utc_t** **utcmp,*
> > **utc_t** **utchp,*
> > **utc_t** **utc);*

Parameters

Input

> *utc*   Binary timestamp or relative binary timestamp. Use NULL if you want this routine to use the current time for this parameter.

Output

> *utclp*   Lowest (earliest) possible absolute time or shortest possible relative time that the input timestamp can represent.

> *utcmp*   Midpoint of the input timestamp.

> *utchp*   Highest (latest) possible absolute time or longest possible relative time that the input timestamp can represent.

Description

The **utc_pointtime( )** routine converts a binary timestamp to three binary timestamps that represent the earliest, latest, and most likely (midpoint) times. If the input is a relative binary time, the outputs represent relative binary times.

utc_pointtime(3dts)

Notes   All outputs have zero inaccuracy. An error is returned if the input binary timestamp has an unspecified inaccuracy.

Return Values

0   Indicates that the routine executed successfully.

-1   Indicates an invalid time argument.

Examples   See the sample program in the **utc_addtime(3dts)** reference page.

Related Information

Functions: **utc_boundtime(3dts)**, **utc_spantime(3dts)**.

utc_reltime

Purpose   Converts a relative binary timestamp to a **tm** structure

Synopsis   **#include <dce/utc.h>**

> **int utc_reltime(**
> > **struct tm ***timetm**,**
> > **long ***tns**,**
> > **struct tm ***inacctm**,**
> > **long ***ins**,**
> > **utc_t ***utc**);**

Parameters

Input

> utc   Relative binary timestamp.

Output

> timetm   Relative time component of the relative binary timestamp. The field **tm_mday** returns a value of -1 and the fields **tm_year** and **tm_mon** return values of 0 (zero). The field **tm_yday** contains the number of days of relative time.
>
> tns   Nanoseconds since the time component of the relative binary timestamp.
>
> inacctm   Seconds of the inaccuracy component of the relative binary timestamp. If the inaccuracy is finite, then **tm_mday** returns a value of -1 and **tm_mon** and **tm_year** return values of 0 (zero). The field **tm_yday** contains the inaccuracy in days. If the inaccuracy is unspecified, all **tm** structure fields return values of -1.
>
> ins   Nanoseconds of the inaccuracy component of the relative binary timestamp.

utc_reltime(3dts)

Description

The **utc_reltime()** routine converts a relative binary timestamp to a **tm** structure. Additional returns include nanoseconds since time and nanoseconds of inaccuracy.

Return Values

0   Indicates that the routine executed successfully.

-1   Indicates an invalid time argument or invalid results.

Examples   See the sample program in the **utc_mulftime(3dts)** reference page.

Related Information

Functions: **utc_mkreltime(3dts)**.

utc_spantime

Purpose   Given two (possibly unordered) binary timestamps, returns a single UTC time interval whose inaccuracy spans the two input binary timestamps

Synopsis   **#include <dce/utc.h>**

int utc_spantime(
   utc_t *_result_,
   utc_t *_utc1_,
   utc_t *_utc2_);

Parameters

Input

utc1   Binary timestamp. Use NULL if you want this routine to use the current time for this parameter.

utc2   Binary timestamp. Use NULL if you want this routine to use the current time for this parameter.

Output

result   Spanning timestamp.

Description

Given two binary timestamps, the **utc_spantime( )** routine returns a single UTC time interval whose inaccuracy spans the two input timestamps (that is, the interval resulting from the earliest possible time of either timestamp to the latest possible time of either timestamp).

Notes   The _tdf_ parameter in the output UTC value is copied from the _utc2_ input. If either input binary timestamp has an unspecified inaccuracy, an error is returned.

utc_spantime(3dts)

Return Values

0   Indicates that the routine executed successfully.

-1   Indicates an invalid time argument.

Examples

The following example computes the earliest and latest times for an array of 10 timestamps.

```
utc_t               time_array[10], testtime, earliest, latest;
int                 i;

/*   Set the running timestamp to the first entry...
 */
testtime = time_array[0];

for (i=1; i<10; i++) {

    /*   Compute the minimum and the maximum against the next
     *   element...
     */
    utc_spantime(&testtime,         /* Out: Resultant interval          */
             &testtime,             /* In:  Largest previous interval   */
             &time_array[i]);       /* In:  Element under test          */
}

/*   Compute the earliest and latest possible times
 */

utc_pointtime(&earliest,            /* Out: Earliest poss time in array */
          (utc_t *)0,               /* Out: Midpoint                    */
          &latest,                  /* Out: Latest poss time in array   */
          &testtime);               /* In:  Spanning interval           */
```

Related Information

Functions: **utc_boundtime(3dts)**, **utc_gettime(3dts)**, **utc_pointtime(3dts)**.

utc_subtime

Purpose   Computes the difference between two binary timestamps

Synopsis   **#include <dce/utc.h>**

int utc_subtime(
utc_t *result,
utc_t *utc1,
utc_t *utc2);

Parameters

Input

utc1   Binary timestamp or relative binary timestamp. Use NULL if you want this routine to use the current time for this parameter.

utc2   Binary timestamp or relative binary timestamp. Use NULL if you want this routine to use the current time for this parameter.

Output

result   Resulting binary timestamp or relative binary timestamp, depending upon the operation performed:

- *absolute time–absolute time=relative time*

- *relative time–relative time=relative time*

- *absolute time–relative time=absolute time*

- *relative time–absolute time* is undefined. (See the note later in this reference page.)

Description

The **utc_subtime( )** routine subtracts one binary timestamp from another. The two binary timestamps express either an absolute time and a relative time, two relative times, or two absolute times. The resulting timestamp is *utc1* minus *utc2*. The inaccuracies of the two input timestamps are combined and included in the output timestamp. The TDF in the first timestamp is copied to the output.

utc_subtime(3dts)

Notes   Although no error is returned, the combination *relative time–absolute time* should *not* be used.

Return Values

       0   Indicates that the routine executed successfully.

      -1   Indicates an invalid time argument or invalid results.

Examples   See the sample program in the **utc_binreltime(3dts)** reference page.

Related Information

Functions: **utc_addtime(3dts)**.

Chapter 3

DCE Security Service

sec_intro

Purpose   Application program interface to the DCE Security Service

Description

The DCE Security Service application program interface (API) allows developers to create network services with complete access to all the authentication and authorization capabilities of DCE Security Service and facilities.

The transaction of a network service generally consists of a client process requesting some action from a server process. The client may itself be a server, or a user, and the server may also be a client of other servers. Before the targeted server executes the specified action, it must be sure of the client's identity, and it must know whether the client is authorized to request the service.

The security service API consists of the following sets of remote procedure calls (RPCs) used to communicate with various security-related services and facilities:

rgy   Maintains the network registry of principal identities.

era   Maintains extended registry attributes.

login   Validates a principal's network identity and establish delegated identities.

epa   Extracts privilege attributes from an opaque binding handle.

acl   Implements an access control list (ACL) protocol for the authorization of a principal to network access and services.

key   Provides facilities for the maintenance of account keys for daemon principals.

id   Maps file system names to universal unique IDs (UUIDs).

pwd_mgmt   Provides facilities for password management.

All the calls in this API have names beginning with the **sec_** prefix. These are the same calls used by various user-level tools provided as part of the DCE. For example, the **sec_create_db(1)** tool is written with **sec_rgy** calls, **acl_edit(1)** is written with **sec_acl** calls, and the **login(1)** program, with which a user logs in to a DCE system, is written using **sec_login** calls. Most sites will find the user-level tools adequate for their needs, and only must use the security service API to customize or replace the functionality of these tools.

Though most of the calls in the security service API represent RPC transactions, code has been provided on the client side to handle much of the overhead involved with making remote calls. These *stubs* handle binding to the requested security server site, the marshalling of data into whatever form is needed for transmission, and other bookkeeping involved with these remote calls. An application programmer can use the security service interfaces as if they were composed of simple C functions.

This reference page introduces each of the following APIs:

- Registry APIs

- Login APIs

- Extended privilege attributes APIs

- Extended registry attributes APIs

- ACL APIs

- Key management APIs

- ID mapping APIs

- Password management APIs

The section for each API is organized as follows:

- Synopsis

- Data Types

- Constants

- Files

REGISTRY API DATA TYPES

Synopsis   #include <dce/rgybase.h>

Data Types

The following data types are used in **sec_rgy_** * calls:

sec_rgy_handle_t
A pointer to the registry server handle. The registry server is bound to a handle with the **sec_rgy_site_open( )** routine.

sec_rgy_bind_auth_info_type_t
A enumeration that defines whether or not the binding is authenticated. This data type is used in conjunction with the **sec_rgy_bind_auth_info_t** data type to set up the authorization method and parameters for a binding. The **sec_rgy_bind_auth_-info_type_t** type consists of the following elements:

sec_rgy_bind_auth_none
The binding is not authenticated.

sec_rgy_bind_auth_dce
The binding uses DCE shared-secret key authentication.

sec_rgy_bind_auth_info_t
A discriminated union that defines authorization and authentication parameters for a binding. This data type is used in conjunction with the **sec_rgy_bind_auth_info_type_t** data type to set up the authorization method and parameters for a binding. The **sec_rgy_bind_auth_info_t** data type consists of the following elements:

info_type A **sec_rgy_bind_auth_info_type_t** data type that specifies whether or not the binding is authenticated. The contents of the union depend on the value of **sec_rgy_bind_auth_info_type_t**.

For unauthenticated bindings (**sec_rgy_bind_auth_-info_type_t** = **sec_rgy_bind_auth_none**), no parameters are supplied.

For authenticated bindings (**sec_rgy_bind_auth_-info_type_t** = **sec_rgy_bind_auth_dce**), the **dce_info** structure is supplied.

dce_info A structure that consists of the following elements:

authn_level An unsigned 32 bit integer indicating the protection level for RPC calls made using the server binding handle.

The protection level determines the degree to which authenticated communications between the client and the server are protected by the authentication service specified by **authn_svc**.

If the RPC runtime or the RPC protocol in the bound protocol sequence does not support a specified level, the level is automatically upgraded to the next higher supported level. The possible protection levels are as follows:

Protection Level	Description
rpc_c_protect_level_default	Uses the default protection level for the specified authentication service. The default protection level for DCE shared-secret key authentication is **rpc_c_protect_level_pkt_value**.
rpc_c_protect_level_none	Performs no authentication: tickets are not exchanged, session keys are not established, client PACs or names are not certified, and transmissions are in the clear. Note that although uncertified PACs should not be trusted, they may be useful for debugging, tracing, and measurement purposes.
rpc_c_protect_level_connect	Authenticates only when the client establishes a relationship with the server.
rpc_c_protect_level_call	Authenticates only at the beginning of each remote procedure call when the server receives the request. This level does not apply to remote procedure calls made over a connection-based protocol sequence (that is, **ncacn_ip_tcp**). If this level is specified and the binding handle uses a connection-based protocol sequence, the routine uses the **rpc_c_protect_level_pkt** level instead.
rpc_c_protect_level_pkt	Ensures that all data received is from the expected client.

sec_intro(3sec)

Protection Level	Description
rpc_c_protect_level_pkt_integ	Ensures and verifies that none of the data transferred between client and server has been modified. This is the highest protection level that is guaranteed to be present in the RPC runtime.
rpc_c_protect_level_pkt_privacy	Authenticates as specified by all of the previous levels and also encrypts each RPC argument value. This is the highest protection level, but is not guaranteed to be present in the RPC runtime.

> **authn_svc**   Specifies the authentication service to use. The exact level of protection provided by the authentication service is specified by **protect_level**. The supported authentication services are as follows:

Authentication Service	Description
rpc_c_authn_none	No authentication: no tickets are exchanged, no session keys established, client PACs or names are not transmitted, and transmissions are in the clear. Specify **rpc_c_authn_none** to turn authentication off for remote procedure calls made using this binding.
rpc_c_authn_dce_secret	DCE shared-secret key authentication.
rpc_c_authn_default	Default authentication service. The current default authentication service is DCE shared-secret key; therefore, specifying **rpc_c_authn_-default** is equivalent to specifying **rpc_c_authn_-dce_secret**.
rpc_c_authn_dce_public	DCE public key authentication (reserved for future use).

> **authz_svc**   Specifies the authorization service implemented by the server for the interface. The validity and trustworthiness of authorization data, like any application data, is dependent on the authentication service and protection level specified. The supported authorization services are as follows:

Authentication Service	Description
rpc_c_authz_none	Server performs no authorization. This is valid only if **authn_svc** is set to **rpc_c_authn_none**, specifying that no authentication is being performed.
rpc_c_authz_name	Server performs authorization based on the client principal name. This value cannot be used if **authn_svc** is **rpc_c_authn_none**.
rpc_c_authz_dce	Server performs authorization using the client's DCE privilege attribute certificate (PAC) sent to the server with each remote procedure call made with this binding. Generally, access is checked against DCE access control lists (ACLs).

        identity   A value of type **sec_login_handle_t** that represents a complete login context.

sec_timeval_sec_t

A 32-bit integer containing the seconds portion of a UNIX **timeval_t**, to be used when expressing absolute dates.

sec_timeval_t

A structure containing the full UNIX time. The structure contains two 32-bit integers that indicate seconds (**sec**) and microseconds (**usec**) since 0:00, January 1, 1970.

sec_timeval_period_t

A 32-bit integer expressing seconds relative to some well-known time.

sec_rgy_acct_key_t

Specifies how many parts (person, group, organization) of an account login name will be enough to specify a unique abbreviation for that account.

sec_rgy_cursor_t

A structure providing a pointer into a registry database. This type is used for iterative operations on the registry information. For example, a call to **sec_rgy_pgo_get_members**( ) might return the 10 account names following the input **sec_rgy_cursor_t** position. Upon return, the cursor position will have been updated, so the next call to that routine will return the next 10 names. The components of this structure are not used by application programs.

sec_rgy_pname_t
>A character string of length **sec_rgy_pname_t_size**.

sec_rgy_name_t
>A character string of length **sec_rgy_name_t_size**.

sec_rgy_login_name_t
>A structure representing an account login name. It contains three strings of type **sec_rgy_name_t**:

>>**pname**   The person name for the account.

>>**gname**   The group name for the account.

>>**oname**   The organization name for the account.

sec_rgy_member_t
>A character string of length **sec_rgy_name_t_size**.

sec_rgy_foreign_id_t
>The representation of a foreign ID. This structure contains two components:

>>**cell**   A string of type **uuid_t** representing the UUID of the foreign cell.

>>**principal** A string of type **uuid_t** representing the UUID of the principal.

sec_rgy_sid_t
>A structure identifying an account. It contains three fields:

>>**person**   The UUID of the person part of the account.

>>**group**   The UUID of the group part of the account.

>>**org**   The UUID of the organization part of the account.

sec_rgy_unix_sid_t
>A structure identifying an account with UNIX ID numbers. It contains three fields:

>>**person**   The UNIX ID of the person part of the account.

>>**group**   The UNIX ID of the group part of the account.

>>**org**   The UNIX ID of the organization part of the account.

sec_rgy_domain_t

This 32-bit integer specifies which naming domain a character string refers to: person, group, or organization.

sec_rgy_pgo_flags_t

A 32-bit bitset containing flags pertaining to registry entries. This type contains the following three flags:

sec_rgy_pgo_is_an_alias

If set, indicates the registry entry is an alias of another entry.

sec_rgy_pgo_is_required

If set, the registry item is required and cannot be deleted. An example of a required account is the one for the registry server itself.

sec_rgy_pgo_projlist_ok

If the accompanying item is a person entry, this flag indicates the person may have concurrent group sets. If the item is a group entry, the flag means this group can appear in a concurrent group set. The flag is undefined for organization items.

sec_rgy_pgo_item_t

The structure identifying a registry item. It contains five components:

id   The UUID of the registry item, in **uuid_t** form.

unix_num   A 32-bit integer containing the UNIX ID number of the registry item.

quota   A 32-bit integer representing the maximum number of user-defined groups the account owner can create.

flags   A **sec_rgy_pgo_flags_t** bitset containing information about the entry.

fullname   A **sec_rgy_pname_t** character string containing a full name for the registry entry. For a person entry, this field might contain the real name of the account owner. For a group, it might contain a description of the group. This is just a data field, and registry queries cannot search on the **fullname** entry.

sec_rgy_acct_admin_flags_t
A 32-bit bitset containing administration flags used as part of the administrator's information for any registry account. The set contains three flags:

sec_rgy_acct_admin_valid
Specifies that the account is valid for login.

sec_rgy_acct_admin_server
If set, the account's name can be used as a server name in a ticket-granting ticket.

sec_rgy_acct_admin_client
If set, the account's name can be used as a client name in a ticket-granting ticket.

Note that you can prevent the principal from being authenticated, by turning off both the **sec_rgy_acct_admin_server** and the **sec_rgy_acct_admin_client flags**.

sec_rgy_acct_auth_flags_t
A 32-bit bitset containing account authorization flags used to implement authentication policy as defined by the Kerberos Version 5 protocol. The set contains six flags:

sec_rgy_acct_auth_post_dated
Allows issuance of post-dated certificates.

sec_rgy_acct_auth_forwardable
Allows issuance of forwardable certificates.

sec_rgy_acct_auth_tgt
Allows issuance of certificates based on ticket-granting ticket (TGT) authentication. If this flag is not set, a client requesting a service may have to supply a password directly to the server.

sec_rgy_acct_auth_renewable
Allows issuance of renewable certificates.

sec_rgy_acct_auth_proxiable
Allows issuance of proxiable certificates.

sec_rgy_acct_auth_dup_session_key
Allows issuance of duplicate session keys.

sec_rgy_acct_admin_t

> The portion of a registry account item containing components relevant to administrators. This structure consists of the fields listed below. Note that only **expiration_date**, **good_since_date**, **flags**, and **authentication_flags** can be modified by an administrator; the remaining fields are set by the security server.

> **creator** This field, in **foreign_id_t format**, identifies the administrator who created the registry account.

> **creation_date**
> > Specifies the creation date of the account, in **sec_timeval_sec_t** format.

> **last_changer** Identifies the last person to change any of the account information, in **foreign_id_t** format.

> **change_date** Specifies the date of the last modification of the account information, in **sec_timeval_sec_t** format.

> **expiration_date**
> > The date after which the account will no longer be valid. In **sec_timeval_sec_t** format.

> **good_since_date**
> > The Kerberos Version 5 TGT revocation date. TGTs issued before this date will not be honored. In **sec_timeval_sec_t** format.

> **flags** Administrative flags in **sec_rgy_acct_admin_flags_t** format.

> **authentication_flags**
> > Authentication flags in **sec_rgy_acct_auth_flags_t** format.

sec_rgy_acct_user_flags_t

> A 32-bit bitset containing flags controlling user-modifiable information. There is only one flag currently implemented. If **sec_rgy_acct_user_passwd_valid** is set, it indicates the user password is valid. If it is not set, this flag prompts the user to change the password on the next login attempt.

sec_rgy_acct_user_t
> A structure containing registry account information. The structure consists of the fields listed below. Note that only the **gecos**, **homedir**, **shell**, and **flags** fields can be modified by the account owner or other authorized useer; the remaining fields are set by the security server.

> **gecos**
>> This is a character string (in **sec_rgy_pname_t** format) containing information about the account user. It generally consists of everything after the full name in the UNIX **gecos** format.

> **homedir**
>> The login directory for the account user, in **sec_rgy_pname_t** format.

> **shell**
>> The default shell for the account user, in **sec_rgy_pname_t** format.

> **passwd_version_number**
>> An unsigned 32-bit integer, indicating the password version number. This value is used as output only.

> **passwd**
>> The UNIX encrypted account password, in **sec_rgy_unix_passwd_buf_t** format. This value is used as output only.

> **passwd_dtm** The date the password was established, in **sec_timeval_sec_t** format.

> **flags**
>> Account user flags, in **sec_rgy_acct_user_flags_t** format.

sec_rgy_plcy_pwd_flags_t
> A 32-bit bitset containing two flags about password policy:

> **sec_rgy_plcy_pwd_no_spaces**
>> If set, will not allow spaces in a password.

> **sec_rgy_plcy_pwd_non_alpha**
>> If set, requires at least one nonalphanumeric character in the password.

sec_rgy_plcy_t

A structure defining aspects of registry account policy. It contains five components:

passwd_min_len

A 32-bit integer describing the minimum number of characters in the account password.

passwd_lifetime

The number of seconds after a password's creation until it expires, in **sec_timeval_period_t** format.

passwd_exp_date

The expiration date of the account password, in **sec_timeval_sec_t** format.

acct_lifespan The number of seconds after the creation of an account before it expires, in **sec_timeval_period_t** format.

passwd_flags Account password policy flags, in **sec_rgy_plcy_-pwd_flags_t** format.

sec_rgy_plcy_auth_t

This type describes authentication policy. It is a structure containing two time periods, in **sec_timeval_period_t** format. One, **max_ticket_lifetime**, specifies the maximum length of the period during which a ticket-granting ticket (TGT) will be valid. The other, **max_renewable_lifetime**, specifies the maximum length of time for which such a ticket may be renewed. This authentication policy applies both to the registry as a whole as well as individual accounts. The effective policy for a given account is defined to be the more restrictive of the site and principal authentication policy.

sec_rgy_properties_t

A structure describing some registry properties. It contains the following:

read_version A 32-bit integer describing the earliest version of the **secd** software that can read this registry.

write_version

A 32-bit integer describing the version of the **secd** software that wrote this registry.

minimum_ticket_lifetime
The minimum lifetime of an authentication certificate, in **sec_timeval_period_t** format.

default_certificate_lifetime
The normal lifetime of an an authentication certificate (ticket-granting ticket in Kerberos parlance), in **sec_timeval_period_t** format. Processes may request authentication certificates with longer lifetimes up to, but not in excess of, the maximum allowable lifetime as determined by the effective policy for the account.

low_unix_id_person
The lowest UNIX number permissible for a person item in the registry.

low_unix_id_group
The lowest UNIX number permissible for a group item in the registry.

low_unix_id_org
The lowest UNIX number permissible for an organization item in the registry.

max_unix_id The largest UNIX number permissible for any registry entry.

flags Property flags, in **sec_rgy_properties_flags_t** format.

realm The name of the cell, in **sec_rgy_name_t** form, for which this registry is the authentication service.

realm_uuid The UUID of the same cell.

sec_rgy_properties_flags_t
A 32-bit bitset, containing flags concerning registry properties:

sec_rgy_prop_readonly
If set (TRUE), indicates that this registry is a query site.

sec_rgy_prop_auth_cert_unbound
If set (TRUE), the registry server will accept requests from any site.

sec_rgy_prop_shadow_passwd

If the shadow password flag is set (TRUE), the registry server will not include the account password when responding to a request for the user data from a specified account. This helps minimize the risk of an account password being intercepted while traveling over the network.

sec_rgy_prop_embedded_unix_id

Indicates that all UUIDs in this registry contain a UNIX number embedded. This implies that the UNIX numbers of objects in the registry cannot be changed, since UUIDs are immutable.

sec_rgy_override_t

A 32-bit integer used as a flag for registry override mode. Currently, its possible values are the constants **sec_rgy_no_-override** and **sec_rgy_override**. When this mode is enabled, override data supplied by the node administrator will replace some of the data gotten from the registry for a given person/account under certain conditions. These conditions are as follows:

1. The registry permits the requested overrides to be set for this machine.

2. The override data is intended for person/account at hand.

When the mode is override off, data from the registry is returned to the end user or the application remains untouched.

sec_rgy_mode_resolve_t

A 32-bit integer used as a flag for resolve mode. Currently, its possible values are the constants **sec_rgy_no_resolve_pname** and **sec_rgy_resolve_pname**. When the mode is enabled, pathnames containing leading **//** (slashes) will be translated into a form understandable by the local machine's NFS.

sec_rgy_unix_passwd_buf_t

A character array of UNIX password strings.

Constants   The following constants are used in **sec_rgy_** calls:

sec_rgy_default_handle
> The value of an unbound registry server handle.

sec_rgy_acct_key_t
> The following 32-bit integer constants are used with the **sec_rgy_acct_key_t** data type:

> > **sec_rgy_acct_key_none**
> > > Invalid key.

> > **sec_rgy_acct_key_person**
> > > The person name alone is enough.

> > **sec_rgy_acct_key_group**
> > > The person and group names are both necessary for the account abbreviation.

> > **sec_rgy_acct_key_org**
> > > The person, group, and organization names are all necessary.

> > **sec rgy_acct_key_last**
> > > Key values must be less than this constant.

sec_rgy_pname_t_size
> The maximum number of characters in a **sec_rgy_pname_t**.

sec_rgy_name_t_size
> The maximum number of characters in a **sec_rgy_name_t**.

sec_rgy_domain_t
> The following 32-bit integer constants are the possible values of the **sec_rgy_domain_t** data type:

> > **sec_rgy_domain_person**
> > > The name in question refers to a person.

> > **sec_rgy_domain_group**
> > > The name in question refers to a group.

> > **sec_rgy_domain_org**
> > > The name in question refers to an organization.

sec_rgy_pgo_flags_t
> A 32-bit constant equal to a variable of type **sec_rgy_pgo_flags_t** with no flags set.

sec_rgy_quota_unlimited
> A 32-bit integer. Set the **quota** field of the **sec_rgy_pgo_item_t** type to this constant to override the registry quota limitation.

sec_rgy_acct_admin_flags_t
> A 32-bit integer. This is the value of the **sec_rgy_acct_admin_-flags_t** bitset when none of its flags are set.

sec_rgy_acct_auth_flags_none
> A 32-bit integer. This is the value of the **sec_rgy_acct_auth_-flags_t** bitset when none of its flags are set.

sec_rgy_acct_user_flags_t
> A 16-bit integer. This is the value of the **sec_rgy_acct_user_-flags_t** bitset when none of its flags are set.

sec_rgy_plcy_pwd_flags_t
> A 16-bit integer. This is the value of the **sec_rgy_policy_pwd_-flags_t** bitset when none of its flags are set.

sec_rgy_properties_flags_t
> A 16-bit integer. This is the value of the **sec_rgy_properties_-flags_t** bitset when none of its flags are set.

sec_rgy_override
> A 32-bit integer, which turns registry override mode on. When this mode is enabled, override data supplied by the node administrator will replace some of the data gotten from the registry for a given person/account under certain conditions.

sec_rgy_no_override
> A 32-bit integer, which turns off registry override mode.

sec_rgy_resolve_pname
> A 32-bit integer, which turns on registry resolve mode. When the mode is enabled, pathnames containing leading // (slashes) will be translated into a form understandable by the local machine's NFS.

sec_rgy_no_resolve_pname
> A 32-bit integer, which turns off registry resolve mode.

Files   **/usr/include/dce/rgybase.idl**
          The **idl** file from which **rgybase.h** was derived.

EXTENDED REGISTRY ATTRIBUTE DATA TYPES

Synopsis   #include <dce/sec_attr_base.h>

Data Types
          The following data types are used in **sec_rgy_attr** calls:

          sec_attr_twr_ref_t
                    A pointer to a tower. This data type is used with the
                    sec_attr_twr_set_t data type to allow a client to pass an
                    unallocated array of towers, which the server must allocate. Both
                    data types are used in conjunction with the **sec_attr_bind_type_t**
                    data type.

          sec_attr_twr_set_t
                    A structure that defines an array of towers. This data type is used
                    with the **sec_attr_twr_ref_t** data type to allow a client to pass a
                    unallocated array of towers, which the server must allocate. Both
                    data types are used in conjunction with the **sec_attr_bind_type_t**
                    data type. The **sec_attr_twr_set_t** structure consists of the
                    following elements:

                    count   An unsigned 32-bit integer specifying the number of
                              towers in the array.

                    towers[ ]   An array of pointers (of type **sec_attr_twr_ref_t**) to
                              towers.

          sec_attr_bind_type_t
                    A 32-bit integer that specifies the type of binding used by an
                    attribute interface. The data type (which is used in conjunction with
                    the **sec_attr_binding_t** data type) uses the following constants:

                    sec_attr_bind_type_string
                              An RPC string binding.

                    sec_attr_bind_type_twrs
                              A DCE protocol tower representation of a bindings.

sec_attr_bind_type_svrname

A name in **rpc_c_ns_syntax** format that identifies a CDS entry containing the server's binding information. This constant has the following structure:

name_syntax

Must be **rpc_c_ns_syntax_dce** to specify that DCE naming rules are used to specify **name**.

name   A pointer to a name of a CDS entry in **rpc_c_ns_syntax_dce** syntax.

sec_attr_binding_t

A discriminated union that supplies information to generate a binding handle for a attribute trigger. This data type, which is used in conjunction with the **sec_attr_bind_info_t** data type, is composed of the following elements:

bind_type   A value of type **sec_attr_bind_type_t** that defines the type of binding used by an attribute interface. The contents of **tagged union** (see table) depend on the value of **sec_attr_bind_type_t**.

tagged_union

A tagged union specifying the binding handle. The contents of the tagged union depend on the value of **bind_type** as follows:

If bind_type is...	Then tagged_union is...
sec_attr_bind_type_string	A pointer to an unsigned 32-bit character string specifying an attribute's RPC string binding.
sec_attr_bind type_twrs	An attribute's tower binding representation of type **sec_attr_twr_set_t**.
sec_attr_bind_svrname	A pointer to a name of type **sec_attr_bind_type_t** that specifies a Cell Directory Service entry containing a attribute trigger's binding information.

sec_attr_binding_p_t

A pointer to a **sec_attr_binding_t** union.

sec_attr_bind_auth_info_type_t
>An enumeration that defines whether or not the binding is authenticated. This data type is used in conjunction with the **sec_attr_bind_auth_info_t** data type to set up the authorization method and parameters for an RPC binding. The **sec_attr_bind_auth_info_type_t** type consists of the following elements:

>**sec_attr_bind_auth_none**
>>The binding is not authenticated.

>**sec_attr_bind_auth_dce**
>>The binding uses DCE shared-secret key authentication.

sec_attr_bind_auth_info_t
>A discriminated union that defines authorization and authentication parameters for a binding. This data type is used in conjunction with the **sec_attr_bind_auth_info_type_t** data type to set up the authorization method and parameters for an RPC binding. The **sec_attr_bind_auth_info_t** data type consists of the following elements:

>**info_type**   A **sec_attr_bind_auth_info_type_t** data type that specifies whether or not the binding is authenticated. The contents of **tagged union** (below) depend on the value of **sec_attr_bind_auth_info_type_t**.

>**tagged_union**
>>A tagged union specifying the method of authorization and the authorization parameters. For unauthenticated bindings (**sec_attr_bind_auth_info_type_t** = **sec_attr_bind_auth_none**), no parameters are supplied. For authenticated bindings (**sec_attr_bind_auth_info_type_t** = **sec_attr_bind_auth_dce**), the following union is supplied:

>>**svr_princ_name**
>>>A pointer to a character string that specifies the principal name of the server referenced by the binding handle.

protect_level An unsigned 32 bit integer indicating the protection level for RPC calls made using the server binding handle. The protection level determines the degree to which authenticated communications between the client and the server are protected by the authentication service specified by **authn_svc**.

If the RPC runtime or the RPC protocol in the bound protocol sequence does not support a specified level, the level is automatically upgraded to the next higher supported level. The possible protection levels are as follows:

Protection Level	Description
rpc_c_protect_level_default	Uses the default protection level for the specified authentication service. The default protection level for DCE shared-secret key authentication is **rpc_c_protect_level_pkt_value**
rpc_c_protect_level_none	Performs no authentication: tickets are not exchanged, session keys are not established, client PACs or names are not certified, and transmissions are in the clear. Note that although uncertified PACs should not be trusted, they may be useful for debugging, tracing, and measurement purposes.
rpc_c_protect_level_connect	Authenticates only when the client establishes a relationship with the server.
rpc_c_protect_level_call	Authenticates only at the beginning of each remote procedure call when the server receives the request. This level does not apply to remote procedure calls made over a connection-based protocol sequence (that is, **ncacn_ip_tcp**). If this level is specified and the binding handle uses a connection-based protocol sequence, the routine uses the **rpc_c_protect_level_pkt** level instead.
rpc_c_protect_level_pkt	Ensures that all data received is from the expected client.

Protection Level	Description
rpc_c_protect_level_pkt_integ	Ensures and verifies that none of the data transferred between client and server has been modified. This is the highest protection level that is guaranteed to be present in the RPC runtime.
rpc_c_protect_level_pkt_privacy	Authenticates as specified by all of the previous levels and also encrypts each RPC argument value. This is the highest protection level, but is not guaranteed to be present in the RPC runtime.

authn_svc Specifies the authentication service to use. The exact level of protection provided by the authentication service is specified by **protect_level**. The supported authentication services are as follows:

Authentication Service	Description
rpc_c_authn_none	No authentication: no tickets are exchanged, no session keys established, client PACs or names are not transmitted, and transmissions are in the clear. Specify **rpc_c_authn_none** to turn authentication off for remote procedure calls made using this binding.
rpc_c_authn_dce_secret	DCE shared-secret key authentication.
rpc_c_authn_default	Default authentication service. The current default authentication service is DCE shared-secret key; therefore, specifying **rpc_c_authn_default** is equivalent to specifying **rpc_c_authn_dce_secret**.
rpc_c_authn_dce_public	DCE public key authentication (reserved for future use).

authz_svc Specifies the authorization service implemented by the server for the interface. The validity and trustworthiness of authorization data, like any application data, is dependent on the authentication service and protection level specified. The supported authorization services are as follows:

Authentication Service	Description
rpc_c_authz_none	Server performs no authorization. This is valid only if **authn_svc** is set to **rpc_c_authn_none**, specifying that no authentication is being performed.
rpc_c_authz_name	Server performs authorization based on the client principal name. This value cannot be used if **authn_svc** is **rpc_c_authn_none**.
rpc_c_authz_dce	Server performs authorization using the client's DCE privilege attribute certificate (PAC) sent to the server with each remote procedure call made with this binding. Generally, access is checked against DCE ACLs.

sec_attr_bind_info_t

A structure that specifies attribute trigger binding information. This data type, which is used in conjunction with the **sec_attr_schema_entry_t** data type, contains of the following elements:

auth_info   The binding authorization information of type **sec_attr_bind_auth_info_t**.

num_bindings

An unsigned 32-bit integer specifying the number of binding handles in **bindings**.

bindings   An array of **sec_attr_binding_t** data types that specify binding handles.

sec_attr_bind_info_p_t

A pointer to a **sec_attr_bind_info_t** union.

sec_attr_encoding_t

An enumerator that contains attribute encoding tags used to define the legal encodings for attribute values. The data type, which is used in conjunction with the **sec_attr_value_t** and **sec_attr_schema_-entry_t** data types, consists of the following elements:

sec_attr_enc_any

The attribute value can be of any legal encoding type. This encoding tag is legal only in a schema entry. An attribute entry must contain a concrete encoding type.

sec_attr_enc_void
> The attribute has no value. It is simple a marker that is either present or absent.

sec_attr_enc_printstring
> The attribute value is a printable IDL string in DCE portable character set.

sec_attr_enc_printstring_array
> The attribute value is an array of printstrings.

sec_attr_enc_integer
> The attribute value is a signed 32-bit integer.

sec_attr_enc_bytes
> The attribute value is a string of bytes. The string is assumed to be a pickle or some other self describing type. (See also the **sec_attr_enc_bytes_t** data type.)

sec_attr_enc_confidential_bytes
> The attribute value is a string of bytes that have been encrypted in the key of the principal object to which the attribute is attached. The string is assumed to be a pickle or some other self describing type. This encoding type is useful only when attached to a principal object, where it is decrypted and encrypted each time the principal's password changes. (See also the **sec_attr_enc_bytes_t** data type.)

sec_attr_enc_i18n_data
> The attribute value is an internationalized string of bytes with a tag identifying the OSF registered codeset used to encode the data. (See also the **sec_attr_i18n_data_t** data type.)

sec_attr_enc_uuid
> The attribute is a value of type **uuid_t**, a DCE UUID.

sec_attr_enc_attr_set
> The attribute value is an attribute set, a vector of attribute UUIDs used to associate multiple related attribute instances which are members of the set. (See also the **sec_attr_enc_attr_set_t** data type.)

sec_attr_enc_binding
> The attribute value is a **sec_attr_bind_info_t** data type that specifies DCE server binding information.

sec_attr_cnc_trig_binding
> This encoding type is returned by **rs_attr_lookup** call. It informs the client agent of the trigger binding information of an attribute with a query trigger.

Unless **sec_attr_enc_void** or **sec_attr_enc_any** is specified, the attribute values must conform to the attribute's encoding type.

sec_attr_enc_bytes_t
> A structure that defines the length of attribute encoding values for attributes encoded as **sec_attr_enc_bytes** and **sec_attr_enc_- confidential_bytes**. The structure, which is used in conjunction with the **sec_attr_value_t** data type, consists of

> **length**
>> An unsigned 32-bit integer that defines the data length.

> **data[ ]**
>> An array of bytes specifying the length of attribute encoding data.

sec_attr_i18n_data_t
> A structure that defines the codeset used for attributes encoded as **sec_attr_enc_il8n_data** and the length of the attribute encoding values. The structure, which is used in conjunction with the **sec_attr_value_t** data type, consists of

> **codeset**
>> An unsigned 32-bit identifier of a codeset registered with the Open Software Foundation.

> **length**
>> An unsigned 32-bit integer that defines the data length.

> **data[ ]**
>> An array of bytes specifying the length of attribute encoding data.

sec_attr_enc_attr_set_t
> A structure that that supplies the UUIDs of each member of an attribute set. The structure, which is used in conjunction with the **sec_attr_value_t** data type, consists of

> **num_members**
>> An unsigned 32-bit integer specifying the total number of attribute's in the set.

members[ ]   An array containing values of type **uuid_t**, the UUID of each member in the set.

sec_attr_enc_printstring_t
A structure that contains a printstring.

sec_attr_enc_printstring_p_t
A pointer to a **sec_attr_enc_printstring_t** structure.

sec_attr_enc_str_array_t
A structure that defines a printstring array. It consists of

num_strings   An unsigned 32-bit integer specifying the number of strings in the array.

strings[ ]   An array of pointers (of type **sec_attr_enc_print_-string_p_t**) to printstrings.

sec_attr_value_t
A discriminated union that defines attribute values. The union, which is used in conjunction with the **sec_attr_t** data type, consists of the following elements:

attr_encoding
A **sec_attr_encoding_t** data type that defines attribute encoding. The contents of **tagged union** depend on the value of **sec_attr_encoding_t**.

tagged_union
A tagged union whose contents depend on **attr_encoding** as follows:

If attr_encoding is...	Then tagged_union is...
sec_attr_enc_void	**NULL**
sec_attr_enc_printstring	A pointer to **printstring**
sec_attr_enc_printstring_array	A pointer to an array of **printstring**s
sec_attr_enc_integer	**signed_int**, a 32-bit signed integer
sec_attr_enc_bytes	**bytes**, a pointer to a structure of type **sec_attr_enc_bytes_t**
sec_attr_enc_confidential_bytes	**bytes**, a pointer to a structure of type **sec_attr_enc_bytes_t**
sec_attr_enc_i18n_data	**idata**, a pointer to a structure of type **sec_attr_i18n_data_t**
sec_attr_end_uuid	**uuid**, a value of type **uuid_t**
sec_attr_enc_attr_set	**attr_set**, a pointer to a structure of type **sec_attr_enc_attr_set_t**
sec_attr_enc_binding	**binding**, a pointer to a structure of type **sec_attr_binding_info_t**

sec_attr_t

A structure that defines an attribute. The structure consists of

attr_id   A value of type **uuid_t**, the UUID of the attribute.

attr_value   A value of type **sec_attr_value_t**.

sec_attr_acl_mgr_info_t

A structure that contains the access control information defined in a schema entry for an attribute. The structure, which is used in conjunction with the **sec_attr_schema_entry_t** data type, consists of the following elements:

acl_mgr_type

The value of type **uuid_t** that specifies the UUID of the ACL manager type that supports the object type to which the attribute can be attached. This field provides a well-defined context for evaluating the permission bits needed to operate on the attribute. The following table lists the ACL manager types for registry objects.

Registry Object Type	ACL manager Type	Valid Permissions
principal	06ab9320-0191-11ca-a9e8-08001e039d7d	rcDnfmaug
group	06ab9640-0191-11ca-a9e8-08001e039d7d	rctDnfmM
organization	06ab9960-0191-11ca-a9e8-08001e039d7d	rctDnfmM
directory	06ab9c80-0191-11ca-a9e8-08001e039d7d	rcidDn
policy	06ab8f10-0191-11ca-a9e8-08001e039d7d	rcma
replist	2ac24970-60c3-11cb-b261-08001e039d7d	cidmAl

query_permset
> Data of type **sec_acl_permset_t** that defines the permission bits needed to access the attribute's value.

update_permset
> Data of type **sec_acl_permset_t** that defines the permission bits needed to update the attribute's value.

test_permset Data of type **sec_acl_permset_t** that defines the permission bits needed to test the attribute's value.

delete_permset
> Data of type **sec_acl_permset_t** that defines the permission bits needed to delete an attribute instance.

sec_attr_acl_mgr_info_p_t
> A pointer to a **sec_attr_acl_mgr_info_t** structure.

sec_attr_acl_mgr_info_set_t
> A structure that defines an attribute's ACL manager set. The structure consists of the following elements:

num_acl_mgrs
> An unsigned 32-bit integer that specifies the number of ACL managers in the ACL manager set.

mgr_info[ ] An array of pointers of type **sec_attr_mgr_info_p_t** that define the ACL manager types in the ACL manager set and the permission sets associated with the ACL manager type.

sec_attr_intercell_action_t

An enumerator that specifies the action that should be taken by the privilege service when it reads acceptable attributes from a foreign cell. A foreign attribute is acceptable only if there is either a schema entry for the foreign cell or if **sec_attr_intercell_act_-accept** is set to **true**.

This enumerator, which is used in conjunction with the **sec_attr_schema_entry_t** data type, is composed of the following elements:

sec_attr_intercell_act_accept

If the **unique** flag in the **sec_attr_schema_entry_t** data type is not set on, retain the attribute. If the **unique** flag is set on, retain the attribute only if its value is unique among all attribute instances of the same attribute type within the cell.

sec_attr_intercell_act_reject

Discard the input attribute.

sec_attr_intercell_act_evaluate

Use the binding information in the **trig_binding** field of this **sec_attr_schema_entry_t** data type to make a **sec_attr_trig_query** call to a trigger server. That server determines whether to retain the attribute value, discard the attribute value, or map the attribute to another value(s).

sec_attr_trig_type_t

Specifies the trigger type, a flag that determines whether an attribute trigger should be invoked for query operations. The data type, which is used in conjunction with the **sec_attr_schema_entry_t** data type, uses the following constants:

sec_attr_trig_type_query

The attribute trigger server is invoked for query operations.

sec_attr_trig_type_query

The attribute trigger server is invoked for update operations.

sec_attr_schema_entry_t

A structure that defines a complete attribute entry for the schema catalog. The entry is identified by both a unique string name and a unique attribute UUID. Although either can either can be used as a retrieval key, the string name should be used for interactive access to the attribute and the UUID for programmatic access. The attribute UUID is used to identify the semantics defined for the attribute type in the schema.

The **sec_attr_schema_entry_t** data type consists of the following elements:

attr_name   A pointer to the attribute name.

attr_id   A value of type **uuid_t** that identifies the attribute type.

attr_encoding

An enumerator of type **sec_attr_encoding_t** that specifies the attribute's encoding.

acl_mgr_set   A structure of type **sec_attr_acl_mgr_info_set_t** that specifies the ACL manager types that support the objects on which attributes of this type can be created and the permission bits supported by that ACL manager type.

schema_entry_flags

An unsigned integer of type **sec_attr_sch_entry_-flags_t** that defines bitsets for the following flags:

unique   When set on, this flag indicates that each instance of this attribute type must have a unique value within the cell for the object type implied by the ACL manager type. If this flag is not set on, uniqueness checks are not performed for attribute writes.

multi_valued When set on, this flag indicates that this attribute type may be multivalued; in other words, multiple instances of the same attribute type can be attached to a single registry object. If this flag is not set on, only one instance of this attribute type can be attached to an object.

reserved When set on, this flag prevents the schema entry from being deleted through any interface or by any user. If this flag is not set on, the entry can be deleted by any authorized principal.

use_defaults When set on, the system-defined default attribute value will be returned on a client query if an instance of this attribute does not exist on the queried object. If this flag is not set on, system defaults are not used.

intercell_action

An enumerator of type **sec_attr_intercell_action_t** that specifies how the privilege service will handle attributes from a foreign cell.

trig_types A flag of type **sec_attr_trig_type_t** that specifies whether whether a trigger can perform update or query operations.

trig_binding A pointer to a structure of type **sec_attr_bind_info_t** that supplies the attribute trigger binding handle.

scope A pointer to a string that defines the objects to which the attribute can be attached.

comment A pointer to a string that contains general comments about the attribute.

sec_attr_schema_entry_parts_t

A 32-bit bitset containing flags that specify the schema entry fields that can be modified on a schema entry update operation. This data type contains the following flags:

> **sec_attr_schema_part_name**
>> If set, indicates that the attribute name (**attr_name**) can be changed.
>
> **sec_attr_schema_part_reserved**
>> If set, indicates that the setting of the flag that determines whether or not the schema entry can be deleted (**reserved**) can be changed.
>
> **sec_attr_schema_part_defaults**
>> If set, indicates that the flag that determines whether or not a query for a nonexistent attribute will not result in a search for a system default (**apply_default**) can be changed.
>
> **sec_attr_schema_part_trig_bind**
>> If set, indicates that the trigger's binding information (**trig_binding**) can be changed.
>
> **sec_attr_schema_part_comment**
>> If set, indicates whether or not comments associated with the schema entry (**comment**) can be changed.

sec_attr_component_name_t
> A pointer to a character string used to further specify the object to which the attribute is attached. (Note that this data type is analogous to the **sec_acl_component_name_t** data type in the ACL interface.)

sec_attr_cursor_t
> A structure that provides a pointer into a registry database and is used for multiple database operations.
>
> This cursor must minimally represent the object indicated by **xattrschema** in the schema interfaces, or *component_name* in the attribute interfaces. The cursor may additionally represent an entry within that schema or an attribute instance on that component.

sec_attr_srch_cursor_t
> A structure that provides a pointer into a registry database and is used for multiple database operations. The cursor must minimally represent the list of all objects managed by this server that possess the search attributes specified in the **sec_attr_srch_cursor_init** routine. It may additionally represent a given object within this list as well as attribute instance(s) possessed by that object.

sec_attr_trig_cursor_t

A structure that provides an attribute trigger cursor for interactive operations. The structure consists of the following elements:

source   A value of type **uuid_t** that provides a UUID to identify the server that initialized the cursor.

object_handle

A signed 32 bit integer that identifies the object (specified by **xattrschema** in the schema interface or *component_name* in the attribute interface) upon which the operation is being performed.

entry_handle A signed 32 bit integer that identifies the current entry (*schema_entry* in the schema interface or *attribute instance* in the attribute interface) for the operation.

valid   A boolean field with the following values:

true (1)   Indicates an initialized cursor.

false (0)   Indicates an uninitialized cursor.

sec_attr_trig_timeval_sec_t

A 32-bit integer containing the seconds portion of a UNIX **timeval_t**, to be used when expressing absolute dates.

Files   **/usr/include/dce/sec_attr_base.idl**

The **idl** file from which **sec_attr_base.h** was derived.

Constants   The following constants are used in **sec_attr** calls:

sec_attr_bind_auth_dce

The binding uses DCE shared-secret key authentication.

sec_attr_bind_auth_none

The binding is not authenticated.

sec_attr_bind_type_string

The attribute uses an rpc string binding.

sec_attr_bind_type_svrname
> The attribute uses a name in **rpc_c_ns_syntax** format that identifies a CDS entry containing the server's binding information. This constant has the following structure:

> **name_syntax**
>> Must be **rpc_c_ns_syntax_dce** to specify that DCE naming rules are used to specify **name**.

> **name**
>> A pointer to a name of a CDS entry in **rpc_c_ns_-syntax_dce** syntax.

sec_attr_bind_type_twr
> The attribute uses a DCE protocol tower binding representation.

sec_attr_trig_type_t
> The following 32-bit constants are used with the **sec_attr_trig_-type_t** data type:

>> **sec_attr_trig_type_query** The trigger server can perform only query operations.

>> **sec_attr_trig_type_update** The trigger server can perform only update operations.

sec_attr_intercell_action_t
> The following constants are used with the **sec_attr_intercell_-action_t** data type:

> **sec_attr_intercell_act_accept**
>> If the **unique** flag in the **sec_attr_schema_entry_t** data type is not set on, retain attributes from a foreign cell. If the **unique** flag is set on, retain the foreign attribute only if its value is unique among all attribute instances of the same attribute type within the cell.

> **sec_attr_intercell_act_reject**
>> Discard attributes from a foreign cell.

> **sec_attr_intercell_act_evaluate**
>> A trigger server determines whether to retain foreign attributes, discard foreign attributes, or map foreign attribute to another value(s).

sec_attr_schema_entry_parts_t
The following constants are used with the **sec_attr_schema_-entry_parts_t** data type:

sec_attr_schema_part_name
Indicates that the attribute name can be changed in an schema update operation.

sec_attr_schema_part_reserved
Indicates that the setting of the **reserved** flag can be changed in a schema entry update.

sec_attr_schema_part_defaults
Indicates that the **apply_default** flag can be changed in a schema entry update operation.

sec_attr_schema_part_trig_bind
Indicates that trigger binding information can be changed in a schema entry update operation.

sec_attr_schema_part_comment
Indicates that comments associated with the schema entry can be changed in a schema entry update.

LOGIN API DATA TYPES

Synopsis   **#include <dce/sec_login.h>**

Data Types

The following data types are used in **sec_login_** calls:

sec_login_handle_t
This is an opaque pointer to a data structure representing a complete login context. The context includes a principal's network credentials, as well as other account information. The network credentials are also referred to as the principal's ticket-granting ticket.

sec_login_flags_t
A 32-bit set of flags describing restrictions on the use of a principal's validated network credentials. Currently, only one flag is implemented, and the set can take on the following two values:

sec_login_no_flags
No special flags are set.

sec_login_credentials_private
Restricts the validated network credentials to the current process. If this flag is not set, it is permissible to share credentials with descendents of current process.

sec_login_auth_src_t
An enumerated set describing how the login context was authorized. The possible values are:

sec_login_auth_src_network
Authentication accomplished through the normal network authority. A login context authenticated this way will have all the network credentials it ought to have.

sec_login_auth_src_local
Authentication accomplished via local data. Authentication occurs locally if a principal's account is tailored for the local machine, or if the network authority is unavailable. Since login contexts authenticated locally have no network credentials, they may not be used for network operations.

sec_login_auth_src_overridden
Authentication accomplished via the override facility.

sec_login_passwd_t
The **sec_login_get_pwent( )** call will return a pointer to a password structure, which depends on the underlying registry structure.

In most cases, the structure will look like that supported by Berkeley 4.4BSD and OSF/1, which looks like this:

```
struct passwd {
char      *pw_name;          * user name *
char      *pw_passwd;        * encrypted password *
int       pw_uid;            * user uid *
int       pw_gid;            * user gid *
time_t    pw_change;         * password change time *
char      *pw_class;         * user access class *
char      *pw_gecos;         * Honeywell login info *
char      *pw_dir;           * home directory *
char      *pw_shell;         * default shell *
time_t    pw_expire;         * account expiration *
};
```

sec_passwd_rec_t

A structure containing either a plaintext password or a preencrypted buffer of password data. The **sec_passwd_rec_t** structure consists of three components:

version_number

The version number of the password.

pepper

A character string combined with the password before an encryption key is derived from the password.

key

A structure consists of the following components:

key_type

The key type can be the following:

sec_passwd_plain

Indicates that a printable string of data is stored in **plain**.

sec_passwd_des

Indicates that an array of data is stored in **des_key.**

tagged_union

A structure specifying the password. The value of the structure depends on **key_type**. If **key_type** is **sec_-passwd_plain**, structure contains **plain**, a character string. If **key_type** is **sec_passwd_des**, the structure contains **des_key**, a DES key of type **sec_passwd_des_key_t**.

Constants   The following constants are used in **sec_login_** calls:

sec_login_default_handle

The value of a login context handle before setup or validation.

sec_login_flags_t

The following two constants are used with the **sec_login_flags_t** type:

sec_login_no_flags

No special flags are set.

sec_login_credentials_private

Restricts the validated network credentials to the current process. If this flag is not set, it is permissible to share credentials with descendents of current process.

sec_login_remote_uid

Used in the **sec_login_passwd_t** structure for users from remote cells.

sec_login_remote_gid

Used in the **sec_login_passwd_t** structure for users from remote cells.

Files   **/usr/include/dce/sec_login.idl**

The **idl** file from which **sec_login.h** was derived.

EXTENDED PRIVILEGE ATTRIBUTE API DATA TYPES

Synopsis **#include <dce/id_epac.h>**

#include <dce/nbase.h>

Data Types

The following data types are used in extended privilege attribute calls and in the **sec_login_cred** calls that implement extended privilege attributes.

sec_cred_cursor_t

A structure that provides an input/output cursor used to iterate through a set of delegates in the **sec_cred_get_delegate**( ) or **sec_login_cred_get_delegate**( ) calls. This cursor is initialized by the **sec_cred_initialize_cursor**( ) or **sec_login_cred_init_cursor**( ) call.

sec_cred_attr_cursor_t

A structure that provides an input/output cursor used to iterate through a set of extended attributes in the **sec_cred_get_-extended_attributes**( ) call. This cursor is initialized by the **sec_cred_initialize_attr_cursor**( ) call.

sec_id_opt_req_t

A structure that specifies application-defined optional restrictions. The **sec_id_opt_req_t** data type is composed of the following elements:

restriction_len

An unsigned 16-bit integer that defines the size of the restriction data.

restrictions A pointer to a **byte_t** that contains the restriction data.

sec_rstr_entry_type_t

An enumerator that specifies the entry types for delegate and target restrictions. This data type is used in conjunction with the **sec_id_restriction_t** data type where the specific UUID(s), if appropriate, are supplied. It consists of the following components:

sec_rstr_e_type_user
> The target is a local principal identified by UUID. This type conforms with the POSIX 1003.6 standard.

sec_rstr_e_type_group
> The target is a local group identified by UUID. This type conforms with the POSIX 1003.6 standard.

sec_rstr_e_type_foreign_user
> The target is a foreign principal identified by principal and cell UUID.

sec_rstr_e_type_foreign_group
> The target is a foreign group identified by group and cell UUID.

sec_rstr_e_type_foreign_other
> The target is any principal that can authenticate to the foreign cell identified by UUID.

sec_rstr_e_type_any_other
> The target is any principal that can authenticate to any cell, but is not identified in any other type entry.

sec_rstr_e_type_no_other
> No pincipal can act as a target or delegate.

sec_id_restriction_t
> A discriminated union that defines delegate and target restrictions. The union, which is used in conjunction with the **sec_restriction_set_t** data type, consists of the following elements:

> **entry_type** A **sec_rstr_entry_type_t** that defines the ACL entry types for delegate and target restrictions. The value of **tagged_union** depends on the value of **entry_type**.

> **tagged_union**
> > A tagged union whose contents depend on **entry_type** as follows:

If entry_type is...	Then tagged_union is...
sec_rstr_e_type_any_other	NULL
sec_rstr_e_type_foreign_other	**foreign_id** that identifies the foreign cell.
sec_rstr_e_type user **sec_rstr_e_type_group**	**id**, a **sec_id_t** that identifies the user or group.
sec_rstr_e_type_foreign_user **sec_rstr_e_type_foreign_group**	**foreign_id**, a **sec_id_foreign_t** that identifies the foreign user or group.

sec_id_restriction_set_t

A structure that that supplies delegate and target restrictions. The structure consists of

num_restrictions

A 16-bit unsigned integer that defines the number of restrictions in **restrictions**.

restrictions   A pointer to a **sec_id_restriction_t** that contains the restrictions.

sec_id_compatibility_mode_t

A unsigned 16 bit integer that defines the compatibility between current and pre-1.1 servers. The data type uses the following constants:

sec_id_compat_mode_none

Compatibility mode is off.

sec_id_compat_mode_initiator

Compatibility mode is on. The 1.0 PAC data extracted from the EPAC of the chain initiator.

sec_id_compat_mode_caller

Compatibility mode is on. The 1.0 PAC data extracted from the last delegate in the delegation chain.

sec_id_delegation_type_t

An unsigned 16 bit integer that defines the delegation type. The data type uses the following constants:

sec_id_deleg_type_none

Delegation is not allowed.

sec_id_deleg_type_traced
Traced delegation is allowed.

sec_id_deleg_type_impersonation
Simple (impersonation) delegation is allowed.

sec_id_pa_t An structure that contains pre-1.1 PAC data extracted from an EPAC of a current version server. This data type, which is used for compatibility with pre-1.1 servers, consists of the following elements:

realm A value of type **sec_id_t** that contains the UUID that identifies the cell in which the principal associated with the PAC exists.

principal A value of type **sec_id_t** that contains the UUID of the principal.

group A value of type **sec_id_t** that contains the UUID of the principal's primary group.

num_groups An unsigned 16-bit integer that specifies the number of groups in the principal's groupset.

groups An array of pointers to **sec_id_t**s that contain the UUIDs of the each group in the principal's groupset.

num_foreign_groupsets
An unsigned 16-bit integer that specifies the number of foreign groups for the principal's groupset.

foreign_groupsets
An array of pointers to **sec_id_t**s that contain the UUIDs of the each group in the principal's groupset.

sec_id_pac_t An structure that contains a pre-1.1 PAC. This data type, which is used as output of the **sec_cred_get_v1_pac** call, consists of the following elements:

pac_type A value of type **sec_id_pac_format_t** that can be used to describe the PAC format.

authenticated
> A boolean field that indicates whether or not the PAC is authenticated (obtained from an authenticated source). FALSE indicates that the PAC is not authenticated. No authentication protocol was used in the rpc that transmitted the identity of the caller. TRUE indicates that the PAC is authenticated.

realm
> A value of type **sec_id_t** that contains the UUID that identifies the cell in which the principal associated with the PAC exists.

principal
> A value of type **sec_id_t** that contains the UUID of the principal.

group
> For local principals, a value of type **sec_id_t** that contains the UUID of the principal's primary group.

num_groups
> An unsigned 16-bit integer that specifies the number of groups in the principal's groupset.

groups
> An array of pointers to **sec_id_t**s that contain the UUIDs of the each group in the principal's groupset.

num_foreign_groups
> An unsigned 16-bit integer that specifies the number of foreign groups in the principal's groupset.

foreign_groups
> An array of pointers to **sec_id_t**s that contain the UUIDs of the each foreign group in the principal's groupset.

sec_id_pac_format_t
An enumerator that can be used to describe the PAC format.

sec_id_t
A structure that contains UUIDs for principals, groups, or organizations and an optional printstring name. Since a UUID is an handle for the object's identity, the **sec_id_t** data type is the basic unit for identifying principals, groups, and organizations.

Because the printstring name is dynamically allocated, this datatype requires a destructor function. Generally, however, the **sec_id_t** is embedded in other data types (ACLs, for example), and these datatypes have a destructor function to release the printstring storage.

The **sec_id_t** data type is composed of the following elements:

uuid	A value of type **uuid_t**, the UUID of the principal, group, or organization.
name	A pointer to a character string containing the name of the principal, group, or organization.

sec_id_foreign_t
A structure that contains UUIDs for principals, groups, or organizations for objects in a foreign cell and the UUID that identifies the foreign cell. The **sec_id_foreign_t** data type is composed of the following elements:

id	A value of type **sec_id_t** that contains the UUIDs of the objects from the foreign cell.
realm	A value of type **sec_id_t** that contains the UUID of the foreign cell.

sec_id_foreign_groupset_t
A structure that contains UUIDs for set of groups in a foreign cell and the UUID that identifies the foreign cell. The **sec_id_foreign_groupset_t** data type is composed of the following elements:

realm	A value of type **sec_id_t** that contain the UUID of the foreign cell.
num_groups	An unsigned 16-bit integer specifying the number of group UUIDs in **groups**.
groups	A printer to a **sec_id_t** that contains the UUIDs of the groupset from the foreign cell.

Constants The following constants are used in the extended privilege attribute calls and in the the **sec_login** calls that implement extended privilege attributes:

sec_id_compat_mode_none
Compatibility mode is off.

sec_id_compat_mode_initiator
Compatibility mode is on. The 1.0 PAC data extracted from the EPAC of the chain initiator.

sec_id_compat_mode_caller
Compatibility mode is on. The 1.0 PAC data extracted from the last delegate in the delegation chain.

sec_id_deleg_type_none
> Delegation is not allowed.

sec_id_deleg_type_traced
> Traced delegation is allowed.

scc_id_deleg_type_impersonation
> Simple (impersonation) delegation is allowed.

sec_rstr_e_type_user
> The delegation target is a local principal identified by UUID. This type conforms with the POSIX 1003.6 standard.

sec_rstr_e_type_group
> The delegation target is a local group identified by UUID. This type conforms with the POSIX 1003.6 standard.

sec_rstr_e_type_foreign_user
> The delegation target is a foreign principal identified by principal and cell UUID.

sec_rstr_e_type_foreign_group
> The delegation target is a foreign group identified by group and cell UUID.

sec_rstr_e_type_foreign_other
> The delegation target is any principal that can authenticate to the foreign cell identified by UUID.

sec_rstr_e_type_any_other
> The delegation target is any principal that can authenticate to any cell, but is not identified in any other type entry.

sec_rstr_e_type_no_other
> No pincipal can act as a target or delegate.

Files **/usr/include/dce/sec_cred.idl**
> The **idl** file from which **sec_cred.h** was derived.

/usr/include/dce/sec_epac.idl
> The **idl** file from which **sec_epac.h** was derived.

/usr/include/dce/sec_nbase.idl
> The **idl** file from which **sec_nbase.h** was derived.

ACL API DATA TYPES

Synopsis   **#include <dce/aclbase.h>**

Data Types

The following data types are used in **sec_acl_** calls:

sec_acl_handle_t
> A pointer to an opaque handle bound to an ACL that is the subject of a test or examination. The handle is bound to the ACL with **sec_acl_bind( )**. An unbound handle has the value **sec_acl_-default_handle**.

sec_acl_posix_semantics_t
> A flag that indicates which, if any, POSIX ACL semantics an ACL manager supports. The following constants are defined for use with the **sec_acl_posix_semantics_t** data type:

> **sec_acl_posix_no_semantics**
>> The manager type does not support POSIX semantics.

> **sec_acl_posix_mask_obj**
>> The manager type supports the **mask_obj** entry type and POSIX 1003.6 Draft 12 ACL mask entry semantics.

sec_acl_t
> This data type is the fundamental type for the ACL manager interfaces. The **sec_acl_t** type contains a complete access control list, made up of a list of entry fields (type **sec_acl_entry_t**). The default cell identifies the authentication authority for simple ACL entries (foreign entries identify their own foreign cells). The **sec_acl_manager_type** identifies the manager to interpret this ACL.

> The **sec_acl_t** type is a structure containing the following fields:

> **default_realm**
>> A structure of type **sec_acl_id_t**, this identifies the UUID and (optionally) the name of the default cell.

> **sec_acl_manager_type**
>> Contains the UUID of the ACL manager type.

num_entries An unsigned 32-bit integer containing the number of ACL entries in this ACL.

sec_acl_entries

An array containing **num_entries** pointers to different ACL entries, each of type **sec_acl_entry_t**.

sec_acl_p_t This data type, simply a pointer to a **sec_acl_t**, is for use with the **sec_acl_list_t** data type.

sec_acl_list_t This data type is a structure containing an unsigned 32-bit integer **num_acls** that describes the number of ACLs indicated by its companion array of pointers, **sec_acls**, of type **sec_acl_p_t**.

sec_acl_entry_t

The **sec_acl_entry_t** type is a structure made up of the following components:

perms A set of flags of type **sec_acl_permset_t** that describe the permissions granted for the principals identified by this ACL entry. Note that if a principal matches more than one ACL entry, the effective permissions will be the most restrictive combination of all the entries.

entry_info A structure containing two members:

entry_type A flag of type **sec_acl_entry_type_t**, indicating the type of ACL entry.

tagged_union

A tagged union whose contents depend on the type of the entry.

The types of entries indicated by **entry_type** can be the following:

sec_acl_e_type_user_obj

The entry contains permissions for the implied user object. This type is described in the POSIX 1003.6 standard.

sec_acl_e_type_group_obj

The entry contains permissions for the implied group object. This type is described in the POSIX 1003.6 standard.

sec_acl_e_type_other_obj
> The entry contains permissions for principals not otherwise named through user or group entries. This type is described in the POSIX 1003.6 standard.

sec_acl_e_type_user
> The entry contains a key that identifies a user. This type is described in the POSIX 1003.6 standard.

sec_acl_e_type_group
> The entry contains a key that identifies a group. This type is described in the POSIX 1003.6 standard.

sec_acl_e_type_mask_obj
> The entry contains the maximum permissions for all entries other than **mask_obj**, **unauthenticated**, **user_obj**, **other_obj**.

sec_acl_e_type_foreign_user
> The entry contains a key that identifies a user and the foreign realm.

sec_acl_e_type_foreign_group
> The entry contains a key that identifies a group and the foreign realm.

sec_acl_e_type_foreign_other
> The entry contains a key that identifies a foreign realm. Any user that can authenticate to the foreign realm will be allowed access.

sec_acl_e_type_any_other
> The entry contains permissions to be applied to any accessor who can authenticate to any realm, but is not identified in any other entry (except **sec_acl_e_type_unauthenticated**).

sec_acl_e_type_unauthenticated
> The entry contains permissions to be applied when the accessor does not pass authentication procedures. A privilege attribute certificate will indicate that the caller's identity is not authenticated. The identity is used to match against the standard entries, but the access rights are masked by this mask. If this mask does not exist in an ACL, the ACL is assumed to grant no access and all unauthenticated access attempts will be denied.

Great care should be exercised when allowing unauthenticated access to an object. Almost by definition, unauthenticated access is very easy to spoof. The presence of this mask on an ACL essentially means that anyone can get at least as much access as allowed by the mask.

sec_acl_e_type_extended

The entry contains additional pickled data. This kind of entry cannot be interpreted, but can be used by an out-of-date client when copying an ACL from one manager to another (assuming that the two managers each understand the data).

The contents of the tagged union depend on the entry type.

For the following entry types, the union contains a UUID and an optional print string (called **entry_info.tagged_union.id** with type **sec_id_t**) for an identified local principal, or for an identified foreign realm.

- **sec_acl_e_type_user**

- **sec_acl_e_type_group**

- **sec_acl_type_foreign_other**

For the following entry types, the union contains two UUIDs and optional print strings (called **entry_info.tagged_union.foreign_id** with type **sec_id_foreign_t**) for an identified foreign principal and its realm.

- **sec_acl_e_type_foreign_user**

- **sec_acl_e_type_foreign_group**

For an extended entry (**sec_acl_e_type_extended**), the union contains **entry_info.tagged_union.extended_info**, a pointer to an information block of type **sec_acl_extend_info_t**.

sec_acl_permset_t

A 32-bit set of permission flags. The flags currently represent the conventional file system permissions (read, write, execute) and the extended DFS permissions (owner, insert, delete).

The unused flags represent permissions that can only be interpreted by the manager for the object. For example, **sec_acl_perm_-unused_00000080** may mean to one ACL manager that withdrawals are allowed, and to another ACL manager that rebooting is allowed.

The following constants are defined for use with the **sec_acl_permset_t** data type:

sec_acl_perm_read
> The ACL allows read access to the protected object.

sec_acl_perm_write
> The ACL allows write access to the protected object.

sec_acl_perm_execute
> The ACL allows execute access to the protected object.

sec_acl_perm_control
> The ACL allows the ACL itself to be modified.

sec_acl_perm_insert
> The ACL allows insert access to the protected object.

sec_acl_perm_delete
> The ACL allows delete access to the protected object.

sec_acl_perm_test
> The ACL allows access to the protected object only to the extent of being able to test for existence.

The bits from 0x00000080 to 0x80000000 are not used by the conventional ACL permission set. Constants of the form **sec_acl_perm_unused_00000080** have been defined so application programs can easily use these bits for extended ACLs.

sec_acl_extend_info_t
> This is an extended information block, provided for future extensibility. Primarily, this allows an out-of-date client to read an ACL from a newer manager and apply it to another (up-to-date) manager. The data cannot be interpreted by the out-of-date client without access to the appropriate pickling routines (that presumably are unavailable to such a client).

In general, ACL managers should not accept ACLs that contain entries the manager does not understand. The manager clearly cannot perform the security service requested by an uninterpretable entry, and it is considered a security breach to lead a client to believe that the manager is performing a particular class of service if the manager cannot do so.

The data structure is made up of the following components:

extension_type
> The UUID of the extension type.

format_label The format of the label, in **ndr_format_t** form.

num_bytes An unsigned 32-bit integer indicating the number of bytes containing the pickled data.

pickled_data The byte array containing the pickled data.

sec_acl_type_t
> The **sec_acl_type_t** type differentiates among the various types of ACLs an object can possess. Most file system objects will only have one ACL controlling the access to that object, but objects that control the creation of other objects (sometimes referred to as *containers*) may have more. For example, a directory can have three different ACLs: the directory ACL, controlling access to the directory; the initial object (or default object) ACL, which serves as a mask when creating new objects in the directory; and the initial directory (or default directory) ACL, which serves as a mask when creating new directories (containers).
>
> The **sec_acl_type_t** is an enumerated set containing one of the following values:

sec_acl_type_object
> The ACL refers to the specified object.

sec_acl_type_default_object
> The ACL is to be used when creating objects in the container.

sec_acl_type_default_container
> The ACL is to be used when creating nested containers.

The following values are defined but not currently used. They are available for application programs that may create an application-specific ACL definition.

- **sec_acl_type_unspecified_3**

- **sec_acl_type_unspecified_4**

- **sec_acl_type_unspecified_5**

- **sec_acl_type_unspecified_6**

- **sec_acl_type_unspecified_7**

sec_acl_printstring_t

A **sec_acl_printstring_t** structure contains a printable representation for a permission in a **sec_acl_permset_t** permission set. This allows a generic ACL editing tool to be used for application-specific ACLs. The tool need not know the printable representation for each permission bit in a given permission set. The **sec_acl_get_printstring( )** function will query an ACL manager for the print strings of the permissions it supports. The structure consists of three components:

printstring   A character string of maximum length **sec_acl_printstring_len** describing the printable representation of a specified permission.

helpstring   A character string of maximum length **sec_acl_printstring_help_len** containing some text that may be used to describe the specified permission.

permissions   A **sec_acl_permset_t** permission set describing the permissions that will be represented with the specified print string.

sec_acl_component_name_t

This type is a pointer to a character string, to be used to specify the entity a given ACL is protecting.

Constants   The following constants are used in **sec_acl_** calls:

sec_acl_default_handle

The value of an unbound ACL manager handle.

sec_rgy_acct_key_t
> The following 32-bit integer constants are used with the **sec_rgy_acct_key_t** data type:
>
> **sec_rgy_acct_key_none**
>> Invalid key.
>
> **sec_rgy_acct_key_person**
>> The person name alone is enough.
>
> **sec_rgy_acct_key_group**
>> The person and group names are both necessary for the account abbreviation.
>
> **sec_rgy_acct_key_org**
>> The person, group, and organization names are all necessary.
>
> **sec_rgy_acct_key_last**
>> Key values must be less than this constant.

sec_rgy_pname_t_size
> The maximum number of characters in a **sec_rgy_pname_t**.

sec_acl_permset_t
> The following constants are defined for use with the **sec_acl_permset_t** data type:
>
> **sec_acl_perm_read**
>> The ACL allows read access to the protected object.
>
> **sec_acl_perm_write**
>> The ACL allows write access to the protected object.
>
> **sec_acl_perm_execute**
>> The ACL allows execute access to the protected object.
>
> **sec_acl_perm_owner**
>> The ACL allows owner-level access to the protected object.
>
> **sec_acl_perm_insert**
>> The ACL allows insert access to the protected object.
>
> **sec_acl_perm_delete**
>> The ACL allows delete access to the protected object.

sec_acl_perm_test
The ACL allows access to the protected object only to the extent of being able to test for existence.

sec_acl_perm_unused_00000080 -
sec_acl_perm_unused_0x80000000
The bits from 0x00000080 to 0x80000000 are not used by the conventional ACL permission set. Constants have been defined so application programs can easily use these bits for extended ACLs.

sec_acl_printstring_len
The maximum length of the printable representation of an ACL permission. (See **sec_acl_printstring_t**.)

sec_acl_printstring_help_len
The maximum length of a help message to be associated with a supported ACL permission. (See **sec_acl_printstring_t**.)

Files   **/usr/include/dce/aclbase.idl**
The **idl** file from which **aclbase.h** was derived.

KEY MANAGEMENT API DATA TYPES

Notes   Key management operations that take a keydata argument expect a pointer to a **sec_passwd_rec_t** structure, and those that take a keytype argument (**void ***) expect a pointer to a **sec_passwd_type_t**. Key management operations that yield a keydata argument as output set the pointer to an array of **sec_passwd_rec_t**. (The array is terminated by an element with a key type of **sec_passwd_none**.)

Operations that take a keydata argument expect a pointer to a **sec_passwd_rec_t** structure. Operations that yield a keydata argument as output set the pointer to an array of **sec_passwd_rec_t**. (The array is terminated by an element with key type **sec_passwd_none**.) Operations that take a keytype argument (**void ***) expect a pointer to a **sec_passwd_type_t**.

Synopsis   **#include <dce/keymgmt.h>**

Data Types

sec_passwd_type_t

An enumerated set describing the currently supported key types. The possible values are as follows:

sec_passwd_none

Indicates no key types are supported.

sec_passwd_plain

Indicates that the key is a printable string of data.

sec_passwd_des

Indicates that the key is DES encrypted data.

sec_passwd_rec_t

A structure containing either a plaintext password or a preencrypted buffer of password data. The **sec_passwd_rec_t** structure consists of three components:

version_number

The version number of the password.

pepper

A character string combined with the password before an encryption key is derived from the password.

key

A structure consists of the following components:

key_type

The key type can be the following:

sec_passwd_plain

Indicates that a printable string of data is stored in **plain**.

sec_passwd_des

Indicates that an array of data is stored in **des_key.**

tagged_union
A structure specifying the password. The value of the structure depends on **key_type**. If **key_type** is **sec_- passwd_plain**, structure contains **plain**, a character string. If **key_type** is **sec_passwd_des**, the structure contains **des_key**, a DES key of type **sec_passwd_des_key_t**.

sec_passwd_version_t
An unsigned 32-bit integer that defines the password version number. You can supply a version number or a 0 for no version number. If you supply the constant **sec_passwd_c_version_none**, the security service supplies a system-generated version number.

sec_key_mgmt_authn_service
A 32-bit unsigned integer whose purpose is to indicate the authentication service in use, since a server may have different keys for different levels of security. The possible values of this data type and their meanings are as follows:

rpc_c_authn_none
No authentication.

rpc_c_authn_dce_private
DCE private key authentication (an implementation of the Kerberos system).

rpc_c_authn_dce_public
DCE public key authentication (reserved for future use).

Constants   There are no constants specially defined for use with the key management API.

Files   **/usr/include/dce/keymgmt.idl**
The **idl** file from which **keymgmt.h** was derived.

ID MAPPING API DATA TYPES

Synopsis   #include <dce/secidmap.h>

Data Types

No special data types are defined for the ID mapping API.

Constants   No special constants are defined for the ID mapping API.

Files   **/usr/include/dce/secidmap.idl**
The **idl** file from which **secidmap.h** was derived.

PASSWORD MANAGEMENT API DATA TYPES

Synopsis   #include <dce/sec_pwd_mgmt.h>

Data Types

The following data types are used in **sec_pwd_mgmt_** calls:

sec_passwd_mgmt_handle_t
A pointer to an opaque handle consisting of password management information about a principal. It is returned by **sec_pwd_mgmt_-setup( )**

Constants   There are no constants specially defined for use with the password management API.

Files   **/usr/include/dce/sec_pwd_mgmt.idl**
The **idl** file from which **sec_pwd_mgmt.h** was derived.

audit_intro

Purpose   Introduction to the DCE audit API runtime

Description

This introduction gives general information about the DCE audit application programming interface (API) and an overview of the following parts of the DCE audit API runtime:

- Runtime services

- Environment variables

- Data types and structures

- Permissions required

Runtime Services

The following is an alphabetical list of the audit API routines. With each routine name is its description. The types of application program that will most likely call the routine are enclosed in parentheses.

dce_aud_close( )

Closes an audit trail (client/server applications, audit trail analysis and examination tools).

dce_aud_commit( )

Performs the audit action(s) (client/server applications).

dce_aud_discard( )

Discards an audit record which releases the memory (client/server applications, audit trail analysis and examination tools).

dce_aud_free_ev_info( )

Frees the memory allocated for an event information structure returned from calling the **dce_aud_get_ev_info( )** function (audit trail analysis and examination tools).

dce_aud_free_header( )

Frees the memory allocated to a designated audit record header structure (audit trail analysis and examination tools).

dce_aud_get_ev_info( )

Gets the event-specific information of a specified audit record (audit trail analysis and examination tools).

dce_aud_get_header( )
> Gets the header of a specified audit record (audit trail analysis and examination tools).

dce_aud_length( )
> Gets the length of a specified audit record (client/server applications, audit trail analysis and examination tools).

dce_aud_next( )
> Reads the next audit record from a specified audit trail into a buffer (audit trail analysis and examination tools).

dce_aud_open( )
> Opens a specified audit trail for read or write (client/server applications, audit trail analysis and examination tools).

dce_aud_print( )
> Formats an audit record into a human-readable form (audit trail analysis and examination tools).

dce_aud_put_ev_info( )
> Adds event-specific information to a specified audit record buffer (client/server applications).

dce_aud_set_trail_size_limit( )
> Sets a limit to the audit trail size (client/server applications).

dce_aud_start( )
> Determines whether a specified event should be audited given the client's binding information and the event outcome. If the event should be audited or if it is not yet known whether the event should be audited because the event outcome is still unknown, memory for the audit record descriptor is allocated and the address of this memory is returned to the caller (client/server applications).

dce_aud_start_with_name( )
> Determines whether a specified event should be audited given the client/server name and the event outcome. If the event should be audited or if it is not yet known whether the event should be audited because the event outcome is still unknown, memory for the audit record descriptor is allocated and the address of this memory is returned to the caller (client/server applications).

dce_aud_start_with_pac( )
> Determines whether a specified event should be audited given the client's privilege attribute certificate (PAC) and the event outcome. If the event should be audited or if it is not yet known whether the event should be audited because the event outcome is still unknown, memory for the audit record descriptor is allocated and the address of this memory is returned to the caller (client/server applications).

dce_aud_start_with_server_binding( )
> Determines whether a specified event should be audited given the server's binding information and the event outcome. If the event should be audited or if it is not yet known whether the event should be audited because the event outcome is still unknown, memory for the audit record descriptor is allocated and the address of this memory is returned to the caller (client/server applications).

dce_aud_start_with_uuid( )
> Determines whether a specified event should be audited given the client/server UUID and the event outcome. If the event must be audited, or if the outcome of the event is not yet known, the memory for the audit record descriptor is allocated and the address of this structure is returned to the caller (client/server applications).

Audit Data Types

The following subsections list the data types and structures used by applications to perform auditing and to analyze audit trails.

Event-Specific Information
> The audit APIs allow applications to include event-specific information in audit records. Event-specific information must be represented as information items using the following data type.

> **typedef struct {**
>   **unsigned16 format;**
>   **union {**
>   **idl_small_int small_int;**
>   **idl_short_int short_int;**
>   **idl_long_int long_int;**
>   **idl_hyper_int hyper_int;**
>   **idl_usmall_int usmall_int;**
>   **idl_ushort_int ushort_int;**
>   **idl_ulong_int ulong_int;**
>   **idl_uhyper_int uhyper_int;**
>   **idl_short_float short_float;**
>   **idl_long_float long_float;**

```
        idl_boolean boolean;
        uuid_t uuid;
        utc_t utc;
        sec_acl_t * acl;
        idl_byte * byte_string;
        idl_char * char_string;
      } data;
  } dce_aud_ev_info_t;
```

The **format** field of the above data structure defines formatting
information that is used to determine the type of the data referenced
by the **data** field. The following table shows possible values of the
format field, their corresponding data types, and their sizes.

Event Data Format Specifiers—intro(3sec)		
Specifier	**Data Type**	**Size**
aud_c_evt_info_small_int	**idl_small_int**	1 byte
aud_c_evt_info_short_int	**idl_short_int**	2 bytes
aud_c_evt_info_long_int	**idl_long_int**	4 bytes
aud_c_evt_info_hyper_int	**idl_hyper_int**	8 bytes
aud_c_evt_info_usmall_int	**idl_usmall_int**	1 bytes
aud_c_evt_info_ushort_int	**idl_ushort_int**	2 bytes
aud_c_evt_info_ulong_int	**idl_ulong_int**	4 bytes
aud_c_evt_info_uhyper_int	**idl_uhyper_int**	8 bytes
aud_c_evt_info_short_float	**idl_short_float**	4 bytes
aud_c_evt_info_long_float	**idl_long_float**	8 bytes
aud_c_evt_info_boolean	**idl_boolean**	1 byte
aud_c_evt_info_uuid	**uuid_t**	16 bytes
aud_c_evt_info_utc	**utc_t**	16 bytes
aud_c_evt_info_acl	**sec_acl_t ***	variable size
aud_c_evt_info_byte_string	**idl_byte ***	variable size
aud_c_evt_info_char_string	**idl_char ***	variable size

Byte strings and character strings are terminated with a 0 (zero)
byte. New data types can be added to this list if they are used
frequently. Servers could use the pickling service of the IDL
compiler to encode complex data types into byte strings that are to
be included in an audit record.

Audit Record Header Data Structure

The following data structure is used to store header information
obtained from an audit record. This structure is normally only used
by audit trail analysis and examination tools. That is, it is hidden
from client/server applications.

```
typedef struct {
      unsigned32              format;
      uuid_t                  server;
      unsigned32              event;
      unsigned16              outcome;
      unsigned16              authz_st;
      uuid_t                  client;
      uuid_t                  cell;
      unsigned16              num_groups;
      utc_t                   time;
      char                    *addr;
      uuid_t                  *groups;
} dce_aud_hdr_t;
```

format   Contains the version number of the tail format of the event used for the event-specific information. With this format version number, the audit analysis tools can accommodate changes in the formats of the event-specific information. For example, the event-specific information of an event may initially be defined to be a 32-bit integer, and later changed to a character string. Format version 0 (zero) is assigned to the initial format for each event.

server   Contains the UUID of the server that generates the audit record.

event   Contains the event number.

outcome   Indicates whether the event failed or succeeded. If the event failed, the reason for the failure is given.

authz_st   Indicates how the client is authorized: by a name or by a DCE privilege attribute certificate (PAC).

client   Contains the UUID of the client.

cell   Contains the UUID of the client's cell.

num_groups   Contains the number of local group privileges the client used for access.

groups   Contains the UUIDs of the local group privileges that
               are used by the client for the access. By default, the
               group information is not be included in the header
               (num_groups is set to 0 in this case), to minimize the
               size of the audit records. If the group information is
               deemed as important, it can be included.

               Information about foreign groups (global groups that
               do not belong to the same cell where the client is
               registered) is not included in this version of audit
               header but may be included in later versions when
               global groups are supported.

time   Contains a timestamp of **utc_t** type that records the
               time when the server committed the audit record (that
               is, after providing the event information through
               audit API function calls). Recording this time, rather
               than recording the time when the audit record is
               appended to an audit trail, will better maintain the
               sequence of events. The implementation of the audit
               subsystem may involve communication between the
               server and a remote audit daemon, incurring
               indefinite delays by network problems or intruders.
               The inaccuracy in the **utc_t** timestamp may be useful
               for correlating events. When searching for events in
               an audit trail that occur within a time interval, if the
               results of the comparisons between the time of an
               event and the interval's starting and ending times is
               maybe (because of inaccuracies), then the event
               should be returned.

addr   Records the client's address (port address of the
               caller). Port addresses are not authenticated. A
               caller can provide a fraudulent port address to a DCE
               server. However, if this unauthenticated port address
               is deemed to be useful information, a DCE server can
               record this information using this field.

The identity of the server cell is not recorded in the header, because
of the assumption that all audit records in an audit trail are for
servers within a single cell, and implicitly, the server cell is the local
cell.

Audit Record Descriptor

An opaque data type, **dce_aud_rec_t**, is used to represent an audit record descriptor. An audit record descriptor may be created, manipulated, or disposed of by the following functions: The functions **dce_aud_start( )**, **dce_aud_start_with_pac( )**, **dce_-aud_start_with_name( )**, **dce_aud_start_with_server_binding( )**, and **dce_aud_next( )** return a record descriptor. The function **dce_aud_put_ev_info( )** adds event information to an audit record through a record descriptor. The functions **dce_aud_get_header( )**, **dce_aud_get_ev_info( )**, and **dce_aud_length( )** get the event and record information through a record descriptor. The function **dce_aud_commit( )** commits an audit record through its descriptor. The function **dce_aud_discard( )** disposes of a record descriptor. The function **dce_aud_discard( )** is necessary only after reading the record (that is, after invoking **dce_aud_next( )**.

Audit Trail Descriptor

An opaque data type, **dce_aud_trail_t**, is used to represent an audit trail descriptor. The **dce_aud_open( )** function opens an audit trail and returns a trail descriptor; **dce_aud_next( )** obtains an audit record from this descriptor; and **dce_aud_commit( )** commits an audit record from and to an opened audit trail through this descriptor. The **dce_aud_close( )** function disposes of this descriptor.

Environment Variables

The audit API routines use the following environment variables:

DCEAUDITOFF

If this environment variable is defined at the time the application is started, auditing is turned off.

DCEAUDITFILTERON

If this environment variable is defined, filtering is enabled.

DCEAUDITTRAILSIZE

Sets the limit of the audit trail size. This variable overrides the limit set by the **dce_aud_set_trail_size_limit( )** function.

Permissions Required

To use an audit daemon's audit record logging service, you need the log (**l**) permission to the audit daemon.

Related Information

Books: *OSF DCE Command Reference*, *OSF DCE Application Development Guide*.

gssapi_intro

Purpose   Generic security service application programming interface

Description

This introduction includes general information about the generic security service application programming interface (GSSAPI) defined in Internet RFC 1508, *Generic Security Service Application Programming Interface*, and RFC 1509, *Generic Security Service API : C-bindings*. It also includes an overview of error handling, data types, and calling conventions, including the following:

- Integer types

- String and similar data

- Object identifiers (OIDs)

- Object identifier sets (OID sets)

- Credentials

- Contexts

- Authentication tokens

- Major status values

- Minor status values

- Names

- Channel bindings

- Optional parameters

General Information

GSSAPI provides security services to applications using peer-to-peer communications (instead of DCE secure RPC). Using OSF DCE GSSAPI routines, applications can perform the following operations:

- Enable an application to determine another application's user

- Enable an application to delegate access rights to another application

- Apply security services, such as confidentiality and integrity, on a per-message basis

GSSAPI represents a secure connection between two communicating applications with a data structure called a *security context*. The application that establishes the secure connection is called the *context indicator* or simply *indicator*. The context initiator is like a DCE RPC client. The application that accepts the secure connection is the *context acceptor* or simply *acceptor*. The context acceptor is like a DCE RPC server.

There are four stages involved in using the GSSAPI:

1. The context initiator acquires a credential with which it can prove its identity to other processes. Similarly, the context acceptor cquires a credential to enable it to accept a security context. Either application may omit this credential acquistion and use their default credentials in subsequent stages. See the section on credentials for more information.

    The applications use credentials to establish their global identity. The global identity can be, but is not necessarily, related to the local user name under which the application is running. Credentials can contain either of the following:

    - Login context

      The login context includes a principal's network credentials, as well as other account information.

    - Principal name and a key

      The key corresponding to the principal name must be registered with the DCE security registration in a key table. A set of DCE GSSAPI routines enables applications to register and use principal names.

2. The communicating applications establish a joint security context by exchanging authentication tokens.

    The *security context* is a pair of GSSAPI data structures that contain information that is shared between the communicating applications. The information describes the state of each application. This security context is required for per-message security services.

    To establish a security context, the context initiator calls the **gss_init_sec_-context()** routine to get a *token*. The token is cryptographically protected, opaque data. The context initiator transfers the token to the context acceptor, which in turn passes the token to the **gss_accept_sec_context()** routine to decode and extract the shared information.

As part of the establishing the the security context, the context initiator is authenticated to the context acceptor. The context initiator can require the context acceptor to authenticate itself in return.

The context initiator can delegate rights to allow the context acceptor to act as its agent. Delegation means the context initiator gives the context acceptor the ability to initiate additional security contexts as an agent of the context initiator. To delegate, the context initiator sets a flag on the **gss_init_sec_context( )** routine indicating that it wants to delegate and sends the returned token in the normal way to the context acceptor. The acceptor passes this token to the **gss_accept_sec_context( )** routine, which generates a delegated credential. The context acceptor can use the credential to initiate additional security contexts.

3. The applications exchange protected messages and data.

The applications can call GSSAPI routines to protect data exchanged in messages. The application sends a protected message by calling the appropriate GSSAPI routine to do the following:

- Apply protection

- Bind the message to the appropriate security context

The application can then send the resulting information to the peer application.

The application that receives the message passes the received data to a GSSAPI routine, which removes the protection and validates the data.

GSSAPI treats application data as arbitrary octet strings. The GSSAPI per-message security services can provide either of the following:

- Integrity and authentication of data origin

- Confidentiality, integrity, and authentication of data origin

4. When the applications have finished communicating, either one may instruct GSSAPI to delete the security context.

There are two sets of GSSAPI routines:

- Standard GSSAPI routines, which are defined in the Internet RFC 1508, *Generic Security Service Application Programming Interface*, and RFC 1509, *Generic Security Service API : C-bindings*. These routines have the prefix **gss_**.

- OSF DCE extensions to the GSSAPI routines. These are additional routines that enable an application to use DCE security services. These routines have the prefix **gssdce_**.

The following sections provide an overview of the GSSAPI error handling and data types.

Error Handling

Each GSSAPI routine returns two status values:

- Major status values

  Major status values are generic API routine errors or calling errors defined in RFC 1509.

- Minor status values

  Minor status values indicate DCE-specific errors.

If a routine has output parameters that contain pointers for storage allocated by the routine, the output parameters will always contain a valid pointer even if the routine returns an error. If no storage was allocated, the routine sets the pointer to NULL and sets any length fields associated with the pointers (such as in the **gss_buffer_desc** structure) to 0 (zero).

Minor status values usually contain more detailed information about the error. They are not, however, portable between GSSAPI implementations. When designing portable applications, use major status values for handling errors. Use minor status values to debug applications and to display error and error-recovery information to users.

GSSAPI Data Types

This section provides an overview of the GSSAPI data types and their definitions.

The GSSAPI defines the following integer data type:

```
OM_uint32     32-bit unsigned integer
```

This integer data type is a portable data type that the GSSAPI routine definitions use for guaranteed minimum bit-counts.

Many of the GSSAPI routines take arguments and return values that describe contiguous multiple-byte data, such as opaque data and character strings. Use the **gss_buffer_t** data type, which is a pointer to the buffer descriptor **gss_buffer_desc**, to pass the data between the GSSAPI routines and applications.

The **gss_buffer_t** data type has the following structure:

```
typedef struct gss_buffer_desc_struct {
        size_t  length;
        void    *value;
} gss_buffer_desc, *gss_buffer_t;
```

The length field contains the total number of bytes in the data and the value field contains a pointer to the actual data.

When using the **gss_buffer_t** data type, the GSSAPI routine allocates storage for any data it passes to the application. The calling application must allocate the **gss_buffer_desc** object. It can initialize unused **gss_buffer_desc** objects with the value **GSS_C_EMPTY_BUFFER**. To free the storage, the application calls the **gss_release_buffer( )** routine.

Applications use the **gss_OID** data type to choose a security mechanism, either DCE security or Kerberos, and to specify name types. Select a security mechanism by using the following two OIDs:

- For DCE security, specify either **GSSDCE_C_OID_DCE_KRBV5_DES** or **GSS_C_NULL_OID**.

- For Kerberos Version 5, specify **GSSDCE_C_OID_KRBV5_DES**.

Use of the default security mechanisms, specified by the constant **GSS_C_NULL_OID**, helps to ensure the portability of the application.

The **gss_OID** data type contains tree-structured values defined by ISO and has the following structure:

```
typedef struct gss_OID_desc_struct {
        OM_uint32 length;
        void    * elements;
}  gss_OID_desc, *gss_OID;
```

The elements field of the structure points to the first byte of an octet string containing the ASN.1 BER encoding of the value of the **gss_OID** data type. The length field contains the number of bytes in the value.

The **gss_OID_desc** values returned from the GSSAPI are read-only values. The application should not try to deallocate them.

The **gss_OID_set** data type represents one or more object identifiers. The values of the **gss_OID_set** data type are used to

- Report the available mechanisms supported by GSSAPI

- Request specific mechanisms

- Indicate which mechanisms a credential supports

The **gss_OID_set** data type has the following structure:

```
typedef struct gss_OID_set_desc_struct {
        int     count
        gss_OID elements
} gss_OID_set_desc, *gss_OID_set;
```

The count field contains the number of OIDs in the set. The elements field is a pointer to an array of **gss_oid_desc** objects, each describing a single OID. The application calls the **gss_release_oid_set()** routine to deallocate storage associated with the **gss_OID_set** values that the GSSAPI routines return to the application.

Credentials establish, or prove, the identity of an application or other principal.

The **gss_cred_id_t** data type is an atomic data type that identifies a GSSAPI credential data structure.

The *security context* is a pair of GSSAPI data structures that contain information shared between the communicating applications. The information describes the cryptographic state of each application. This security context is required for per-message security services and is created by a successful authentication exchange.

The **gss_ctx_id_t** data type contains an atomic value that identifies one end of a GSSAPI security context. The data type is opaque to the caller.

GSSAPI uses tokens to maintain the synchronization between the applications sharing a security context. The token is a cryptographically protected bit string generated by DCE Security at one end of the GSSAPI security context for use by the peer application at the other end of the security context. The data type is opaque to the caller.

The applications use the **gss_buffer_t** data type as tokens to GSSAPI routines.

GSSAPI routines return GSS status codes as their **OM_uint32** function value. These codes indicate either generic API routine errors or calling errors.

A GSS status code can indicate a single, fatal generic API error from the routine and a single calling error. Additional status information can also be contained in the GSS status code. The errors are encoded into a 32-bit GSS status code, as follows:

```
MSB                                                     LSB
+----------------------------------------------------+
| Calling Error | Routine Error | Supplementary Info|
+----------------------------------------------------+
Bit 31          24 23            16 15                0
```

If a GSSAPI routine returns a GSS status code whose upper 16 bits contain a nonzero value, the call failed. If the calling error field is nonzero, the context initiator's use of the routine was in error. In addition, the routine can indicate additional information by setting bits in the supplementary information field of the status code. The tables that follow describe the routine errors, calling errors, and supplementary information status bits and their meanings.

The following table lists the GSSAPI routine errors and their meanings:

Name	Value	Meaning
GSS_S_BAD_MECH	1	The required mechanism is unsupported.
GSS_S_NAME	2	The name passed is invalid.
GSS_S_NAMETYPE	3	The name passed is unsupported.
GSS_S_BAD_BINDINGS	4	The channel bindings are incorrect.
GSS_S_BAD_STATUS	5	A status value was invalid.
GSS_S_BAD_SIG	6	A token had an invalid signature.
GSS_S_NO_CRED	7	No credentials were supplied.
GSS_S_NO_CONTEXT	8	No context has been established.
GSS_S_DEFECTIVE_TOKEN	9	A token was invalid.
GSS_S_DEFECTIVE_CREDENTIAL	10	A credential was invalid.
GSS_S_CREDENTIALS_EXPIRED	11	The referenced credentials expired.
GSS_S_CONTEXT_EXPIRED	12	The context expired.
GSS_S_FAILURE	13	The routine failed. Check minor status codes.

The following table lists the calling error values and their meanings:

Name	Value	Meaning
GSS_S_CALL_INACCESSIBLE_READ	1	Could not read a required input parameter.
GSS_S_CALL_INACCESSIBLE_WRITE	2	Could not write a required output parameter.
GSS_S_BAD_STRUCTURE	3	A parameter was incorrectly structured.

The following table lists the supplementary bits and their meanings.

Name	Number	Meaning
GSS_S_CONTINUE_NEEDED	0 (LSB)	Call the routine again to complete its function.
GSS_S_DUPLICATE_TOKEN	1	The token was a duplicate of an earlier token.
GSS_S_OLD_TOKEN	2	The token's validity period expired; the routine cannot verify that the token is not a duplicate of an earlier token.
GSS_S_UNSEQ_TOKEN	3	A later token has been processed.

All **GSS_S_** symbols equate to complete **OM_uint32** status codes, rather than to bitfield values. For example, the actual value of **GSS_S_BAD_NAMETYPE** (value 3 in the routine error field) is 3 << 16.

The major status code **GSS_S_FAILURE** indicates that DCE security detected an error for which no major status code is available. Check the minor status code for details about the error. See the section on minor status values for more information.

The GSSAPI provides three macros:

- **GSS_CALLING_ERROR( )**

- **GSS_ROUTINE_ERROR( )**

- **GSS_SUPPLEMENTARY_INFO( )**

Each macro takes a GSS status code and masks all but the relevant field. For example, when you use the **GSS_ROUTINE_ERROR( )** macro on a status code, it returns a value. The value of the macro is arrived at by using only the routine errors field and zeroing the values of the calling error and the supplementary information fields.

An additional macro, **GSS_ERROR( )**, lets you determine whether the status code indicated a calling or routine error. If the status code indicated a calling or routine error, the macro returns a nonzero value. If no calling or routine error is indicated, the routine returns a 0 (zero).

Note: At times, a GSSAPI routine that is unable to access data can generate a platform-specific signal, instead of returning a **GSS_S_CALL_-INACCESSIBLE_READ** or **GSS_S_CALL_INACCESSIBLE_-WRITE** status value.

The GSSAPI routines return a *minor_status* parameter to indicate errors from either DCE Security or Kerberos. The parameter can contain a single error, indicated by an **OM_uint32** value. The **OM_uint32** data type is equivalent to the DCE data type **error_status_t** and can contain any DCE-defined error.

Names identify principals. The GSSAPI authenticates the relationship between a name and the principal claiming the name.

Names are represented in two forms:

- A printable form, for presentation to an application

- An internal, canonical form that is used by the API and is opaque to applications

The **gss_import_name( )** and **gss_display_name( )** routines convert names between their printable form and their **gss_name_t** data type. DCE GSSAPI supports only DCE principal names, which are identified by the constant OID, **GSSCDE_C_OID_DCENAME**.

The **gss_compare_names( )** routine compares internal form names.

You can define and use channel bindings to associate the security context with the communications channel that carries the context. Channel bindings are communicated to the GSSAPI by using the following structure:

```
typedef struct gss_channel_binding_struct {
        OM_uint32        initiator_addrtype;
        gss_buffer_desc initiator_address;
        OM_uint32        acceptor_addrtype;
        gss_buffer_desc aceptor_address;
        gss_buffer_desc application_data;
} *gss_channel_bindings_t;
```

Use the **initiator_addrtype** and **acceptor_addrtype** fields to initiate the type of
addresses contained in the **initiator_address** and **acceptor_address** buffers. The
following table lists the address types and their **addrtype** values:

Address Type	addrtype Value
Unspecified	**GSS_C_AF_UNSPEC**
Host-local	**GSS_C_AF_LOCAL**
DARPA Internet	**GSS_C_AF_INET**
ARPAnet IMP	**GSS_C_AF_IMPLINK**
pup protocols (for example, BSP)	**GSS_C_AF_PUP**
MIT CHAOS protocol	**GSS_C_AF_CHAOS**
XEROX NS	**GSS_C_AF_NS**
nbs	**GSS_C_AF_NBS**
ECMA	**GSS_C_AF_ECMA**
datakit protocols	**GSS_C_AF_DATAKIT**
CCITT protocols (for example, X.25)	**GSS_C_AF_CCITT**
IBM SNA	**GSS_C_AF_SNA**
Digital DECnet	**GSS_C_AF_DECnet**
Direct data link interface	**GSS_C_AF_DLI**
LAT	**GSS_C_AF_LAT**
NSC Hyperchannel	**GSS_C_AF_HYLINK**
AppleTalk	**GSS_C_AF_APPLETALK**
BISYNC 2780/3780	**GSS_C_AF_BSC**
Distributed system services	**GSS_C_AF_DSS**
OSI TP4	**GSS_C_AF_OSI**
X25	**GSS_C_AF_X25**
No address specified	**GSS_C_AF_NULLADDR**

The tags specify address families rather than addressing formats. For address families that contain several alternative address forms, the **initiator_address** and the **acceptor_address** fields should contain sufficient information to determine which address form is used. Format the bytes that contain the addresses in the order in which the bytes are transmitted across the network.

The GSSAPI creates an octet string by concatenating all the fields (**initiator_addrtype**, **initiator_address**, **acceptor_addrtype**, **acceptor_address**, and **application_data**). The security mechanism signs the octet string and binds the signature to the token generated by the **gss_init_sec_context( )** routine. The context acceptor presents the same bindings to the **gss_accept_sec_context( )** routine, which evaluates the signature and compares it to the signature in the token. If the signatures differ, the **gss_accept_sec_context( )** routine returns a **GSS_S_BAD_BINDINGS** error, and the context is not established.

Some security mechanisms check that the **initiator_address** field of the channel bindings presented to the **gss_init_sec_context( )** routine contains the correct network address of the host system. Therefore portable applications should use either the correct address type and value or the **GSS_C_AF_NULLADDR** for the **initiator_addrtype** address field. Some security mechanisms include the channel binding data in the token instead of a signature, so portable applications should not use confidential data as channel-binding components. The DCE GSSAPI does not verify the address or include the plain text bindings information in the token.

In routine descriptions, *optional parameters* allow the application to request default behaviors by passing a default value for the parameter. The following conventions are used for optional parameters:

Convention	Value Default	Explanation
gss_buffer_t types	**GSS_C_NO_BUFFER**	For an input parameter, indicates no data is supplied. For an output parameter, indicates that the information returned is not required by the application.
Integer types (input)		Refer to the reference pages for default values.
Integer types (output)	NULL	Indicates that the application does not require the information.
Pointer types (output)	NULL	Indicates that the application does not require the information.
OIDs	**GSS_C_NULL_OID**	Indicates the default choice for name type or security mechanism.
OID sets	**GSS_C_NULL_OID_SET**	Indicates the default set of security mechanisms, DCE security and Kerberos.
Credentials	**GSS_C_NO_CREDENTIAL**	Indicates that the application should use the default credential handle.
Channel bindings	**GSS_C_NO_CHANNEL_BINDINGS**	Indicates that no channel bindings are used.

Related Information

Books: *OSF DCE Application Development Guide—Core Components.*

dce_acl_copy_acl

Purpose   Copies an ACL

Synopsis   #include <dce/dce.h>
#include <dce/aclif.h>

void dce_acl_copy_acl(
    sec_acl_t *source,
    sec_acl_t *target,
    error_status_t *status);

Parameters

Input

source   A pointer to the ACL to be copied.

target   A pointer to the new ACL that is to receive the copy.

Output

status   A pointer to the completion status. On successful completion, the
routine returns **error_status_ok**. Otherwise, it returns an error.

Description

The **dce_acl_copy_acl( )** routine makes a copy of a specified ACL. The caller
passes the space for the target ACL, but the space for the **sec_acl_entries** array is
allocated. To free the allocated space, call **dce_acl_obj_free_entries( )**, which
frees the entries, but not the ACL itself.

Errors   **rpc_s_no_memory**
The **rpc_sm_allocate( )** routine could not obtain memory.

error_status_ok
The call was successful.

Related Information

Functions: **dce_acl_obj_free_entries(3sec)**.

dce_acl_inq_acl_from_header

Purpose   Retrieves the UUID of an ACL from an item's header in a backing store

Synopsis   **#include <dce/dce.h>**
#include <dce/aclif.h>

void dce_acl_inq_acl_from_header(
  dce_db_header_t *db_header*,
  sec_acl_type_t *sec_acl_type*,
  uuid_t *acl_uuid,
  error_status_t *status);

Parameters

Input

db_header   The backing store header containing the ACL object.

sec_acl_type   The type of ACL to be identified:

- **sec_acl_type_object**

- **sec_acl_type_default_object**

- **sec_acl_type_default_container**

Output

acl_uuid   A pointer to the UUID of the ACL object.

status   A pointer to the completion status. On successful completion, the routine returns **error_status_ok**. Otherwise, it returns an error.

Description

The **dce_acl_inq_acl_from_header( )** routine gets the UUID for an ACL object of the specified type from the specified backing store header.

Errors   **db_s_key_not_found**
        The specified key was not found in the backing store. (This error is passed through from **dce_db_fetch( )**.)

dce_acl_inq_acl_from_header(3sec)

db_s_bad_index_type
The key's type is wrong, or else the backing store is not by name or by UUID. (This error is passed through from **dce_db_fetch( )**.)

sec_acl_invalid_type
The *sec_acl_type* parameter does not contain a valid type.

error_status_ok
The call was successful.

Related Information

Functions: **dce_acl_resolve_by_name(3sec)**, **dce_acl_resolve_by_uuid(3sec)**.

dce_acl_inq_client_creds

Purpose   Returns the client's credentials

Synopsis   **#include <dce/dce.h>**
#include <dce/aclif.h>

void dce_acl_inq_client_creds(
    handle_t *handle*,
    sec_cred_pa_handle_t **creds*,
    error_status_t **status*);

Parameters

Input

    handle   The remote procedure call binding handle.

Output

    creds   A pointer to the returned credentials, or NULL if unauthorized.

    status   A pointer to the completion status. On successful completion, the routine returns **error_status_ok**. Otherwise, it returns an error.

Description

The **dce_acl_inq_client_creds( )** routine returns the client's security credentials found through the RPC binding handle.

Errors   **error_status_ok**
        The call was successful.

    rpc_s_authn_authz_mismatch
        Either the client, or the server, or both is not using the **rpc_c_authz_dce** authorization service.

    rpc_s_invalid_binding
        Invalid RPC binding handle.

    rpc_s_wrong_kind_of_binding
        Wrong kind of binding for operation.

dce_acl_inq_client_creds(3sec)

rpc_s_binding_has_no_auth
Binding has no authentication information. The client or the server
should have called **rpc_binding_set_auth_info( )**.

Related Information

Functions: **dce_acl_inq_client_permset(3sec)**,
dce_acl_inq_permset_for_creds(3sec), **dce_acl_register_object_type(3sec)**.

dce_acl_inq_client_permset

Purpose   Returns the client's permissions corresponding to an ACL

Synopsis   **#include <dce/dce.h>**
#include <dce/aclif.h>

void dce_acl_inq_client_permset(
   handle_t *handle*,
   uuid_t **mgr_type*,
   uuid_t **acl_uuid*,
   sec_acl_permset_t **permset*,
   error_status_t **status*);

Parameters

Input

handle	The remote procedure call binding handle.
mgr_type	A pointer to the UUID identifying the type of the ACL manager in question. There may be more than one type of ACL manager protecting the object whose ACL is bound to the input handle. Use this parameter to distinguish them.
acl_uuid	A pointer to the UUID of the ACL.

Output

permset	The set of permissions allowed to the client.
status	A pointer to the completion status. On successful completion, the routine returns **error_status_ok**. Otherwise, it returns an error.

dce_acl_inq_client_permset(3sec)

Description

The **dce_acl_inq_client_permset( )** routine returns the client's permissions that correspond to the ACL. It finds the ACL in the database as defined for this ACL manager type with **dce_acl_register_object_type( )**. The client's credentials are determined from the binding handle. The ACL and credentials determine the permission set.

Errors

acl_s_bad_manager_type

The *mgr_type* parameter does not match the manager type in the ACL itself.

error_status_ok

The call was successful.

Related Information

Functions: **dce_acl_inq_client_pac(3sec)**, **dce_acl_inq_permset_for_pac(3sec)**, **dce_acl_register_object_type(3sec)**.

dce_acl_inq_permset_for_creds

Purpose   Determines a principal's complete extent of access to an object

Synopsis   **#include <dce/dce.h>**
                #include <dce/aclif.h>

                void dce_acl_inq_permset_for_creds(
                   sec_cred_pa_handle_t **creds,**
                   sec_acl_t **ap,**
                   uuid_t **owner_id,**
                   uuid_t **group_id,**
                   sec_acl_posix_semantics_t *posix_semantics,*
                   sec_acl_permset_t **perms,**
                   error_status_t **status);**

Parameters

Input

    creds   The security credentials that represent the principal.

    ap   The ACL that represents the object.

    owner_id   Identifies the owner of the object that is protected by the specified ACL. If the **sec_acl_e_type_user_obj** ACLE (ACL entry) exists, then the **owner_id** (**uuid_t** pointer) can not be NULL. If it is, then the error **sec_acl_expected_user_obj** is returned.

    group_id   Identifies the group in which the object that is protected by the specified ACL belongs. If the a **sec_acl_e_type_group_obj** ACLE exists, the **group_id** (**uuid_t** pointer) can not be NULL. If it is, the error **sec_acl_expected_group_obj** is returned.

    posix_semantics
              This parameter is currently unused in OSF's implementation.

Output

    perms   A bit mask containing a 1 bit for each permission granted by the ACL and 0 (zero) bits elsewhere.

    status   A pointer to the completion status. On successful completion, the routine returns **error_status_ok**.

Description

The **dce_acl_inq_permset_for_creds( )** routine returns a principal's complete extent of access to some object. This routine is useful for implementing operations such as the conventional UNIX access function.

The values allowed for the credentials representing the principal include NULL or unauthenticated.

The routine normally returns TRUE, even when the access permissions are determined to be all 0 (zero) bits (**dce_acl_c_no_permissions**). It returns FALSE only on illogical error conditions (such as unsupported ACL entry types), in which case the status output gets the error status code and the *perms* is set to **dce_acl_c_no_permissions**.

The following ACL entry types (of type **sec_acl_entry_type_t**) are supported by this routine. The categories are checked in the order shown.

ACL Entry Type	Meaning
sec_acl_e_type_user sec_acl_e_type_foreign_user	At most, one can match.
sec_acl_e_type_group sec_acl_e_type_foreign_group	The union of all permissions for each matching group.
sec_acl_e_type_other_obj	Matching local realm accesses.
sec_acl_e_type_foreign_other	At most, one can match.
sec_acl_e_type_any_other	Anything not in the other types.
sec_acl_e_type_unauthenticated	The **sec_acl_e_type_unauthenticated** type is a mask that is used for all matches on unauthenticated credentials. It is also intersected with **sec_acl_e_type_any_other** for NULL credentials.

Notes

The meanings of the permission bits have no effect on the action of the **dce_acl_inq_permset_for_creds( )** routine. The interpretation of the bits is left entirely to the application.

Errors

error_status_ok
The call was successful.

Related Information

Functions: **dce_acl_inq_client_creds(3sec)**, **dce_acl_inq_client_permset(3sec)**, **dce_acl_register_object_type(3sec)**.

dce_acl_inq_prin_and_group

Purpose   Inquires the principal and group of an RPC caller

Synopsis   **#include <dce/dce.h>**
                #include <dce/aclif.h>

        void dce_acl_inq_prin_and_group(
          handle_t *handle,*
          uuid_t **principal,*
          uuid_t **group,*
          error_status_t *status);

Parameters

Input

    handle   The remote procedure call binding handle.

Output

    principal   The UUID of the principal of the caller of the RPC.

    group   The UUID of the group of the caller of the RPC.

    status   A pointer to the completion status. On successful completion, the routine returns **error_status_ok**. Otherwise, it returns an error.

Description

The **dce_acl_inq_prin_and_group**( ) routine finds the principal and group of the caller of a remote procedure call. This information is useful for filling in the **owner_id** and **group_id** fields of standard data or object headers. Setting the owner and group make sense only if your ACL manager will handle owners and groups, which you specify with the **dce_acl_c_has_owner** and **dce_acl_c_has_-groups** flags to **dce_acl_register_object_type**( ).

If the caller is unauthenticated, the principal and group are filled with the **NIL** UUID, generated through **uuid_create_nil**( ).

dce_acl_inq_prin_and_group.3sec( )

Examples
```
dce_db_std_header_init(db, &data, ..., &st);
dce_acl_inq_prin_and_group(h, &data.h.owner_id, &data.h.group_id, &st);
```

Errors
The **dce_acl_inq_prin_and_group**( ) routine can return errors from **dce_acl_- inq_client_creds**( ), **sec_cred_get_initiator**( ), and **sec_cred_get_pa_data**( ). It generates no error messages of its own.

Related Information

Functions: **dce_acl_register_object_type(3sec)**.

dce_acl_is_client_authorized

Purpose   Checks whether a client's credentials are authenticated

Synopsis   **#include <dce/dce.h>**
#include <dce/aclif.h>

void dce_acl_is_client_authorized(
    handle_t *handle*,
    uuid_t *mgr_type,
    uuid_t *acl_uuid,
    sec_acl_permset_t *desired_perms*,
    boolean32 *authorized,
    error_status_t *status);

Parameters

Input

    handle   The client's binding handle.

    mgr_type   A pointer to the UUID identifying the type of the ACL manager in
                    question. There may be more than one type of ACL manager
                    protecting the object whose ACL is bound to the input handle. Use
                    this parameter to distinguish them.

    acl_uuid   A pointer to the UUID of the ACL.

    desired_perms
                    A permission set containing the desired privileges. This is a 32-bit
                    set of permission flags. The flags may represent the conventional
                    file system permissions (read, write, and execute), the extended AFS
                    permissions (owner, insert, and delete), or some other permissions
                    supported by the specific application ACL manager. For example, a
                    bit that is unused for file system permissions may mean withdrawals
                    are allowed for a bank ACL manager, while it may mean matrix
                    inversions are allowed for a CPU ACL manager. The *mgr_type*
                    identifies the semantics of the bits.

Output

    authorized   A pointer to the TRUE or FALSE return value of the routine.

dce_acl_is_client_authorized(3sec)

        status   A pointer to the completion status. On successful completion, the routine returns **error_status_ok**. Otherwise, it returns an error.

Description

The **dce_acl_is_client_authorized**( ) routine returns TRUE in the *authorized* parameter if and only if all of the desired permissions (represented as bits in *desired_perms*) are included in the actual permissions corresponding to the *handle*, the *mgr_type*, and the *acl_uuid* UUID. Otherwise, the returned value is FALSE.

Notes   The routine's return value is **void**. The returned **boolean32** value is in the *authorized* parameter.

Errors   **acl_s_bad_manager_type**
            The *mgr_type* does not match the manager type in the ACL itself.

        error_status_ok
            The call was successful.

dce_acl_obj_add_any_other_entry

Purpose   Adds permissions for any_other ACL entry to a given ACL

Synopsis   #include <dce/dce.h>
#include <dce/aclif.h>

void dce_acl_obj_add_any_other_entry(
    sec_acl_t *acl,
    sec_acl_permset_t permset,
    error_status_t *status);

Parameters

Input

acl   A pointer to the ACL that is to be modified.

permset   The permissions to be granted to **sec_acl_e_type_any_other**.

Output

status   A pointer to the completion status. On successful completion, the routine returns **error_status_ok**. Otherwise, it returns an error.

Description

The **dce_acl_obj_add_any_other_entry**() routine adds an ACL entry for **sec_acl_e_type_any_other** access to the specified ACL. It is equivalent to calling the **dce_acl_obj_add_obj_entry**() routine with the **sec_acl_e_type_any_other** entry type, but is more convenient.

Errors

error_status_ok
    The call was successful.

Related Information

Functions: **dce_acl_obj_add_obj_entry(3sec)**.

dce_acl_obj_add_foreign_entry

Purpose   Adds permissions for an ACL entry for a foreign user or group to the given ACL

Synopsis   **#include <dce/dce.h>**
#include <dce/aclif.h>

void dce_acl_obj_add_foreign_entry(
  sec_acl_t **acl,*
  sec_acl_entry_type_t *entry_type,*
  sec_acl_permset_t *permset,*
  uuid_t **realm,*
  uuid_t **id,*
  error_status_t **status*);

Parameters

Input

acl	A pointer to the ACL that is to be modified.
entry_type	Must be one of the following types:

  - **sec_acl_e_type_foreign_user**
  - **sec_acl_e_type_foreign_group**.
  - **sec_acl_e_type_for_user_deleg**
  - **sec_acl_e_type_for_group_deleg**

permset	The permissions to be granted to the foreign group or foreign user.
realm	The UUID of the foreign cell.
id	The UUID identifying the foreign group or foreign user.

Output

status	A pointer to the completion status. On successful completion, the routine returns **error_status_ok**. Otherwise, it returns an error.

Description

The **dce_acl_obj_add_foreign_entry**( ) routine adds an ACL entry for **sec_acl_e_type_foreign_xxx** access to the specified ACL.

Errors

sec_acl_invalid_entry_type

The type specified in *entry_type* is not one of the four specified types.

error_status_ok

The call was successful.

Related Information

Functions: **dce_acl_obj_add_id_entry(3sec)**, **sec_id_parse_name(3sec)**.

dce_acl_obj_add_group_entry

Purpose   Adds permissions for a group ACL entry to the given ACL

Synopsis   **#include <dce/dce.h>**
#include <dce/aclif.h>

void dce_acl_obj_add_group_entry(
  sec_acl_t **acl,*
  sec_acl_permset_t *permset,*
  uuid_t **group,*
  error_status_t **status*)**;**

Parameters

Input

acl	A pointer to the ACL that is to be modified.
permset	The permissions to be granted to the group.
group	The UUID identifying the group.

Output

status	A pointer to the completion status. On successful completion, the routine returns **error_status_ok**. Otherwise, it returns an error.

Description

The **dce_acl_obj_add_group_entry( )** routine adds a group ACL entry to the given ACL. It is equivalent to calling the **dce_acl_obj_add_id_entry( )** routine with the **sec_acl_e_type_group** entry type, but is more convenient.

Errors

error_status_ok
The call was successful.

Related Information

Functions: **dce_acl_obj_add_id_entry(3sec)**.

dce_acl_obj_add_id_entry

Purpose   Adds permissions for an ACL entry to the given ACL

Synopsis   **#include <dce/dce.h>**
                #include <dce/aclif.h>

        void dce_acl_obj_add_id_entry(
          sec_acl_t **acl,*
          sec_acl_entry_type_t *entry_type,*
          sec_acl_permset_t *permset,*
          uuid_t **id,*
          error_status_t **status*);

Parameters

Input

    acl   A pointer to the ACL that is to be modified.

    entry_type   Must be one of the following types:

- **sec_acl_e_type_user**

- **sec_acl_e_type_group**

- **sec_acl_e_type_foreign_other**

- **sec_acl_e_type_user_deleg**

- **sec_acl_e_type_group_deleg**

- **sec_acl_e_type_for_other_deleg**

    permset   The permissions to be granted to the **user**, **group**, or **foreign_other**.

    id   The UUID identifying the **user**, **group**, or **foreign_other** to be added

Output

    status   A pointer to the completion status. On successful completion, the routine returns **error_status_ok**. Otherwise, it returns an error.

dce_acl_obj_add_id_entry(3sec)

Description

The **dce_acl_obj_add_id_entry( )** routine adds an ACL entry (user or group, domestic or foreign) to the given ACL.

Errors   **sec_acl_invalid_entry_type**
The type specified in *entry_type* is not one of the six specified types.

error_status_ok
The call was successful.

Related Information

Functions: **dce_acl_obj_add_group_entry(3sec)**,
dce_acl_obj_add_user_entry(3sec).

dce_acl_obj_add_obj_entry

Purpose   Adds permissions for an object (obj) ACL entry to the given ACL

Synopsis   **#include <dce/dce.h>**
#include <dce/aclif.h>

void dce_acl_obj_add_obj_entry(
  **sec_acl_t ***acl,
  sec_acl_entry_type_t entry_type,
  sec_acl_permset_t permset,
  **error_status_t ***status);

Parameters

Input

  acl   A pointer to the ACL that is to be modified.

  entry_type   Must be one of these types:

    - **sec_acl_e_type_unauthenticated**

    - **sec_acl_e_type_any_other**

    - **sec_acl_e_type_user_obj_deleg**

    - **sec_acl_e_type_group_obj_deleg**

    - **sec_acl_e_type_other_obj_deleg**

    - **sec_acl_e_type_any_other_deleg**

  permset   The permissions to be granted.

Output

  status   A pointer to the completion status. On successful completion, the
               routine returns **error_status_ok**. Otherwise, it returns an error.

dce_acl_obj_add_obj_entry(3sec)

Description

The **dce_acl_obj_add_obj_entry( )** routine adds an **obj** ACL entry to the given ACL.

Errors   **sec_acl_invalid_entry_type**
The type specified in *entry_type* is not one of the six specified types.

error_status_ok
The call was successful.

Related Information

Functions: **dce_acl_obj_add_any_other_entry(3sec)**, **dce_acl_obj_add_unauth_entry(3sec)**.

dce_acl_obj_add_unauth_entry

Purpose   Adds permissions for unauthenticated ACL entry to the given ACL

Synopsis   **#include <dce/dce.h>**
                 #include <dce/aclif.h>

                 void dce_acl_obj_add_unauth_entry(
                   sec_acl_t **acl*,
                   sec_acl_permset_t *permset*,
                   error_status_t **status*);

Parameters

Input

    acl   A pointer to the ACL that is to be modified.

    permset   The permissions to be granted for **sec_acl_e_type_-unauthenticated**.

Output

    status   A pointer to the completion status. On successful completion, the routine returns **error_status_ok**. Otherwise, it returns an error.

Description

The **dce_acl_obj_add_unauth_entry( )** routine adds ACL entry for **sec_acl_e_type_unauthenticated** to the given ACL. It is equivalent to calling the **dce_acl_obj_add_obj_entry( )** routine with the **sec_acl_e_type_unauthenticated** entry type, but it is more convenient.

Errors   **error_status_ok**
                 The call was successful.

Related Information

Functions: **dce_acl_obj_add_obj_entry(3sec)**.

dce_acl_obj_add_user_entry

Purpose Adds permissions for a user ACL entry to the given ACL

Synopsis #include <dce/dce.h>
#include <dce/aclif.h>

void dce_acl_obj_add_user_entry(
    sec_acl_t *acl,
    sec_acl_permset_t permset,
    uuid_t *user,
    error_status_t *status);

Parameters

Input

acl   A pointer to the ACL that is to be modified.

permset   The permissions to be granted to the user.

user   The UUID identifying the user to be added.

Output

status   A pointer to the completion status. On successful completion, the routine returns **error_status_ok**. Otherwise, it returns an error.

Description

The **dce_acl_obj_add_user_entry()** routine adds a user ACL entry to the given ACL. It is equivalent to calling the **dce_acl_obj_add_id_entry()** routine with the **sec_acl_e_type_user** entry type, but it is more convenient.

Errors error_status_ok
            The call was successful.

Related Information

Functions: **dce_acl_obj_add_id_entry(3sec)**.

dce_acl_obj_free_entries

Purpose   Frees space used by an ACL's entries

Synopsis   **#include <dce/dce.h>**
#include <dce/aclif.h>

void dce_acl_obj_free_entries(
  sec_acl_t **acl,*
  error_status_t **status*);

Parameters

Input

  acl   A pointer to the ACL that is to be freed.

Output

  status   A pointer to the completion status. On successful completion, the
                 routine returns **error_status_ok**. Otherwise, it returns an error.

Description

The **dce_acl_obj_free_entries( )** routine frees space used by an ACL's entries,
then sets the pointer to the ACL entry array to NULL and the entry count to 0
(zero).

Errors   **error_status_ok**
              The call was successful.

Related Information

Functions: **dce_acl_obj_init(3sec)**.

dce_acl_obj_init

Purpose   Initializes an ACL

Synopsis   **#include <dce/dce.h>**
                 #include <dce/aclif.h>

                 void dce_acl_obj_init(
                   uuid_t * *mgr_type*,
                   sec_acl_t * *acl*,
                   error_status_t * *status*);

Parameters

   Input

   mgr_type   A pointer to the UUID identifying the type of the ACL manager in
                   question. There may be more than one type of ACL manager
                   protecting the object whose ACL is bound to the input handle. Use
                   this parameter to distinguish them.

   acl   A pointer to the ACL that is to be created.

   Output

   status   A pointer to the completion status. On successful completion, the
                   routine returns **error_status_ok**. Otherwise, it returns an error.

Description

             The **dce_acl_obj_init( )** routine initializes an ACL. The caller passes in the
             pointer to the already-existing ACL structure (of type **sec_acl_t**), for which the
             caller provides the space.

Examples   This example shows the use of **dce_acl_obj_init( )** and the corresponding routine
             to free the entries, **dce_acl_obj_free_entries( )**.

```
sec_acl_t acl;
extern uuid_t my_mgr_type;
error_status_t status;
dce_acl_obj_init(&my_mgr_type, &acl, &status);
/* ... use the ACL ... */
dce_acl_obj_free_entries(&acl, &status);
```

Errors   **error_status_ok**

The call was successful.

Related Information

Functions: **dce_acl_obj_free_entries(3sec)**.

dce_acl_register_object_type

Purpose   Registers an ACL manager's object type

Synopsis   **#include <dce/dce.h>**
            #include <dce/aclif.h>

            void dce_acl_register_object_type(
              dce_db_handle_t *db*,
              uuid_t **mgr_type*,
              unsigned32 *printstring_size*,
              sec_acl_printstring_t **printstring*,
              sec_acl_printstring_t **mgr_info*,
              sec_acl_permset_t *control_perm*,
              sec_acl_permset_t *test_perm*,
              dce_acl_resolve_func_t *resolver*,
              void **resolver_arg*,
              unsigned32 *flags*,
              error_status_t **status*);

Parameters

Input

> *db*   The *db* parameter specifies the handle to the backing store database in which the ACL objects are stored. It must be indexed by UUID and not use backing store headers. The database is obtained through **dce_db_open( )**, which is called prior to this routine.

> *mgr_type*   A pointer to the UUID identifying the type of the ACL manager in question. There may be more than one type of ACL manager protecting the object whose ACL is bound to the input handle. Use this parameter to distinguish them.

> *printstring_size*
> The number of items in the *printstring* array.

> *printstring*   An array of **sec_acl_printstring_t** structures containing the printable representation of each specified permission. These are the printstrings used by **dcecp** or other ACL editors.

> *mgr_info*   A single **sec_acl_printstring_t** containing the name and short description for the given ACL manager.

control_perm The permission set needed to change an ACL, typically **sec_acl_perm_control**. If the value is 0, then anyone is allowed to change the ACL. The permission must be listed in the **printstring**.

test_perm The permission set needed to test an ACL, typically **sec_acl_perm_test**. If the value is 0, then anyone is allowed to test the ACL. The permissions must be listed in the **printstring**.

resolver The function for finding an ACL's UUID.

resolver_arg The argument to pass to the *resolver* function. If using **dce_acl_resolve_by_name( )** or **dce_acl_resolve_by_uuid( )**, then pass the database handle to the name or UUID backing store database. The backing store must use the standard backing store header. See **dce_db_open(3dce)**.

flags A bit mask with the following possible bit values:

> **dce_acl_c_orphans_ok**
> > If this bit is specified, it is possible to replace an ACL with one in which no control bits are turned on in any of the ACL entries. (Use the **rdacl_replace** operation to replace an ACL.) This is a write-once operation, and once it has been done, no one can change the ACL.

> **dce_acl_c_has_owner**
> > If this bit is set, then the ACL manager supports the concept of user owners of objects. This is required to use ACL entries of type **user_obj** and **user_obj_deleg**. entries such as **sec_acl_e_type_-user_obj**.

> **dce_acl_c_has_groups**
> > A similar bit for group owners of objects.

Output

status A pointer to the completion status. On successful completion, the routine returns **error_status_ok**. Otherwise, it returns an error.

Description

The **dce_acl_register_object_type( )** routine registers an ACL manager's object types with the ACL library.

The *resolver* function may be the **dce_acl_resolve_by_name( )** or the **dce_acl_resolve_by_uuid( )** routine, if the application uses the standard header in the backing store database, or it may be some other user-supplied routine, as appropriate. A user-supplied routine must be of type **dce_acl_resolve_func_t**. The *resolver* function finds the UUID of the ACL of the given object. The *resolver*'s parameters must match the type **dce_db_convert_func_t** defined in the file **<dce/aclif.h>**. Observe the use of the resolver function **dce_acl_convert_func( )** in **EXAMPLES**.

Unless the **dce_acl_c_orphans_ok** bit is set in the *flags* parameter, all ACLs must always have *someone* able to modify the ACL.

Another way to express this is that if **dce_acl_c_orphans_ok** is cleared in a call to **dce_acl_register_object_type( )** where a *control_perm* value is specified, then a subsequent ACL replacement using an ACL that has no control bits set in any nondelegation entry will fail, resulting in the **acl_s_no_control_entries** error. If **dce_acl_c_orphans_ok** is set, but no *control_perm* bits are specified, then **dce_acl_c_orphans_ok** is ignored, and the replacement works in all cases.

Files   **/usr/include/dce/aclif.h**
          Definition of **dce_acl_resolve_func_t**.

Examples   The **dce_acl_register_object_type( )** routine should be called once for each type of object that the server manages. A typical call is shown below. The sample code defines three variables: the manager printstring, the ACL printstrings, and the ACL database. Note that the manager printstring does not define any permission bits; they will be set by the library to be the union of all permissions in the ACL printstring. The code also uses the global **my_uuid** as the ACL manager type UUID. The ACL printstring uses the standard **sec_acl_perm_XXX** bits.

```
include <dce/aclif.h>

/* Manager help. */
sec_acl_printstring_t my_acl_help = {
    "me", "My manager"
};


/*
 * ACL permission descriptions; these are from /usr/include/dce/aclbase.idl
 * This example refrains from redefining any of the conventionally
 * established bits.
 */
```

```
sec_acl_printstring_t my_printstring[] = {
    { "r", "read", sec_acl_perm_read },
    { "f", "foobar", sec_acl_perm_unused_00000080 },
    { "w", "write", sec_acl_perm_write },
    { "d", "delete, sec_acl_perm_delete },
    { "c", "control", sec_acl_perm_control }
};

dce_db_open("my_acldb", NULL,
    dce_db_c_std_header | dce_db_c_index_by_uuid,
    (dce_db_convert_func_t)dce_acl_convert_func,
    &dbh, &st);

dce_acl_register_object_type(dbh, &my_manager_uuid,
    sizeof my_printstring / sizeof my_printstring[0],
    my_printstring, &my_acl_help, sec_acl_perm_control,
    0, xxx_resolve_func, NULL, 0, &st);
```

If the ACL manager can use the standard collection of ACL bits (that is, has not defined any special ones), then it can use the global variable **dce_acl_g_printstring** that predefines a printstring. Here is an example of its use:

```
dce_acl_register_object_type(acl_db, &your_mgr_type,
    sizeof dce_acl_g_printstring / sizeof dce_acl_g_printstring[0],
    dce_acl_g_printstring, &your_acl_help,
    dced_perm_control, dced_perm_test, your_resolver, NULL, 0, st);
```

Errors

error_status_ok

The call was successful.

acl_s_owner_not_allowed

In a **rdacl_replace** operation an attempt was made to add an ACL entry of type **sec_acl_e_type_user_obj** or **sec_acl_e_type_user_obj_deleg** to a manager that does not support object users ownership.

acl_s_owner_not_allowed

In a **rdacl_replace** operation an attempt was made to add an ACL entry of type **sec_acl_e_type_user_obj** or **sec_acl_e_type_user_obj_deleg** to a manager that does not support object users ownership.

acl_s_group_not_allowed

In a **rdacl_replace** operation an attempt was made to add an ACL entry of type **sec_acl_e_type_group_obj** or **sec_acl_e_type_group_obj_deleg** to a manager that does not support object group ownership.

dce_acl_register_object_type(3sec)

acl_s_no_control_entries
> In a **rdacl_replace** operation an attempt was made to replace the ACL where no entries have control permission.

acl_s_owner_not_allowed
> In a **rdacl_replace** operation an attempt was made to add an ACL entry of type **sec_acl_e_type_user_obj** or **sec_acl_e_type_user_-obj_deleg** to a manager that does not support object users ownership.

acl_s_group_not_allowed
> In a **rdacl_replace** operation an attempt was made to add an ACL entry of type **sec_acl_e_type_group_obj** or **sec_acl_e_type_-group_obj_deleg** to a manager that does not support object group ownership.

acl_s_no_control_entries
> In a **rdacl_replace** operation an attempt was made to replace the ACL where no entries have control permission. CL entry of type **sec_acl_e_type_group_obj** or **sec_acl_e_type_group_obj_deleg** to a manager that does not support object group ownership.

acl_s_no_control_entries
> In a **rdacl_replace** operation an attempt was made to replace the ACL where no entries have control permission.

Related Information

Functions: **dce_acl_resolve_by_name(3sec)**, **dce_acl_resolve_by_uuid(3sec)**, **dce_db_open(3dce)**.

dce_acl_resolve_by_name

Purpose   Finds an ACL's UUID, given an object's name

Synopsis   **#include <dce/dce.h>**
#include <dce/aclif.h>

void dce_acl_resolve_by_name(
  handle_t *handle*,
  sec_acl_component_name_t *component_name*,
  sec_acl_type_t *sec_acl_type*,
  uuid_t **mgr_type*,
  boolean32 *writing*,
  void **resolver_arg*,
  uuid_t **acl_uuid*,
  error_status_t **status*);

Parameters

Input

handle   A client binding handle passed into the server stub. Use **sec_acl_bind( )** to create this handle.

component_name
        A character string containing the name of the target object.

sec_acl_type   The type of ACL to be resolved:

- **sec_acl_type_object**

- **sec_acl_type_default_object**

- **sec_acl_type_default_container**

mgr_type   A pointer to the UUID identifying the type of the ACL manager in question. There may be more than one type of ACL manager protecting the object whose ACL is bound to the input handle. Use this parameter to distinguish them.

writing   This parameter is ignored in OSF's implementation.

resolver_arg   This argument is passed into **dce_acl_register_object_type( )**. It should be a handle for a backing store indexed by name.

Output

acl_uuid The ACL UUID, as resolved by **dce_acl_resolve_by_name( )**.

status A pointer to the completion status. On successful completion, the routine returns **error_status_ok**. Otherwise, it returns an error.

Description

The **dce_acl_resolve_by_name( )** routine finds an ACL's UUID, given an object's name, as provided in the *component_name* parameter. The user does not call this function directly. It is an instance of the kind of function provided to the *resolver* argument of **dce_acl_register_object_type( )**.

If **dce_acl_resolve_by_name( )** and **dce_acl_resolve_by_uuid( )** are inappropriate, the user of **dce_acl_register_object_type( )** must provide some other *resolver* function.

Errors

error_status_ok

The call was successful.

Related Information

Functions: **dce_acl_register_object_type(3sec),
dce_acl_resolve_by_uuid(3sec), dce_db_open(3dce),
dce_db_std_header_fetch(3dce)**.

dce_acl_resolve_by_uuid

Purpose   Finds an ACL's UUID, given an object's UUID

Synopsis   **#include <dce/dce.h>**
#include <dce/aclif.h>

dce_acl_resolve_func_t dce_acl_resolve_by_uuid(
    handle_t *handle,*
    sec_acl_component_name_t *component_name,*
    sec_acl_type_t *sec_acl_type,*
    uuid_t **mgr_type,*
    boolean32 *writing,*
    void **resolver_arg,*
    uuid_t **acl_uuid,*
    error_status_t **status*);

Parameters

Input

handle   A client binding handle passed into the server stub. Use **sec_acl_bind**( ) to create this handle.

component_name
    A character string containing the name of the target object. (The **dce_acl_resolve_by_uuid**( ) routine ignores this parameter.)

sec_acl_type   The type of ACL to be resolved:

- **sec_acl_type_object**

- **sec_acl_type_default_object**

- **sec_acl_type_default_container**

mgr_type   A pointer to the UUID identifying the type of the ACL manager in question. There may be more than one type of ACL manager protecting the object whose ACL is bound to the input handle. Use this parameter to distinguish them.

writing   This parameter is ignored in OSF's implementation.

resolver_arg   This argument is passed into **dce_acl_register_object_type**( ). It should be a handle for a backing store indexed by UUID.

Output

acl_uuid   The ACL UUID, as resolved by **dce_acl_resolve_by_uuid( )**.

status   A pointer to the completion status. On successful completion, the routine returns **error_status_ok**. Otherwise, it returns an error.

Description

The **dce_acl_resolve_by_uuid( )** routine finds an ACL's UUID, given an object's UUID, as provided through the *handle* parameter. The user does not call this function directly. It is an instance of the kind of function provided to the *resolver* argument of **dce_acl_register_object_type( )**.

If **dce_acl_resolve_by_uuid( )** and **dce_acl_resolve_by_name( )** are inappropriate, the user of **dce_acl_register_object_type( )** must provide some other *resolver* function.

Errors

error_status_ok

The call was successful.

Related Information

Functions: **dce_acl_register_object_type(3sec)**, **dce_acl_resolve_by_name(3sec)**, **dce_db_open(3dce)**, **dce_db_std_header_fetch(3dce)**.

dce_aud_close

Purpose   Closes an audit trail file

Used by client/server applications and audit trail analysis and examination tools

Synopsis   **#include <dce/audit.h>**

void dce_aud_close(
        dce_aud_trail_t *at*,
        unsigned32 **status*);

Parameters

Input

at   A pointer to an audit trail descriptor returned by a previous call to **dce_aud_open( )**.

Output

status   The status code returned by this routine.

Description

The **dce_aud_close( )** function releases data structures of file openings, RPC bindings, and other memory associated with the audit trail that is specified by the audit trail descriptor.

Return Values

No value is returned.

Errors   **aud_s_ok**   The call was successful.

Related Information

Functions: **dce_aud_open(3sec)**.

dce_aud_commit

Purpose   Writes the audit record in the audit trail file

Used by client/server applications

Synopsis   **#include <dce/audit.h>**

void dce_aud_commit(
        dce_aud_trail_t *at*,
        dce_aud_rec_t *ard*,
        unsigned32 *options*,
        unsigned16 *format*,
        unsigned32 *outcome*,
        unsigned32 **status*);

Parameters

Input

at   Designates an audit trail file to which the completed audit record will be written. The audit trail file must have been previously opened by a successful call to the **dce_aud_open**( ) function.

ard   Designates an audit record descriptor that was returned by a previously successful call to one of the **dce_aud_start_*( )** functions. The content of this record buffer will be appended to the audit trail specified by *at*.

options   Bitwise **OR** of option values described below. A value of 0 (zero) for *options* results in the default operation (normal writing to the file without flushing to stable storage). The possible option value is

aud_c_evt_commit_sync
        Flushes the audit record to stable storage before the function returns.

aud_c_evt_always_log
        Unconditionally logs the audit record to the audit trail.

aud_c_evt_always_alarm
        Unconditionally displays the audit record on the console.

format   Event's tail format used for the event-specific information. This format can be configured by the user. With this format version number, the servers and audit analysis tools can accommodate changes in the formats of the event specific information, or use different formats dynamically.

outcome   The event outcome to be stored in the header. The possible event-outcome values are as follows:

aud_c_esl_cond_success
> The event completed successfully.

aud_c_esl_cond_denial
> The event failed because of access denial.

aud_c_esl_cond_failure
> The event failed because of reasons other than access denial.

aud_c_esl_cond_pending
> The event is in an intermediate state, and the outcome is pending, being one in a series of connected events, where the application desires to record the real outcome only after the last event.

aud_c_esl_cond_unknown
> The event outcome (denial, failure, pending, or success) is not known. This outcome exists only between a **dce_aud_start( )** (all varieties of this routine) call and the next **dce_aud_commit( )** call. You can also use **0** to specify this outcome.

Output

status   Returns the status code from this routine. This status code indicates whether the routine completed successfully or not. If the routine did not complete successfully, the reason for the failure is given.

Description

The **dce_aud_commit( )** function determines whether the event should be audited given the event outcome. If it should be audited, the function completes the audit record identified by **ard** and writes it to the audit trail designated by **at**. If any of the **aud_c_evt_always_log** or **aud_c_evt_always_alarm** options is selected, the event is always audited (logged or an alarm message is sent to the standard output).

If the **aud_c_evt_commit_sync** option is selected, the function attempts to flush the audit record to stable storage. If the stable storage write cannot be performed, the function either continues to try until the stable-storage write is completed or returns an error status.

Upon successful completion, **dce_aud_commit()** calls **dce_aud_discard()** internally to release the memory of the audit record that is being committed.

The caller should not change the outcome between the **dce_aud_start()** and **dce_aud_commit()** calls arbitrarily. In this case, the outcome can be made more specific, for example, from **aud_c_esl_cond_unknown** to **aud_c_esl_cond_-success** or from **aud_c_esl_cond_pending** to **aud_c_esl_cond_success**.

An outcome change from **aud_c_esl_cond_success** to **aud_c_esl_cond_denial** is not logically correct because the outcome **aud_c_esl_cond_success** may have caused a NULL *ard* to be returned in this function. If the final outcome can be **aud_c_esl_cond_success**, then it should be specified in this function, or use **aud_c_esl_cond_unknown**.

Return Values

No value is returned.

Errors

aud_s_wrong_protection_level
Client used the wrong protection level.

aud_s_dmn_disabled
The daemon is disabled for logging.

aud_s_log_access_denied
The client's access to the Audit log was denied.

aud_s_cannot_gettime
The audit library cannot backup a trail file due to failure of the **utc_gettime()** call.

aud_s_cannot_getgmtime
The audit library cannot backup a trail file due to failure of the **utc_gmtime()** call.

aud_s_rename_trail_file_rc
Cannot rename the audit trail file.

aud_s_cannot_reopen_trail_file_rc
Internally, the audit trail file was being reopened and the reopening of the file failed.

aud_s_rename_trail_index_file_rc
>Internally, the audit trail index file was being renamed and the renaming of the file failed.

aud_s_cannot_reopen_trail_index_file_rc
>Internally, the audit trail index file was being reopened and the reopening of the file failed.

aud_s_invalid_record_descriptor
>The audit record descriptor is invalid.

aud_s_invalid_outcome
>The event outcome parameter that was provided is invalid.

aud_s_outcomes_inconsistent
>The event outcome parameter is inconsistent with the outcome parameter provided in the **dce_aud_start( )** call.

aud_s_trl_write_failure
>The audit record cannot be written to stable storage.

aud_s_ok   The call was successful.

Status codes passed from **dce_aud_discard( )**

Status codes passed from **rpc_binding_inq_auth_caller( )**

Status codes passed from **dce_acl_is_client_authorized( )**

Status codes passed from **audit_pickle_dencode_ev_info( )** (RPC idl compiler)

Related Information

Functions: **dce_aud_open(3sec), dce_aud_put_ev_info(3sec), dce_aud_start(3sec), dce_aud_start_with_name(3sec), dce_aud_start_with_pac(3sec), dce_aud_start_with_server_binding(3sec)**.

dce_aud_discard

Purpose   Discards an audit record (releases the memory)

Used by client/server applications and trail analysis and examination tools

Synopsis   **#include <dce/audit.h>**

void dce_aud_discard(
        dce_aud_rec_t *ard*,
        unsigned32 **status*)**;**

Parameters

Input

ard   Designates an audit record descriptor that was returned by a previously successful call to one of the **dce_aud_start_*( )** functions or the **dce_aud_next( )** function.

Output

status   The status code returned by this routine. This status code indicates whether the routine was completed successfully or not. If the routine was not completed successfully, the reason for the failure is   given.

Description

The **dce_aud_discard( )** function releases the memory used by the audit record descriptor and the associated audit record that is to be discarded.

Return Values

No value is returned.

Errors   **aud_s_ok**   The call was successful.

Status codes passed from **dce_aud_free_header( )**

Related Information

Functions: **dce_aud_open(3sec)**, **dce_aud_start(3sec)**,
dce_aud_start_with_name(3sec), **dce_aud_start_with_pac(3sec)**,
dce_aud_start_with_server_binding(3sec).

dce_aud_free_ev_info

Purpose   Frees the memory allocated for an event information stucture returned from calling **dce_aud_get_ev_info( )**

Used by the audit trail analysis and examination tools

Synopsis   **#include <dce/audit.h>**

void dce_aud_free_ev_info(
    dce_aud_ev_info_t *_event_info_,
    unsigned32 *_status_);

Parameters

Input

> _event_info_   Designates an event-specific information item returned from a previous successful call to the **dce_aud_get_ev_info( )** function.

Output

> _status_   The status code returned by this routine.

Description

> The **dce_aud_free_ev_info( )** function frees the memory allocated for an event information stucture returned by a previous successful call to the **dce_aud_get_ev_info( )** function.

Return Values

> No value is returned.

Errors   **aud_s_ok**   The call was successful.

Related Information

> Functions: **dce_aud_get_ev_info(3sec)**, **dce_aud_next(3sec)**.

dce_aud_free_header

Purpose   Frees the memory allocated to a designated audit record header structure

Used by the audit trail analysis and examination tools

Synopsis   **#include <dce/audit.h>**

void dce_aud_free_header(
    dce_aud_hdr_t **header*,
    unsigned32 **status*);

Parameters

Input

ard   Designates a pointer to an audit record header structure that was
returned by a previous successful call to the **dce_aud_get_header( )**
function.

Output

status   The status code returned by this routine.

Description

The **dce_aud_free_header( )** frees the memory allocated to a designated audit
record header structure. The designated audit record header is usually obtained
from an audit record by calling **dce_aud_get_header( )**.

Return Values

No value is returned.

Errors   **aud_s_ok**   The call was successful.

Related Information

Functions: **dce_aud_get_header(3sec)**, **dce_aud_next(3sec)**,
dce_aud_open(3sec).

dce_aud_get_ev_info

Purpose   Returns a pointer to an event information stucture (**dce_aud_ev_info_t**)

Used by the audit trail analysis and examination tools

Synopsis   **#include <dce/audit.h>**

void dce_aud_get_ev_info(
          dce_aud_rec_t *ard*,
          dce_aud_ev_info_t **event_info,
          unsigned32 *status)**;**

Parameters

Input

> *ard*   Designates an audit record descriptor that was returned by a previously successful call to the **dce_aud_next( )** function.

Output

> *event_info*   Returns an event-specific information item of the designated audit record. Returns NULL if there are no more information items.

> *status*   The status code returned by this routine. This status code indicates whether the routine was completed successfully or not. If the routine was not completed successfully, the reason for the failure is given.

Description

The **dce_aud_get_ev_info( )** function returns a pointer to an event information structure. The designated record is usually obtained from an audit trail by calling **dce_aud_open( )** and **dce_aud_next( )**. If there is more than one item of event-specific information in the audit record, then one item is returned through one call to **dce_aud_get_ev_info( )**. The order in which the items are returned is the same as the order in which they were included in the audit record through **dce_aud_put_ev_info( )** calls. This function allocates the memory to hold the human-readable representation of the audit record and returns the address of this memory.

Return Values

No value is returned.

Errors

aud_s_invalid_record_descriptor
    The audit record descriptor is invalid.

aud_s_ok   The call was successful.

Related Information

Functions: **dce_aud_next(3sec)**, **dce_aud_open(3sec)**.

dce_aud_get_header

Purpose   Gets the header of a specified audit record

Used by the audit trail analysis and examination tools

Synopsis   **#include <dce/audit.h>**

void dce_aud_get_header(
    dce_aud_rec_t *ard,*
    dce_aud_hdr_t ****header,*
    unsigned32 **status);*

Parameters

Input

ard   Designates an audit record descriptor that was returned by a previously successful call to the **dce_aud_next( )** function.

Output

header   Returns the header information of the designated audit record.

status   The status code returned by this routine. This status code indicates whether the routine was completed successfully or not. If the routine was not completed successfully, the reason for the failure is given.

Description

The **dce_aud_get_header( )** function gets the header information of a designated audit record. The designated record is usually obtained from an audit trail by calling **dce_aud_open( )** and **dce_aud_next( )**.

Return Values

No value is returned.

Errors   **aud_s_invalid_record_descriptor**
                        The audit record descriptor is invalid.

        aud_s_ok   The call was successful.

Related Information

        Functions: **dce_aud_next(3sec)**, **dce_aud_open(3sec)**.

dce_aud_length

Purpose   Gets the length of a specified audit record

Used by client/server applications and trail analysis and examination tools

Synopsis   **#include <dce/audit.h>**

unsigned32 dce_aud_length(
dce_aud_rec_t *ard*,
unsigned32 **status*);

Parameters

Input

ard   Designates an audit record descriptor that was returned by a previously successful call to **dce_aud_next( )**, or one of the **dce_aud_start_*( )** functions.

Output

status   The status code returned by this routine. This status code indicates whether the routine was completed successfully or not. If the routine was not completed successfully, the reason for the failure is given.

Description

The **dce_aud_length( )** function gets the length of a designated audit record. The designated record (in binary format) may be obtained from an audit trail by calling the **dce_aud_open( )** and **dce_aud_next( )** functions.

Applications can use this function to know how much space an audit record will use before it is committed. This function can also be used by audit trail analysis and examination tools to determine the space that a previously committed audit record uses before it is read.

Return Values

The size of the specified audit record in number of bytes.

Errors

aud_s_invalid_record_descriptor
The audit record descriptor is invalid.

aud_s_ok   The call was successful.

Status codes passed from **idl_es_encode_dyn_buffer( )**

Status codes passed from **audit_pickle_dencode_ev_info( )**
(RPC IDL compiler)

Status codes passed from **idl_es_handle_free( )**

Status codes passed from **rpc_sm_client_free( )**

Related Information

Functions: **dce_aud_next(3aud), dce_aud_open(3aud),
dce_aud_put_ev_info(3aud), dce_aud_start(3aud),
dce_aud_start_with_name(3aud), dce_aud_start_with_pac(3aud),
dce_aud_start_with_server_binding(3aud).**

dce_aud_next

Purpose   Reads the next audit record from a specified audit trail file into a buffer

Used by the trail analysis and examination tools

Synopsis   **#include <dce/audit.h>**

void dce_aud_next(
> **dce_aud_trail_t** *at*,
> **char ****predicate*,
> **unsigned16** *format*,
> **dce_aud_rec_t ****ard*,
> **unsigned32 ****status*);

Parameters

Input

at   A pointer to the descriptor of an audit trail file previously opened for reading by the function **dce_aud_open( )**.

predicate   Criteria for selecting the audit records that are to be read from the audit trail file. A predicate statement consists of an attribute and its value, separated by any of the following operators: = (equal to), < (less than), and > (greater than):

- *attribute=value*

- *attribute>value*

- *attribute<value*

Attribute names are case sensitive, and no space is allowed within a predicate expression. Multiple predicates are delimited by a comma, of the form:

attribute1=value1,attribute2>value2, ...

No space is allowed between predicates. Note that when multiple predicates are defined, the values are logically ANDed together.

The possible attribute names, their values, and allowable operators are as follows:

SERVER   The UUID of the server principal that generated the record. The attribute value must be a UUID string. Operator allowed: =

EVENT   The audit event number. The attribute value must be an integer. Operator allowed: =

OUTCOME   The event outcome of the record. The possible attribute values are **SUCCESS**, **FAILURE**, or **DENIAL**. Operator allowed: =

STATUS   The authorization status of the client. The possible attribute values are **DCE** for DCE authorization (PAC based), and **NAME** for name-based authorization. Operator allowed: =

CLIENT   The UUID of the client principal. The attribute value must be a UUID string. Operator allowed: =

TIME   The time the record was generated. The attribute value must be a null-terminated string that expresses an absolute time. Operators allowed: =, <, and >

CELL   The UUID of the client's cell. The attribute value must be a UUID string. Operator allowed: =

GROUP   The UUID of one of the client's group(s). The attribute value must be a UUID string. Operator allowed: =

ADDR   The address of the client. The attribute is typically the string representation of an RPC binding handle. Operator allowed: =

FORMAT   The format version number of the audit event record. The attribute value must be an integer. Operators allowed: =, <, and >

If the **predicate** parameter is a NULL pointer, the next record in the audit trail file is returned.

format   Event's tail format used for the event-specific information. This format can be configured by the user. With this format version number, the servers and audit analysis tools can accomodate changes in the formats of the event-specific information, or use different formats dynamically.

Output

> *ard*　　　　A pointer to the audit record descriptor containing the returned record.

> *status*　　Returns the status code from this routine. This status code indicates whether the routine was completed successfully or not. If the routine was not completed successfully, the reason for the failure is given.

Description

The **dce_aud_next( )** function attempts to read the next record from the audit trail that is specified by the audit trail descriptor, **at**. This function also defines the predicate to be used to search for the next record and returns a matching record if one exists. The **dce_aud_next( )** function can be used to search for successive records in the trail that match the defined predicate. By default, if no predicate is explicitly defined, the function returns the next record read from the audit trail.

If no record satisfies the predicate specified for the call, a value of zero is returned in *ard*.

The value returned in **ard** can be supplied as an input parameter to the functions **dce_aud_get_header( )**, **dce_aud_length( )**, **dce_aud_get_ev_info( )**, and **dce_-aud_discard( )**.

Storage allocated by this function must be explicitly freed by a call to **dce_aud_discard( )** with *ard* as the input parameter.

If the function successfully reads an audit trail record, the cursor associated with the audit trail descriptor **at** will be advanced to the next record in the audit trail.

If no appropriate record can be found in the audit trail, an *ard* value of zero is returned and the cursor is advanced to the end of the audit trail. If a call is unsuccessful, the position of the cursor does not change.

Return Values

No value is returned.

Errors   **aud_s_invalid_trail_descriptor**
The audit trail descriptor is invalid.

aud_s_trail_file_corrupted
The trail file is corrupted.

aud_s_cannot_allocate_memory
The **malloc( )** call failed.

aud_s_ok   The call was successful.

Status codes passed from **idl_es_decode_buffer( )**

Status codes passed from **idl_es_handle_free( )**

Status codes passed from **audit_pickle_dencode_ev_info( )**
(RPC IDL compiler)

Related Information

Functions: **dce_aud_discard(3sec)**, **dce_aud_get_ev_info(3sec)**,
dce_aud_get_header(3sec), **dce_aud_length(3sec)**, **dce_aud_open(3sec)**.

dce_aud_open

Purpose   Opens a specified audit trail file for read or write

Used by client/server applications and trail analysis and examination tools

Synopsis   **#include <dce/audit.h>**

void dce_aud_open(
      unsigned32 *flags,*
      char **description,*
      unsigned32 *first_evt_number,*
      unsigned32 *num_of_evts,*
      dce_aud_trail_t **at,*
      unsigned32 **status);*

Parameters

Input

    flags   Specifies the mode of opening. The flags parameter is set to the bitwise OR of the following values:

- **aud_c_trl_open_read**

- **aud_c_trl_open_write**

- **aud_c_trl_ss_wrap**

    description   A character string specifying an audit trail file to be opened. If **description** is NULL, the default audit trail file is opened. When the audit trail file is opened for write, the default audit trail is an RPC interface to a local audit daemon.

    first_evt_num The lowest assigned audit event number used by the calling server.

    num_of_evts   The number of audit events defined for the calling server.

Output

    at   A pointer to an audit trail descriptor. When the audit trail descriptor is no longer needed, it must be released by calling the **dce_aud_close( )** function.

status   Returns the status code from this routine. This status code indicates whether the routine was completed successfully or not. If the routine was not completed successfully, the reason for the failure is given.

Description

The **dce_aud_open( )** function opens the audit trail file specified by the **description** parameter. If **description** is NULL, the function uses the default audit trail which is an RPC interface to the local audit daemon.

This function must be invoked after the server has finished registering with RPC and before calling **rpc_server_listen( )**.

If the **flags** parameter is set to **aud_c_trl_open_read**, the specified file (**description** cannot be null in this case) is opened for reading audit records, using the **dce_aud_next( )** function. If **flags** is set to **aud_c_trl_open_write**, the specified file or the default audit trail device is opened and initialized for appending audit records using the **dce_aud_commit( )** function. Only one of the **aud_c_trl_open_read** and **aud_c_trl_open_write** flags may be specified in any call to **dce_aud_open( )**. If the **flags** parameter is set to **aud_c_trl_ss_wrap**, the audit trail operation is set to **wrap** mode. The **aud_c_trl_ss_wrap** flag has meaning only if you specify the **aud_c_trl_open_write** flag.

If the audit trail specified is a file and the calling server does not have the read and write permissions to the file, a NULL pointer is returned in **at**, and **status** is set to **aud_s_cannot_open_trail_file_rc**. The same values will be returned if the default audit trail file is used (that is, through an audit daemon) and if the calling server is not authorized to use the audit daemon to log records.

Return Values

No value is returned.

Errors

aud_s_ok   The call was successful.

aud_s_trl_invalid_open_flags
                The flags argument must include either **aud_c_trl_open_read** or **aud_c_trl_open_write** flag, but not both.

aud_s_cannot_open_dmn_binding_file
                The local audit daemon trail file is designated, but the daemon's binding file cannot be opened.

Status codes passed from **sec_login_get_current_context( )**
When the local audit daemon trail file is designated, a login context is needed for making secure audit logging RPC to the audit daemon.

aud_s_cannot_open_dmn_identity_file
The local audit daemon trail file is designated, but the daemon's identity file cannot be opened.

Status codes passed from **rpc_binding_set_auth_info( )**
When the local audit daemon trail file is designated, **dce_aud_open( )** sets authentication information in the RPC binding handle for making secure audit logging RPC to the audit daemon. This is done by calling **rpc_binding_set_auth_info( )**.

aud_s_cannot_open_trail_file_rc
Cannot open a local trail file.

aud_s_cannot_allocate_memory
Memory allocation failed.

aud_s_cannot_init_trail_mutex
Audit trail mutex initialization failed.

Status codes passed from **rpc_server_inq_bindings( )**
When filtering is turned on, **dce_aud_open( )** gets the caller's RPC bindings to be used for registering an RPC interface in receiving filter update notification from the local audit daemon. This is done by calling **rpc_server_inq_bindings( )**.

Status codes passed from **rpc_binding_to_string_binding( )**
When filtering is turned on, the caller's RPC bindings are converted to string bindings before they are stored in a file. This is done by calling **rpc_binding_to_string_binding( )**.

aud_s_cannot_mkdir
Cannot create a directory for storing the bindings file for the filter update notification interface.

Related Information

Functions: **dce_aud_commit(3sec)**, **dce_aud_next(3sec)**, **dce_aud_start(3sec)**, **dce_aud_start_with_name(3sec)**, **dce_aud_start_with_pac(3sec)**, **dce_aud_start_with_server_binding(3sec)**.

dce_aud_print

Purpose   Formats an audit record into human-readable form

Used by audit trail examination and analysis tools

Synopsis   **#include <dce/audit.h>**

void dce_aud_print(
  dce_aud_rec_t *ard*,
  unsigned32 *options*,
  char ******buffer*,
  unsigned32 *status);

Parameters

Input

ard   An audit record descriptor. This descriptor can be obtained from an opened audit trail by calling **dce_aud_next**( ) or it can be a new record established by calling one of the **dce_aud_start_***( ) functions.

options   The options governing the transformation of the binary audit record information into a character string. The value of the *options* parameter is the bitwise OR of any selected combination of the following option values:

aud_c_evt_all_info
        Includes all the optional information (that is, groups, address, and event specific information).

aud_c_evt_groups_info
        Includes the groups' information.

aud_c_evt_address_info
        Includes the address information.

aud_c_evt_specific_info
        Includes the event specific information.

Output

buffer   Returns the pointer to a character string converted from the audit record specified by *ard*.

status   The status code returned by this routine. This status code indicates whether the routine was completed successfully or not. If the routine was not completed successfully, the reason for the failure is given.

Description

The **dce_aud_print( )** function transforms the audit record specified by *ard* into a character string and places it in a buffer. The buffer is allocated using **malloc( )**, and must later be freed by the caller. (This function allocates the memory to hold the human-readable text of the audit record and returns the address of this memory in the *buffer* parameter.)

The *options* parameter is set to the bitwise OR of flag values defined in the **dce/audit.h** header file. A value of 0 (zero) for options will result in default operation, that is, no group, address, and event-specific information is included in the output string.

Return Values

No value is returned.

Errors

aud_s_invalid_record_descriptor
>The audit record descriptor is invalid.

aud_s_cannot_allocate_memory
>The **malloc( )** call failed.

aud_s_ok   The call was successful.

Status codes passed from **sec_login_get_current_context( )**

Status codes passed from **sec_login_inquire_net_info( )**

Related Information

Functions: **dce_aud_next(3sec), dce_aud_open(3sec), dce_aud_put_ev_info(3sec), dce_aud_start(3sec), dce_aud_start_with_name(3sec), dce_aud_start_with_pac(3sec), dce_aud_start_with_server_binding(3sec).**

dce_aud_put_ev_info

Purpose   Adds event-specific information to a specified audit record buffer

Used by client/server applications

Synopsis   **#include <dce/audit.h>**

void dce_aud_put_ev_info(
        dce_aud_rec_t *ard*,
        dce_aud_ev_info_t *info*,
        unsigned32 **status*);

Parameters

Input

ard   A pointer to an audit record descriptor initialized by one of the **dce_aud_start_*( )** functions.

info   A data structure containing an event-specific information item that is to be appended to the tail of the audit record identified by **ard**. The possible formats of the event-specific information are listed in the **sec_intro(3sec)** reference page of this book.

Output

status   The status code returned by this routine. This status code indicates whether the routine was completed successfully or not. If the routine was not completed successfully, the reason for the failure is given.

Description

The **dce_aud_put_ev_info( )** function adds event-specific information to an audit record. The event-specific information is included in an audit record by calling **dce_aud_put_ev_info( )** one or more times. The order of the information items included by multiple calls is preserved in the audit record, so that they may be read in the same order by the **dce_aud_get_ev_info( )** function. This order is also observed by the **dce_aud_print( )** function. The **info** parameter is a pointer to an instance of the self-descriptive **dce_aud_ev_info_t** structure.

dce_aud_put_ev_info(3sec)

Return Values

No value is returned.

Errors

aud_s_invalid_record_descriptor
The input audit record descriptor is invalid.

aud_s_evt_tail_info_exceeds_limit
The tail portion of the audit trail record has exceeded its limit of 4K.

aud_s_ok   The call was successful.

Related Information

Functions: **dce_aud_commit(3sec)**, **dce_aud_open(3sec)**, **dce_aud_start(3sec)**, **dce_aud_start_with_name(3sec)**, **dce_aud_start_with_pac(3sec)**, **dce_aud_start_with_server_binding(3sec)**.

dce_aud_set_trail_size_limit

Purpose   Sets a limit to the audit trail size

Used by client/server applications

Synopsis   **#include <dce/audit.h>**

void dce_aud_set_trail_size_limit (
    dce_aud_trail_t *at*,
    unsigned32 *file_size_limit_value*,
    unsigned32 * *status*)

Parameters

Input

at   A pointer to the descriptor of an audit trail file previously opened for reading by the function **dce_aud_open( )**.

file_size_limit_value
    The desired maximum size of the audit trail file, in bytes.

Output

status   Returns the status code of this routine. This status code indicates whether the routine completed successfully or not. If the routine did not complete successfully, the reason for the failure is given.

Description

The **dce_aud_set_trail_size_limit( )** function can be used by an application that links with **libaudit** to set the maximum size of the audit trail. This function must be called immediately after calling **dce_aud_open( )**.

For added flexibility, the environment variable **DCEAUDITTRAILSIZE** can also be used to set the maximum trail size limit.

If none of these methods are used for setting the trail size, then a hardcoded limit of 2 megabytes will be assumed.

If set, the value of the environment variable **DCEAUDITTRAILSIZE** overrides the value set by this function. Any of the values set by **DCEAUDITTRAILSIZE** or this function overrides the hardcoded default.

When the size limit is reached, the current trail file is copied to another file. The name of this new file is the original filename appended by a timestamp. For example, if the name of the original trail file is **central_trail**, its companion trail file is named **central_trail.md_index**. These two files will be copied to the following locations:

central_trail.1994-09-26-16-38-15
central_trail.1994-09-26-16-38-15.md_index

When a trail file is copied to a new file by the audit library because it has reached the size limit, a serviceability message is issued to the console notifying the user that an audit trail file (and its companion index file) is available to be backed up. Once the backup is performed, it is advisable to remove the old trail file, so as to prevent running out of disk space.

Auditing will then continue, using the original name of the file, (in our example, **central_trail**).

Return Values

No value is returned.

Errors

aud_s_invalid_trail_descriptor
        The audit trail descriptor *at* is null.

aud_s_ok   The call is successful.

Related Information

Functions: **dce_aud_open(3sec)**.

dce_aud_start

Purpose   Determines whether a specified event should be audited given the client binding information and the event outcome

Used by client/server applications

Synopsis   **#include <dce/audit.h>**

void dce_aud_start(
      unsigned32 *event*,
      rpc_binding_handle_t *binding*,
      unsigned32 *options*,
      unsigned32 *outcome*,
      dce_aud_rec_t **ard*,
      unsigned32 **status*);

Parameters

Input

event	Specifies the event to be audited. This is a 32-bit event number. The **event** field in the audit record header will be set to this number.
binding	Specifies the client's RPC binding handle from which the client identification information is retrieved to set the **client**, **cell**, **num_groups**, **groups**, and **addr** fields in the audit record header.
options	Specifies the optional header information desired (**aud_c_evt_all_info**, **aud_c_evt_group_info**, or **aud_c_evt_-address_info**).

It can also be used to specify whether the audit records are always logged (**aud_c_evt_always_log**) or that an alarm message is always sent to the standard output (**aud_c_evt_always_alarm**). If any of these two options is selected, the filter is bypassed.

The value of the **options** parameter is the bitwise OR of any selected combination of the following option values:

aud_c_evt_all_info
            Includes all optional information (groups and address) in the audit record header.

aud_c_evt_groups_info
Includes the groups information in the audit record header.

aud_c_evt_address_info
Includes the client address information in the audit record header.

aud_c_evt_always_log
Bypasses the filter mechanism and indicates that the event must be logged.

aud_c_evt_always_alarm
Bypasses the filter mechanism and indicates that an alarm message must be sent to the system console for the event.

outcome The event outcome to be stored in the header. The following event outcome values are defined:

aud_c_esl_cond_success
The event was completed successfully.

aud_c_esl_cond_denial
The event failed because of access denial.

aud_c_esl_cond_failure
The event failed because of reasons other than access denial.

aud_c_esl_cond_pending
The event is in an intermediate state, and the outcome is pending, being one in a series of connected events, where the application desires to record the real outcome only after the last event.

aud_c_esl_cond_unknown
The event outcome (denial, failure, pending, or success) is still unknown. This outcome exists only between a **dce_aud_start( )** (all varieties of this routine) call and the next **dce_aud_commit( )** call. You can also use **0** to specify this outcome.

Output

ard   Returns a pointer to an audit record buffer. If the event does not need to be audited because it is not selected by the filters, or if the environment variable **DCEAUDITOFF** has been set, a NULL pointer is returned. If the function is called with *outcome* set to **aud_c_esl_cond_unknown**, it is possible that the function cannot determine whether the event should be audited. In this case, the audit record descriptor is still allocated and its address is returned to the caller. An *outcome* other than **aud_c_esl_cond_unknown** must be provided when calling the **dce_aud_commit( )** function.

status   The status code returned by this function. This status code indicates whether the routine was completed successfully or not. If the routine was not completed successfully, the reason for the failure is given.

Description

The **dce_aud_start( )** function determines if an audit record should be generated for the specified event. The decision is based on the event filters, an environment variable (**DCEAUDITOFF**), the client's identity provided in the **binding** parameter, and the event outcome (if it is provided in the **outcome** parameter). If this event needs to be audited, the function allocates an audit record descriptor and returns a pointer to it, (that is, *ard*). If the event does not need to be audited, a NULL *ard* is returned. If an internal error(s) has occurred, a NULL pointer is returned in *ard*. If the **aud_c_evt_always_log** or **aud_c_evt_always_alarm** option is selected, an audit record descriptor will always be created and returned.

The **dce_aud_start( )** function is designed to be used by RPC applications. Non-RPC applications that use the DCE authorization model (that is, DCE ACL and PAC) must use **dce_aud_start_with_pac( )**. Non-RPC applications that do not use the DCE authorization model must use **dce_aud_start_with_name( )**.

This function obtains the client identity information from the RPC binding handle and records it in the newly-created audit record descriptor.

Event-specific information can be added to the record by calling the **dce_aud_put_ev_info( )** function. This function can be called multiple times after calling **dce_aud_start( )** and before calling **dce_aud_commit( )**. A completed audit record will be appended to an audit trail file or sent to the audit daemon (depending on the value of the **description** parameter used in the previous call to **dce_aud_open**) by calling **dce_aud_commit( )**.

This function searches for all relevant filters (for the specified subject and outcome, if these are specified), summarizes the actions for each possible event outcome, and records an outcome-action table with *ard*. If the outcome is specified when calling this function and the outcome does not require any action according to filters, then this function returns a NULL *ard*.

If the *outcome* is not specified in the **dce_aud_start( )** call, **dce_aud_start( )** returns a NULL *ard* if no action is required for all possible outcomes.

The caller should not change the outcome between the **dce_aud_start( )** and **dce_aud_commit( )** calls arbitrarily. In this case, the outcome can be made more specific, for example, from **aud_c_esl_cond_unknown** to **aud_c_esl_cond_-success** or from **aud_c_esl_cond_pending** to **aud_c_esl_cond_success**.

An outcome change from **aud_c_esl_cond_success** to **aud_c_esl_cond_denial** is not logically correct because the outcome **aud_c_esl_cond_success** may have caused a NULL *ard* to be returned in this function. If the final outcome can be **aud_c_esl_cond_success**, then it should be specified in this function, or use **aud_c_esl_cond_unknown**.

This function can be called with the *outcome* parameter taking a value of zero or the union (logical OR) of selected values from the set of constants **aud_c_esl_cond_success**, **aud_c_esl_cond_failure**, **aud_c_esl_cond_denial**, and **aud_c_esl_cond_pending**. The *outcome* parameter used in the **dce_aud_commit( )** function should take one value from the same set of constants.

If **dce_aud_start( )** used a nonzero value for *outcome*, then the constant used for *outcome* in the **dce_aud_commit( )** call should have been selected in the **dce_aud_start( )** call.

Return Values

No value is returned.

Errors

aud_s_ok   The call was successful.

Status codes passed from **rpc_binding_to_string_binding( )**

Status codes passed from **rpc_string_free( )**

Status codes passed from **dce_aud_start_with_name( )**

Status codes passed from **sec_cred_get_initiator( )**

Status codes passed from **sec_cred_get_v1_pac( )**

Status codes passed from **dce_aud_start_with_pac( )**

Status codes passed from **sec_cred_get_delegate( )**

Related Information

Functions: **dce_aud_commit(3sec), dce_aud_open(3sec),
dce_aud_put_ev_info(3sec), dce_aud_start_with_name(3sec),
dce_aud_start_with_pac(3sec), dce_aud_start_with_server_binding(3sec).**

dce_aud_start_with_name

Purpose Determines whether a specified event should be audited given the client/server name and the event outcome

Used by non-RPC based client/server applications that do not use the DCE authorization model

Synopsis **#include <dce/audit.h>**

void dce_aud_start_with_name(
    unsigned32 *event,*
    unsigned_char_t **client,*
    unsigned_char_t **address,*
    unsigned32 *options,*
    unsigned32 *outcome,*
    dce_aud_rec_t **ard,*
    unsigned32 **status);*

Parameters

Input

event Specifies the event to be audited. This is a 32-bit event number. The **event** field in the audit record header will be set to this number.

client Specifies the principal name of the remote client/server.

address Specifies the address of the remote client/server. The address could be in any format of the underlying transport protocol.

options Specifies the optional header information desired (**aud_c_evt_all_info,** **aud_c_evt_group_info,** **aud_c_evt_-address_info**).

It can also be used to specify any of two options: to always log an audit record (**aud_c_evt_always_log**) or to always send an alarm message to the standard output (**aud_c_evt_always_alarm**). If any of these two options is selected, the filter is bypassed. The value of the **options** parameter is the bitwise OR of any selected combination of the following option values:

aud_c_evt_all_info
            Includes all optional information (groups and address) in the audit record header.

aud_c_evt_groups_info
Includes the groups information in the audit record header.

aud_c_evt_address_info
Includes the client address information in the audit record header.

aud_c_evt_always_log
Bypasses the filter mechanism and indicates that the event must be logged.

aud_c_evt_always_alarm
Bypasses the filter mechanism and indicates that an alarm message must be sent to the system console for the event.

outcome   The event outcome to be stored in the header. The following event outcome values are defined:

aud_c_esl_cond_success
The event was completed successfully.

aud_c_esl_cond_denial
The event failed because of access denial.

aud_c_esl_cond_failure
The event failed because of reasons other than access denial.

aud_c_esl_cond_pending
The event is in an intermediate state, and the outcome is pending, being one in a series of connected events, where the application desires to record the real outcome only after the last event.

aud_c_esl_cond_unknown
The event outcome (denial, failure, pending, or success) is still unknown. This outcome exists only between a **dce_aud_start( )** (all varieties of this routine) call and the next **dce_aud_commit( )** call. You can also use **0** to specify this outcome.

Output

ard   Returns a pointer to an audit record buffer. If the event does not need to be audited because it is not selected by the filters or if the environment variable **DCEAUDITOFF** has been set, a NULL pointer is returned. If the function is called with *outcome* set to **aud_c_esl_cond_unknown**, the function may not be able to determine whether the event should be audited. In this case, the audit record descriptor is still allocated and its address is returned to the caller. An *outcome* must be provided prior to logging the record with the **dce_aud_commit( )** function.

status   The status code returned by this routine. This status code indicates whether the routine was completed successfully or not. If the routine was not completed successfully, the reason for the failure is given.

Description

The **dce_aud_start_with_name( )** function determines if an audit record must be generated for the specified event. The decision is based on the event filters, an environment variable (**DCEAUDITOFF**), the client's identity provided in the input parameters, and the event outcome (if it is provided in the **outcome** parameter). If this event needs to be audited, the function allocates an audit record descriptor and returns a pointer to it, (that is, **ard**). If the event does not need to be audited, NULL is returned in the *ard* parameter. If either the **aud_c_evt_always_log** or **aud_c_evt_always_alarm** option is selected, an audit record descriptor will always be created and returned.

The **dce_aud_start_with_name( )** function is designed to be used by non-RPC applications that do not use the DCE authorization model (that is, DCE PAC and ACL). RPC applications must use **dce_aud_start( )**. Non-RPC applications that use the DCE authorization model must use **dce_aud_start_with_pac( )**.

This function records the input identity parameters in the newly created audit record descriptor.

Event-specific information can be added to the record by using the **dce_aud_put_ev_info( )** function, which can be called multiple times after calling any of the **dce_aud_start_*** and before calling **dce_aud_commit( )**. A completed audit record can either be appended to an audit trail file or sent to the audit daemon by calling **dce_aud_commit( )**.

This function searches for all relevant filters (for the specified subject and outcome, if these are specified), summarizes the actions for each possible event outcome, and records an outcome-action table with *ard*. If the outcome is specified when calling this function and the outcome does not require any action according to filters, then this function returns a NULL *ard*.

If the *outcome* is not specified in the **dce_aud_start_with_name()** call, **dce_aud_start_with_name()** returns a NULL *ard* if no action is required for all possible outcomes.

The caller should not change the outcome between the **dce_aud_start_with_name()** and **dce_aud_commit()** calls arbitrarily. In this case, the outcome can be made more specific, for example, from **aud_c_esl_cond_unknown** to **aud_c_esl_cond_success** or from **aud_c_esl_cond_pending** to **aud_c_esl_cond_success**.

An outcome change from **aud_c_esl_cond_success** to **aud_c_esl_cond_denial** is not logically correct because the outcome **aud_c_esl_cond_success** may have caused a NULL *ard* to be returned in this function. If the final outcome can be **aud_c_esl_cond_success**, then it should be specified in this function, or use **aud_c_esl_cond_unknown**.

This function can be called with the *outcome* parameter taking a value of zero or the union (logical OR) of selected values from the set of constants **aud_c_esl_cond_success, aud_c_esl_cond_failure, aud_c_esl_cond_denial**, and **aud_c_esl_cond_pending**. The *outcome* parameter used in the **dce_aud_commit()** function should take one value from the same set of constants.

If **dce_aud_start_with_name()** used a nonzero value for *outcome*, then the constant used for *outcome* in the **dce_aud_commit()** call should have been selected in the **dce_aud_start_with_name()** call.

Return Values

No value is returned.

Errors

aud_s_ok   The call was successful.

Status codes passed from **sec_rgy_site_open()**

Status codes passed from **sec_id_parse_name()**

Status codes passed from **dce_aud_start_with_pac()**

dce_aud_start_with_name(3sec)

Related Information

Functions: **dce_aud_commit(3sec)**, **dce_aud_open(3sec)**,
dce_aud_put_ev_info(3sec), **dce_aud_start(3sec)**,
dce_aud_start_with_pac(3sec), **dce_aud_start_with_server_binding(3sec)**.

dce_aud_start_with_pac

Purpose   Determines whether a specified event must be audited given the client's privilege attribute certificate (PAC) and the event outcome

Used by non-RPC based client/server applications that use the DCE authorization model

Synopsis   **#include <dce/audit.h>**

void dce_aud_start_with_pac(
      unsigned32 *event*,
      sec_id_pac_t *pac,
      unsigned_char_t *address,
      unsigned32 *options*,
      unsigned32 *outcome*,
      dce_aud_rec_t *ard,
      unsigned32 **status***);**

Parameters

Input

event   Specifies the event to be audited. This is a 32-bit event number. The **event** field in the audit record header will be set to this number.

pac   Specifies the client's PAC from which the client's identification information is retrieved to set the **client**, **cell**, **num_groups**, and **groups** fields in the audit record header.

address   Specifies the client's address. The address can be in any format that is native to the underlying transport protocol.

options   Specifies the optional header information desired (**aud_c_evt_all_info**, **aud_c_evt_group_info**, **aud_c_evt_-address_info**). It can also be used to specify any of two options: to always log an audit record (**aud_c_evt_always_log**) or to always send an alarm message to the standard output (**aud_c_evt_always_-alarm**). If any of these two options is selected, the filter is bypassed.

dce_aud_start_with_pac(3sec)

The value of the **options** parameter is the bitwise OR of any selected combination of the following option values:

aud_c_evt_all_info

Includes all optional information (groups and address) in the audit record header.

aud_c_evt_groups_info

Includes the groups' information in the audit record header.

aud_c_evt_address_info

Includes the client address information in the audit record header.

aud_c_evt_always_log

Bypasses the filter and indicates that the event must be logged.

aud_c_evt_always_alarm

Bypasses the filter and indicates that an alarm message must be sent to the system console for the event.

outcome   The event outcome to be stored in the header. The following event outcome values are defined:

aud_c_esl_cond_success

The event was completed successfully.

aud_c_esl_cond_denial

The event failed because of access denial.

aud_c_esl_cond_failure

The event failed because of reasons other than access denial.

aud_c_esl_cond_pending

The event is in an intermediate state, and the outcome is pending, being one in a series of connected events, where the application desires to record the real outcome only after the last event.

aud_c_esl_cond_unknown

The event outcome (denial, failure, pending, or success) is still unknown. This outcome exists only between a **dce_aud_start( )** (all varieties of this routine) call and the next **dce_aud_commit( )** call. You can also use **0** to specify this outcome.

Output

ard

Returns a pointer to an audit record buffer. If the event does not need to be audited because it is not selected by the filters, or if the environment variable **DCEAUDITOFF** has been set, a NULL pointer is returned. If the function is called with *outcome* set to **aud_c_esl_cond_unknown**, it is possible that the function cannot determine whether the event should be audited. In this case, the audit record descriptor is still allocated and its address is returned to the caller. An *outcome* must be provided prior to logging the record with the **dce_aud_commit( )** function.

status

The status code returned by this routine. This status code indicates whether the routine was completed successfully or not. If the routine was not completed successfully, the reason for the failure is given.

Description

The **dce_aud_start_with_pac( )** function determines if an audit record must be generated for the specified event. The decision is based on the event filters, an environment variable (**DCEAUDITOFF**), the client's identity provided in the **pac** parameter, and the event outcome (if it is provided in the **outcome** parameter). If this event needs to be audited, the function allocates an audit record descriptor and returns a pointer to it, (that is, **ard**). If the event does not need to be audited, NULL is returned in the *ard* parameter. If either the **aud_c_evt_always_log** or **aud_c_evt_always_alarm** option is selected, then an audit record descriptor will always be created and returned.

The **dce_aud_start_with_pac( )** function is designed to be used by non-RPC applications that use the DCE authorization model (that is, DCE PAC and ACL). RPC applications must use **dce_aud_start( )**. Non-RPC applications that do not use the DCE authorization model must use **dce_aud_start_with_name( )**.

This function obtains the client's identity information from the client's privilege attribute certificate (PAC) and records it in the newly created audit record descriptor.

Event-specific information can be added to the record by calling the **dce_aud_put_ev_info( )** function. This function can be called multiple times after calling any of the **dce_aud_start_*** functions and before calling **dce_aud_commit( )**. A completed audit record can either be appended to an audit trail file or sent to the audit daemon by calling the **dce_aud_commit( )** function.

This function searches for all relevant filters (for the specified subject and outcome, if these are specified), summarizes the actions for each possible event outcome, and records an outcome-action table with *ard*. If the outcome is specified when calling this function and the outcome does not require any action according to filters, then this function returns a NULL *ard*.

If the *outcome* is not specified in the **dce_aud_start_with_pac( )** call, **dce_aud_start_with_pac( )** returns a NULL *ard* if no action is required for all possible outcomes.

The caller should not change the outcome between the **dce_aud_start_with_pac( )** and **dce_aud_commit( )** calls arbitrarily. In this case, the outcome can be made more specific, for example, from **aud_c_esl_cond_unknown** to **aud_c_esl_cond_success** or from **aud_c_esl_cond_pending** to **aud_c_esl_cond_success**.

An outcome change from **aud_c_esl_cond_success** to **aud_c_esl_cond_denial** is not logically correct because the outcome **aud_c_esl_cond_success** may have caused a NULL *ard* to be returned in this function. If the final outcome can be **aud_c_esl_cond_success**, then it should be specified in this function, or use **aud_c_esl_cond_unknown**.

This function can be called with the *outcome* parameter taking a value of zero or the union (logical OR) of selected values from the set of constants **aud_c_esl_cond_success**, **aud_c_esl_cond_failure**, **aud_c_esl_cond_denial**, and **aud_c_esl_cond_pending**. The *outcome* parameter used in the **dce_aud_commit( )** function should take one value from the same set of constants.

If **dce_aud_start_with_pac( )** used a nonzero value for *outcome*, then the constant used for *outcome* in the **dce_aud_commit( )** call should have been selected in the **dce_aud_start_with_pac( )** call.

Return Values

No value is returned.

Errors   **aud_s_ok**   The call was successful.

Status codes passed from **sec_rgy_site_open( )**

Status codes passed from **sec_rgy_properties_get_info( )**

Status codes passed from **uuid_create_nil( )**

Related Information

Functions: **dce_aud_commit(3sec)**, **dce_aud_open(3sec)**,
dce_aud_put_ev_info(3sec), **dce_aud_start(3sec)**,
dce_aud_start_with_name(3sec), **dce_aud_start_with_server_binding(3sec)**.

dce_aud_start_with_server_binding

Purpose   Determines whether a specified event must be audited given the server binding information and the event outcome

Used by client/server applications

Synopsis   **#include <dce/audit.h>**

void dce_aud_start_with_server_binding(
        unsigned32 *event*,
        rpc_binding_handle_t *binding*,
        unsigned32 *options*,
        unsigned32 *outcome*,
        dce_aud_rec_t **ard*,
        unsigned32 **status*);

Parameters

Input

event   Specifies the event to be audited. This is a 32-bit event number. The **event** field in the audit record header will be set to this number.

binding   Specifies the server's RPC binding handle from which the server identification information is retrieved to set the client, cell, and addr fields in the audit record header. Note that when an application client issues an audit record, the server identity is represented in the *client* field of the record.

options   This parameter can be used to specify the optional header information desired (**aud_c_evt_all_info**, **aud_c_evt_group_info**, **aud_c_evt_address_info**). It can also be used to specify any of two options: to always log an audit record (**aud_c_evt_always_log**) or to always send an alarm message to the standard output (**aud_c_evt_always_alarm**). If any of these two options is selected, the filter is bypassed.

The value of the **options** parameter is the bitwise OR of any selected combination of the following option values:

aud_c_evt_address_info
                Includes the server address information in the audit record header.

aud_c_evt_always_log

Bypasses the filter and indicates that the event must be logged.

aud_c_evt_always_alarm

Bypasses the filter and indicates that an alarm message must be sent to the system console for the event.

outcome The event outcome to be stored in the header. The following event outcome values are defined:

aud_c_esl_cond_success

The event was completed successfully.

aud_c_esl_cond_denial

The event failed because of access denial.

aud_c_esl_cond_failure

The event failed because of reasons other than access denial.

aud_c_esl_cond_pending

The event is in an intermediate state, and the outcome is pending, being one in a series of connected events, where the application desires to record the real outcome only after the last event.

aud_c_esl_cond_unknown

The event outcome (denial, failure, pending, or success) is still unknown. This outcome exists only between a **dce_aud_start( )** (all varieties of this routine) call and the next **dce_aud_commit( )** call. You can also use **0** to specify this outcome.

Output

ard Returns a pointer to an audit record buffer. If the event does not need to be audited because it is not selected by the filters, or if the environment variable **DCEAUDITOFF** has been set, a NULL pointer is returned. If the function is called with **outcome** set to **aud_c_esl_cond_unknown**, it is possible that the function cannot determine whether the event should be audited. In this case, the audit record descriptor is still allocated and its address is returned to the caller. An *outcome* must be provided prior to logging the record with the **dce_aud_commit( )** function.

status   The status code returned by this routine. This status code indicates whether the routine was completed successfully or not. If the routine was not completed successfully, the reason for the failure is given.

Description

The **dce_aud_start_with_server_binding( )** function determines if an audit record must be generated for the specified event. The decision is based on the event filters, an environment variable (**DCEAUDITOFF**), the server's identity provided in the **binding** parameter, and the event outcome (if it is provided in the **outcome** parameter). If this event needs to be audited, the function allocates an audit record descriptor and returns a pointer to it (that is, **ard**). If the event does not need to be audited, NULL is returned in the *ard* parameter. If the **aud_c_evt_always_log** or **aud_c_evt_always_alarm** option is selected, an audit record descriptor will always be created and returned.

The **dce_aud_start_with_server_binding( )** function is designed to be used by RPC applications. Non-RPC applications that use the DCE authorization model must use the **dce_aud_start_with_pac( )** function. Non-RPC applications that do not use the DCE authorization model must use the **dce_aud_start_with_name( )** function.

This function obtains the server identity information from the RPC binding handle and records it in the newly created audit record descriptor.

Event-specific information can be added to the record by calling the **dce_aud_put_ev_info( )** function. The **dce_aud_put_ev_info( )** function can be called multiple times after calling any of the **dce_aud_start_*** functions and before calling **dce_aud_commit( )**. A completed audit record can either be appended to an audit trail file or sent to the audit daemon by calling **dce_aud_commit( )**.

This function searches for all relevant filters (for the specified subject and outcome, if these are specified), summarizes the actions for each possible event outcome, and records an outcome-action table with *ard*. If the outcome is specified when calling this function and the outcome does not require any action according to filters, then this function returns a NULL *ard*.

If the *outcome* is not specified in the **dce_aud_start_with_server_binding( )** call, **dce_aud_start_with_server_binding( )** returns a NULL *ard* if no action is required for all possible outcomes.

The caller should not change the outcome between the **dce_aud_start_with_-server_binding( )** and **dce_aud_commit( )** calls arbitrarily. In this case, the outcome can be made more specific, for example, from **aud_c_esl_cond_-unknown** to **aud_c_esl_cond_success** or from **aud_c_esl_cond_pending** to **aud_c_esl_cond_success**.

An outcome change from **aud_c_esl_cond_success** to **aud_c_esl_cond_denial** is not logically correct because the outcome **aud_c_esl_cond_success** may have caused a NULL *ard* to be returned in this function. If the final outcome can be **aud_c_esl_cond_success**, then it should be specified in this function, or use **aud_c_esl_cond_unknown**.

This function can be called with the *outcome* parameter taking a value of 0 (zero) or the union (logical OR) of selected values from the set of constants **aud_c_esl_cond_success**, **aud_c_esl_cond_failure**, **aud_c_esl_cond_denial**, and **aud_c_esl_cond_pending**. The *outcome* parameter used in the **dce_aud_commit( )** function should take one value from the same set of constants.

If **dce_aud_start_with_server_binding( )** used a nonzero value for *outcome*, then the constant used for *outcome* in the **dce_aud_commit( )** call should have been selected in the **dce_aud_start_with_server_binding( )** call.

Return Values

No value is returned.

Errors

aud_s_ok   The call was successful.

Status codes passed from **rpc_binding_inq_auth_info( )**

Status codes passed from **rpc_binding_to_string_binding( )**

Status codes passed from **dce_aud_start_with_name( )**

Related Information

Functions: **dce_aud_commit(3sec)**, **dce_aud_open(3sec)**, **dce_aud_put_ev_info(3sec)**, **dce_aud_start(3sec)**, **dce_aud_start_with_name(3sec)**, **dce_aud_start_with_pac(3sec)**.

dce_aud_start_with_uuid

Purpose   Determines whether a specified event should be audited given the client/server UUID and the event outcome

Used by client/server applications which already know the UUIDs of their clients and wish to avoid the overhead of the audit library acquiring them

Synopsis   **#include <dce/audit.h>**

void dce_aud_start_with_uuid(
>   **unsigned32** *event*,
>   **uuid_t** *server_uuid*,
>   **uuid_t** *client_uuid*,
>   **uuid_t** *realm_uuid*,
>   **unsigned_char_t *** *address*,
>   **unsigned32** *options*,
>   **unsigned32** *outcome*,
>   **dce_aud_rec_t *** *ard*,
>   **unsigned32 ****status*);

Parameters

Input

event   Specifies the event to be audited. This is a 32-bit event number. The **event** field in the audit record header will be set to this number.

server_uuid   Specifies the calling application's principal uuid.

client_uuid   Specifies the remote client/server's principal uuid.

realm_uuid   Specifies the remote client/server's cell uuid.

address   Specifies the remote client/server's address. The address could be in any format of the underlying transport protocol.

options   Specifies the optional header information desired (**aud_c_evt_all_info**, **aud_c_evt_group_info**, **aud_c_evt_-address_info**).

It can also be used to specify any of two options: to always log an audit record (**aud_c_evt_always_log**) or to always send an alarm message to the standard output (**aud_c_evt_always_alarm**). If any of these two options is selected, the filter is bypassed. The value of the **options** parameter is the bitwise OR of any selected combination of the following option values:

aud_c_evt_all_info
> Includes all optional information (groups and address) in the audit record header.

aud_c_evt_groups_info
> Includes the groups information in the audit record header.

aud_c_evt_address_info
> Includes the client address information in the audit record header.

aud_c_evt_always_log
> Bypasses the filter mechanism and indicates that the event must be logged.

aud_c_evt_always_alarm
> Bypasses the filter mechanism and indicates that an alarm message must be sent to the system console for the event.

outcome   The event outcome to be stored in the header. The following event outcome values are defined:

aud_c_esl_cond_unknown
> The event outcome (denial, failure, or success) is still unknown.

aud_c_esl_cond_success
> The event completed successfully.

aud_c_esl_cond_denial
> The event failed due to access denial.

aud_c_esl_cond_failure
> The event failed due to reasons other than access denial.

aud_c_esl_cond_pending
> The event outcome is pending, being one in a series of connected events, where the application desires to record the real outcome only after the last event.

Output

ard
> Returns a pointer to an audit record buffer. If the event does not need to be audited because it is not selected by the filters, or if the environment variable **DCEAUDITOFF** has been set, a NULL pointer is returned. If the function is called with *outcome* set to **aud_c_esl_cond_unknown**, it is possible that the function cannot determine whether the event should be audited. In this case, the audit record descriptor is still allocated and its address is returned to the caller. An *outcome*, different from **unknown**, must be provided prior to logging the record with the **dce_aud_commit( )** function.

status
> The status code returned by this routine. This status code indicates whether the routine completed successfully or not. If the routine did not complete successfully, the reason for the failure is given.

Description

The **dce_aud_start_with_uuid( )** function determines if an audit record must be generated for the specified event. The decision is based on the event filters, an environment variable (**DCEAUDITOFF**), the client's identity provided in the input parameters, and the event outcome (if it is provided in the **outcome** parameter). If this event needs to be audited, the function allocates an audit record descriptor and returns a pointer to it, (that is, **ard**). If the event does not need to be audited, NULL is returned in the *ard* parameter. If either the **aud_c_evt_always_log** or **aud_c_evt_always_alarm** option is selected, an audit record descriptor will always be created and returned.

The **dce_aud_start_with_uuid( )** function is designed to be used by RPC applications that know their client's identity in UUID form. Otherwise, RPC applications should use **dce_aud_start( )**. Non-RPC applications that use the DCE authorization model should use **dce_aud_start_with_pac( )**. The **dce_aud_start_with_name( )** function should be used by non-RPC applications that do not use the DCE authorization model.

This function records the input identity parameters in the newly-created audit record descriptor.

Event-specific information can be added to the record by using the **dce_aud_put_ev_info( )** function, which can be called multiple times after calling any of the **dce_aud_start_*** and before calling **dce_aud_commit( )**. A completed audit record can either be appended to an audit trail file or sent to the audit daemon by calling **dce_aud_commit( )**.

This function searches for all relevant filters (for the specified subject and outcome, if these are specified), summarizes the actions for each possible event outcome, and records an outcome-action table with *ard*. If the outcome is specified when calling this function and the outcome does not require any action according to filters, then this function returns a NULL *ard*.

If the *outcome* is not specified in the **dce_aud_start_with_uuid( )** call, **dce_aud_start_with_uuid( )** returns a NULL *ard* if no action is required for all possible outcomes.

The caller should not change the outcome between the **dce_aud_start_with_-uuid( )** and **dce_aud_commit( )** calls arbitrarily. In this case, the outcome can be made more specific, for example, from **aud_c_esl_cond_unknown** to **aud_c_esl_-cond_success** or from **aud_c_esl_cond_pending** to **aud_c_esl_cond_success**.

An outcome change from **aud_c_esl_cond_success** to **aud_c_esl_cond_denial** is not logically correct because the outcome **aud_c_esl_cond_success** may have caused a NULL *ard* to be returned in this function. If the final outcome can be **aud_c_esl_cond_success**, then it should be specified in this function, or use **aud_c_esl_cond_unknown**.

This function can be called with the *outcome* parameter taking a value of zero or the union (logical OR) of selected values from the set of constants **aud_c_esl_cond_success**, **aud_c_esl_cond_failure**, **aud_c_esl_cond_denial**, and **aud_c_esl_cond_pending**. The *outcome* parameter used in the **dce_aud_-commit( )** function should take one value from the same set of constants.

If **dce_aud_start_with_uuid( )** used a nonzero value for *outcome*, then the constant used for *outcome* in the **dce_aud_commit( )** call should have been selected in the **dce_aud_start_with_uuid( )** call.

Return Values

No value is returned.

dce_aud_start_with_uuid(3sec)

Errors   **aud_s_ok**   The call was successful.

Status codes passed from **dce_aud_start_with_pac( )**

Related Information

Functions: **dce_aud_commit(3sec)**, **dce_aud_open(3sec)**,
dce_aud_put_ev_info(3sec), **dce_aud_start(3sec)**,
dce_aud_start_with_name(3sec), **dce_aud_start_with_pac(3sec)**,
dce_aud_start_with_server_binding(3sec).

gss_accept_sec_context

Purpose   Establishes a security context between the application and a context acceptor

Synopsis   **#include <dce/gssapi.h>**

> **OM_uint32 gss_accept_sec_context (**
> **OM_uint32** **minor_status,*
> **gss_ctx_id_t** **context_handle,*
> **gss_cred_id_t** *verifier_cred_handle,*
> **gss_buffer_t** *input_token_buffer,*
> **gss_channel_bindings_t** *input_chan_bindings,*
> **gss_name_t** **src_name,*
> **gss_OID** **actual_mech_type,*
> **gss_buffer_t** *output_token,*
> **int** **ret_flags,*
> **OM_uint32** **time_rec*
> **gss_cred_id_t** **delegated_cred_handle)*

Parameters

Input

verifier_cred_handle
> Specifies the credential handle (the identity) claimed by the context acceptor. This is optional information. The credential must be either an **ACCEPT** type credential or a **BOTH** type credential. If you do not specify a credential handle and specify instead **GSS_C_NO_CREDENTIAL**, the application can accept a context under any registered identity. Use the **gssdce_register_acceptor_-identity**( ) routine to register an identity before specifying **GSS_C_NO_CREDENTIAL**.

input_token_buffer
> Specifies the token received from the context acceptor.

input_chan_bindings
> Specifies bindings supplied by the context initiator.
>
> Allows the context initiator to bind the channel identification information securely to the security context.

Input/Output

context_handle

Specifies a context handle for a new context. The first time the context initiator uses the routine, specify **GSS_C_NO_CONTEXT** to set up a specific context. In subsequent calls, use the value returned by this parameter.

Output

src_name Returns the authenticated name of the context initiator. This information is optional. If the authenticated name is not required, specify NULL.

To deallocate the authenticated name, pass it to the **gss_release_name( )** routine.

actual_mech_type

Returns the security mechanism with which the context was established. The security mechanism will be one of the following:

- **GSS_C_OID_DCE_KRBV5_DES**, for DCE security

- **GSS_C_OID_KRBV5_DES**, for Kerberos Version 5

output_token Returns a token to pass to the context acceptor. If no token is to be passed to the context acceptor, the routine sets the length field of the returned token buffer to 0 (zero).

ret_flags Returns a bitmask containing six independent flags, each of which requests that the context support a service option. The following symbolic names are provided to correspond to each flag. The symbolic names should be logically ANDed with the value of *ret_flags* to test whether the context supports the service option.

GSS_C_DELEG_FLAG

TRUE Delegated credentials are available from the *delegated_cred_handle* parameter.

FALSE No credentials were delegated.

GSS_C_MUTUAL_FLAG

TRUE   The context acceptor requested mutual authentication.

FALSE   The context acceptor did not request mutual authentication.

GSS_C_REPLAY_FLAG

TRUE   Replayed signed or sealed messages will be detected.

FALSE   Replayed messages will not be detected.

GSS_C_SEQUENCE_FLAG

TRUE   Out-of-sequence signed or sealed messages will be detected.

FALSE   Out-of-sequence signed or sealed messages will not be detected.

GSS_C_CONF_FLAG

TRUE   Confidentiality services are available by calling the **gss_seal( )** routine.

FALSE   Confidentiality services are not available. However, the application can call the **gss_seal( )** routine to provide message encapsulation, data-origin authentication, and integrity services.

GSS_C_INTEG_FLAG

TRUE   Integrity services can be invoked by calling either the **gss_sign( )** or **gss_seal( )** routine.

FALSE   Integrity services for individual messages are not available.

time_rec   Returns the number of seconds for which the context remains valid. This is optional information. If the time is not required, specify NULL.

gss_accept_sec_context(3sec)

delegated_cred_handle
Returns the credential handle for credentials received from the context initiator. The credential handle is valid only if delegated credentials are available. If the *ret_flags* parameter is true, the flag **GSS_C_DELEG_FLAG** is set, indicating that delegated credentials are available.

minor_status Returns a status code from the security mechanism.

Description

The **gss_accept_sec_context( )** routine is the second step in establishing a security context between the context initiator and a context acceptor. In the first step, the context initiator calls the **gss_init_sec_context( )** routine. The **gss_init_sec_context( )** routine generates a token for the security context and passes it to the context initiator. The context initiator sends the token to the context acceptor.

In the second step, the context acceptor accepts the call from the context initiator and calls the **gss_accept_sec_context( )** routine. The **gss_accept_sec_context( )** routine expects a value for the *input_token* parameter. The value for the *input_token* parameter is generated by the **gss_init_sec_context( )** routine and passed by the initiator to the acceptor.

The **gss_accept_sec_context( )** routine can also return a value for the *output_token* parameter. The context acceptor presents the token to the **gss_init_sec_context( )** routine. If the acceptor does not need to send a token to the initiator, **gss_accept_sec_context( )** sets the length field of the *output_token* parameter to 0 (zero).

To complete establishing the context, the context initiator can require one or more reply tokens from the context acceptor. If the application requires reply tokens, the **gss_accept_sec_context( )** routine returns a status value containing **GSS_S_CONTINUE_NEEDED**. The application calls the routine again when the reply token is received from the context acceptor. The application passes the token to the **gss_accept_sec_context( )** routine via the *output_token* parameters.

The **gss_accept_sec_context( )** routine must find a key to decrypt the token. The token contains the unencrypted principal name of the context acceptor. The acceptor's principal name identifies the key that the context initiator used to encrypt the rest of the token. The **gss_accept_sec_context( )** routine matches the principal name with the key in the following way:

- If you specify a credential, the credential and the name in the token must match. The acceptor's principal name (contained in the token) has been registered by a call to the **gssdec_register_acceptor_identity( )** routine. The **gss_accept_sec_context( )** routine looks in the registered key table.

- If you specify **GSS_C_NO_CRED** and the principal name in the token is registered, the **gss_accept_sec_context( )** routine, using either the **rpc_server_register_auth_info( )** routine or the **gssdcc_register_- acceptor_identity( )** routine, looks in the table specified when you registered the token name.

- If you specify **GSS_C_NO_CRED** and the principal name in the token is not registered, the **gss_accept_sec_context( )** routine fails and returns the status **GSS_S_FAILURE** because the generic security service application programming interface (GSSAPI) does not know where to find the key.

The following table summarizes how the **gss_accept_sec_context( )** routine determines the key for the credential:

You specify...	Is the principal's name registered?	Then the routine...
A credential	Yes	Looks in the key table specified in **gssdce_- register_acceptor_- identity( )** or the default key table.
GSS_C_NO_CRED	Yes	Looks in the key table specified in **gssdce_- register_acceptor_- identity( )**.
	No	Fails because the principal is not registered. It returns the status code **GSS_S_FAILURE**.

The values returned using the *src_name*, *ret_flags*, *time_rec*, and *delegated_cred_handle* parameters are not defined unless the routine returns the status **GSS_S_COMPLETE**.

Errors **GSS_S_COMPLETE**

The routine was completed successfully.

GSS_S_BAD_BINDINGS

The *input_token* parameter contains different channel bindings from those specified with the *input_chan_bindings* parameter.

GSS_S_BAD_SIG

The *input_token* parameter contains an invalid signature.

GSS_S_CONTINUE_NEEDED
> To complete the context, the **gss_accept_sec_context( )** routine must be called again with a token required from the context acceptor.

GSS_S_CREDENTIALS_EXPIRED
> The referenced credentials have expired.

GSS_S_DEFECTIVE_CREDENTIAL
> Consistency checks performed on the credential failed.

GSS_S_DEFECTIVE_TOKEN
> Consistency checks performed on the *input_token* parameter failed.

GSS_S_DUPLICATE_TOKEN
> The *input_token* parameter was already processed. This is a fatal error that occurs during context establishment.

GSS_S_FAILURE
> The routine failed. See the *minor_status* parameter return value for more information.

GSS_S_NO_CONTEXT
> The supplied context handle did not refer to a valid context.

GSS_S_NO_CRED
> Indicates either the supplied credentials were not valid for context acceptance or the credential handle did not reference any credentials.

GSS_S_OLD_TOKEN
> The *input_token* parameter was too old. This is a fatal error that occurs during context establishment.

Related Information

Functions: **gss_acquire_cred(3sec), gss_delete_sec_context(3sec), gss_init_sec_context(3sec), gssdce_register_acceptor_identity(3sec)**.

gss_acquire_cred

Purpose   Allows an application to acquire a handle for an existing named credential

Synopsis   **#include <dce/gssapi.h>**

> **OM_uint32 gss_acquire_cred (**
> **OM_uint32** **minor_status,*
> **gss_name_t** *desired_name,*
> **OM_uint32** *time_req,*
> **gss_OID_set** *desired_mechs,*
> **int** *cred_usage,*
> **gss_cred_id_t** **output_cred_handle,*
> **gss_OID_set** **actual_mechs,*
> **OM_int32** **time_rec)*

Parameters

Input

desired_name Specifies the principal name to use for the credential.

time_req   Specifies the number of seconds that credentials remain valid.

desired_mechs
> Specifies the OID set for the security mechanism to use with the credential, as follows:

To use...	Specify...
DCE security	**GSS_C_NULL_OID_SET**
Kerberos	**GSS_C_OID_KRBV5_DES**
Both DCE security and Kerberos	**GSS_C_OID_DCE_KRBV5_DES** and **GSS_C_OID_KRBV5_DES**

> To help ensure portability of your application, request the default security mechanism by specifying **GSS_C_NULL_OID_SET**.

cred_usage   Specify one of the following:

> **GSS_C_BOTH**
> > Specifies credentials that the context initiator can use to either initiate or accept security contexts.

GSS_C_ACCEPT
Specifies credentials that the context initiator can use only to accept security contexts.

Output

output_cred_handle
Returns the handle for the return credential.

actual_mechs Returns a set of mechanisms for which the credential is valid. This information is optional. If you do not want a set of mechanisms returned, specify NULL.

time_rec Returns the actual number of seconds for which the return credential remains valid. This information is optional. If the actual number of seconds is not required, specify NULL.

minor_status Returns a status code from the security mechanism.

Description

The **gss_acquire_cred( )** routine allows an application to obtain a handle for either an **ACCEPT** or **BOTH** credential. The application then passes the credential handle to either the **gss_init_sec_context( )** or **gss_accept_sec_context( )** routine.

Credential handles created by the **gss_acquire_cred( )** routine contain a principal name. If the principal name is unregistered, the **gss_acquire_cred( )** routine automatically registers the principal in the default key table. You can change the principal's key table by calling the **gssdce_register_acceptor_identify( )** routine.

To create an **INITIATE** credential, you must use the **gssdce_login_context_to_-cred( )** routine.

Errors

GSS_S_COMPLETE
The routine was completed successfully.

GSS_S_BAD_MECH
The requested security mechanism is unsupported or unavailable.

GSS_S_BAD_NAMETYPE
The name passed by the *desired_name* parameter is unsupported.

GSS_S_BAD_NAME

An invalid name was passed by the *desired_name* parameter.

GSS_S_FAILURE

The routine failed. See the *minor_status* parameter return value for more information.

Related Information

Functions: **gss_init_sec_context(3sec), gssdce_accept_sec_context(3sec), gssdce_create_empty_oid_set(3sec), gssdce_login_context_to_credential(3sec), gssdce_register_acceptor_identity(3sec).**

gss_compare_name

Purpose   Allows an application to compare two internal names to determine whether they refer to the same object

Synopsis   **#include <dce/gssapi.h>**

        OM_uint32 gss_compare_name (
        OM_uint32 **minor_status,*
        gss_name_t *name1,*
        gss_name_t *name2,*
        int **name_equal)*

Parameters

Input

    name1   Specifies the first internal name.

    name2   Specifies the second internal name.

Output

    name_equal   Returns one of the following values:

        TRUE   The names refer to the same object.

        FALSE   The names are not known to refer to the same object.

    minor_status   Returns a status code from the security mechanism.

Description

The **gss_compare_name( )** routine lets an application compare two internal names to determine whether they refer to the same object.

Errors

GSS_S_COMPLETE
    The routine was completed successfully.

GSS_S_BAD_NAMETYPE
    The name passed by the *name1* or *name2* parameter is unsupported.

GSS_S_BAD_NAME
    An invalid name was passed by the *name1* or *name2* parameter.

GSS_S_FAILURE

The routine failed. Check the *minor_status* parameter for details.

Related Information

Functions: **gss_display_name(3sec)**, **gss_import_name(3sec)**, **gss_release_name(3sec)**.

gss_context_time

Purpose   Checks the number of seconds for which the context will remain valid

Synopsis   #include <dce/gssapi.h>

> **OM_uint32 gss_context_time (**
> **OM_uint32** **minor_status,*
> **gss_ctx_id_t** *context_handle,*
> **OM_int32** **time_rec)*

Parameters

Input

context_handle
> Specifies the context to be checked.

Output

time_rec   Returns the number of seconds that the context will remain valid. Returns a 0 (zero) if the context has already expired.

minor_status Returns a status code from the security mechanism.

Description

The **gss_context_time( )** routine checks the number of seconds for which the context will remain valid.

Errors

GSS_S_COMPLETE
> The routine was completed successfully.

GSS_S_CONTEXT_EXPIRED
> The context has already expired.

GSS_S_CREDENTIALS_EXPIRED
> The context is recognized but the associated credentials have expired.

GSS_S_NO_CONTEXT

The context identified in the *context_handle* parameter was not valid.

GSS_S_FAILURE

The routine failed. See the *minor_status* parameter return value for more information.

gss_delete_sec_context

Purpose   Deletes a security context

Synopsis   **#include <dce/gssapi.h>**

> **OM_uint32 gss_delete_sec_context (**
> **OM_uint32** **minor_status,*
> **gss_ctx_id_t** **context_handle,*
> **gss_buffer_t** *output_token_buffer)*

Parameters

Output

context_handle
> Returns the context handle for the context to delete.

output_token_buffer
> Returns a token to tell the application to delete the context.

minor_status   Returns a status code from the security mechanism.

Description

The **gss_delete_sec_context( )** routine deletes a security context. It also deletes the local data structures associated with the security context. When it deletes the context, the routine can generate a token. The application passes the token to the context acceptor. The context acceptor then passes the token to the **gss_process_context_token( )** routine, telling it to delete the context and all associated local data structures.

When the context is deleted, the applications cannot use the *context_handle* parameter for additional security services.

Errors

GSS_S_COMPLETE
> The routine was completed successfully.

GSS_S_FAILURE
> The routine failed. See the *minor_status* parameter return value for more information.

GSS_S_NO_CONTEXT
> The supplied context handle did not refer to a valid context.

Related Information

Functions: **gss_accept_sec_context(3sec)**, **gss_init_sec_context(3sec)**, **gss_process_context_token(3sec)**.

gss_display_name

Purpose   Provides to an application the textual representation of an opaque internal name

Synopsis   **#include <dce/gssapi.h>**

> **OM_uint32 gss_display_name (**
> **OM_uint32** **minor_status,*
> **gss_name_t** *input_name,*
> **gss_buffer_t** *output_name_buffer,*
> **gss_OID** **output_name_type)*

Parameters

Input

> *input_name*   Specifies the name to convert to text.

Output

> *output_name_buffer*
> Returns the name as a character string.

> *output_name_type*
> Returns the type of name to display as a pointer to static storage. The application should treat this as read-only.

> *minor_status* Returns a status code from the security mechanism.

Description

The **gss_display_name( )** routine provides an application with the text form of an opaque internal name. The application can use the text to display the name but not to print it.

Errors   **GSS_S_COMPLETE**
The routine was completed successfully.

GSS_S_BAD_NAMETYPE
The name passed by the *input_name* parameter is recognized.

GSS_S_BAD_NAME

An invalid name was passed by the *input_name* parameter.

GSS S_FAILURE

The routine failed. Check the *minor_status* parameter for details.

Related Information

Functions: **gss_compare_name(3sec), gss_import_name(3sec),
gss_release_name(3sec)**.

gss_display_status

Purpose   Provides an application with the textual representation of a GSSAPI status code that can be displayed to a user or used for logging

Synopsis   **#include <dce/gssapi.h>**

> **OM_uint32 gss_display_status (**
> **OM_uint32** **minor_status,*
> **int** *status_value,*
> **int** *status_type,*
> **gss_OID** *mech_type,*
> **int** **message_context,*
> **gss_buffer_t** *status_string)*

Parameters

Input

status_value   Specifies the status value to convert.

status_type   Specifies one of the following status types:

- **GSS_C_GSS_CODE**

  Major status; a GSS status code

- **GSS_C_MECH_CODE**

  Minor status; either DCE security or Kerberos status code

mech_type   Specifies the security mechanism. To use DCE security, specify either of the following:

- **GSS_C_OID_DCE_KRBV5_DES**

- **GSS_C_NULL_OID_SET**

To use Kerberos, specify **GSS_C_OID_KRBV5_DES**.

Input/Output

message_context
Indicates whether the status code has multiple messages to read.

The first time an application calls the routine, you initialize the parameter to 0 (zero). The routine returns the first message. If there are more messages, the routine sets the parameter to a nonzero value. The application calls the routine repeatedly to get the next message, until the *message_context* parameter is zero again.

Output

status_string   Returns the status value as a text message.

minor_status   Returns a status code from the security mechanism.

Description

The **gss_display_status( )** routine provides the context initiator with a textual representation of a status code so that the application can display the message to a user or log the message. Because some status values can indicate more than one error, the routine enables the calling application to process status codes with multiple messages.

The *message_context* parameter indicates which error message the application should extract from the *status_value* parameter. The first time an application calls the routine, it should initialize the *message_context* parameter to 0 (zero) and return the first message. If there are additional messages to read, the **gss_display_status( )** routine returns a nonzero value. The application can call **gss_display_status( )** repeatedly to generate a single text string for each call.

Errors

GSS_S_COMPLETE
The routine was completed successfully.

GSS_S_BAD_MECH
The translation requires a mechanism that is unsupported or unavailable.

GSS_S_BAD_STATUS
Indicates either the status value was not recognized or the status type was something other than **GSS_C_GSS_CODE** or **GSS_C_MECH_CODE**.

GSS_S_FAILURE
The routine failed. Check the *minor_status* for details.

gss_import_name

Purpose   Converts a printable name to an internal form

Synopsis   **#include <dce/gssapi.h>**

    OM_uint32 gss_import_name (
    OM_uint32 **minor_status,*
    gss_buffer_t *input_buffer_name,*
    gss_OID *input_name_type,*
    gss_name_t **output_name)*

Parameters

Input

input_name_buffer
    Specifies the buffer containing the printable name to convert.

input_name_type
    Specifies the object identifier for the type of printable name. Specify **GSS_C_NULL_OID** to use the DCE name.

    You can explicitly request the DCE name by using **GSS_C_OID_DCE_NAME**. To help ensure portability of your application, use the default, **GSS_C_NULL_OID**.

Output

output_name   Returns the name in an internal form.

minor_status   Returns a status code from the security mechanism.

Description

The **gss_import_name( )** routine converts a printable name to an internal form.

Errors   **GSS_S_COMPLETE**

The routine was completed successfully.

GSS_S_BAD_NAMETYPE

The name passed by the *input_name* parameter is not recognized.

GSS_S_BAD_NAME

The routine could not interpret the *input_name* parameter as a name of the type specified.

GSS_S_FAILURE

Check the minor status for details.

Related Information

Functions: **gss_compare_name(3sec)**, **gss_display_name(3sec)**, **gss_release_name(3sec)**.

gss_indicate_mechs

Purpose   Allows an application to determine which underlying security mechanisms are available

Synopsis   **#include <dce/gssapi.h>**

> **OM_uint32 gss_indicate_mechs (**
> **OM_uint32 *_minor_status_,**
> **gss_OID_set *_mech_set_)**

Parameters

Output

> _mech_set_   Returns the set of supported security mechanisms. The value of **gss_OID_set** is a pointer to a static storage and should be treated as read-only by the context initiator.

> _minor_status_   Returns a status code from the security mechanism.

Description

> The **gss_indicate_mechs( )** routine enables an application to determine which underlying security mechanisms are available. These are DCE security and Kerberos Version 5.

> You can use the **gssdce_test_oid_set_member( )** routine to check whether a specific security mechanism is available.

Errors

GSS_S_COMPLETE
> The routine was completed successfully.

GSS_S_FAILURE
> The routine failed. Check the _minor_status_ parameter for details.

Related Information

> Functions: **gssdce_test_oid_set_member(3sec)**.

gss_init_sec_context

Purpose   Establishes a security context between the context initiator and a context acceptor

Synopsis   **#include <dce/gssapi.h>**

> **OM_uint32 gss_init_sec_context (**
> **OM_uint32** **minor_status,*
> **gss_cred_id_t** *claimant_cred_handle,*
> **gss_ctx_id_t** **context_handle*
> **gss_name_t** *target_name,*
> **gss_OID** *mech_type,*
> **int** *req_flags,*
> **int** *time_req,*
> **gss_channel_bindings_t** *input_channel_bindings,*
> **gss_buffer_t** *input_token,*
> **gss_OID** **actual_mech_types,*
> **gss_buffer_t** *output_token,*
> **nt** **ret_flags,*
> **OM_int32** **time_rec)*

Parameters

Input

claimant_cred_handle
> Specifies an optional handle for the credential. To use the default credential, supply **GSS_C_NO_CREDENTIAL**. The credential handle created refers to the DCE default login context. The credential must be either an **INITIATE** or **BOTH** type credential.

target_name   Specifies the name of the context acceptor.

mech_type   Specifies the security mechanism. To use DCE security, specify either of the following:

- **GSS_C_OID_DCE_KRBV5_DES**

- **GSS_C_NULL_OID**

To use Kerberos, specify **GSS_C_OID_KRBV5_DES**.

req_flags   Specifies four independent flags, each of which requests that the context support a service option. The following symbolic names are provided to correspond to each flag. The symbolic names should be logically ORed to form a bit-mask value.

GSS_C_DELEG_FLAG

TRUE   Credentials were delegated to the context acceptor.

FALSE   No credentials were delegated.

GSS_C_MUTUAL_FLAG

TRUE   The context acceptor has been asked to authenticate itself.

FALSE   The context initiator has not been asked to authenticates itself.

GSS_C_REPLAY_FLAG

TRUE   Replayed signed or sealed messages will be detected.

FALSE   Replayed messages will not be detected.

GSS_C_SEQUENCE_FLAG

TRUE   Out-of-sequence signed or sealed messages will be detected.

FALSE   Out-of-sequence signed or sealed messages will not be detected.

time_req   Specifies the desired number of seconds for which the context should remain valid. To specify the default validity period, use 0 (zero).

input_chan_bindings
        Specifies the bindings set by the context initiator. Allows the context initiator to bind the channel identification information securely to the security context.

input_token   Specifies the token received from the context acceptor.

        The first time the application calls the routine, you specify **GSS_NO_BUFFER**. Subsequent calls require a token from the context acceptor.

Input/Output

context_handle

Specifies the context handle for the new context.

The first time the application calls the routine, you specify **GSS_C_NO_CONTEXT**. Subsequent calls use the value returned by the first call.

Output

actual_mech_type

Returns one of the following values indicating the security mechanism:

- **GSS_C_OID_DCE_KRBV5_DES** for DCE security

- **GSS_C_OID_KRBV5_DES** for Kerberos

output_token   Returns the token to send to the context acceptor.

If the length field of the returned buffer is 0 (zero), no token is sent.

ret_flags   Returns six independent flags, each of which indicates that the context supports a service option. The following symbolic names are provided to correspond to each flag:

GSS_C_DELEG_FLAG

TRUE	Credentials were delegated to the context acceptor.
FALSE	No credentials were delegated.

GSS_C_MUTUAL_FLAG

TRUE	The context acceptor has been asked to authenticate itself.
FALSE	The context acceptor has not been asked to authenticate itself.

GSS_C_REPLAY_FLAG

TRUE	Replayed signed or sealed messages will be detected.
FALSE	Replayed messages will not be detected.

GSS_C_SEQUENCE_FLAG

TRUE	Out-of-sequence signed or sealed messages will be detected.
FALSE	Out-of-sequence signed or sealed messages will not be detected.

GSS_C_CONF_FLAG

TRUE	Confidentiality service can be invoked by calling the **gss_seal( )** routine.
FALSE	No confidentiality service is available. (Confidentiality can be provided using the **gss_seal( )** routine, which provides only message encapsulation, data-origin authentication, and integrity services.)

GSS_C_INTEG_FLAG

TRUE	Integrity service can be invoked by calling either the **gss_sign( )** or **gss_seal( )** routine.
FALSE	Integrity service for individual messages is unavailable.

time_rec   Returns the number of seconds for which the context will be valid. If the mechanism does not support credential expiration, the routine returns the value **GSS_C_INDEFINITE**. If the credential expiration time is not required, specify NULL.

minor_status   Returns a status code from the security mechanism.

Description

The **gss_init_sec_context( )** routine is the first step in the establishment of a security context between the context initiator and the context acceptor. To ensure the portability of the application, use its default credential by supplying **GSS_C_NO_CREDENTIAL** to the *claimant_cred_handle* parameter. Specify an explicit credential when the application needs an additional credential; for example, to use delegation.

The first time the application calls the **gss_init_sec_context( )** routine, specify the *input_token* parameter as **GSS_NO_BUFFER**. Calls to the routine can return an *output_token* for transfer to the context acceptor. The context acceptor presents the token to the **gss_accept_sec_context( )** routine.

If the context initiator does not require a token, **gss_init_sec_context( )** sets the length field of the *output_token* argument to 0 (zero).

To complete establishing the context, the calling application can require one or more reply tokens from the context acceptor. If the application requires reply tokens, the **gss_init_sec_context( )** routine returns a status value of **GSS_S_CONTINUE_NEEDED**. The application calls the routine again when the reply token is received from the context acceptor and passes the token to the **gss_init_sec_context( )** routine via the *input_token* parameter.

The values returned by the *ret_flags* and *time_rec* parameters are not defined unless the routine returns the status **GSS_S_COMPLETE**.

Errors

GSS_S_COMPLETE
:   The routine was completed successfully.

GSS_S_BAD_BINDINGS
:   The *input_token* parameter contains different channel bindings from those specified with the *input_chan_bindings* parameter.

GSS_S_BAD_NAMETYPE
:   The *target_name* parameter contains an invalid or unsupported name type.

GSS_S_BAD_NAME
:   The *target_name* parameter was incorrectly formed.

GSS_S_BAD_SIG
:   Indicates either that the *input_token* parameter contains an invalid signature or that the *input_token* parameter contains a signature that could not be verified.

GSS_S_CONTINUE_NEEDED
:   To complete the context, the **gss_init_sec_context( )** routine must be called again with a token required from the context acceptor.

GSS_S_CREDENTIALS_EXPIRED
:   The referenced credentials have expired.

GSS_S_DEFECTIVE_CREDENTIAL
:   Consistency checks performed on the credential failed.

GSS_S_DEFECTIVE_TOKEN
> Consistency checks performed on the *input_token* parameter failed.

GSS_S_DUPLICATE_TOKEN
> The *input_token* parameter was already processed. This is a fatal error that occurs during context establishment.

GSS_S_FAILURE
> The routine failed. See the *minor_status* parameter return value for more information.

GSS_S_NO_CONTEXT
> The supplied context handle did not refer to a valid context.

GSS_S_OLD_TOKEN
> The *input_token* parameter was too old. This is a fatal error that occurs during context establishment.

Related Information

Functions: **gss_accept_sec_context(3sec)**, **gss_delete_sec_context(3sec)**.

gss_inquire_cred

Purpose   Provides the calling application information about a credential

Synopsis   **#include <dce/gssapi.h>**

> **OM_uint32 gss_inquire_cred (**
> **OM_uint32** **minor_status,*
> **gss_cred_id_t** *cred_handle,*
> **gss_name_t** **name,*
> **OM_uint32** **lifetime,*
> **int** **cred_usage,*
> **gss_OID_set** **mechs)*

Parameters

Input

> *cred_handle*   Specifies a handle for the target credential. To get information about the default credential, specify **GSS_C_NO_CREDENTIAL**.

Output

> *name*   Returns the principal name asserted by the credential. If the principal name is not required, specify NULL.

> *lifetime*   Returns the number of seconds for which the credential will remain valid.
>
> If the credential expired, the parameter returns a 0 (zero). If there is no credential expiration, the parameter returns the value **GSS_C_INDEFINITE**. If an expiration time is not required, specify NULL.

> *cred_usage*   Returns one of the following values describing how the application can use the credential:
>
> - **GSS_C_INITIATE**
>
> - **GSS_C_ACCEPT**
>
> - **GSS_C_BOTH**
>
> If no usage information is required, specify NULL.

gss_inquire_cred(3sec)

    mechs   Returns a set of security mechanisms supported by the credential, as follows:

- **GSS_C_OID_DCE_KRBV5_DES** for DCE security

- **GSS_C_OID_KRBV5_DES** for Kerberos

minor_status Returns a status code from the security mechanism.

Description

The **gss_inquire_cred( )** routine provides information about a credential to the calling application. The calling application must first have called the **gss_acquire_cred( )** routine for a handle for the credential.

Errors

GSS_S_COMPLETE
> The routine was completed successfully.

GSS_S_CREDENTIALS_EXPIRED
> The credentials expired. If the *lifetime* parameter was passed as NULL, it is set to 0 (zero).

GSS_S_DEFECTIVE_CREDENTIAL
> The credentials were invalid.

GSS_S_FAILURE
> The routine failed. Check the *minor_status* parameter for details.

GSS_S_NO_CRED
> The routine could not access the credentials.

Related Information

Functions: **gss_acquire_cred(3sec)**.

gss_process_context_token

Purpose   Passes a context to the security service

Synopsis   **#include <dce/gssapi.h>**

    OM_uint32 gss_process_context_token (
    OM_uint32 **minor_status,*
    gss_ctx_id_t **context_handle,*
    gss_buffer_t *input_token_buffer)*

Parameters

Input

context_handle

    Specifies the context handle on which the security service processes the token.

input_token_buffer

    Specifies an opaque pointer to the first byte of the token to be processed.

Output

minor_status   Returns a status code from the security mechanism.

Description

The **gss_process_context_token( )** routine passes tokens generated by the **gss_delete_security_context( )** routine to the security service.

Usually, tokens are associated with either the context establishment or with per-message security services. If the tokens are associated with the context establishment, they are passed to the **gss_init_sec_context( )** or **gss_accept_sec_context( )** routine. If the tokens are associated with the per-message security service, they are passed to the **gss_verify( )** or **gss_unseal( )** routine. Tokens generated by the **gss_delete_security_context( )** routine are passed by the **gss_process_context_token( )** routine to the security service for processing.

gss_process_context_token(3sec)

Errors   **GSS_S_COMPLETE**
The routine was completed successfully.

GSS_S_DEFECTIVE_TOKEN
Consistency checks performed on the *input_token* parameter failed.

GSS_S_FAILURE
The routine failed. See the *minor_status* parameter return value for more information.

GSS_S_NO_CONTEXT
The supplied context handle did not refer to a valid context.

Related Information
Functions: **gss_delete_security_context(3sec)**.

gss_release_buffer

Purpose   Frees storage associated with a buffer

Synopsis   **#include <dce/gssapi.h>**

> **OM_uint32 gss_release_buffer (**
> **OM_uint32 ***minor_status*,
> **gss_buffer_t** *buffer*)

Parameters

Input

> *buffer*   The buffer to delete.

Output

> *minor_status* Returns a status code from the security mechanism.

Description

> The **gss_release_buffer()** routine deletes the buffer by freeing the storage associated with it.

Errors

GSS_S_COMPLETE
> The routine was completed successfully.

GSS_S_FAILURE
> The routine failed. See the *minor_status* parameter for details.

gss_release_cred

Purpose   Marks a credential for deletion

Synopsis   **#include <dce/gssapi.h>**

> **OM_uint32 gss_release_cred (**
> **OM_uint32** **minor_status,*
> **gss_cred_id_t** **cred_handle,*

Parameters

Input

> *cred_handle*   Specifies the buffer containing the opaque credential handle. This information is optional. To release the default credential, specify **GSS_C_NO_CREDENTIAL**.

Output

> *minor_status*   Returns a status code from the security mechanism.

Description

> The **gss_release_cred( )** routine informs the GSSAPI that a credential is no longer required and marks it for deletion.

Errors   **GSS_S_COMPLETE**
> The routine was completed successfully.

> **GSS_S_FAILURE**
> The routine failed. Check the *minor_status* parameter for details.

> **GSS_S_NO_CRED**
> The credentials could not be accessed.

gss_release_name

Purpose   Frees storage associated with an internal name that was allocated by a GSSAPI routine.

Synopsis   **#include <dce/gssapi.h>**

> **OM_uint32 gss_release_name (**
> **OM_uint32** **minor_status,*
> **gss_name_t** **name)*

Parameters

Input

> *name*   The name to delete.

Output

> *minor_status* Returns a status code from the security mechanism.

Description

The **gss_release_name( )** routine deletes the internal name by freeing the storage associated with that internal name.

Errors

GSS_S_COMPLETE

> The routine was completed successfully.

GSS_S_BAD_NAME

> The *name* parameter did not contain a valid name.

GSS_S_FAILURE

> The routine failed. Check the *minor_status* parameter for details.

Related Information

Functions: **gss_compare_name(3sec)**, **gss_display_name(3sec)**, **gss_import_name(3sec)**.

gss_release_oid_set

Purpose   Frees storage associated with a **gss_OID_set** object

Synopsis   **#include <dce/gssapi.h>**

> **OM_uint32 gss_release_oid_set (**
> **OM_uint32** **minor_status,*
> **gss_OID_set** *set)*

Parameters

Input

> *set*   The OID set to delete.

Output

> *minor_status* Returns a status code from the security mechanism.

Description

The **gss_release_oid_set( )** routine frees storage that is associated with the **gss_OID_set** parameter and was allocated by a GSSAPI routine.

Errors

GSS_S_COMPLETE
> The routine was completed successfully.

GSS_S_FAILURE
> The routine failed. Check the *minor_status* parameter for details.

gss_seal

Purpose   Cryptographically signs and optionally encrypts a message

Synopsis   **#include <dce/gssapi.h>**

> **OM_uint32 gss_seal (**
> **OM_uint32** **minor_status,*
> **gss_ctx_id_t** *context_handle,*
> **int** *conf_req_flag,*
> **int** *qop_req,*
> **gss_buffer_t** *input_message_buffer,*
> **int** **conf_state,*
> **gss_buffer_t** *output_message_buffer)*

Parameters

Input

context_handle
> Specifies the context on which the message is sent.

conf_req_flag Specifies the requested level of confidentiality and integrity services, as follows:

> | | |
> |---|---|
> | TRUE | Both confidentiality and integrity services are requested. |
> | FALSE | Only integrity services are requested. |

qop_req   Specifies the cryptographic algorithm, or quality of protection. Specify **GSS_C_QOP_DEFAULT**. The DCE GSSAPI supports only one quality of protection.

input_message_buffer
> Specifies the message to seal.

Output

conf_state   Returns the requested level of confidentiality and integrity services, as follows:

> | | |
> |---|---|
> | TRUE | Confidentiality, data origin, authentification, and integrity services have been applied. |

FALSE   Only integrity and data origin services have been
             applied.

output_message_buffer
             Returns the buffer to receive the sealed message.

minor_status Returns a status code from the security mechanism.

Description

The **gss_seal( )** routine cryptographically signs and optionally encrypts a message.
The *output_message* parameter contains both the signature and the message.

Although the *qop_req* parameter enables a choice between several qualities of
protection, DCE GSSAPI supports only one quality of protection. If you specify an
unsupported   protection,   the   **gss_seal( )**   routine   returns   a   status   of
GSS_S_FAILURE.

Errors

GSS_S_COMPLETE
             The routine was completed successfully.

GSS_S_CONTEXT_EXPIRED
             The context has already expired.

GSS_S_CREDENTIALS_EXPIRED
             The context is recognized but the associated credentials have
             expired.

GSS_S_FAILURE
             The routine failed. Check the *minor_status* parameter for details.

GSS_S_NO_CONTEXT
             The context identified in the *context_handle* parameter was not
             valid.

gss_sign

Purpose   Generates a cryptographic signature for a message

Synopsis   **#include <dce/gssapi.h>**

OM_uint32 gss_sign (
OM_uint32 *_minor_status_,
gss_ctx_id_t _context_handle_,
int _qop_req_,
gss_buffer_t _message_buffer_,
gss_buffer_t _msg_token_)

Parameters

Input

_context_handle_
Specifies the context on which the message is sent.

_qop_req_   Specifies the cryptographic algorithm, or quality of protection.
Specify **GSS_C_QOP_DEFAULT**. DCE GSSAPI supports only
one quality of protection.

_message_buffer_
Specifies the message to send.

Output

_msg_token_   Returns the buffer to receive the signature token to transfer to the
context acceptor.

_minor_status_   Returns a status code from the security mechanism.

Description

The **gss_sign( )** routine generates an encrypted signature for a message. It places
the signature in a token for transfer to the context acceptor.

Although the _qop_req_ parameter enables a choice between several qualities of
protection, DCE GSSAPI supports only one quality of protection. If you specify an
unsupported protection, the **gss_sign( )** routine returns a status of
GSS_S_FAILURE.

Errors　　**GSS_S_COMPLETE**
　　　　　　　　The routine was completed successfully.

　　　　　　GSS_S_CONTEXT_EXPIRED
　　　　　　　　The context has already expired.

　　　　　　GSS_S_CREDENTIALS_EXPIRED
　　　　　　　　The context is recognized but the associated credentials have
　　　　　　　　expired.

　　　　　　GSS_S_FAILURE
　　　　　　　　The routine failed. Check the *minor_status* parameter for details.

　　　　　　GSS_S_NO_CONTEXT
　　　　　　　　The context identified in the *context_handle* parameter was not
　　　　　　　　valid.

gss_unseal

Purpose   Converts a sealed message into a usable form and verifies the embedded signature

Synopsis   **#include <dce/gssapi.h>**

> **OM_uint32 gss_unseal (**
> **OM_uint32** **minor_status,*
> **gss_ctx_id_t** *context_handle,*
> **gss_buffer_t** *input_message_buffer,*
> **gss_buffer_t** *output_message_buffer,*
> **int** **conf_state,*
> **int** **qop_state)*

Parameters

Input

> *context_handle*
> > Specifies the context on which the message arrived.
>
> *input_message_buffer*
> > Specifies the sealed message.
>
> *output_message_buffer*
> > Specifies the buffer to receive the unsealed message.

Output

> *conf_state*   Returns the requested level of confidentiality and integrity services, as follows:
>
> > TRUE   Both confidentiality and integrity services are requested.
> >
> > FALSE   Only integrity services are requested.
>
> *qop_state*   Returns the cryptographic algorithm, or quality of protection.
>
> *minor_status*   Returns a status code from the security mechanism.

Description

The **gss_unseal( )** routine converts a sealed message to a usable form and verifies the embedded signature. The *conf_state* parameter indicates whether the message was encrypted. The *qop_state* parameter indicates the quality of protection.

Errors

GSS_S_COMPLETE

The routine was completed successfully.

GSS_S_BAD_SIG

The signature was incorrect.

GSS_S_CONTEXT_EXPIRED

The context has already expired.

GSS_S_CREDENTIALS_EXPIRED

The context is recognized but the associated credentials have expired.

GSS_S_DEFECTIVE_TOKEN

The token failed consistency checks.

GSS_S_DUPLICATE_TOKEN

The token was valid and contained the correct signature but it had already been processed.

GSS_S_FAILURE

The routine failed. The context specified in the *context_handle* parameter was not valid.

GSS_S_NO_CONTEXT

The context identified in the *context_handle* parameter was not valid.

GSS_S_OLD_TOKEN

The token was valid and contained the correct signature but it is too old.

GSS_S_UNSEQ_TOKEN

The token was valid and contained the correct signature but it has been verified out of sequence. An earlier token signed or sealed by the remote application has not been processed locally.

Related Information

Functions: **gss_seal(3sec)**, **gss_sign(3sec)**.

gss_verify

Purpose   Checks that the cryptographic signature fits the supplied message

Synopsis   **#include <dce/gssapi.h>**

> **OM_uint32 gss_verify(**
> **OM_uint32** **minor_status,*
> **gss_ctx_id_t** *context_handle,*
> **gss_buffer_t** *message_buffer,*
> **gss_buffer_t** *token_buffer)*
> **int** *qop_state)*

Parameters

Input

context_handle
> Specifies the context on which the message arrived.

message_buffer
> Specifies the message to be verified.

token_buffer   Specifies the signature token to be associated with the message.

Output

qop_state   Returns the cryptographic algorithm, or quality of protection, from the signature.

minor_status   Returns a status code from the security mechanism.

Description

The **gss_verify( )** routine checks that an encrypted signature, in the *token_buffer* parameter, fits the message in the *message_buffer* buffer. The application receiving the message can use the *qop_state* parameter to check the message's protection.

gss_verify(3sec)

Errors   **GSS_S_COMPLETE**
: The routine was completed successfully.

GSS_S_CONTEXT_EXPIRED
: The context has already expired.

GSS_S_CREDENTIALS_EXPIRED
: The context is recognized but the associated credentials have expired.

GSS_S_FAILURE
: The routine failed.   Check the *minor_status* parameter for details.

GSS_S_NO_CONTEXT
: The context identified in the *context_handle* parameter was not valid.

Related Information

Functions: **gss_seal(3sec)**, **gss_sign(3sec)**.

gssapi_intro

Purpose   Generic security service application programming interface

Description

This introduction includes general information about the generic security service application programming interface (GSSAPI) defined in Internet RFC 1508, *Generic Security Service Application Programming Interface*, and RFC 1509, *Generic Security Service API : C-bindings*. It also includes an overview of error handling, data types, and calling conventions, including the following:

- Integer types

- String and similar data

- Object identifiers (OIDs)

- Object identifier sets (OID sets)

- Credentials

- Contexts

- Authentication tokens

- Major status values

- Minor status values

- Names

- Channel bindings

- Optional parameters

General Information

GSSAPI provides security services to applications using peer-to-peer communications (instead of DCE secure RPC). Using OSF DCE GSSAPI routines, applications can perform the following operations:

- Enable an application to determine another application's user

- Enable an application to delegate access rights to another application

- Apply security services, such as confidentiality and integrity, on a per-message basis

GSSAPI represents a secure connection between two communicating applications with a data structure called a *security context*. The application that establishes the secure connection is called the *context indicator* or simply *indicator*. The context initiator is like a DCE RPC client. The application that accepts the secure connection is the *context acceptor* or simply *acceptor*. The context acceptor is like a DCE RPC server.

There are four stages involved in using the GSSAPI:

1. The context initiator acquires a credential with which it can prove its identity to other processes. Similarly, the context acceptor cquires a credential to enable it to accept a security context. Either application may omit this credential acquistion and use their default credentials in subsequent stages. See the section on credentials for more information.

    The applications use credentials to establish their global identity. The global identity can be, but is not necessarily, related to the local user name under which the application is running. Credentials can contain either of the following:

    *   Login context

        The login context includes a principal's network credentials, as well as other account information.

    *   Principal name and a key

        The key corresponding to the principal name must be registered with the DCE security registration in a key table. A set of DCE GSSAPI routines enables applications to register and use principal names.

2. The communicating applications establish a joint security context by exchanging authentication tokens.

    The *security context* is a pair of GSSAPI data structures that contain information that is shared between the communicating applications. The information describes the state of each application. This security context is required for per-message security services.

    To establish a security context, the context initiator calls the **gss_init_sec_-context( )** routine to get a *token*. The token is cryptographically protected, opaque data. The context initiator transfers the token to the context acceptor, which in turn passes the token to the **gss_accept_sec_context( )** routine to decode and extract the shared information.

As part of the establishing the the security context, the context initiator is authenticated to the context acceptor. The context initiator can require the context acceptor to authenticate itself in return.

The context initiator can delegate rights to allow the context acceptor to act as its agent. Delegation means the context initiator gives the context acceptor the ability to initiate additional security contexts as an agent of the context initiator. To delegate, the context initiator sets a flag on the **gss_init_sec_context( )** routine indicating that it wants to delegate and sends the returned token in the normal way to the context acceptor. The acceptor passes this token to the **gss_accept_sec_context( )** routine, which generates a delegated credential. The context acceptor can use the credential to initiate additional security contexts.

3. The applications exchange protected messages and data.

   The applications can call GSSAPI routines to protect data exchanged in messages. The application sends a protected message by calling the appropriate GSSAPI routine to do the following:

   - Apply protection

   - Bind the message to the appropriate security context

   The application can then send the resulting information to the peer application.

   The application that receives the message passes the received data to a GSSAPI routine, which removes the protection and validates the data.

   GSSAPI treats application data as arbitrary octet strings. The GSSAPI per-message security services can provide either of the following:

   - Integrity and authentication of data origin

   - Confidentiality, integrity, and authentication of data origin

4. When the applications have finished communicating, either one may instruct GSSAPI to delete the security context.

There are two sets of GSSAPI routines:

- Standard GSSAPI routines, which are defined in the Internet RFC 1508, *Generic Security Service Application Programming Interface*, and RFC 1509, *Generic Security Service API : C-bindings*. These routines have the prefix **gss_**.

- OSF DCE extensions to the GSSAPI routines. These are additional
  routines that enable an application to use DCE security services. These
  routines have the prefix **gssdce_**.

The following sections provide an overview of the GSSAPI error handling and data
types.

Error Handling

Each GSSAPI routine returns two status values:

- Major status values

  Major status values are generic API routine errors or calling errors defined
  in RFC 1509.

- Minor status values

  Minor status values indicate DCE-specific errors.

If a routine has output parameters that contain pointers for storage allocated by the
routine, the output parameters will always contain a valid pointer even if the
routine returns an error. If no storage was allocated, the routine sets the pointer to
NULL and sets any length fields associated with the pointers (such as in the
gss_buffer_desc structure) to 0 (zero).

Minor status values usually contain more detailed information about the error.
They are not, however, portable between GSSAPI implementations. When
designing portable applications, use major status values for handling errors. Use
minor status values to debug applications and to display error and error-recovery
information to users.

GSSAPI Data Types

This section provides an overview of the GSSAPI data types and their definitions.

The GSSAPI defines the following integer data type:

```
OM_uint32       32-bit unsigned integer
```

This integer data type is a portable data type that the GSSAPI routine definitions
use for guaranteed minimum bit-counts.

Many of the GSSAPI routines take arguments and return values that describe
contiguous multiple-byte data, such as opaque data and character strings. Use the
gss_buffer_t data type, which is a pointer to the buffer descriptor **gss_buffer_desc**,
to pass the data between the GSSAPI routines and applications.

The **gss_buffer_t** data type has the following structure:

```
typedef struct gss_buffer_desc_struct {
        size_t  length;
        void    *value;
} gss_buffer_desc, *gss_buffer_t;
```

The length field contains the total number of bytes in the data and the value field contains a pointer to the actual data.

When using the **gss_buffer_t** data type, the GSSAPI routine allocates storage for any data it passes to the application. The calling application must allocate the **gss_buffer_desc** object. It can initialize unused **gss_buffer_desc** objects with the value **GSS_C_EMPTY_BUFFER**. To free the storage, the application calls the **gss_release_buffer( )** routine.

Applications use the **gss_OID** data type to choose a security mechanism, either DCE security or Kerberos, and to specify name types. Select a security mechanism by using the following two OIDs:

- For DCE security, specify either **GSSDCE_C_OID_DCE_KRBV5_DES** or **GSS_C_NULL_OID**.

- For Kerberos Version 5, specify **GSSDCE_C_OID_KRBV5_DES**.

Use of the default security mechanisms, specified by the constant **GSS_C_NULL_OID**, helps to ensure the portability of the application.

The **gss_OID** data type contains tree-structured values defined by ISO and has the following structure:

```
typedef struct gss_OID_desc_struct {
        OM_uint32 length;
        void    * elements;
}  gss_OID_desc, *gss_OID;
```

The elements field of the structure points to the first byte of an octet string containing the ASN.1 BER encoding of the value of the **gss_OID** data type. The length field contains the number of bytes in the value.

The **gss_OID_desc** values returned from the GSSAPI are read-only values. The application should not try to deallocate them.

The **gss_OID_set** data type represents one or more object identifiers. The values of the **gss_OID_set** data type are used to

- Report the available mechanisms supported by GSSAPI

- Request specific mechanisms

- Indicate which mechanisms a credential supports

The **gss_OID_set** data type has the following structure:

```
typedef struct gss_OID_set_desc_struct {
        int     count
        gss_OID elements
} gss_OID_set_desc, *gss_OID_set;
```

The count field contains the number of OIDs in the set. The elements field is a pointer to an array of **gss_oid_desc** objects, each describing a single OID. The application calls the **gss_release_oid_set( )** routine to deallocate storage associated with the **gss_OID_set** values that the GSSAPI routines return to the application.

Credentials establish, or prove, the identity of an application or other principal.

The **gss_cred_id_t** data type is an atomic data type that identifies a GSSAPI credential data structure.

The *security context* is a pair of GSSAPI data structures that contain information shared between the communicating applications. The information describes the cryptographic state of each application. This security context is required for per-message security services and is created by a successful authentication exchange.

The **gss_ctx_id_t** data type contains an atomic value that identifies one end of a GSSAPI security context. The data type is opaque to the caller.

GSSAPI uses tokens to maintain the synchronization between the applications sharing a security context. The token is a cryptographically protected bit string generated by DCE Security at one end of the GSSAPI security context for use by the peer application at the other end of the security context. The data type is opaque to the caller.

The applications use the **gss_buffer_t** data type as tokens to GSSAPI routines.

GSSAPI routines return GSS status codes as their **OM_uint32** function value. These codes indicate either generic API routine errors or calling errors.

A GSS status code can indicate a single, fatal generic API error from the routine and a single calling error. Additional status information can also be contained in the GSS status code. The errors are encoded into a 32-bit GSS status code, as follows:

```
MSB                                                        LSB
+-------------------------------------------------------+
| Calling Error | Routine Error | Supplementary Info|
+-------------------------------------------------------+
Bit 31          24 23              16 15                 0
```

If a GSSAPI routine returns a GSS status code whose upper 16 bits contain a nonzero value, the call failed. If the calling error field is nonzero, the context initiator's use of the routine was in error. In addition, the routine can indicate additional information by setting bits in the supplementary information field of the status code. The tables that follow describe the routine errors, calling errors, and supplementary information status bits and their meanings.

The following table lists the GSSAPI routine errors and their meanings:

Name	Value	Meaning
GSS_S_BAD_MECH	1	The required mechanism is unsupported.
GSS_S_NAME	2	The name passed is invalid.
GSS_S_NAMETYPE	3	The name passed is unsupported.
GSS_S_BAD_BINDINGS	4	The channel bindings are incorrect.
GSS_S_BAD_STATUS	5	A status value was invalid.
GSS_S_BAD_SIG	6	A token had an invalid signature.
GSS_S_NO_CRED	7	No credentials were supplied.
GSS_S_NO_CONTEXT	8	No context has been established.
GSS_S_DEFECTIVE_TOKEN	9	A token was invalid.
GSS_S_DEFECTIVE_CREDENTIAL	10	A credential was invalid.
GSS_S_CREDENTIALS_EXPIRED	11	The referenced credentials expired.
GSS_S_CONTEXT_EXPIRED	12	The context expired.
GSS_S_FAILURE	13	The routine failed. Check minor status codes.

The following table lists the calling error values and their meanings:

Name	Value	Meaning
GSS_S_CALL_INACCESSIBLE_READ	1	Could not read a required input parameter.
GSS_S_CALL_INACCESSIBLE_WRITE	2	Could not write a required output parameter.
GSS_S_BAD_STRUCTURE	3	A parameter was incorrectly structured.

The following table lists the supplementary bits and their meanings.

Name	Number	Meaning
GSS_S_CONTINUE_NEEDED	0 (LSB)	Call the routine again to complete its function.
GSS_S_DUPLICATE_TOKEN	1	The token was a duplicate of an earlier token.
GSS_S_OLD_TOKEN	2	The token's validity period expired; the routine cannot verify that the token is not a duplicate of an earlier token.
GSS_S_UNSEQ_TOKEN	3	A later token has been processed.

All **GSS_S_** symbols equate to complete **OM_uint32** status codes, rather than to bitfield values. For example, the actual value of **GSS_S_BAD_NAMETYPE** (value 3 in the routine error field) is $3 \ll 16$.

The major status code **GSS_S_FAILURE** indicates that DCE security detected an error for which no major status code is available. Check the minor status code for details about the error. See the section on minor status values for more information.

The GSSAPI provides three macros:

- **GSS_CALLING_ERROR( )**

- **GSS_ROUTINE_ERROR( )**

- **GSS_SUPPLEMENTARY_INFO( )**

Each macro takes a GSS status code and masks all but the relevant field. For example, when you use the **GSS_ROUTINE_ERROR( )** macro on a status code, it returns a value. The value of the macro is arrived at by using only the routine errors field and zeroing the values of the calling error and the supplementary information fields.

An additional macro, **GSS_ERROR( )**, lets you determine whether the status code indicated a calling or routine error. If the status code indicated a calling or routine error, the macro returns a nonzero value. If no calling or routine error is indicated, the routine returns a 0 (zero).

Note: At times, a GSSAPI routine that is unable to access data can generate a platform-specific signal, instead of returning a **GSS_S_CALL_- INACCESSIBLE_READ** or **GSS_S_CALL_INACCESSIBLE_- WRITE** status value.

The GSSAPI routines return a *minor_status* parameter to indicate errors from either DCE Security or Kerberos. The parameter can contain a single error, indicated by an **OM_uint32** value. The **OM_uint32** data type is equivalent to the DCE data type **error_status_t** and can contain any DCE-defined error.

Names identify principals. The GSSAPI authenticates the relationship between a name and the principal claiming the name.

Names are represented in two forms:

- A printable form, for presentation to an application

- An internal, canonical form that is used by the API and is opaque to applications

The **gss_import_name( )** and **gss_display_name( )** routines convert names between their printable form and their **gss_name_t** data type. DCE GSSAPI supports only DCE principal names, which are identified by the constant OID, **GSSCDE_C_OID_DCENAME**.

The **gss_compare_names( )** routine compares internal form names.

You can define and use channel bindings to associate the security context with the communications channel that carries the context. Channel bindings are communicated to the GSSAPI by using the following structure:

```
typedef struct gss_channel_binding_struct {
        OM_uint32       initiator_addrtype;
        gss_buffer_desc initiator_address;
        OM_uint32       acceptor_addrtype;
        gss_buffer_desc aceptor_address;
        gss_buffer_desc application_data;
} *gss_channel_bindings_t;
```

Use the **initiator_addrtype** and **acceptor_addrtype** fields to initiate the type of addresses contained in the **initiator_address** and **acceptor_address** buffers. The following table lists the address types and their **addrtype** values:

Address Type	addrtype Value
Unspecified	**GSS_C_AF_UNSPEC**
Host-local	**GSS_C_AF_LOCAL**
DARPA Internet	**GSS_C_AF_INET**
ARPAnet IMP	**GSS_C_AF_IMPLINK**
pup protocols (for example, BSP)	**GSS_C_AF_PUP**
MIT CHAOS protocol	**GSS_C_AF_CHAOS**
XEROX NS	**GSS_C_AF_NS**
nbs	**GSS_C_AF_NBS**
ECMA	**GSS_C_AF_ECMA**
datakit protocols	**GSS_C_AF_DATAKIT**
CCITT protocols (for example, X.25)	**GSS_C_AF_CCITT**
IBM SNA	**GSS_C_AF_SNA**
Digital DECnet	**GSS_C_AF_DECnet**
Direct data link interface	**GSS_C_AF_DLI**
LAT	**GSS_C_AF_LAT**
NSC Hyperchannel	**GSS_C_AF_HYLINK**
AppleTalk	**GSS_C_AF_APPLETALK**
BISYNC 2780/3780	**GSS_C_AF_BSC**
Distributed system services	**GSS_C_AF_DSS**
OSI TP4	**GSS_C_AF_OSI**
X25	**GSS_C_AF_X25**
No address specified	**GSS_C_AF_NULLADDR**

The tags specify address families rather than addressing formats. For address families that contain several alternative address forms, the **initiator_address** and the **acceptor_address** fields should contain sufficient information to determine which address form is used. Format the bytes that contain the addresses in the order in which the bytes are transmitted across the network.

The GSSAPI creates an octet string by concatenating all the fields (**initiator_addrtype**, **initiator_address**, **acceptor_addrtype**, **acceptor_address**, and **application_data**). The security mechanism signs the octet string and binds the signature to the token generated by the **gss_init_sec_context( )** routine. The context acceptor presents the same bindings to the **gss_accept_sec_context( )** routine, which evaluates the signature and compares it to the signature in the token. If the signatures differ, the **gss_accept_sec_context( )** routine returns a **GSS_S_BAD_BINDINGS** error, and the context is not established.

Some security mechanisms check that the **initiator_address** field of the channel bindings presented to the **gss_init_sec_context( )** routine contains the correct network address of the host system. Therefore portable applications should use either the correct address type and value or the **GSS_C_AF_NULLADDR** for the **initiator_addrtype** address field. Some security mechanisms include the channel binding data in the token instead of a signature, so portable applications should not use confidential data as channel-binding components. The DCE GSSAPI does not verify the address or include the plain text bindings information in the token.

In routine descriptions, *optional parameters* allow the application to request default behaviors by passing a default value for the parameter. The following conventions are used for optional parameters:

Convention	Value Default	Explanation
gss_buffer_t types	**GSS_C_NO_BUFFER**	For an input parameter, indicates no data is supplied. For an output parameter, indicates that the information returned is not required by the application.
Integer types (input)		Refer to the reference pages for default values.
Integer types (output)	NULL	Indicates that the application does not require the information.
Pointer types (output)	NULL	Indicates that the application does not require the information.
OIDs	**GSS_C_NULL_OID**	Indicates the default choice for name type or security mechanism.
OID sets	**GSS_C_NULL_OID_SET**	Indicates the default set of security mechanisms, DCE security and Kerberos.
Credentials	**GSS_C_NO_CREDENTIAL**	Indicates that the application should use the default credential handle.
Channel bindings	**GSS_C_NO_CHANNEL_BINDINGS**	Indicates that no channel bindings are used.

Related Information

Books: *OSF DCE Application Development Guide—Core Components.*

gssdce_add_oid_set_member

Purpose   Adds an OID to an OID set

Synopsis   **#include <dce/gssapi.h>**

>   **OM_uint32 gssdce_add_oid_set_member (**
>   **OM_uint32*** *minor_status***,**
>   **gss_OID*** *member_OID***,**
>   **gss_OID_set*** *OID_set***);**

Parameters

Input

>   *member_OID*   Specifies the OID you want to add to the OID set.
>
>   *OID_set*   Specifies an OID set.

Output

>   *minor_status*   Returns a status code from the security mechanism.

Description

The **gssdce_add_oid_set_member( )** routine adds a new OID to an OID set. If an OID set does not exist, you can create a new, empty OID set with the **gssdce_create_empty_oid_set( )** routine.

Errors

GSS_S_COMPLETE
>   The routine was completed successfully.

GSS_S_FAILURE
>   The routine failed. Check the *minor_status* parameter for details.

Related Information

Functions: **gss_acquire_cred(3sec)**, **gssdce_create_empty_oid_set(3sec)**.

gssdce_create_empty_oid_set

Purpose   Creates a new, empty OID set to which members can be added by calling **gssdce_add_oid_set_member( )**

Synopsis   #include <dce/gssapi.h>

OM_uint32 **gssdce_create_empty_oid_set** (
OM_uint32 *minor_status*,
gss_OID_set *OID_set*);

Parameters

Input

OID_set   Specifies the OID set you want to create.

Output

minor_status   Returns a status code from the security mechanism.

Description

The **gssdce_create_empty_oid_set( )** routine creates a new, empty OID set to which the context initiator can add members. Use the **gssdce_add_oid_set_-member( )** routine to add members to the OID set.

Use the **gssdce_create_empty_oid_set( )** routine to specify a set of security mechanisms with which you can use an acquired credential. To create a credential that can accept a security context using DCE security, Kerberos, or a combination of the two, use the **gss_acquire_cred( )** routine.

Errors   GSS_S_COMPLETE
The routine was completed successfully.

GSS_S_FAILURE
The routine failed. Check the *minor_status* parameter for details.

Related Information

Functions: **gss_acquire_cred(3sec)**, **gssdce_add_oid_set_member(3sec)**.

gssdce_cred_to_login_context

Purpose   Obtains the DCE login context associated with a GSSAPI credential

Synopsis   **#include <dce/gssapi.h>**

> **OM_uint32 gssdce_cred_to_login_context (**
> **OM_uint32 *****minor_status**,
> **cred_id_t *****cred_handle**,
> **sec_login_handle_t** login_context**);**

Parameters

Input

  cred_handle   Specifies the credential handle.

Output

  login_context   Returns the DCE login context associated with the credential.

  minor_status   Returns a status code from the security mechanism.

Description

Using the **gssdce_cred_to_login_context( )** routine, an application can obtain the DCE login context associated with a GSSAPI credential. Only credentials with usage-types **INIT** or **BOTH** have associated login contexts.

Use this routine in the following situations:

- If you want to add delegation notes to a login context

- To use an **INITIATE** or **BOTH** credential to initiate an authenticated RPC call

The application must delete the login context when it no longer needs the credentials or the login context.

Errors   **GSS_S_COMPLETE**
                    The routine was completed successfully.

               GSS_S_CREDENTIALS_EXPIRED
                    The credentials have expired.

               GSS_S_DEFECTIVE_CREDENTIAL
                    The credential is defective in some way.

               GSS_S_FAILURE
                    The routine failed. Check the *minor_status* parameter for details.

               GSS_S_NO_CRED
                    The routine requested the default login context, but no default login
                    context was available.

Related Information
               Functions: **gssdce_login_context_to_cred(3sec)**,
               sec_login_purge_contexts(3sec), **sec_login_release_context(3sec)**.

gssdce_extract_creds_from_sec_context

Purpose   Extracts a DCE credential from a GSSAPI security context

Synopsis   **#include <dce/gssapi.h>**

> **OM_uint32 gssdce_extract_creds_from_sec_context (**
> **OM_uint32** *minor_status,*
> **gss_ctx_id_t** *context_handle,*
> **rpc_authz_cred_handle_t** *output_cred*);

Parameters

Input

> *context_handle*
>> Specifies the handle of the security context containing the DCE credential.

Output

> *output_cred*   Returns the DCE credential.
>
> *minor_status*   Returns a status code from the security mechanism.

Description

> The **gssdce_extract_creds_from_sec_context( )** routine extracts the context initiator's DCE credential from a context acceptor's security context. Use this routine if the underlying mechanism type is DCE security (**GSS_C_OID_DCE_-KRBV5_DES**).
>
> The context acceptor calls the **gssdce_extract_creds_from_sec_context( )** routine to get the DCE credential containing the privilege attributes of the context initiator. DCE credentials are used by DCE ACL managers to determine whether the initiator has the right to access the object to which an ACL refers.
>
> The principal contained in the DCE credential may not be the same as the *src_name* parameter value from the **gss_accept_sec_context( )** routine. The principal in the DCE credential may be a compound principal.

gssdce_extract_creds_from_sec_context(3sec)

If the context was established by calling the **gss_init_set_context( )** routine and specifying **GSS_C_OID_KRBV5_DES** to use Kerberos (instead of DCE security), the **gssdce_extract_creds_from_sec_context( )** routine returns a major status of

Errors **GSS_S_COMPLETE**
The routine was completed successfully.

GSS_S_FAILURE
The routine failed. Check the *minor_status* parameter for details.

GSS_S_NO_CONTEXT
The routine could not access the security context.

Related Information
Functions: **gss_init_sec_context(3sec)**.

gssdce_login_context_to_cred

Purpose   Creates a GSSAPI credential handle for a context initiator or context acceptor from a DCE login context

Synopsis   **#include <dce/gssapi.h>**

OM_uint32 gssdce_login_context_to_cred (
OM_uint32 **minor_status,*
sec_login_handle_t *login_context,*
OM_uint32 *lifetime_req,*
OID_set *desired_mechs,*
cred_id_t **output_cred_handle,*
OID_set **actual_mechs,*
OM_uint32 *lifetime_rec***);**

Parameters

Input

login_context   Specifies the DCE login context handle. To use the default login context handle, specify NULL.

lifetime_req   Specifies the number of seconds that the credential should remain valid.

desired_mechs
Specifies the OID set for the security mechanism to use with the credential, as follows:

To use...	Specify...
DCE security	**GSS_C_NULL_OID_SET**
Kerberos	**GSS_C_OID_KRBV5_DES**
Both DCE security and Kerberos	**GSS_C_OID_DCE_KRBV5_DES** and **GSS_C_OID_KRBV5_DES**

To help ensure portability of your application, use the default security mechanism by specifying **GSS_C_NULL_OID_SET**.

Output

output_cred_handle
Returns the credential handle.

actual_mechs Returns the set specifying the security mechanisms with which the credential can be used. The set can contain one or both of the following:

- **GSS_C_OID_DCE_KRBV5_DES** for DCE security

- **GSS_C_OID_KRBV5_DES** for Kerberos

lifetime_rec Returns the number of seconds that the credential will remain valid.

minor_status Returns a status code from the security mechanism.

Description

The **gssdce_login_context_to_cred**( ) routine creates a GSSAPI credential handle for the context initiator or context acceptor from a DCE login context. The routine creates a credential that can be used to initiate or acquire a security context. Use this routine if you need to create a GSSAPI credential for delegation.

Errors   GSS_S_COMPLETE
The routine was completed successfully.

GSS_S_DEFECTIVE_CREDENTIAL
The credential is defective in some way.

GSS_S_NO_CRED
The routine requested the default login context, but no default login context was available.

GSS_S_FAILURE
The routine failed. Check the *minor_status* parameter for details.

Related Information

Functions: **gss_acquire_cred(3sec)**, **gssdce_cred_to_login_context(3sec)**.

gssdce_register_acceptor_identity

Purpose   Registers a context acceptor's identity

Synopsis   **#include <dce/gssapi.h>**

> **OM_uint32 gss_register_acceptor_indentity (**
> **OM_uint32 ***minor_status,*
> **unsigned_char_t ****acceptor_principal_name,*
> **rpc_auth_key_retrieval_fn_t** *get_key_fn,*
> **void ***arg);*

Parameters

Input

acceptor_principal_name
> Specifies the principal name to use for the context acceptor.

get_key_fn   Specifies either the DCE default key-retrieval routine or the address of a routine that returns encryption keys.

arg   Specifies an argument to pass to the *get_key_fn* key acquisition routine. To specify the DCE default, use NULL.

Output

minor_status   Returns a status code from the security mechanism.

Description

The **gssdce_register_acceptor_identity( )** routine registers the server principal name as an identity claimed by the context acceptor and informs DCE security where to find the key table containing the principal's key information.

The **gssdce_register_acceptor_identity( )** routine uses the *get_key_fn* and *arg* parameters of the **rpc_server_register_auth_info( )** routine to find the key for the token for the context acceptor's principal name. The following table lists the values for the parameters and which key tables they point to:

Retrieval Routine	Key Table	Explanation
NULL	NULL	Uses the default DCE retrieval routine to get the key from the DCE key table. This is accomplished via the default key table, **/krb/v5srvtab**.
NULL	*string=key_table_name*	Uses the default DCE retrieval routine to get the key from the a key table whose name you specify using the argument string.
routine_address	*user_written_routine*	Uses a user-written retrieval routine to get the key from a key table specified in the routine.

For more information on registering a server with DCE, refer to the **rpc_server_register_auth_info(3rpc)** reference page.

Errors   **GSS_S_COMPLETE**
The routine was completed successfully.

GSS_S_FAILURE
The routine failed. Check the minor status for details.

Related Information
Functions: **gss_accept_sec_context(3sec)**, **rpc_server_register_auth_info(3rpc)**.

gssdce_set_cred_context_ownership

Purpose   Changes the ownership of a DCE credential's login context

Synopsis   **#include <dce/gssapi.h>**

> **OM_uint32 gssdce_set_cred_context_ownership (**
> **OM_uint32 *___minor_status___,**
> **gss_cred_id_t** ___credential_handle___**,**
> **int** ___ownership___**);**

Parameters

Input

___credential_handle___
> Specifies the handle of the DCE credential to be modified.

___ownership___   Specifies the owner of the DCE credential. Specify one of the following:

> **GSSDCE_C_OWNWERSHIP_GSSAPI**
> > Specifies that the credential's login context is owned by GSSAPI.

> **GSSDCE_C_OWNERSHIP_APPLICATION**
> > Specifies that the credential's login context is owned by the application.

Output

___minor_status___   Returns a status code from the security mechanism.

Description

The **gssdce_set_cred_context_ownership( )** routine modifies the ownership of a DCE credential's login context. **INIT** type and **BOTH** type credentials have DCE login contexts. Normally, these internal login contexts are deleted when the credential is released (when the application calls the **gss_release_cred( )** routine).

gssdce_set_cred_context_ownership(3sec)

For credentials created by the **gssdce_cred_to_login_context( )** and credentials passsed to the **gsscdce_cred_to_login_context( )** routine, the application may have an external reference to the credential's login context and may still be using the login context. GSSAPI will not delete internal login contexts of these credentials when they are released.

This routine allows the application to modify the ownership of a credential's login context. If ownership is changed to **GSSDCE_C_OWNERSHIP_GSSAPI**, the login context is deleted when GSSAPI releases the credential. If ownership is changed to **GSSDCE_C_OWNERSHIP_APPLICATION**, the application is responsible for deleting the login context. DCE credential login contexts that are owned by an application must not be deleted until the credential is released since GSSAPI may still need to access the credential's login context.

Related Information

Functions: **gss_acquire_cred(3sec)**, **gss_release_buffer(3sec)**, **gssdce_cred_to_login_context(3sec)**.

gssdce_test_oid_set_member

Purpose   Checks an OID set to see if a specified OID is in the set

Synopsis   #include <dce/gssapi.h>

OM_uint32 gssdce_test_oid_set_member (
OM_uint32 *minor_status,
gss_OID member_OID,
gss_OID_set set,
int* is_present /* 1 = present, 0 = absent */);

Parameters

Input

member_OID   Specifies the OID to search for in the OID set.

set   Specifies the OID set to check.

Output

is_present   Returns one of the following values to indicate whether the OID is a member of the OID set:

Returns...	If...
1	The OID is present as a member of the OID set
0	The OID is absent, not a member of the OID set

minor_status Returns a status code from the security mechanism.

Description

The **gssdce_test_oid_set_member( )** routine checks an OID set to see if the specified OID is a member of the set. To add a member to an OID set, use the **gssdce_add_oid_set_member( )** routine.

The **gssdce_test_oid_set_member( )** routine uses the value of the *actual_mechs* output parameter from the **gss_acquire_cred( )** routine to get the list of OIDs. It checks this list to see if any of the OIDs are members of the OID set.

gssdce_test_oid_set_member (3sec)

Errors   **GSS_S_COMPLETE**

The routine was completed successfully.

GSS_S_FAILURE

The routine failed. Check the *minor_status* parameter for details.

Related Information

Functions: **gss_acquire_cred(3sec), gss_indicate_mechs(3sec), gssdce_add_oid_set_member(3sec)**.

priv_attr_trig_query

Purpose   Retrieves attributes stored by a trigger server for a specified principal for inclusion
in the principal's EPAC

Synopsis   **#include <dce/priv_attr_trig.h>**

void priv_attr_trig_query (
        handle_t *h,*
        sec_id_foreign_t *principal,*
        unsigned32 *num_upstream_delegates,*
        sec_id_foreign_t *upstream_delegates*[ ],
        priv_attr_trig_cursor_t **cursor,*
        unsigned32 *num_attr_keys,*
        unsigned32 *space_avail,*
        sec_attr_t *attr_keys*[ ],
        unsigned32 **num_returned,*
        sec_attr_t *attrs*[ ],
        priv_attr_trig_timeval_sec_t *time_to_live*[ ],
        unsigned32 **num_left,*
        error_status_t **status*);

Parameters

Input

h	An opaque handle bound to a trigger server. Use the trigger binding information specified in the attribute encoding to acquire a bound handle.
principal	A value of type **sec_id_foreign_t** that identifies the UUID, name, and cell of the principal(s) whose attributes are to be retrieved.

num_upstream_delegates
                If *principal* is a member of a delegation chain, an unsigned 32-bit
                integer that specifies the number of delegates in the chain upstream
                from (before) this principal. The upstream delegate chain ordering
                reflects the sequence in which delegates were added to the chain.
                For example, the delegation initiator will always be first in the
                chain.

       upstream_delegates

If the privilege sever is adding *principal* to a delegation chain, an array of values of type **sec_id_foreign_t** that identify the UUID and cell of each delegate in the upstream delegation chain. Note that principal names are not provided.

       num_attr_keys

An unsigned 32-bit integer that specifies the number of elements in the *attr_keys* array. Set this parameter to 0 (zero) to return all of the principal's attributes that the caller is authorized to see.

space_avail   An unsigned 32-bit integer that specifies the size of the *attr_keys* array.

attr_keys[ ]   An array of values of type **sec_attr_t** that identify the attribute type ID of the attribute instance(s) to be looked up. The size of the *attr_keys[ ]* array is determined by the *num_attr_keys* parameter.

Input/Output

cursor   A pointer to a **priv_attr_trig_cursor_t**. As an input parameter, *cursor* is a pointer to a **priv_attr_trig_cursor_t** initialized by a the **sec_attr_cursor_init( )** call. As an output parameter, *cursor* is a pointer to a **priv_attr_trig_cursor_t** that is positioned past the components returned in this call.

Output Parameters

num_returned A pointer to a 32-bit unsigned integer that specifies the number of attribute instances returned in the *attrs[ ]* array.

attrs   An array of values of type **sec_attr_t** that contains the attributes retrieved by UUID. The size of the array is determined by *space_avail* and the length by *num_returned*.

       time_to_live[ ]

An array of values of type **priv_attr_trig_timeval_sec_t** that specifies, for each attribute in the **attrs[ ]** array The size of the array is determined by *space_avail* and the length by *num_returned*.

num_left   A pointer to a 32-bit unsigned integer that supplies the number of attributes that were found but could not be returned because of space constraints in the *attrs[ ]* buffer. To ensure that all the attributes will be returned, increase the size of the *attrs[ ]* array by increasing the size of *space_avail* and *num_returned*.

status A pointer to the completion status. On successful completion, the
routine returns **error_status_ok**, or, if the requested attributes were
not available, it returns the message **not_all_available**. Otherwise,
it returns an error.

Description

The **priv_attr_trig_query( )** function is used by the privilege server to retrieve
attributes for a principal specified by UUID and include them in the principal's
EPAC. The privilege server calls this function when it gets a request for ERAs in
an EAPC.

Although generally this routine it is not called directly, this reference page is
provided for users who are writing the attribute trigger servers that will receive
priv_attr_trig_query( ) input and supply its output.

If the *num_attr_keys* parameter is set to 0 (zero), all of the object's attributes that
the caller is authorized to see are returned. This routine is useful for programmatic
access.

For multivalued attributes, the call returns a **sec_attr_t** for each value as an
individual attribute instance. For attribute sets, the call returns a **sec_attr_t** for
each member of the set; it does not return the set instance.

The *attr_keys*[ ] array, which specifies the attributes to be returned, contains values
of type **sec_attr_t**. These values consist of

- **attr_id**, a UUID that identifies the attribute type

- **attr_value**, values of **sec_attr_value_t** that specify the attribute's encoding
  type and values.

Use the **attr_id** field of each *attr_keys* array element, to specify the UUID that
identifies the attribute type to be returned.

If the attribute instance to be read is associated with a query attribute trigger that
requires additional information before it can process the query request, use a
sec_attr_value_t to supply the requested information. To do this

- Set the **sec_attr_encoding_t** to an encoding type that is compatible with
  the information required by the query attribute trigger.

- Set the **sec_attr_value_t** to hold the required information.

Note that if you set *num_attr_keys* to zero to return all of the object's attributes and
that attribute is associated with a query attribute trigger, the attribute trigger will be
called with no input attribute information (that would normally have been passed in
via the **attr_value** field).

The *cursor* parameter specifies a cursor of type **priv_attr_trig_cursor_t** initialized to the point in the attribute list at which to start processing the query. Use the **sec_attr_cursor_init( )** function to initialize *cursor*. If *cursor* is uninitialized, the server begins processing the query at the first attribute that satisfies the search criteria.

The *num_left* parameter contains the number of attributes that were found but could not be returned because of space constraints of the *attrs*[ ] array. (Note that this number may be inaccurate if the target server allows updates between successive queries.) To obtain all of the remaining attributes, set the size of the *attrs*[ ] array so that it is large enough to hold the number of attributes listed in *num_left*.

Permissions Required

The **priv_attr_trig_query( )** routine requires the query permission set for each attribute type identified in the *attr_keys*[ ] array. These permissions are defined as part of the ACL manager set in the schema entry of each attribute type.

Files

/usr/include/dce/priv_attr_trig.idl

The **idl** file from which **dce/priv_attr_trig.h** was derived.

Errors

unauthorized

registry server unavailable

trigger server unavailable

error_status_ok

Related Information

Functions: **sec_rgy_attr_cursor_init(3sec)**, **sec_intro(3sec)**.

rdacl_get_access

Purpose   Reads a privilege attribute certificate

Synopsis   **#include <dce/rdaclif.h>**

    void rdacl_get_access(
        handle_t *h*,
        sec_acl_component_name_t *component_name*,
        uuid_t **manager_type*,
        sec_acl_permset_t **net_rights*,
        error_status_t **status*);

Parameters

Input

h   A handle referring to the object whose ACL is to be accessed.

component_name
        A character string containing the name of the target object.

manager_type
        A pointer to the UUID identifying the type of the ACL manager in question. There may be more than one type of ACL manager protecting the object whose ACL is bound to the input handle. Use this parameter to distinguish them. Use **sec_acl_get_manager_-types( )** to acquire a list of the manager types protecting a given object.

Output

net_rights   The output list of access rights, in **sec_acl_permset_t** form. This is a 32-bit set of permission flags supported by the manager type.

status   A pointer to the completion status. On successful completion, the routine returns **error_status_ok**. Otherwise, it returns an error.

Description

The **rdacl_get_access( )** routine determines the complete extent of access to the specified object by the calling process. Although the **rdacl_test_access( )** routines are the preferred method of testing access, this routine is useful for implementing operations like the conventional UNIX access function.

Notes

This call is not intended to be used by application programs. The **sec_acl** application programming interface (API) provides all the functionality necessary to use the ACL facility. This reference page is provided for programmers who wish to write an ACL manager. In order to write an ACL manager, a programmer must implement the entire **rdacl** interface.

This network interface is called on the client side via the **sec_acl** local interface. Developers are responsible for implementing the server side of this interface. Test server code is included as a sample implementation.

Files

/usr/include/dce/rdaclif.idl
> The **idl** file from which **dce/rdaclif.h** was derived.

Errors

sec_acl_invalid_manager_type
> The manager type is not valid.

sec_acl_invalid_acl_type
> The ACL type is not valid.

sec_acl_not_authorized
> The requested operation is not allowed.

sec_acl_object_not_found
> The requested object could not be found.

error_status_ok
> The call was successful.

Related Information

Functions: **rdacl_test_access(3sec)**, **sec_intro(3sec)**.

rdacl_get_manager_types

Purpose   Lists the types of ACLs protecting an object

Synopsis   **#include <dce/rdaclif.h>**

void rdacl_get_manager_types(
        handle_t *h*,
        sec_acl_component_name_t *component_name*,
        sec_acl_type_t *sec_acl_type*,
        unsigned32 *size_avail*,
        unsigned32 * *size_used*,
        unsigned32 * *num_types*,
        uuid_t *manager_types*[ ],
        error_status_t * *status*);

Parameters

Input

h   A handle referring to the target object.

component_name
                A character string containing the name of the target object.

sec_acl_type   The ACL type. The **sec_acl_type_t** data type distinguishes the various types of ACLs an object can possess for a given manager type. The possible values are as follows:

- **sec_acl_type_object**

- **sec_acl_type_default_object**

- **sec_acl_type_default_container**

size_avail   An unsigned 32-bit integer containing the allocated length of the *manager_types*[ ] array.

Output

size_used   An unsigned 32-bit integer containing the number of output entries returned in the *manager_types*[ ] array.

num_types   An unsigned 32-bit integer containing the number of types returned in the *manager_types*[ ] array. This is always equal to *size_used*.

manager_types[ ]

An array of length *size_avail* to contain UUIDs (of type **uuid_t**) identifying the different types of ACL managers protecting the target object.

status   A pointer to the completion status. On successful completion, the routine returns **error_status_ok**. Otherwise, it returns an error.

Description

The **rdacl_get_manager_types( )** routine returns a list of the types of ACLs protecting an object. For example, in addition to the regular file system ACL, a file representing the stable storage of some database could have an ACL manager that supported permissions allowing database updates only on certain days of the week.

ACL editors and browsers can use this operation to determine the ACL manager types that a particular reference monitor is using to protect a selected entity. Then, using the **rdacl_get_printstring( )** routine, they can determine how to format for display the permissions supported by a specific manager.

Notes

This call is not intended to be used by application programs. The **sec_acl** application programming interface (API) provides all the functionality necessary to use the ACL facility. This reference page is provided for programmers who wish to write an ACL manager. In order to write an ACL manager, a programmer must implement the entire **rdacl** interface.

This network interface is called on the client side via the **sec_acl** local interface. Developers are responsible for implementing the server side of this interface. Test server code is included as a sample implementation.

Files

/usr/include/dce/rdaclif.idl

The **idl** file from which **dce/rdaclif.h** was derived.

Errors

error_status_ok

The call was successful.

Related Information

Functions: **rdacl_get_printstring(3sec)**, **sec_intro(3sec)**.

rdacl_get_manager_types_semantics

Purpose   Lists the ACL manager types protecting an object and the POSIX semantics supported by each manager type

Synopsis   **#include <dce/rdaclif.h>**

void rdacl_get_mgr_types_semantics(
   handle_t *h,*
   sec_acl_component_name_t *component_name,*
   sec_acl_type_t *sec_acl_type,*
   unsigned32 *size_avail,*
   unsigned32 * *size_used,*
   unsigned32 * *num_types,*
   uuid_t *manager_types*[ ],
   sec_acl_posix_semantics_t *posix_semantics*[ ],
   error_status_t * *status*);

Parameters

Input

   h   A handle referring to the target object.

   component_name
              A character string containing the name of the target object.

   sec_acl_type The ACL type used to limit the function's output to ACL managers that control the specified types of ACLs. The possible values are as follows:

   - **sec_acl_type_object**

       Object ACL, the ACL controlling access to an object.

   - **sec_acl_type_default_object**

       Initial Object ACL, the default ACL for objects created in a container object.

   - **sec_acl_type_default_container**

       Initial Container ACL, the default ACL for containers created in a container object.

> *size_avail*   An unsigned 32-bit integer containing the allocated length of the *manager_types*[ ] and the *posix_semantics*[ ] arrays.

Output

> *size_used*   An unsigned 32-bit integer containing the number of output entries returned in the *manager_types*[ ] array.

> *num_types*   An unsigned 32-bit integer containing the number of types returned in the *manager_types*[ ] array. This is always equal to *size_used*.

> *manager_types*[ ]
> An array of length *size_avail* containing the returned UUIDs (of type **uuid_t**) identifying the different ACL manager types protecting the target object.

> *posix_semantics*[ ]
> An array of length *size_avail* containing the POSIX semantics (of type **sec_acl_posix_semantics_t**) that are supported by each returned ACL manager type.

> *status*   A pointer to the completion status. On successful completion, the routine returns **error_status_ok**. Otherwise, it returns an error.

Description

The **rdacl_get_manager_types_semantics( )** routine returns a list of the ACL manager types protecting an object and a list of the POSIX semantics supported by those ACL manager types. Access to an object can be controlled by multiple ACL manager types. For example, access to a file representing the stable storage of a database could be controlled by two ACL manager types each with completely different sets of permissions: one to provide standard file system access (read, write, execute, etc.) and one to provide access that allows database updates only on certain days of the week.

ACL editors and browsers can use this operation to determine the ACL manager types that a particular reference monitor is using to protect a selected entity. Then, using the **rdacl_get_printstring( )** routine, they can determine how to format for display the permissions supported by a specific manager.

Notes　　This call is not intended to be used by application programs. The **sec_acl** application programming interface (API) provides all the functionality necessary to use the ACL facility. This reference page is provided for programmers who wish to write an ACL manager. In order to write an ACL manager, a programmer must implement the entire **rdacl** interface.

This network interface is called on the client side via the **sec_acl** local interface. Developers are responsible for implementing the server side of this interface. Test server code is included as a sample implementation.

Files　　**/usr/include/dce/rdaclif.idl**

　　　　The **idl** file from which **dce/rdaclif.h** was derived.

Errors　　**error_status_ok**

　　　　The call was successful.

Related Information

Functions: **rdacl_get_printstring(3sec)**, **sec_intro(3sec)**.

rdacl_get_printstring

Purpose   Returns printable ACL strings

Synopsis   **#include <dce/rdaclif.h>**

> **void rdacl_get_printstring(**
> > **handle_t** *h,*
> > **uuid_t** **manager_type,*
> > **unsigned32** *size_avail,*
> > **uuid_t** **manager_type_chain,*
> > **sec_acl_printstring_t** **manager_info,*
> > **boolean32** **tokenize,*
> > **unsigned32** **total_num_printstrings,*
> > **unsigned32** **size_used,*
> > **sec_acl_printstring_t** *printstrings[ ],*
> > **error_status_t** **status);*

Parameters

Input

h   A handle referring to the target object.

manager_type
> A pointer to the UUID identifying the type of the ACL manager in question. There may be more than one type of ACL manager protecting the object whose ACL is bound to the input handle. Use this parameter to distinguish them. Use **rdacl_get_manager_types( )** to acquire a list of the manager types protecting a given object.

size_avail   An unsigned 32-bit integer containing the allocated length of the *printstrings[ ]* array.

Output

manager_type_chain
If the target object ACL contains more than 32 permission bits, multiple manager types are used, one for each 32-bit wide slice of permissions. The UUID returned in *manager_type_chain* refers to the next ACL manager in the chain. If there are no more ACL managers for this ACL, **uuid_nil** is returned.

manager_info Provides a name and helpstring for the given ACL manager.

tokenize When FALSE this variable indicates that the returned permission printstrings are unambiguous and therefore may be concatenated when printed without confusion. When TRUE, however, this property does not hold, and the strings need to be separated when printed or passed.

total_num_printstrings
An unsigned 32-bit integer containing the total number of permission printstrings supported by this ACL manager type.

size_used An unsigned 32-bit integer containing the number of permission entries returned in the *printstrings*[ ] array.

printstrings[ ] An array of permission printstrings of type **sec_acl_printstring_t**. Each entry of the array is a structure containing three components:

printstring A character string of maximum length **sec_acl_printstring_len** containing the printable representation of a specified permission.

helpstring A character string of maximum length **sec_acl_printstring_help_len** containing some text that can be used to describe the specified permission.

permissions A **sec_acl_permset_t** permission set describing the permissions that are to be represented with the companion printstring.

The array consists of one such entry for each permission supported by the ACL manager identified by *manager_type*.

status A pointer to the completion status. On successful completion, the routine returns **error_status_ok**. Otherwise, it returns an error.

Description

The **rdacl_get_printstring( )** routine returns an array of printable representations (called printstrings) for each permission bit or combination of permission bits the specified ACL manager will support. The ACL manager type specified must be one of the types indicated by the ACL handle.

In addition to returning the printstrings, this routine also returns instructions about how to print the strings. When the *tokenize* variable is set to FALSE, a print string might be **r** or **w**, which could be concatenated in the display as **rw** without any confusion. However, when the *tokenize* variable is TRUE, it implies the printstrings might be of a form like **read** or **write**, which must be displayed separated by spaces or colons or something.

In any list of permission printstrings, there may appear to be some redundancy. ACL managers often define aliases for common permission combinations. By convention, however, simple entries need to appear at the beginning of the *printstrings*[ ] array, and combinations need to appear at the end.

Notes

This call is not intended to be used by application programs. The **sec_acl** application programming interface (API) provides all the functionality necessary to use the ACL facility. This reference page is provided for programmers who wish to write an ACL manager. In order to write an ACL manager, a programmer must implement the entire **rdacl** interface.

This network interface is called on the client side via the **sec_acl** local interface. Developers are responsible for implementing the server side of this interface. Test server code is included as a sample implementation.

Files

/usr/include/dce/rdaclif.idl
The **idl** file from which **dce/rdaclif.h** was derived.

Errors

sec_acl_unknown_manager_type
The manager type selected is not among those referenced by the input handle.

error_status_ok
The call was successful.

Related Information

Functions: **rdacl_get_manager_types(3sec)**, **sec_acl_bind(3sec)**, **sec_intro(3sec)**.

rdacl_get_referral

Purpose   Gets a referral to an ACL update site

Synopsis   **#include <dce/rdaclif.h>**

> **void rdacl_get_referral(**
>   **handle_t** *h*,
>   **sec_acl_component_name_t** *component_name*,
>   **uuid_t ****manager_type*,
>   **sec_acl_type_t** *sec_acl_type*,
>   **sec_acl_tower_set_t ****towers*[ ],
>   **error_status_t ****status*);

Parameters

Input

h   A handle referring to the target object.

component_name
                         A character string containing the name of the target object.

manager_type
                         A pointer to the UUID identifying the type of the ACL manager in question. There may be more than one type of ACL manager protecting the object whose ACL is bound to the input handle. Use this parameter to distinguish them. Use **sec_acl_get_manager_-types( )** to acquire a list of the manager types protecting a given object.

sec_acl_type   The ACL type. The **sec_acl_type_t** data type distinguishes the various types of ACLs an object can possess for a given manager type. The possible values are as follows:

- **sec_acl_type_object**

- **sec_acl_type_default_object**

- **sec_acl_type_default_container**

Output

towers[ ]   A pointer to address information indicating an ACL update site. This information, obtained from the RPC runtime, is used by the client-side code to construct a new ACL binding handle indicating a site that will not return the **sec_acl_site_readonly** error.

The **sec_acl_tower_set_t** structure contains an array of towers (called *towers*[ ]) and an unsigned 32-bit integer indicating the number of array elements (called *count*). This type enables the client to pass in an unallocated array of towers and have the server allocate the correct amount.

status   A pointer to the completion status. On successful completion, the routine returns **error_status_ok**. Otherwise, it returns an error.

Description

The **rdacl_get_referral( )** routine obtains a referral to an ACL update site. This function is used when the current ACL site yields a **sec_acl_site_readonly** error. Some replication managers will require all updates for a given object to be directed to a given replica. If clients of the generic ACL interface know they are dealing with an object that is replicated in this way, this function allows them to recover from the problem and rebind to the proper update site. The DCE network registry, for example, is replicated this way.

Notes

This call is not intended to be used by application programs. The **sec_acl** application programming interface (API) provides all the functionality necessary to use the ACL facility. This reference page is provided for programmers who wish to write an ACL manager. In order to write an ACL manager, a programmer must implement the entire **rdacl** interface.

This network interface is called on the client side via the **sec_acl** local interface. Developers are responsible for implementing the server side of this interface. Test server code is included as a sample implementation.

Files

/usr/include/dce/rdaclif.idl
        The **idl** file from which **dce/rdaclif.h** was derived.

Errors

sec_acl_unknown_manager_type
        The manager type selected is not an available option.

error_status_ok
        The call was successful.

Related Information

Functions: **sec_intro(3sec)**.

rdacl_lookup

Purpose   Returns the ACL for an object

Synopsis   **#include <dce/rdaclif.h>**

void rdacl_lookup(
      handle_t *h,*
      sec_acl_component_name_t *component_name,*
      uuid_t **manager_type,*
      sec_acl_type_t *sec_acl_type,*
      sec_acl_result_t **result*);

Parameters

Input

h   A handle referring to the target object.

component_name
      A character string containing the name of the target object.

manager_type
      A pointer to the UUID identifying the type of the ACL manager in question. There may be more than one type of ACL manager protecting the object whose ACL is bound to the input handle. Use this parameter to distinguish them. Use **sec_acl_get_manager_-types( )** to acquire a list of the manager types protecting a given object.

sec_acl_type   The ACL type. The **sec_acl_type_t** data type distinguishes the various types of ACLs an object can possess for a given manager type. The possible values are as follows:

- **sec_acl_type_object**

- **sec_acl_type_default_object**

- **sec_acl_type_default_container**

Output

result A pointer to a tagged union of type **sec_acl_result_t**. The tag is the completion status, **result.st**. If **result.st** is equal to **error_status_ok**, the union contains an ACL. Otherwise, the completion status indicates an error, and the union is empty.

If the call returned successfully, the **result.tagged_union.sec_acl_-list_t** structure contains a **sec_acl_list_t**. This data type is an array of pointers to **sec_acl_t**s that define ACLs. If the permission set of the returned ACL is 32 bits or smaller, **sec_acl_list_t** points to only one **sec_acl_t**. If the permission set of the returned ACL is larger than 32 bits, multiple **sec_acl_t**s are used to hold them, and the **sec_acl_list_t** points to multiple **sec_acl_t**s.

Description

The **rdacl_lookup()** routine loads into memory a copy of an object's ACL corresponding to the specified manager type. The routine returns a pointer to the ACL. This routine is only used by ACL editors and browsers; an application would use **sec_acl_test_access()** or **sec_acl_test_access_on_behalf()** to process the contents of an ACL.

Notes

This call is not intended to be used by application programs. The **sec_acl** application programming interface (API) provides all the functionality necessary to use the ACL facility. This reference page is provided for programmers who wish to write an ACL manager. In order to write an ACL manager, a programmer must implement the entire **rdacl** interface.

This network interface is called on the client side via the **sec_acl** local interface. Developers are responsible for implementing the server side of this interface. Test server code is included as a sample implementation.

Files

/usr/include/dce/rdaclif.idl
The **idl** file from which **dce/rdaclif.h** was derived.

Errors

sec_acl_unknown_manager_type
The manager type selected is not an available option.

sec_acl_cant_allocate_memory
The requested operation requires more memory than is available.

error_status_ok
The call was successful.

Related Information

Functions: **sec_acl_bind(3sec)**, **sec_acl_test_access(3sec)**, **sec_acl_test_access_on_behalf(3sec)**, **sec_intro(3sec)**.

rdacl_replace

Purpose   Replaces an ACL

Synopsis   **#include <dce/rdaclif.h>**

void rdacl_replace(
      handle_t *h*,
      sec_acl_component_name_t *component_name*,
      uuid_t *manager_type,
      sec_acl_type_t *sec_acl_type*,
      sec_acl_list_t *sec_acl_list,
      error_status_t *status);

Parameters

Input

h   A handle referring to the target object.

component_name
A character string containing the name of the target object.

manager_type
A pointer to the UUID identifying the type of the ACL manager in question. There may be more than one type of ACL manager protecting the object whose ACL is bound to the input handle. Use this parameter to distinguish them. Use **sec_acl_get_manager_-types( )** to acquire a list of the manager types protecting a given object.

sec_acl_type   The ACL type. The **sec_acl_type_t** data type distinguishes the various types of ACLs an object can possess for a given manager type. The possible values are as follows:

- **sec_acl_type_object**

- **sec_acl_type_default_object**

- **sec_acl_type_default_container**

rdacl_replace(3sec)

          sec_acl_list   The new ACL to use for the target object. This is represented by a pointer to the **sec_acl_list_t** structure containing the complete access control list. An ACL contains a list of ACL entries, the UUID of the default cell where authentication takes place (foreign entries in the ACL contain the name of their parent cell), and the UUID of the ACL manager to interpret the list.

Output

          status   A pointer to the completion status. On successful completion, the routine returns **error_status_ok**. Otherwise, it returns an error.

Description

The **rdacl_replace( )** routine replaces the ACL indicated by the input handle with the information in the *sec_acl_list* parameter. ACLs are thought of as immutable, and in order to modify them, an editing application must read an entire ACL (using the **sec_acl_lookup( )** routine), modify it as needed, and replace it using this routine.

Notes

This call is not intended to be used by application programs. The **sec_acl** application programming interface (API) provides all the functionality necessary to use the ACL facility. This reference page is provided for programmers who wish to write an ACL manager. In order to write an ACL manager, a programmer must implement the entire **rdacl** interface.

This network interface is called on the client side via the **sec_acl** local interface. Developers are responsible for implementing the server side of this interface. Test server code is included as a sample implementation.

Files

/usr/include/dce/rdaclif.idl

    The **idl** file from which **dce/rdaclif.h** was derived.

Errors

sec_acl_unknown_manager_type

    The manager type selected is not an available option.

error_status_ok

    The call was successful.

Related Information

Functions: **sec_acl_bind(3sec)**, **sec_acl_lookup(3sec)**, **sec_intro(3sec)**.

rdacl_test_access

Purpose   Tests access to an object

Synopsis   **#include <dce/rdaclif.h>**

boolean32 rdacl_test_access(
   handle_t *h,*
   sec_acl_component_name_t *component_name,*
   uuid_t **manager_type,*
   sec_acl_permset_t *desired_permset,*
   error_status_t **status);*

Parameters

Input

h   A handle referring to the target object.

component_name
                A character string containing the name of the target object.

manager_type
                A pointer to the UUID identifying the type of the ACL manager in question. There may be more than one type of ACL manager protecting the object whose ACL is bound to the input handle. Use this parameter to distinguish them. Use **sec_acl_get_manager_-types( )** to acquire a list of the manager types protecting a given object.

desired_permset
                A permission set in **sec_acl_permset_t** form containing the desired privileges. This is a 32-bit set of permission flags supported by the manager type.

Output

status   A pointer to the completion status. On successful completion, the routine returns **error_status_ok**. Otherwise, it returns an error.

rdacl_test_access(3sec)

Description

The **rdacl_test_access**( ) routine determines if the specified ACL contains entries granting privileges to the calling process matching those in *desired_permset*. An application generally only inquires after the minimum set of privileges needed to accomplish a specific task.

Notes

This call is not intended to be used by application programs. The **sec_acl** application programming interface (API) provides all the functionality necessary to use the ACL facility. This reference page is provided for programmers who wish to write an ACL manager. In order to write an ACL manager, a programmer must implement the entire **rdacl** interface.

This network interface is called on the client side via the **sec_acl** local interface. Developers are responsible for implementing the server side of this interface. Test server code is included as a sample implementation.

Files

/usr/include/dce/rdaclif.idl
> The **idl** file from which **dce/rdaclif.h** was derived.

Errors

sec_acl_unknown_manager_type
> The manager type selected is not an available option.

error_status_ok
> The call was successful.

Related Information

Functions: **rdacl_test_access_on_behalf(3sec)**, **sec_intro(3sec)**.

rdacl_test_access_on_behalf

Purpose Tests access to an object on behalf of another process

Synopsis **#include <dce/rdaclif.h>**

boolean rdacl_test_access_on_behalf(
  handle_t *h*,
  sec_acl_component_name_t *component_name*,
  uuid_t *manager_type,
  sec_id_pac_t *subject,
  sec_acl_permset_t *desired_permset*,
  error_status_t *status);

Parameters

Input

  h   A handle referring to the target object.

  component_name
         A character string containing the name of the target object.

  manager_type
         A pointer to the UUID identifying the type of the ACL manager in
         question. There may be more than one type of ACL manager
         protecting the object whose ACL is bound to the input handle. Use
         this parameter to distinguish them. Use **sec_acl_get_manager_-**
         types( ) to acquire a list of the manager types protecting a given
         object.

  subject   A privilege attribute certificate (PAC) for the subject process. The
         PAC contains the name and UUID of the principal and parent cell of
         the subject process, as well as a list of any groups to which it
         belongs. The PAC also contains a flag (named **authenticated**).
         When set, it indicates that the certificate was obtained from an
         authenticated source. When not set, the certificate must not be
         trusted.

The field is FALSE when it was obtained from the **rpc_auth** layer and the protect level was set to **rpc_c_protect_level_none**. This indicates that no authentication protocol was actually used in the remote procedure call; the identity was simply transmitted from the caller to the callee. If an authentication protocol was used, then the flag is set to TRUE. A server uses **rpc_binding_inq_auth_client**( ) to acquire a certificate for the client process.

desired_permset

A permission set in **sec_acl_permset_t** form containing the desired privileges. This is a 32-bit set of permission flags supported by the manager type.

Output

status   A pointer to the completion status. On successful completion, the routine returns **error_status_ok**. Otherwise, it returns an error.

Description

The **rdacl_test_access_on_behalf**( ) routine determines if the specified ACL contains entries granting privileges to the subject, a process besides the calling process, matching those in *desired_permset*. This routine succeeds only if the access is available to both the caller process as well as the subject identified in the call. An application will generally only inquire after the minimum set of privileges needed to accomplish a specific task.

Notes

This call is not intended to be used by application programs. The **sec_acl** application programming interface (API) provides all the functionality necessary to use the ACL facility. This reference page is provided for programmers who wish to write an ACL manager. In order to write an ACL manager, a programmer must implement the entire **rdacl** interface.

This network interface is called on the client side via the **sec_acl** local interface. Developers are responsible for implementing the server side of this interface. Test server code is included as a sample implementation.

Files

/usr/include/dce/rdaclif.idl

The **idl** file from which **dce/rdaclif.h** was derived.

Errors   **sec_acl_unknown_manager_type**
    The manager type selected is not an available option.

error_status_ok
    The call was successful.

Related Information

Functions: **rdacl_test_access(3sec)**, **rpc_binding_inq_auth_client(3rpc)**, **sec_intro(3sec)**.

rsec_pwd_mgmt_gen_pwd

Purpose   Generates a set of passwords

Synopsis   **#include <dce/rsec_pwd_mgmt.h>**

void rsec_pwd_mgmt_gen_pwd(
        handle_t *pwd_mgmt_svr_h,*
        sec_rgy_name_t *princ_name,*
        unsigned32 *plcy_args,*
        sec_attr_t *plcy[ ],*
        sec_bytes_t *gen_info_in,*
        unsigned32 *num_pwds,*
        unsigned32 **num_returned,*
        sec_passwd_rec_t *gen_pwd_set[ ],*
        sec_bytes_t **gen_info_out,*
        error_status_t **stp*
)

Parameters

Input

> *pwd_mgmt_svr_h*
> > An RPC binding handle to the password management server exporting this operation.
>
> *princ_name*   The name of the principal requesting the generated passwords.
>
> *plcy_args*   The size of the plcy array.
>
> *plcy*   An array of extended registry attributes, each specifying a password management policy of some sort. The contents of this array are as follows:
>
> > **plcy[0]**   Effective registry password minimum length for the principal.
> >
> > **plcy[1]**   Effective registry password policy flags for the principal, describing limitations on password characters.

gen_info_in   An NDR pickle containing additional information needed to generate the passwords. There are currently no encoding types defined.

num_pwds   The number of generated passwords requested.

Output

num_returned The number of generated passwords returned.

gen_pwd_set An array of generated passwords, each stored in a **sec_passwd_- rec_t** structure.

gen_info_out An NDR pickle containing additional information returned by the password management server. There are currently no encoding types defined.

stp   A pointer to the completion status. On successful completion, the routine returns **error_status_ok**. Otherwise, it returns an error.

Description

The **rsec_pwd_mgmt_gen_pwd**( ) routine returns a set of generated passwords.

Notes

This function is not intended to be called by application programmers. The **sec_pwd_mgmt**( ) API provides all the functionality necessary to retrieve generated passwords. This reference page is provided for programmers who want to write their own password management servers.

This network interface is called on the client side via the **sec_pwd_mgmt_gen_pwd**( ) operation. Developers are responsible for implementing the server side of this interface. (**pwd_strengthd(8sec)** is provided as a sample implementation.)

The **plcy**[ ] parameter is intended to be expandable to allow administrators to attach new password policy ERAs to a principal. This feature is, however, currently unsupported, and the **plcy**[ ] parameter consists only of the entries described in this reference page.

rsec_pwd_mgmt_gen_pwd(3sec)

Files   **/usr/include/dce/sec_pwd_mgmt.idl**

The **idl** file from which **dce/sec_pwd_mgmt.h** was derived.

Errors   **sec_pwd_mgmt_not_authorized**

The user is not authorized to call this API.

sec_pwd_mgmt_svr_error

Password management server generic error. Additional information is usually logged by the password management server.

error_status_ok

The call was successful.

Related Information

Functions: **pwd_strengthd(8sec)**, **rsec_pwd_mgmt_str_chk(3sec)**, **sec_intro(3sec)**, **sec_pwd_mgmt_gen_pwd(3sec)**.

rsec_pwd_mgmt_str_chk

Purpose   Strength-checks a password

Synopsis   **#include <dce/rsec_pwd_mgmt.h>**

boolean32 rsec_pwd_mgmt_str_chk(
    handle_t *handle*,
    sec_rgy_name_t *princ*,
    sec_passwd_rec_t **pwd*,
    signed32 *pwd_val_type*,
    unsigned32 *plcy_args*,
    sec_attr_t *plcy*[ ],
    sec_bytes_t *str_info_in*,
    sec_bytes_t **str_info_out*,
    error_status_t **stp*
)

Parameters

Input

handle   An RPC binding handle to the password management server exporting this operation.

princ   The name of the principal requesting the generated passwords.

pwd   A pointer to the password to be strength checked.

pwd_val_type The value of the user's password validation type (as stored in the **pwd_val_type** ERA).

plcy_args   The size of the **plcy** array.

plcy   An array of extended registry attributes, each specifying a password management policy of some sort. The contents of this array are as follows:

        plcy[0]   Effective registry password minimum length for the principal.

        plcy[1]   Effective registry password policy flags for the principal, describing limitations on password characters.

str_info_in   An NDR pickle containing additional information needed to strength check the password. There are currently no encoding types defined.

Output

str_info_out   An NDR pickle containing additional information returned by the password management server. There are currently no encoding types defined.

stp   A pointer to the completion status. On successful completion, the routine returns **error_status_ok**. Otherwise, it returns an error.

Description

The **rsec_pwd_mgmt_str_chk( )** routine strength checks a password.

Notes

This function is not intended to be called by application programmers. The registry server provides all the functionality necessary to strength check passwords. This reference page is provided for programmers who wish to write their own password management servers.

This network interface is called on the client side via **secd(8)**. Developers are responsible for implementing the server side of this interface. (**pwd_strengthd(8sec)** is provided as a sample implementation.)

The **plcy**[ ] parameter is intended to be expandable to allow administrators to attach new password policy ERAs to a principal. This feature is, however, currently unsupported, and the **plcy**[ ] parameter consists only of the entries described in this reference page.

Return Value

The **rsec_pwd_mgmt_str_chk( )** routine returns TRUE if the user's password passes the server's strength checking algorithm and FALSE if it does not.

Files

/usr/include/dce/sec_pwd_mgmt.idl
The **idl** file from which **dce/sec_pwd_mgmt.h** was derived.

Errors

sec_pwd_mgmt_str_check_failed
The password failed the server's strength checking algorithm.

sec_pwd_mgmt_not_authorized
The user is not authorized to call this API.

sec_pwd_mgmt_svr_error
Password management server generic error. Additional information is usually logged by the password management server.

error_status_ok
The call was successful

Related Information

Functions: **pwd_strengthd(8sec)**, **rsec_pwd_mgmt_gen_pwd(3sec)**, **sec_intro(3sec)**.

sec_acl_bind

Purpose   Returns a handle for an object's ACL

Synopsis   **#include <dce/daclif.h>**

> **void sec_acl_bind(**
> > **unsigned char ****entry_name***,
> > **boolean32** *bind_to_entry*,
> > **sec_acl_handle_t ****h***,
> > **error_status_t ****status***);**

Parameters

Input

> *entry_name*   The name of the target object. Subsequent ACL operations using the returned handle will affect the ACL of this object.
>
> *bind_to_entry*   Bind indicator, for use when *entry_name* identifies both an entry in the global namespace and an actual object. A TRUE value binds the handle to the entry in the namespace, while FALSE binds the handle to the actual object.

Output

> *h*   A pointer to the **sec_acl_handle_t** variable to receive the returned ACL handle. The other **sec_acl** routines use this handle to refer to the ACL for the object specified with *entry_name*.
>
> *status*   A pointer to the completion status. On successful completion, the routine returns **error_status_ok**. Otherwise, it returns an error.

Description

The **sec_acl_bind( )** routine returns a handle bound to the indicated object's ACL. This routine is central to all the other **sec_acl** routines, each of which requires this handle to identify the ACL on which to operate.

Notes   If the specified name is both an actual object, and an entry in the global namespace, there are two ACLs associated with it. For example, in addition to the ACL normally attached to file system objects, the root directory of a file system has an ACL corresponding to its entry in the global namespace. This controls access by outsiders to the entire file system, whereas the resident ACL for the root directory only controls access to the directory and, by inheritance, its subdirectories. The ambiguity must be resolved with the *bind_to_entry* parameter.

Files   **/usr/include/dce/daclif.idl**
> The **idl** file from which **dce/daclif.h** was derived.

Errors   **sec_acl_object_not_found**
> The requested object could not be found.

sec_acl_no_acl_found
> There is no ACL associated with the specified object.

error_status_ok
> The call was successful.

Related Information

Functions: **sec_intro(3sec)**.

sec_acl_bind_to_addr

Purpose   Returns a handle to an object identified by its network address

Synopsis   #include <dce/daclif.h>

void sec_acl_bind_to_addr(
        unsigned char *site_addr,
        sec_acl_component_name_t component_name,
        sec_acl_handle_t *h,
        error_status_t *status);

Parameters

Input

site_addr   An RPC string binding to the fully qualified network address of the target object.

component_name
                The name of the target object. Subsequent ACL operations using the returned handle will affect the ACL of this object.

Output

h   A pointer to the **sec_acl_handle_t** variable to receive the returned ACL handle. The other **sec_acl** routines use this handle to refer to the ACL for the object specified with *entry_name*.

status   A pointer to the completion status. On successful completion, the routine returns **error_status_ok**. Otherwise, it returns an error.

Description

The **sec_acl_bind_to_addr( )** routine returns a handle bound to the indicated object's ACL manager. This routine and the **sec_acl_bind( )** routine are central to all the other **sec_acl** routines, each of which requires a handle to identify the ACL on which to operate.

This routine differs from **sec_acl_bind( )** in that it binds to the network address of the target object, rather than to a cell namespace entry. Therefore, unlike **sec_acl_bind( )**, it is possible to pass **sec_acl_bind_to_addr( )** a null string as a component name and to bind with a nonexistent name. The purpose of this call is to eliminate the necessity of looking up an object's name. To validate the name, use **sec_acl_bind( )**.

Files   **/usr/include/dce/daclif.idl**
        The **idl** file from which **dce/daclif.h** was derived.

Errors   **sec_acl_object_not_found**
        The requested object could not be found.

        sec_acl_no_acl_found
        There is no ACL associated with the specified object.

        sec_acl_unable_to_authenticate
        The call could not authenticate to the server that manages the target object's ACL.

        sec_acl_bind_error
        The call could not bind to the requested site.

        sec_acl_invalid_site_name
        The *site_addr* parameter is invalid.

        sec_acl_cant_allocate_memory
        Memory allocation failure.

        error_status_ok
        The call was successful.

Related Information
        Functions: **sec_intro(3sec)**.

sec_acl_calc_mask

Purpose   Returns the **sec_acl_type_mask_obj** entry for the specified ACL list

Synopsis   #include <dce/daclif.h>

void sec_acl_calc_mask(
        sec_acl_list_t *sec_acl_list,
        error_status_t *status);

Parameters

Input/Output

sec_acl_list   A pointer to a **sec_acl_type_t** the specifies the number of ACLs of each ACL type. The **sec_acl_type_t** data type distinguishes between the various types of ACLs an object can possess for a given manager. In the file system, for example, most objects have only one ACL, controlling the access to that object, but objects that control the creation of other objects (sometimes referred to as *containers*) may have more. A directory, for example, can have ACLs to be used as initial values when member objects are created.

Do not confuse ACL types with the permissions corresponding to different ACL manager types or with the ACL manager types themselves.

Output

status   A pointer to the completion status. On successful completion, the routine returns **error_status_ok**. Otherwise, it returns an error.

Description

The **sec_acl_calc_mask( )** routine calculates and sets the **sec_acl_e_type_mask_-obj** entry of the specified ACL list. The value of the **sec_acl_e_type_mask_obj** entry is the union of the permissions of all ACL entries that refer to members of the file group class.

This operation is performed locally, within the client. The function does not check to determine if the manager to which the specified ACL list will be submitted supports the **sec_acl_e_type_mask_obj** entry type. The calling application must determine whether to call this routine, after obtaining the required, if any, POSIX semantics, via the **sec_acl_get_mgr_types_semantics( )** routine.

Notes   This call is provided in source code form.

Files   **/usr/include/dce/daclif.idl**
   The **idl** file from which **dce/daclif.h** was derived.

Errors   **sec_acl_cant_allocate_memory**
   Requested operation requires more memory than is available.

   error_status_ok
   The call was successful.

Related Information

Functions: **sec_intro(3sec)**.

sec_acl_get_access

Purpose   Lists the access (permission set) that the caller has for an object

Synopsis   **#include <dce/daclif.h>**

void sec_acl_get_access(
        sec_acl_handle_t *h*,
        uuid_t *manager_type,
        sec_acl_permset_t *net_rights,
        error_status_t *status);

Parameters

Input

h
    A handle referring to the object whose ACL is to be accessed. Use **sec_acl_bind( )** to create this handle.

manager_type
    A pointer to the UUID identifying the manager type of the ACL in question. There may be more than one type of ACL manager protecting the object whose ACL is bound to the input handle. Use this parameter to distinguish them. Use **sec_acl_get_manager_-types( )** to acquire a list of the manager types protecting a given object.

Output

net_rights
    The output list of access rights in **sec_acl_permset_t** form. This is a 32-bit set of permission flags supported by the manager type.

status
    A pointer to the completion status. On successful completion, the routine returns **error_status_ok**. Otherwise, it returns an error.

Description

The **sec_acl_get_access( )** routine determines the complete extent of access to the specified object by the calling process. Although the **scc_acl_test_access( )** and **sec_acl_test_access_on_behalf( )** routines are the preferred method of testing access, this routine is useful for implementing operations like the conventional UNIX access function.

Permissions Required

The **sec_acl_get_access( )** routine requires at least one permission of any kind on the object for which the access is to be returned.

Files

/usr/include/dce/daclif.idl

The **idl** file from which **dce/daclif.h** was derived.

Errors

error_status_ok

The call was successful.

Related Information

Functions: **sec_acl_test_access(3sec)**, **sec_acl_test_access_on_behalf(3sec)**.

sec_acl_get_error_info

Purpose   Returns error information from an ACL handle

Synopsis   **#include <dce/daclif.h>**

        error_status_t sec_acl_get_error_info(
            sec_acl_handle_t *h*);

Parameters

Input

    h   A handle referring to the target ACL. The handle is bound to the ACL with the **sec_acl_bind( )** routine, which also specifies the name of the object to which the target ACL belongs.

Description

The **sec_acl_get_error_info( )** routine returns error information from the specified ACL handle.

During a call to a routine in the **sec_acl** application programming interface (API), error codes received from the RPC runtime or other APIs are saved in the ACL handle and a corresponding error code from the **sec_acl** set is passed back by the ACL API. The **sec_acl_get_error_info( )** routine returns the last error code stored in the ACL handle for those clients who need to know exactly what went wrong.

Files   **/usr/include/dce/daclif.idl**
        The **idl** file from which **dce/daclif.h** was derived.

Return Values

This routine returns a value of type **error_status_t**, indicating the cause of the last error issued by the RPC runtime.

Errors   **sec_acl_invalid_handle**

The ACL handle specified by **sec_acl_handle_t** is invalid.

Related Information

Functions: **sec_acl_bind(3sec)**, **sec_acl_lookup(3sec)**, **sec_intro(3sec)**.

sec_acl_get_manager_types

Purpose   Lists the manager types of the ACLs protecting an object

Synopsis   **#include <dce/daclif.h>**

void sec_acl_get_manager_types(
      sec_acl_handle_t *h*,
      sec_acl_type_t *sec_acl_type*,
      unsigned32 *size_avail*,
      unsigned32 **size_used*,
      unsigned32 **num_types*,
      uuid_t *manager_types*[ ],
      error_status_t **status*);

Parameters

Input

h   A handle referring to the target object. Use **sec_acl_bind( )** to create this handle.

sec_acl_type   The ACL type. The **sec_acl_type_t** data type distinguishes the various types of ACLs an object can possess for a given manager type. The possible values are as follows:

- **sec_acl_type_object**

- **sec_acl_type_default_object**

- **sec_acl_type_default_container**

size_avail   An unsigned 32-bit integer containing the allocated length of the *manager_types*[ ] array.

Output

size_used   An unsigned 32-bit integer containing the number of output entries returned in the *manager_types*[ ] array.

num_types   An unsigned 32-bit integer containing the number of types returned in the *manager_types*[ ] array. This may be greater than *size_used* if there was not enough space allocated in the *manager_types*[ ] array for all the manager types.

manager_types[ ]
                An array of length *size_avail* to contain UUIDs (of type **uuid_t**) identifying the different types of ACL managers protecting the target object.

status   A pointer to the completion status. On successful completion, the routine returns **error_status_ok**. Otherwise, it returns an error.

Description

The **sec_acl_get_manager_types( )** routine returns a list of the manager types of ACLs of type *sec_acl_type* that are protecting the object identified by *h*. For example, in addition to the regular file system ACL, a file representing the stable storage of some database could have an ACL manager that supported permissions allowing database updates only on certain days of the week.

ACL editors and browsers can use this operation to determine the ACL manager types that a particular reference monitor is using to protect a selected entity. Then, using the **sec_acl_get_printstring( )** routine, they can determine how to format for display the permissions supported by a specific manager.

Permissions Required

The **sec_acl_get_manager_types( )** routine requires at least one permission of any kind on the object for which the ACL manager types are to be returned.

Files

/usr/include/dce/daclif.idl
                The **idl** file from which **dce/daclif.h** was derived.

Errors

error_status_ok
                The call was successful.

Related Information

Functions: **sec_acl_bind(3sec)**, **sec_acl_get_printstring(3sec)**, **sec_intro(3sec)**.

sec_acl_get_mgr_types_semantics

Purpose   Lists the manager types of the ACLs protecting an object

Synopsis   **#include <dce/daclif.h>**

    void sec_acl_get_mgr_types_semantics(
        sec_acl_handle_t *h*,
        sec_acl_type_t *sec_acl_type*,
        unsigned32 *size_avail*,
        unsigned32 **size_used*,
        unsigned32 **num_types*,
        uuid_t *manager_types*[ ],
        sec_acl_posix_semantics_t *posix_semantics*[ ],
        error_status_t **status*);

Parameters

Input

    h   A handle referring to the target object. Use **sec_acl_bind( )** to create this handle.

    sec_acl_type The ACL type. The **sec_acl_type_t** data type distinguishes the various types of ACLs an object can possess for a given manager type. The possible values are as follows:

        • **sec_acl_type_object**

        • **sec_acl_type_default_object**

        • **sec_acl_type_default_container**

    size_avail An unsigned 32-bit integer containing the allocated length of the *manager_types*[ ] array.

Output

    size_used An unsigned 32-bit integer containing the number of output entries returned in the *manager_types*[ ] array.

num_types   An unsigned 32-bit integer containing the number of types returned in the *manager_types*[ ] array. This may be greater than *size_used* if there was not enough space allocated in the *manager_types*[ ] array for all the manager types.

manager_types[ ]

An array of length *size_avail* to contain UUIDs (of type **uuid_t**) identifying the different types of ACL managers protecting the target object.

posix_semantics[ ]

An array of POSIX semantics supported by each manager type with entries of type **sec_acl_posix_semantics_t**.

status   A pointer to the completion status. On successful completion, the routine returns **error_status_ok**. Otherwise, it returns an error.

Description

The **sec_acl_get_mgr_types_semantics( )** routine returns a list of the manager types of ACLs of type *sec_acl_type* that are protecting the object identified by *h*. For example, in addition to the regular file system ACL, a file representing the stable storage of some database could have an ACL manager that supported permissions allowing database updates only on certain days of the week.

ACL editors and browsers can use this operation to determine the ACL manager types that a particular reference monitor is using to protect a selected entity. Then, using the **sec_acl_get_printstring( )** routine, they can determine how to format for display the permissions supported by a specific manager.

Permissions Required

The **sec_acl_get_mgr_types_semantics( )** routine requires at least one permission of any kind on the object for which the ACL manager types are to be returned.

Files
/usr/include/dce/daclif.idl

The **idl** file from which **dce/daclif.h** was derived.

Errors
error_status_ok

The call was successful.

sec_acl_get_mgr_types_semantics(3sec)

Related Information

Functions: **sec_acl_bind(3sec), sec_acl_get_printstring(3sec), sec_intro(3sec).**

sec_acl_get_printstring

Purpose   Returns printable ACL strings

Synopsis   **#include <dce/daclif.h>**

void sec_acl_get_printstring(
        sec_acl_handle_t *h,*
        uuid_t **manager_type,*
        unsigned32 *size_avail,*
        uuid_t **manager_type_chain,*
        sec_acl_printstring_t **manager_info,*
        boolean32 **tokenize,*
        unsigned32 **total_num_printstrings,*
        unsigned32 **size_used,*
        sec_acl_printstring_t *printstrings*[ ],
        error_status_t **status*);

Parameters

Input

h
        A handle referring to the target object. Use **sec_acl_bind**( ) to create this handle.

manager_type
        A pointer to the UUID identifying the type of the ACL manager in question. There may be more than one type of ACL manager protecting the object whose ACL is bound to the input handle. Use this parameter to distinguish them. Use **sec_acl_get_manager_-types**( ) to acquire a list of the manager types protecting a given object.

size_avail
        An unsigned 32-bit integer containing the allocated length of the *printstrings*[ ] array.

Output

manager_type_chain
> If the target object ACL contains more than 32 permission bits, multiple manager types are used, one for each 32-bit wide "slice" of permissions. The UUID returned in *manager_type_chain* refers to the next ACL manager in the chain. If there are no more ACL managers for this ACL, **uuid_nil** is returned.

manager_info Provides a name and help string for the given ACL manager.

tokenize
> When FALSE, this variable indicates that the returned permission printstrings are unambiguous and therefore may be concatenated when printed without confusion. When TRUE, however, this property does not hold, and the strings need to be separated when printed or passed.

total_num_printstrings
> An unsigned 32-bit integer containing the total number of permission printstrings supported by this ACL manager type.

size_used
> An unsigned 32-bit integer containing the number of permission entries returned in the *printstrings*[ ] array.

printstrings[ ] An array of permission printstrings of type **sec_acl_printstring_t**. Each entry of the array is a structure containing the following three components:

> **printstring** A character string of maximum length **sec_acl_printstring_len** describing the printable representation of a specified permission.

> **helpstring** A character string of maximum length **sec_acl_printstring_help_len** containing some text that can be used to describe the specified permission.

> **permissions** A **sec_acl_permset_t** permission set describing the permissions that are represented with the companion printstring.

> The array consists of one such entry for each permission supported by the ACL manager identified by *manager_type*.

status
> A pointer to the completion status. On successful completion, the routine returns **error_status_ok**. Otherwise, it returns an error.

Description

The **sec_acl_get_printstring( )** routine returns an array of printable representations (called *printstrings*) for each permission bit or combination of permission bits the specified ACL manager supports. The ACL manager type specified must be one of the types protecting the object indicated by *h*.

In addition to returning the printstrings, this routine also returns instructions about how to print the strings. When the *tokenize* variable is set to FALSE, a printstring might be **r** or **w**, which could be concatenated in the display as **rw** without any confusion. However, when the *tokenize* variable is TRUE, it implies the printstrings might be of a form like **read** or **write**, which must be displayed separated by spaces or colons or something.

In any list of permission printstrings, there may appear to be some redundancy. ACL managers often define aliases for common permission combinations. By convention, however, simple entries should appear at the beginning of the *printstrings*[ ] array, and combinations should appear at the end.

Files

/usr/include/dce/daclif.idl
> The **idl** file from which **dce/daclif.h** was derived.

Errors

sec_acl_unknown_manager_type
> The manager type selected is not among those referenced by the input handle.

error_status_ok
> The call was successful.

Related Information

Functions: **sec_acl_bind(3sec)**, **sec_acl_get_manager_types(3sec)**, **sec_intro(3sec)**.

sec_acl_lookup

Purpose   Returns the ACL for an object

Synopsis   **#include <dce/daclif.h>**

void sec_acl_lookup(
        sec_acl_handle_t *h*,
        uuid_t *manager_type,
        sec_acl_type_t *sec_acl_type*,
        sec_acl_list_t *sec_acl_list,
        error_status_t *status);

Parameters

Input

h   A handle referring to the target object. Use **sec_acl_bind( )** to create this handle.

manager_type
A pointer to the UUID identifying the type of the ACL manager in question. There may be more than one type of ACL manager protecting the object whose ACL is bound to the input handle. Use this parameter to distinguish them. Use **sec_acl_get_manager_-types( )** to acquire a list of the manager types protecting a given object.

sec_acl_type   The ACL type. The **sec_acl_type_t** data type distinguishes the various types of ACLs an object can possess for a given manager type. The possible values are as follows:

- **sec_acl_type_object**

- **sec_acl_type_default_object**

- **sec_acl_type_default_container**

Output

sec_acl_list   A pointer to the **sec_acl_list_t** structure to receive the complete access control list. An ACL contains a list of ACL entries, the UUID of the default cell where authentication takes place (foreign entries in the ACL contain the name of their home cell), and the UUID of the ACL manager to interpret the list.

status   A pointer to the completion status. On successful completion, the routine returns **error_status_ok**. Otherwise, it returns an error.

Description

The **sec_acl_lookup()** routine loads into memory a copy of an object's ACL corresponding to the specified manager type. The routine returns a pointer to the ACL. This routine is only used by ACL editors and browsers; an application would use **sec_acl_test_access()** or **sec_acl_test_access_on_behalf()** to process the contents of an ACL.

Permissions Required

The **sec_acl_lookup()** routine requires at least one permission of any kind on the object for which the ACL is to be returned.

Notes

The memory containing the **sec_acl_t** structure for each ACL is dynamically allocated. Use the **sec_acl_release()** routine to return each ACL's memory block to the pool when an application is finished with the ACLs.

Files

/usr/include/dce/daclif.idl
          The **idl** file from which **dce/daclif.h** was derived.

Errors

sec_acl_unknown_manager_type
          The manager type selected is not an available option.

sec_acl_cant_allocate_memory
          The requested operation requires more memory than is available.

Related Information

Functions: **sec_acl_bind(3sec), sec_acl_test_access(3sec),
sec_acl_test_access_on_behalf(3sec), sec_intro(3sec)**.

sec_acl_release

Purpose   Releases ACL storage

Synopsis   **#include <dce/daclif.h>**

void sec_acl_release(
          sec_acl_handle_t *h*,
          sec_acl_t **sec_acl*,
          error_status_t **status*);

Parameters

Input

h   A handle referring to the target object. Use **sec_acl_bind( )** to create this handle.

sec_acl   A pointer to the complete ACL associated with the target object.

Output

status   A pointer to the completion status. On successful completion, the routine returns **error_status_ok**. Otherwise, it returns an error.

Description

The **sec_acl_release( )** routine releases any local storage associated with the ACL object, returning it to the pool. This is strictly a local operation (since the storage in question is local), and has no effect on the remote object or its ACL. The ACL handle is in the argument list only for consistency with other **sec_acl** routines.

Files

/usr/include/dce/daclif.idl
          The **idl** file from which **dce/daclif.h** was derived.

Errors   error_status_ok
                     The call was successful.

Related Information

Functions: **sec_acl_bind(3sec)**, **sec_acl_lookup(3sec)**, **sec_intro(3sec)**.

sec_acl_release_handle

Purpose   Removes an ACL handle

Synopsis   **#include <dce/daclif.h>**

void sec_acl_release_handle(
        sec_acl_handle_t *h,
        error_status_t *status);

Parameters

Input

h   The handle to be removed. The handle is bound to the object to
             which the ACL belongs with the **sec_acl_bind( )** routine.

Output

status   A pointer to the completion status. On successful completion, the
             routine returns **error_status_ok**. Otherwise, it returns an error.

Description

The **sec_acl_release_handle( )** routine removes the specified handle. This is
strictly a local operation, and has no effect on the remote object or its ACL.

Files   **/usr/include/dce/daclif.idl**
             The **idl** file from which **dce/daclif.h** was derived.

Errors   error_status_ok
             The call was successful.

Related Information

Functions: **sec_acl_bind(3sec)**, **sec_intro(3sec)**.

sec_acl_replace

Purpose   Replaces an ACL

Synopsis   **#include <dce/daclif.h>**

   void sec_acl_replace(
       sec_acl_handle_t *h*,
       uuid_t *manager_type,
       sec_acl_type_t *sec_acl_type*,
       sec_acl_list_t *sec_acl_list,
       error_status_t *status);

Parameters

Input

h
A handle referring to the target object. Use **sec_acl_bind( )** to create this handle.

manager_type
A pointer to the UUID identifying the type of the ACL manager in question. There may be more than one type of ACL manager protecting the object whose ACL is bound to the input handle. Use this parameter to distinguish them. Use **sec_acl_get_manager_-types( )** to acquire a list of the manager types protecting a given object.

sec_acl_type   The ACL type. The **sec_acl_type_t** data type distinguishes the various types of ACLs an object can possess for a given manager type. The possible values are as follows:

- **sec_acl_type_object**

- **sec_acl_type_default_object**

- **sec_acl_type_default_container**

sec_acl_list   The new ACL to use for the target object. This is represented by a pointer to the **sec_acl_list_t** structure containing the complete access control list. An ACL contains a list of ACL entries, the UUID of the default cell where authentication will take place (foreign entries in the ACL contain the name of their parent cell), and the UUID of the ACL manager to interpret the list.

sec_acl_replace(3sec)

Output

    status   A pointer to the completion status. On successful completion, the routine returns **error_status_ok**. Otherwise, it returns an error.

Description

The **sec_acl_replace( )** routine replaces the ACL indicated by the input handle with the information in the *sec_acl_list* parameter. ACLs are thought of as immutable, and in order to modify them, an editing application must read an entire ACL (using the **sec_acl_lookup( )** routine), modify it as needed, and replace it using this routine.

Permissions Required

The **sec_acl_replace( )** routine requires the **c** (control) permission on the object for which the ACL is to be replaced.

Files
/usr/include/dce/daclif.idl
      The **idl** file from which **dce/daclif.h** was derived.

Errors
sec_acl_unknown_manager_type
      The manager type selected is not an available option.

error_status_ok
      The call was successful.

Related Information

Functions: **sec_acl_bind(3sec)**, **sec_acl_lookup(3sec)**, **sec_intro(3sec)**.

sec_acl_test_access

Purpose   Tests access to an object

Synopsis   **#include <dce/daclif.h>**

boolean32 sec_acl_test_access(
sec_acl_handle_t *h*,
uuid_t **manager_type*,
sec_acl_permset_t *desired_permset*,
error_status_t **status*);

Parameters

Input

h   A handle referring to the target object. Use **sec_acl_bind()** to create this handle.

manager_type

A pointer to the UUID identifying the type of the ACL manager in question. There may be more than one type of ACL manager protecting the object whose ACL is bound to the input handle. Use this parameter to distinguish them. Use **sec_acl_get_manager_-types()** to acquire a list of the manager types protecting a given object.

desired_permset

A permission set in **sec_acl_permset_t** form containing the desired privileges. This is a 32-bit set of permission flags supported by the manager type.

Output

status   A pointer to the completion status. On successful completion, the routine returns **error_status_ok**. Otherwise, it returns an error.

sec_acl_test_access(3sec)

Description

The **sec_acl_test_access( )** routine determines if the specified ACL contains entries granting privileges to the calling process matching those in *desired_permset*. An application generally only inquires after the minimum set of privileges needed to accomplish a specific task.

Permissions Required

The **sec_acl_test_access( )** routine requires at least one permission of any kind on the object for which the privileges are to be tested.

Files /usr/include/dce/daclif.idl
The **idl** file from which **dce/daclif.h** was derived.

Return Values

The routine returns TRUE if the calling application program is authorized to access the target object with the privileges in *desired_permset*.

Errors **sec_acl_unknown_manager_type**
The manager type selected is not an available option.

error_status_ok
The call was successful.

Related Information

Functions: **sec_acl_bind(3sec)**, **sec_acl_test_access_on_behalf(3sec)**, **sec_intro(3sec)**.

sec_acl_test_access_on_behalf

Purpose   Tests access to an object on behalf of another process

Synopsis   **#include <dce/daclif.h>**

boolean32 sec_acl_test_access_on_behalf(
  sec_acl_handle_t *h*,
  uuid_t **manager_type*,
  sec_id_pac_t **subject*,
  sec_acl_permset_t *desired_permset*,
  error_status_t **status*);

Parameters

Input

h   A handle referring to the target object. Use **sec_acl_bind**( ) to create this handle.

manager_type
              A pointer to the UUID identifying the type of the ACL manager in question. There may be more than one type of ACL manager protecting the object whose ACL is bound to the input handle. Use this parameter to distinguish them. Use **sec_acl_get_manager_- types**( ) to acquire a list of the manager types protecting a given object.

subject   A privilege attribute certificate (PAC) for the subject process. The PAC contains the name and UUID of the principal and cell of the subject process, as well as a list of any groups to which it belongs. The PAC also contains a flag (named **authenticated**). When set, it indicates that the certificate was obtained from an authenticated source. When not set, the certificate must not be trusted. (The field is FALSE when it was obtained from the **rpc_auth(3rpc)** layer and the protect level was set to **rpc_c_protect_level_none**. This indicates that no authentication protocol was actually used in the remote procedure call; the identity was simply transmitted from the caller to the callee. If an authentication protocol was used, then the flag is set to TRUE.)

If a null PAC is passed, the subject is treated as an anonymous user, matching only the **any_other** and **unauthenticated** entries (if they exist) on the ACL.

A server uses **rpc_binding_inq_auth_client**( ) to acquire a certificate for the client process.

desired_permset

A permission set in **sec_acl_permset_t** form containing the desired privileges. This is a 32-bit set of permission flags supported by the manager type.

Output

status   A pointer to the completion status. On successful completion, the routine returns **error_status_ok**. Otherwise, it returns an error.

Description

The **sec_acl_test_access_on_behalf**( ) routine determines if the specified ACL contains entries that grant the privileges specified in *desired_permset* to the subject process. An application generally inquires about only the minimum set of privileges needed to accomplish a specific task.

Permissions Required

The **sec_acl_test_access_on_behalf**( ) routine requires at least one permission of any kind on the object for which the privileges are to be tested. Both the calling process and the identified subject must have permission on the object.

Files   /usr/include/dce/daclif.idl

The **idl** file from which **dce/daclif.h** was derived.

Return Values

If the routine completes successfully (with a completion status of **error_status_ok**) it returns a value of

- TRUE, if the caller has any access (at least one permission of any kind), and the subject has the *desired_permset* privileges.

- FALSE, if both the caller and the subject have any access, but the subject does not have the *desired_permset* privileges.

If the routine does not complete successfully, it returns a bad completion status code and a return value of FALSE.

Errors   **sec_acl_unknown_manager_type**
              The manager type selected is not an available option.

              error_status_ok
              The call was successful.

Related Information

Functions: **rpc_binding_inq_auth_client(3rpc)**, **sec_acl_bind(3sec)**,
sec_acl_test_access(3sec), **sec_intro(3sec)**.

sec_attr_trig_query

Purpose   Reads attributes coded with an attribute trigger type of query

Synopsis   **#include <dce/sec_attr_trig.h>**

void sec_attr_trig_query (
    handle_t *h*,
    sec_attr_component_name_t *cell_name*,
    sec_attr_component_name_t *component_name*,
    sec_attr_trig_cursor_t **cursor*,
    unsigned32 *num_attr_keys*,
    unsigned32 *space_avail*,
    sec_attr_t *attr_keys*[ ],
    unsigned32 **num_returned*,
    sec_attr_t *attrs*[ ],
    sec_attr_trig_timeval_sec_t *time_to_live*[ ],
    unsigned32 **num_left*,
    error_status_t **status*);

Parameters

Input

    h   A handle referring to the trigger server to be accessed Use the trigger binding information specified in the attribute encoding to acquire a bound handle.

    cell_name   A value of **sec_attr_component_name_t** that identifies the cell in which the object whose attribute is to be accessed resides. Supply a NULL *cell_name* to specify the local cell (*/.:*).

    component_name
        A value of **sec_attr_component_name_t** that identifies the name of the object whose attribute is to be accessed. If *cell_name* specifies a foreign cell, *component_name* is interpreted as a UUID in string format since the caller of this interface knows only the UUID, not the name, of the foreign principal.

    num_attr_keys
        An unsigned 32-bit integer that specifies the number of elements in the *attr_keys*[ ] array. This integer must be greater than 0 (zero).

    space_avail   An unsigned 32-bit integer that specifies the size of the *attr_keys*[ ] array.

    attr_keys[ ]   An array of values of type **sec_attr_t**. For each attribute instance, the **sec_attr_t** array contains an **attr_id** (a UUID of type **uuid_t**) to identify the attribute to be queried and an **attr_value**. **attr_value** can be used to pass in optional information required by the attribute trigger query. If no additional information is to be passed, set **attr_value** to **sec_attr_enc_void**. This is actually accomplished by setting the **sec_attr_encoding_t** data type to **sec_attr_enc_void**.

    The size of the *attr_keys*[ ] array is determined by *num_attr_keys*.

Input/Output

    cursor   A pointer to a cursor of type **sec_attr_trig_cursor_t**. As an input parameter, *cursor* can be initialized (by the **sec_addr_trig_cursor_init** routine) or uninitialized. As an output parameter, *cursor* is positioned past the attributes returned in this call.

Output

    num_returned A pointer to an unsigned 32-bit integer that specifies the number of attribute instances returned in the *attr_keys*[ ] array.

    attrs[ ]   An array of values of type **sec_attr_t**. The size of this array is determined by the *space_avail* parameter and the length by the *num_returned* parameter.

    time_to_live[ ]

        An array of values of type **sec_attr_trig_timeval_sec_t**. For each attribute in the *attrs*[ ] array, The *time_to_live*[ ] array specifies the time in seconds that the attribute can be safely cached.

    num_left   A pointer to an unsigned 32-bit integer that supplies the number of attributes found but not returned because of space constraints in the *attrs*[ ] buffer.

    status   A pointer to the completion status. On successful completion, the routine returns **error_status_ok**. Otherwise, it returns an error.

Description

The **sec_attr_trig_query**( ) routine reads attributes coded with a attribute trigger type of query.

The **sec_attr_trig_query**( ) routine is called by the DCE attribute lookup code for all schema entries that specify a query attribute trigger (**sec_attr_trig_type_query** specified with the **sec_attr_trig_type_flags_t** data type). The attribute query code passes the **sec_attr_trig_query**( ) input parameters to a user-written query attribute trigger server and receives the output parameters back from the server. Although generally this routine it is not called directly, this reference page is provided for users who are writing the attribute trigger servers that will receive **sec_attr_trig_query**( ) input and supply its output.

Multivalued attributes are returned as independent attribute instances sharing the same attribute UUID. A read of an attribute set returns all instances of members of the set; the attribute set instance is not returned.

For objects in the local cell, set the *cell_name* parameter to **null**, and the *component_name* parameter to specify the object's name.

For objects in a foreign cell, set the *cell_name* parameter to identify the name of the foreign cell, and the *component_name* parameter to the UUID in string format that identifies the object in the foreign cell.

The *cursor* parameter specifies a cursor of type **sec_attr_trig_cursor_t** that establishes the point in the attribute list at which to start processing the query. Use the **sec_attr_trig_cursor_init** function to initialize a list cursor. If *cursor* is uninitialized, the server begins processing the query at the first attribute that satisfies the search criteria. Note that generally, **sec_attr_trig_cursor_init** function makes a remote call to the specified server. To initialize the cursor without making this remote call, set the **sec_attr_trig_cursor_init** function *valid* parameter to 0 (zero).

The *num_left* parameter contains the number of attributes that were found but could not be returned because of space constraints of the *attrs*[ ] array. (Note that this number may be inaccurate if the target server allows updates between successive queries.) To obtain all of the remaining attributes, set the size of the *attrs*[ ] array so that it is large enough to hold the number of attributes listed in *num_left*.

Files

/usr/include/dce/sec_attr_trig.idl
The **idl** file from which **dce/sec_attr_trig.h** was derived.

Errors   not_all_available

unauthorized

error status_ok

Related Information

Functions: **sec_attr_trig_cursor_init**, **sec_attr_trig_update(3sec)**, **sec_intro(3sec)**.

sec_attr_trig_update

Purpose   For attributes coded with an attribute trigger type of update, passes attribute updates to an update attribute trigger server for evaluation

Synopsis   **#include <dce/sec_attr_trig.h>**

   void sec_attr_trig_update (
           handle_t *h*,
           sec_attr_component_name_t *cell_name*,
           sec_attr_component_name_t *component_name*,
           unsigned32 *num_to_write*,
           unsigned32 *space_avail*,
           sec_attr_t *in_attrs*[ ],
           unsigned32 **num_returned*,
           sec_attr_t *out_attrs*[ ],
           unsigned32 **num_left*,
           signed32 **failure_index*,
           error_status_t **status*);

Parameters

Input

   h   A handle referring to the trigger server to be accessed. Use the trigger binding information specified in the attribute encoding to acquire a bound handle.

   cell_name   A value of **sec_attr_component_name_t** that identifies the cell in which the object whose attribute is to be accessed resides. Supply a NULL *cell_name* to specify the local cell (**/.:**).

   component_name
                    A value of **sec_attr_component_name_t** that identifies the name of the object whose attribute is to be accessed. If *cell_name* specifies a foreign cell, *component_name* is interpreted as a UUID in string format since the caller of this interface knows only the UUID, not the name, of the foreign principal.

   num_to_write   An unsigned 32-bit integer that specifies the number of elements in the *in_attrs* array. This integer must be greater than 0 (zero).

space_avail   An unsigned 32-bit integer that specifies the size of the *out_attrs* array.

in_attrs[ ]   An array of values of type **sec_attr_t** that specifies the attribute instances to be written. The size of *in_attrs*[ ] is determined by *num_to_write*.

Output

num_returned A pointer to an unsigned 32-bit integer that specifies the number of attribute instances returned in the *out_attrs*[ ] array.

out_attrs[ ]   An array of values of type **sec_attr_t**. These values, supplied by the update attribute trigger server, are in a form suitable for storage in the registry database.

num_left   A pointer to an unsigned 32-bit integer that supplies the number of attributes that were found but not returned because of space constraints in the *out_attrs*[ ] buffer.

failure_index In the event of an error, *failure_index* is a pointer to the element in the *in_attrs*[ ] array that caused the update to fail. If the failure cannot be attributed to a specific attribute, the value of *failure_index* is -1.

status   A pointer to the completion status. On successful completion, the routine returns **error_status_ok**. Otherwise, it returns an error.

Description

The **sec_attr_trig_update( )** routine passes attributes coded with an attribute trigger type of update to a user-written update attribute trigger server for evaluation before the updates are made to the registry.

Although generally this routine it is not called directly, this reference page is provided for users who are writing the attribute trigger servers that will receive **sec_attr_trig_update( )** input and supply its output.

The **sec_attr_trig_update( )** routine is called by the DCE attribute update code for all schema entries that specify an update attribute trigger (**sec_attr_trig_type_-update** specified with the **sec_attr_trig_type_flags_t** data type). The attribute update code passes the **sec_attr_trig_update( )** input parameters to a user-written update attribute trigger server and receives the output parameters back from the server.

The attribute trigger server is responsible for evaluating the semantics of the entry in order to reject or accept it, and the attribute trigger server may even make changes in the output it sends back to the update code to ensure the entry adheres to the semantics. The output received from the attribute trigger server is in a form to be stored in the registry. (Note that update attribute trigger servers do not store attribute values. Attribute values are stored in the registry database.)

This is an atomic operation: if the update of any attribute in the array fails to pass the evaluation, all updates are aborted. The attribute causing the update to fail is identified in *failure_index*. If the failure cannot be attributed to a given attribute, *failure_index* contains -1.

For objects in the local cell, set the *cell_name* parameter to **null**, and the *component_name* parameter to specify the object's name.

For objects in a foreign cell, set the *cell_name* parameter the the name of the foreign cells, and the *component_name* parameter to specify the UUID in string format that identifies the object in the foreign cell.

Files   **/usr/include/dce/sec_attr_trig.idl**
The **idl** file from which **dce/sec_attr_trig.h** was derived.

Errors   **database read only**

server unavailable

invalid/unsupported attribute type

invalid encoding type

value not unique

site read only

unauthorized

error_status_ok

Related Information

Functions: **sec_attr_trig_query(3sec)**, **sec_intro(3sec)**.

sec_cred_free_attr_cursor

Purpose   Frees the local resources allocated to a **sec_attr_cursor_t**

Synopsis   **#include <dce/sec_cred.h>**

void sec_cred_free_attr_cursor (
        sec_cred_attr_cursor_t *cursor*,
        error_status_t *status*);**

Parameters

Input/Output

cursor   As input, a pointer to a **sec_cred_attr_cursor_t** whose resources
                are to be freed. As output a pointer to an initialized
                sec_cred_attr_cursor_t with allocated resources freed.

Output

status   A pointer to the completion status. On successful completion, the
                routine returns **error_status_ok**. Otherwise, it returns an error.

Description

The **sec_cred_free_attr_cursor( )** routine frees the resources assoicated with a
cursor of type **sec_cred_attr_cursor_t** used by the **sec_cred_get_extended_-
attrs( )** call.

Errors   error_status_ok

Related Information

Functions: **sec_cred_get_extended_attrs(3sec)**,
sec_cred_initialize_attr_cursor(3sec), **sec_intro(3sec)**.

sec_cred_free_cursor

Purpose   Releases local resources allocated to a **sec_cred_cursor_t**

Synopsis   **#include <dce/sec_cred.h>**

void sec_cred_free_cursor (
           sec_cred_cursor_t **cursor,*
           error_status_t **status)*;

Parameters

Input/Output

    cursor   As input, a **sec_cred_cursor_t** whose resources are to be freed. As output, a **sec_cred_cursor_t** whose resources are freed.

Output

    status   A pointer to the completion status. On successful completion, the routine returns **error_status_ok**. Otherwise, it returns an error.

Description

The **sec_cred_free_cursor( )** routine releases local resources allocated to a **sec_cred_cursor_t** used by the **sec_cred_get_delegate( )** call.

Errors   **sec_login_s_no_memory**

           error_status_ok

Related Information

Functions: **sec_cred_get_delegate(3sec)**, **sec_cred_initialize_cursor(3sec)**, **sec_intro(3sec)**.

sec_cred_free_pa_handle

Purpose   Frees the local resources allocated to a privilege attribute handle of type **sec_cred_pa_handle_t**

Synopsis   **#include <dce/sec_cred.h>**

void sec_cred_free_pa_handle (
          sec_cred_pa_handle__t *_pa_handle_,
          error_status_t *_status_**);**

Parameters

Input/Output

_pa_handle_   As input, a pointer to a **sec_cred_pa_handle_t** whose resources are to be freed. As output a pointer to a **sec_cred_pa_handle_t** with allocated resources freed.

Output

status   A pointer to the completion status. On successful completion, the routine returns **error_status_ok**. Otherwise, it returns an error.

Description

The **sec_cred_free_pa_handle( )** routine frees the resources assoicated with a privilege attribute handle of type **sec_cred_pa_handle_t** used by the **sec_cred_get_initiator( )** and **sec_cred_get_delegate( )** calls.

Errors   error_status_ok

Related Information

Functions: **sec_cred_get_delegate(3sec)**, **sec_cred_get_initiator(3sec)**, **sec_intro(3sec)**.

sec_cred_get_authz_session_info

Purpose   Returns session-specific information that represents an authenticated client's credentials

Synopsis   **#include <dce/sec_cred.h>**

void sec_cred_get_authz_session_info(
            rpc_authz_cred_handle_t *callers_identity,*
            uuid_t **session_id,*
            sec_timeval_t **session_expiration,*
            error_status_t **status);*

Parameters

Input

callers_identity
                A credential handle of type **rpc_authz_cred_handle_t**. This handle is supplied as output of the **rpc_binding_inq_auth_caller( )** call.

Output

session_ID   A pointer to a **uuid_t** that identifies the client's DCE authorization session.

session_expiration
                A pointer to a **sec_timeval_t** that specifies the expiration time of the authenticated client's credentials.

status   A pointer to the completion status. On successful completion, *status* is assigned **error_status_ok**. Otherwise, it returns an error.

Description

The **sec_cred_get_authz_session_info( )** routine retrieves session-specific information that represents the credentials of authenticated client specified by *callers_identity*. If the client is a member of a delegation chain, the information represents the credentials of all members of the chain.

The information can aid application servers in the construction of identity-based caches. For example, it could be used as a key into a cache of previously allocated delegation contexts and thus avoid the overhead of allocating a new login context on every remote operation. It could also be used as a key into a table of previously computed authorization decisions.

Before you execute this call, you must execute an **rpc_binding_inq_auth_-caller( )** call to obtain an **rpc_authz_cred_handle_t** for the *callers_identity* parameter.

Errors   **sec_cred_s_authz_cannot_comply**

error_status_ok

Related Information

Functions: **rpc_binding_inq_auth_caller(rpc)**, **sec_intro(3sec)**.

sec_cred_get_client_princ_name

Purpose   Returns the principal name associated with a credential handle

Synopsis   **#include <dce/sec_cred.h>**

void sec_cred_get_client_princ_name(
        rpc_authz_cred_handle_t *callers_identity*,
        unsigned_char_p_t **client_princ_name*,
        error_status_t *status);

Parameters

Input

callers_identity
        A handle of type **rpc_authz_cred_handle_t** to the credentials for
        which to return the principal name. This handle is supplied as
        output of the **rpc_binding_inq_auth_caller()** call.

Output

client_princ_name
        A pointer to the principal name of the server's RPC client.

status   A pointer to the completion status. On successful completion, *status*
        is assigned **error_status_ok**. Otherwise, it returns an error.

Description

The **sec_cred_get_client_princ_name()** routine extracts the principal name
associated with the credentials identified by **callers_pas**.

Before you execute **sec_cred_get_client_princ_name()**, you must execute an
rpc_binding_inq_auth_caller() call to obtain an **rpc_authz_cred_handle_t** for
the *callers_identity* parameter.

Errors sec_cred_s_authz_cannot_comply

error_status_ok

Related Information

Functions: **rpc_binding_inq_auth_caller(3sec)**, **sec_intro(3sec)**.

sec_cred_get_deleg_restrictions

Purpose   Returns delegate restrictions from a privilege attribute handle

Synopsis   **#include <dce/sec_cred.h>**

sec_id_restriction_set_t *sec_cred_get_deleg_restrictions(
 sec_cred_pa_handle_t *callers_pas*,
 error_status_t ***status*);**

Parameters

Input

callers_pas   A value of type **sec_cred_pa_handle_t** that provides a handle to a principal's privilege attributes. This handle is supplied as output of the **sec_cred_get_initiator( )** call, the **sec_cred_get_delegate( )** call and the **sec_login_cred** calls.

Output

status   A pointer to the completion status. On successful completion, *status* is assigned **error_status_ok**.

Description

The **sec_cred_get_deleg_restrictions** ( ) routine extracts delegate restrictions from the privilege attribute handle identified by *callers_pas*. The restrictions are returned in a **sec_id_restriction_set_t**.

Before you execute **sec_cred_get_pa_data( )**, you must execute a **sec_cred_get_-initiator( )** or **sec_cred_get_delegate( )** call to obtain a **sec_cred_pa_handle_t** for the *callers_pas* parameter.

Errors

sec_cred_s_invalid_pa_handle

error_status_ok

Related Information

Functions: **sec_cred_get_delegate(3sec)**, **sec_cred_get_initiator(3sec)**, **sec_intro(3sec)**.

sec_cred_get_delegate

Purpose   Returns a handle to the privilege attributes of an intermediary in a delegation chain

Synopsis   **#include <dce/sec_cred.h>**

     sec_cred_pa_handle_t sec_cred_get_delegate(
        rpc_authz_cred_handle_t *callers_identity,*
        sec_cred_cursor_t **cursor,*
        error_status_t **status*);

Parameters

Input

callers_identity

     A handle of type **rpc_authz_cred_handle_t**. This handle is supplied as output of the **rpc_binding_inq_auth_caller( )** call.

Input/Output

cursor   As input, a pointer to a cursor of type **sec_cred_cursor_t** that has been initialized by the **sec_cred_initialize_cursor( )** call. As an output parameter, *cursor* is a pointer to a cursor of type **sec_attr_srch_cursor_t** that is positioned past the principal whose privilege attributes have been returned in this call.

Output

status   A pointer to the completion status. On successful completion, *status* is assigned **error_status_ok**.

Description

The **sec_cred_get_delegate( )** routine returns a handle to the the privilege attributes of an intermediary in a delegation chain that performed an authenticated RPC operation.

This call is used by servers. Clients use the **sec_login_cred_get_delegate( )** routine to return the privilege attribute handle of an intermediary in a delegation chain.

The credential handle identified by *callers_identity* contains authentication and authorization information for all delegates in the chain. This call returns a handle (**sec_cred_pa_handle_t**) to the privilege attributes of one of the delegates in the binding handle. The **sec_cred_pa_handle_t** returned by this call is used in other **sec_cred_get_** * calls to obtain privilege attribute information for a single delegate.

To obtain the privilege attributes of each delegate in the credential handle identified by *callers_identity*, execute this call until the message **sec_cred_s_no_more_entries** is returned.

Before you execute **sec_cred_get_delegate( )**, you must execute

- An **rpc_binding_inq_auth_caller( )** call to obtain an **rpc_authz_cred_handle_t** for the *callers_identity* parameter.

- A **sec_cred_initialize_cursor( )** call to initialize a cursor of type **sec_cred_cursor_t**.

Use the **sec_cred_free_pa_handle( )** all to free the resources associated with the **sec_cred_pa_handle_t**.

Errors   sec_cred_s_invalid_auth_handle

sec_cred_s_invalid_cursor

sec_cred_s_no_more_entries

error_status_ok

Related Information

Functions: **rpc_binding_inq_auth_caller(3rpc)**, **sec_cred_free_pa_handle( )**, **sec_cred_get_deleg_restrictions(3sec)**, **sec_cred_get_delegation_type(3sec)**, **sec_cred_get_extended_attrs(3sec)**, **sec_cred_get_opt_restrictions(3sec)**, **sec_cred_get_pa_date**, **sec_cred_get_req_restrictions(3sec)**, **sec_cred_get_tgt_restrictions(3sec)**, **sec_cred_get_v1_pac(3sec)** **sec_cred_initialize_cursor(3sec)**, **sec_intro(3sec)**.

sec_cred_get_delegation_type

Purpose   Returns the delegation type from a privilege attribute handle

Synopsis   **#include <dce/sec_cred.h>**

sec_id_delegation_type_t *sec_cred_get_delegation_type(
    sec_cred_pa_handle_t *callers_pas,*
    error_status_t **status***);**

Parameters

Input

callers_pas   A value of type **sec_cred_pa_handle_t** that provides a handle to a principal's privilege attributes. This handle is supplied as output of either the **sec_cred_get_initiator**() call or **sec_cred_get_-delegate**() call.

Output

status   A pointer to the completion status. On successful completion, *status* is assigned **error_status_ok**.

Description

The **sec_cred_get_delegation_type** () routine extracts the delegation type from the privilege attribute handle identified by *callers_pas* and returns it in a **sec_id_delegation_type_t**.

Before you execute **sec_cred_get_delegation_type**(), you must execute a **sec_cred_get_initiator**() or **sec_cred_get_delegate**() call to obtain a **sec_cred_pa_handle_t** for the *callers_pas* parameter.

Errors   **sec_cred_s_invalid_pa_handle**

error_status_ok

Related Information

Functions: **sec_cred_get_delegate(3sec)**, **sec_cred_get_initiator(3sec)**, **sec_intro(3sec)**.

sec_cred_get_extended_attrs

Purpose   Returns extended attributes from a privilege handle

Synopsis   **#include <dce/sec_cred.h>**

        void sec_cred_get_extended_attrs(
            sec_cred_pa_handle_t *callers_pas*,
            sec_cred_attr_cursor_t **cursor*
            sec_attr_t **attr*
            error_status_t **status***);**

Parameters

Input

    callers_pas   A handle of type **sec_cred_pa_handle_t** to the caller's privilege attributes. This handle is supplied as output of either the **sec_cred_get_initiator**( ) call or **sec_cred_get_delegate**( ) call.

Input/Output

    cursor   A cursor of type **sec_cred_attr_cursor_t** that has been initialized by the **sec_cred_initialize_attr_cursor**( ) routine. As input *cursor* must be initialized. As output, *cursor* is positioned at the first attribute after the returned attribute.

Output

    attr   A pointer to a value of **sec_attr_t** that contains extended registry attributes.

    status   A pointer to the completion status. On successful completion, *status* is assigned **error_status_ok**.

Description

The **sec_cred_get_extended_attrs**( ) routine extracts extended registry initialized from the privilege attribute handle identified by *callers_pas*.

sec_cred_get_extended_attrs(3sec)

Before you execute call, you must execute

- A **sec_cred_get_initiator( )** or **sec_cred_get_delegate( )** call to obtain a **sec_cred_pa_handle_t** for the *callers_pas* parameter.

- A **sec_cred_initialize_attr_cursor( )** to initialize a **sec_attr_t**.

To obtain all the extended registry attributes in the privilege attribute handle, repeat **sec_cred_get_extended_attrs( )** calls until the status message **no_more_entries_available** is returned.

Errors   **sec_cred_s_invalid_pa_handle**

sec_cred_s_invalid_cursor

sec_cred_s_no_more_entries

error_status_ok

Related Information

Functions: **sec_cred_get_initiator(3sec), sec_cred_get_delegate(3sec), sec_cred_initialize_attr_cursor(3sec), sec_intro(3sec).**

sec_cred_get_initiator

Purpose   Returns the privilege attributes of the initiator of a delegation chain

Synopsis   **#include <dce/sec_cred.h>**

sec_cred_pa_handle_t sec_cred_get_initiator(
        rpc_authz_cred_handle_t *callers_identity*,
        error_status_t *status);

Parameters

Input

callers_identity
        A credential handle of type **rpc_authz_cred_handle_t**. This handle
        is supplied as output of the **rpc_binding_inq_auth_caller( )** call.

Output

status   A pointer to the completion status. On successful completion, *status*
        is assigned **error_status_ok**.

Description

The **sec_cred_get_initiator( )** routine returns a handle to the the privilege
attributes of the initiator of a delegation chain that performed an authenticated
RPC operation.

The credential handle identified by *callers_identity* contains authentication and
authorization information for all delegates in the chain. This call returns a handle
(**sec_cred_pa_handle_t**) to the privilege attributes of the client that initiated the
delegation chain. The **sec_cred_pa_handle_t** returned by this call is used in other
sec_cred_get_ * calls to obtain privilege attribute information for the initiator.

Before you execute **sec_cred_get_initiator( )**, you must execute an
rpc_binding_inq_auth_caller( ) call to obtain an **rpc_authz_cred_handle_t** for
the *callers_identity* parameter.

Errors   sec_cred_s_invalid_auth_handle

error_status_ok

Related Information

Functions: **rpc_binding_inq_auth_caller(3rpc)**,
sec_cred_get_deleg_restrictions(3sec), **sec_cred_get_delegation_type(3sec)**,
sec_cred_get_extended_attrs(3sec), **sec_cred_get_opt_restrictions(3sec)**,
sec_cred_get_pa_date, **sec_cred_get_req_restrictions(3sec)**,
sec_cred_get_tgt_restrictions(3sec), **sec_cred_get_v1_pac(3sec)**,
sec_intro(3sec).

sec_cred_get_opt_restrictions

Purpose   Returns optional restrictions from a privilege handle

Synopsis   **#include <dce/sec_cred.h>**

> **sec_id_opt_req_t *sec_cred_get_opt_restrictions(**
>   **sec_cred_pa_handle_t** *callers_pas*,
>   **error_status_t ***status*);

Parameters

Input

callers_pas   A handle of type **sec_cred_pa_handle_t** to a principal's privilege attributes. This handle is supplied as output of either the **sec_cred_get_initiator( )** call or **sec_cred_get_delegate( )** call.

Output

status   A pointer to the completion status. On successful completion, *status* is assigned **error_status_ok**.

Description

The **sec_cred_get_opt_restrictions** ( ) routine extracts optional restrictions from the privilege attribute handle identified by *callers_pas* and returns them in a **sec_id_restriction_set_t**.

Before you execute **sec_cred_get_pa_data( )**, you must execute a **sec_cred_get_-initiator( )** or **sec_cred_get_delegate( )** call to obtain a **sec_cred_pa_handle_t** for the *callers_pas* parameter.

Errors   **sec_cred_s_invalid_pa_handle**

error_status_ok

Related Information

Functions: **sec_cred_get_delegate(3sec)**, **sec_cred_get_initiator(3sec)**, **sec_intro(3sec)**.

sec_cred_get_pa_data

Purpose   Returns identity information from a privilege attribute handle

Synopsis   **#include <dce/sec_cred.h>**

sec_id_pa_t *sec_cred_get_pa_data(
   sec_cred_pa_handle_t *callers_pas***,**
   error_status_t **status***);**

Parameters

Input

callers_pas   A handle of type **sec_cred_pa_handle_t** to a principal's privilege attributes. This handle is supplied as output of either the **sec_cred_get_initiator( )** call or **sec_cred_get_delegate( )** call.

Output

status   A pointer to the completion status. On successful completion, *status* is assigned **error_status_ok**.

Description

The **sec_cred_get_pa_data( )** routine extracts identity information from the privilege attribute handle specified by *callers_pas* and returns it in a **sec_id_pa_t**. The identity information includes an identifier of the princpal's locall cell and the principal's local and foreign group sets.

Before you execute **sec_cred_get_pa_data( )**, you must execute a **sec_cred_get_-initiator( )** or **sec_cred_get_delegate( )** call to obtain a **sec_cred_pa_handle_t** for the *callers_pas* parameter.

Errors   **sec_cred_s_invalid_pa_handle**

error_status_ok

Related Information

Functions: **sec_cred_get_delegate(3sec)**, **sec_cred_get_initiator(3sec)**, **sec_intro(3sec)**.

sec_cred_get_req_restrictions

Purpose Returns required restrictions from a privilege attribute handle

Synopsis **#include <dce/sec_cred.h>**

sec_id_opt_req_t *sec_cred_get_req_restrictions (
      sec_cred_pa_handle_t *callers_pas***,**
      error_status_t **status***);**

Parameters

Input

callers_pas   A handle of type **sec_cred_pa_handle_t** to a principal's privilege attributes. This handle is supplied as output of either the **sec_cred_get_initiator**( ) call or **sec_cred_get_delegate**( ) call.

Output

status   A pointer to the completion status. On successful completion, *status* is assigned **error_status_ok**.

Description

The **sec_cred_get_req_restrictions**( ) routine extracts required restrictions from the privilege attribute handle identified by *callers_pas* and returns them in a **sec_id_opt_req_t**.

Before you execute **sec_cred_get_req_restrictions**( ), you must execute a **sec_- cred_get_initiator**( ) or **sec_cred_get_delegate**( ) call to obtain a **sec_cred_pa_- handle_t** for the *callers_pas* parameter.

Errors   **sec_cred_s_invalid_pa_handle**

error_status_ok

Related Information

Functions: **sec_cred_get_delegate(3sec)**, **sec_cred_get_initiator(3sec)**, **sec_intro(3sec)**.

sec_cred_get_tgt_restrictions

Purpose Returns target restrictions from a privilege attribute handle

Synopsis #include <dce/sec_cred.h>

sec_id_restriction_set_t *sec_cred_get_tgt_restrictions(
    sec_cred_pa_handle_t *callers_pas*,
    error_status_t *status*);

Parameters

Input

callers_pas A handle of type **sec_cred_pa_handle_t** to a principal's privilege attributes. This handle is supplied as output of either the **sec_cred_get_initiator( )** call or **sec_cred_get_delegate( )** call.

Output

status A pointer to the completion status. On successful completion, *status* is assigned **error_status_ok**.

Description

The **sec_cred_get_tgt_restrictions( )** routine extracts target restrictions from the privilege attribute handle identified by *callers_pas* and returns them in a **sec_id_restriction_set_t**.

Before you execute **sec_cred_get_tgt_restrictions( )**, you must execute a **sec_cred_get_initiator( )** or **sec_cred_get_delegate( )** call to obtain a **sec_cred_pa_handle_t** for the *callers_pas* parameter.

Errors **sec_cred_s_invalid_pa_handle**

error_status_ok

Related Information

Functions: **sec_cred_get_delegate(3sec)**, **sec_cred_get_initiator(3sec)**, **sec_intro(3sec)**.

sec_cred_get_v1_pac

Purpose   Returns pre-1.1 PAC from a privilege attribute handle

Synopsis   **#include <dce/sec_cred.h>**

sec_id_pac_t *sec_cred_get_v1_pac(
       sec_cred_pa_handle_t *callers_pas,*
       error_status_t **status***);**

Parameters

Input

callers_pas   A handle of type **sec_cred_pa_handle_t** to the principal's privilege attributes. This handle is supplied as output of either the **sec_cred_get_initiator( )** call or **sec_cred_get_delegate( )** call.

Output

status   A pointer to the completion status. On successful completion, *status* is assigned **error_status_ok**.

Description

The **sec_cred_get_v1_pac( )** routine extracts the privilege attributes from a pre-1.1 PAC for the privilege attribute handle specified by *callers_pas* and returns them in a **sec_id_pa_t**.

Before you execute **sec_cred_get_v1_pac( )**, you must execute a **sec_cred_get_-initiator( )** or **sec_cred_get_delegate( )** call to obtain a **sec_cred_pa_handle_t** for the *callers_pas* parameter.

Errors   **sec_cred_s_invalid_pa_handle**

error_status_ok

Related Information

Functions: **sec_cred_get_delegate(3sec)**, **sec_cred_get_initiator(3sec)**, **sec_intro(3sec)**.

sec_cred_initialize_attr_cursor

Purpose   Initializes a **sec_attr_cursor_t**

Synopsis   **#include <dce/sec_cred.h>**

void sec_cred_initialize_attr_cursor (
            sec_cred_attr_cursor_t **cursor,*
            error_status_t **status*)**;**

Parameters

Input/Output

cursor   As input, a pointer to a **sec_cred_attr_cursor_t** to be initialized. As output a pointer to an initialized **sec_cred_attr_cursor_t**.

Output

status   A pointer to the completion status. On successful completion, the routine returns **error_status_ok**. Otherwise, it returns an error.

Description

The **sec_cred_initialize_attr_cursor( )** routine allocates and initializes a cursor of type **sec_cred_attr_cursor_t** for use with the **sec_cred_get_extended_attrs( )** call. Use the **sec_cred_free_attr_cursor( )** call to free the resources allocated to *cursor.*

Errors   **sec_login_s_no_memory**

error_status_ok

Related Information

Functions: **sec_cred_free_attr_cursor( )**, **sec_cred_get_extended_attrs(3sec)**, **sec_intro(3sec)**.

sec_cred_initialize_cursor

Purpose   Initializes a **sec_cred_cursor_t**

Synopsis   **#include <dce/sec_cred.h>**

void sec_cred_initialize_cursor (
        sec_cred_cursor_t **cursor**,
        error_status_t **status**);

Parameters

Input/Output

cursor   As input, a **sec_cred_cursor_t** to be initialized. As output, an
                initialized **sec_cred_cursor_t**.

Output

status   A pointer to the completion status. On successful completion, the
                routine returns **error_status_ok**. Otherwise, it returns an error.

Description

The **sec_cred_initialize_cursor( )** routine initializes a cursor of type **sec_cursor_t**
for use with the **sec_cred_get_delegate( )** call. Use the **sec_cred_free_cursor( )**
call to free the resources allocated to cursor.

Errors   **sec_login_s_no_memory**

                error_status_ok

Related Information

Functions: **sec_cred_free_cursor(3sec)**, **sec_cred_get_delegate(3sec)**,
sec_intro(3sec).

sec_cred_is_authenticated

Purpose   Returns TRUE if the supplied credentials are authenticated, and FALSE if they are not

Synopsis   **#include <dce/sec_cred.h>**

boolean32 sec_cred_is_authenticated(
        rpc_authz_cred_handle_t *callers_identity*,
        error_status_t *status);

Parameters

Input

callers_identity
                A handle of type **rpc_authz_cred_handle_t** to the credentials to check for authentication. This handle is supplied as output of the **rpc_binding_inq_auth_caller( )** call.

Output

status   A pointer to the completion status. On successful completion, *status* is assigned **error_status_ok**. Otherwise, it returns an error.

Description

The **sec_cred_is_authenticated( )** routine returns TRUE if the credentials identified by *callers_identity* are authenticated or FALSE if they are not.

Before you execute this call, you must execute an **rpc_binding_inq_auth_-caller( )** call to obtain an **rpc_authz_cred_handle_t** for the *callers_identity* parameter.

Files   **/usr/include/dce/sec_cred.idl**
                The **idl** file from which **dce/sec_cred.h** was derived.

Return Values

The routine returns **true** if the credentials are authenticated; **false** if they are not.

Related Information

Functions: **rpc_binding_inq_auth_caller(3rpc)**, **sec_intro(3sec)**.

sec_id_gen_group

Purpose   Generates a global name from cell and group UUIDs

Synopsis   **#include <dce/secidmap.h>**

> **void sec_id_gen_group(**
>   **sec_rgy_handle_t** *context*,
>   **uuid_t** **cell_idp*,
>   **uuid_t** **group_idp*,
>   **sec_rgy_name_t** *global_name*,
>   **sec_rgy_name_t** *cell_namep*,
>   **sec_rgy_name_t** *group_namep*,
>   **error_status_t** **status*);

Parameters

Input

context	An opaque handle bound to a registry server. Use **sec_rgy_site_-open( )** to acquire a bound handle.
cell_idp	A pointer to the UUID of the home cell of the group whose name is in question.
group_idp	A pointer to the UUID of the group whose name is in question.

Output

global_name	The global (full) name of the group in **sec_rgy_name_t** form.
cell_namep	The name of the group's home cell in **sec_rgy_name_t** form.
group_namep	The local (with respect to the home cell) name of the group in **sec_rgy_name_t** form.
status	A pointer to the completion status. On successful completion, the function returns **error_status_ok**. Otherwise, it returns an error.

Description

The **sec_id_gen_group( )** routine generates a global name from input cell and group UUIDs. For example, given a UUID specifying the cell **/.../world/hp/brazil**, and a UUID specifying a group resident in that cell named **writers**, the routine would return the global name of that group, in this case, **/.../world/hp/brazil/writers**. It also returns the simple names of the cell and group, translated from the UUIDs.

The routine will not produce translations to any name for which a NULL pointer has been supplied.

Files

/usr/include/dce/secidmap.idl

The **idl** file from which **dce/secidmap.h** was derived.

Errors

sec_id_e_name_too_long

The name is too long for current implementation.

sec_id_e_bad_cell_uuid

The cell UUID is not valid.

sec_rgy_object_not_found

The registry server could not find the specified group.

sec_rgy_server_unavailable

The DCE registry server is unavailable.

error_status_ok

The call was successful.

Related Information

Functions: **sec_id_gen_name(3sec)**, **sec_id_parse_group(3sec)**, **sec_id_parse_name(3sec)**, **sec_intro(3sec)**.

sec_id_gen_name

Purpose   Generates a global name from cell and principal UUIDs

Synopsis   **#include <dce/secidmap.h>**

void sec_id_gen_name(
        sec_rgy_handle_t *context*,
        uuid_t **cell_idp*,
        uuid_t **princ_idp*,
        sec_rgy_name_t *global_name*,
        sec_rgy_name_t *cell_namep*,
        sec_rgy_name_t *princ_namep*,
        error_status_t **status*);

Parameters

Input

context   An opaque handle bound to a registry server. Use **sec_rgy_site_-open( )** to acquire a bound handle.

cell_idp   A pointer to the UUID of the home cell of the principal whose name is in question.

princ_idp   A pointer to the UUID of the principal whose name is in question.

Output

global_name   The global (full) name of the principal in **sec_rgy_name_t** form.

cell_namep   The name of the principal's home cell in **sec_rgy_name_t** form.

princ_namep   The local (with respect to the home cell) name of the principal in **sec_rgy_name_t** form.

status   A pointer to the completion status. On successful completion, the function returns **error_status_ok**. Otherwise, it returns an error.

Description

The **sec_id_gen_name( )** routine generates a global name from input cell and principal UUIDs. For example, given a UUID specifying the cell **/.../world/hp/brazil**, and a UUID specifying a principal resident in that cell named **writers/tom**, the routine would return the global name of that principal, in this case, **/.../world/hp/brazil/writers/tom**. It also returns the simple names of the cell and principal, translated from the UUIDs.

The routine will not produce translations to any name for which a NULL pointer has been supplied.

Permissions Required

The **sec_id_gen_name( )** routine requires at least one permission of any kind on the account associated with the input cell and principal UUIDs.

Files

/usr/include/dce/secidmap.idl
> The **idl** file from which **dce/secidmap.h** was derived.

Errors

sec_id_e_name_too_long
> The name is too long for current implementation.

sec_id_e_bad_cell_uuid
> The cell UUID is not valid.

sec_rgy_object_not_found
> The registry server could not find the specified principal.

sec_rgy_server_unavailable
> The DCE registry server is unavailable.

error_status_ok
> The call was successful.

Related Information

Functions: **sec_id_gen_group(3sec)**, **sec_id_parse_group(3sec)**, **sec_id_parse_name(3sec)**, **sec_intro(3sec)**.

sec_id_parse_group

Purpose   Translates a global name into group and cell names and UUIDs

Synopsis   **#include <dce/secidmap.h>**

> **void sec_id_parse_group(**
>   **sec_rgy_handle_t** *context*,
>   **sec_rgy_name_t** *global_name*,
>   **sec_rgy_name_t** *cell_namep*,
>   **uuid_t** **cell_idp*,
>   **sec_rgy_name_t** *group_namep*,
>   **uuid_t** **group_idp*,
>   **error_status_t** **status*);

Parameters

Input

context   An opaque handle bound to a registry server. Use **sec_rgy_site_-open( )** to acquire a bound handle.

global_name   The global (full) name of the group in **sec_rgy_name_t** form.

Output

cell_namep   The output name of the group's home cell in **sec_rgy_name_t** form.

cell_idp   A pointer to the UUID of the home cell of the group whose name is in question.

group_namep   The local (with respect to the home cell) name of the group in **sec_rgy_name_t** form.

group_idp   A pointer to the UUID of the group whose name is in question.

status   A pointer to the completion status. On successful completion, the function returns **error_status_ok**. Otherwise, it returns an error.

Description

The **sec_id_parse_group( )** routine translates a global group name into a cell name and a cell-relative group name. It also returns the UUIDs associated with the group and its home cell.

The routine will not produce translations to any name for which a NULL pointer has been supplied.

Files

/usr/include/dce/secidmap.idl

The **idl** file from which **dce/secidmap.h** was derived.

Errors

sec_id_e_name_too_long

The name is too long for current implementation.

sec_id_e_bad_cell_uuid

The cell UUID is not valid.

sec_rgy_object_not_found

The registry server could not find the specified group.

sec_rgy_server_unavailable

The DCE registry server is unavailable.

error_status_ok

The call was successful.

Related Information

Functions: **sec_id_gen_group(3sec)**, **sec_id_gen_name(3sec)**, **sec_id_parse_group(3sec)**, **sec_id_parse_name(3sec)**, **sec_intro(3sec)**.

sec_id_parse_name

Purpose   Translates a global name into principal and cell names and UUIDs

Synopsis   **#include <dce/secidmap.h>**

        void sec_id_parse_name(
                sec_rgy_handle_t *context,*
                sec_rgy_name_t *global_name,*
                sec_rgy_name_t *cell_namep,*
                uuid_t **cell_idp,*
                sec_rgy_name_t *princ_namep,*
                uuid_t **princ_idp,*
                error_status_t **status)*;

Parameters

Input

    context   An opaque handle bound to a registry server. Use **sec_rgy_site_-open( )** to acquire a bound handle.

    global_name The global (full) name of the principal in **sec_rgy_name_t** form.

Output

    cell_namep   The output name of the principal's home cell in **sec_rgy_name_t** form.

    cell_idp   A pointer to the UUID of the home cell of the principal whose name is in question.

    princ_namep The local (with respect to the home cell) name of the principal in **sec_rgy_name_t** form.

    princ_idp   A pointer to the UUID of the principal whose name is in question.

    status   A pointer to the completion status. On successful completion, the function returns **error_status_ok**. Otherwise, it returns an error.

Description

The **sec_id_parse_name( )** routine translates a global principal name into a cell name and a cell-relative principal name. It also returns the UUIDs associated with the principal and its home cell.

The routine will not produce translations to any name for which a NULL pointer has been supplied.

Permissions Required

Only if *princ_idp* is requested as output does the **sec_id_parse_name( )** routine require a permission. In this case, the routine requires at least one permission of any kind on the account whose global principal name is to be translated.

Files

/usr/include/dce/secidmap.idl

The **idl** file from which **dce/secidmap.h** was derived.

Errors

sec_id_e_name_too_long

The name is too long for current implementation.

sec_id_e_bad_cell_uuid

The cell UUID is not valid.

sec_rgy_object_not_found

The registry server could not find the specified principal.

sec_rgy_server_unavailable

The DCE registry server is unavailable.

error_status_ok

The call was successful.

Related Information

Functions: **sec_id_gen_name(3sec)**, **sec_intro(3sec)**.

sec_key_mgmt_change_key

Purpose   Changes a principal's key

Synopsis   **#include <dce/keymgmt.h>**

void sec_key_mgmt_change_key(
          sec_key_mgmt_authn_service *authn_service,*
          void **arg,*
          idl_char **principal_name,*
          unsigned32 *key_vno,*
          void **keydata,*
          sec_timeval_period_t **garbage_collect_time,*
          error_status_t **status);*

Parameters

Input

authn_service Identifies the authentication protocol using this key. The possible
          authentication protocols are as follows:

          rpc_c_authn_dce_secret
                    DCE shared-secret key authentication.

          rpc_c_authn_dce_public
                    DCE public key authentication (reserved for future
                    use).

arg   This parameter can specify either the local key file or an argument
          to the *get_key_fn* key acquisition routine of the **rpc_server_-
          register_auth_info** routine.

          A value of NULL specifies that the default key file (**/krb/v5srvtab**)
          should be used. A key filename specifies that file should be used as
          the key file. You must prepend the file's absolute filename with
          FILE: and the file must have been created with the **rgy_edit ktadd**
          command or the **sec_key_mgmt_set_key** function.

          Any other value specifies an argument for the *get_key_fn* key
          acquisition routine. See the **rpc_server_register_auth_info( )**
          reference page for more information.

principal_name
> A pointer to a character string indicating the name of the principal whose key is to be changed.

key_vno
> The version number of the new key. If 0 (zero) is specified, the routine will select the next appropriate key version number.

keydata
> A pointer to a structure of type **sec_passwd_rec_t**.

Output

garbage_collect_time
> The number of seconds that must elapse before all currently valid tickets (which are encoded with the current or previous keys) expire. At that time, all obsolete keys may be "garbage collected," since no valid tickets encoded with those keys will remain outstanding on the network.

status
> A pointer to the completion status. On successful completion, the routine returns **error_status_ok**. Otherwise, it returns an error.

Description

The **sec_key_mgmt_change_key()** routine performs all activities necessary to update a principal's key to the specified value. This includes updating any local storage for the principal's key and also performing any remote operations needed to keep the authentication protocol (or network registry) current. Old keys for the principal are garbage collected if appropriate.

Files

/usr/include/dce/keymgmt.idl
> The **idl** file from which **dce/keymgmt.h** was derived.

Errors

Any error condition will leave the key state unchanged.

sec_key_mgmt_e_key_unavailable
> The old key is not present and therefore cannot be used to set a client side authentication context.

sec_key_mgmt_e_authn_invalid
> The authentication protocol is not valid.

sec_key_mgmt_e_auth_unavailable
> The authentication protocol is not available to update the network database or to obtain the necessary network credentials.

sec_key_mgmt_change_key(3sec)

sec_key_mgmt_e_unauthorized
> The caller is not authorized to perform the operation.

sec_key_mgmt_e_key_unsupported
> The key type is not supported.

sec_key_mgmt_e_key_version_ex
> A key with this version number already exists.

sec_rgy_server_unavailable
> The DCE registry server is unavailable.

sec_rgy_object_not_found
> No principal was found with the given name.

sec_login_s_no_memory
> A memory allocation error occurred.

error_status_ok
> The call was successful.

Related Information

Functions: **sec_intro(3sec)**, **sec_key_mgmt_generate_key(3sec)**, **sec_key_mgmt_set_key(3sec)**.

sec_key_mgmt_delete_key

Purpose   Deletes a key from the local storage

Synopsis   **#include <dce/keymgmt.h>**

void sec_key_mgmt_delete_key(
          sec_key_mgmt_authn_service *authn_service*,
          void *arg,
          idl_char *principal_name,
          unsigned32 *key_vno*,
          error_status_t *status);

Parameters

Input

authn_service   Identifies the authentication protocol using this key. The possible authentication protocols are as follows:

rpc_c_authn_dce_secret
          DCE shared-secret key authentication.

rpc_c_authn_dce_public
          DCE public key authentication (reserved for future use).

arg   This parameter can specify either the local key file or an argument to the *get_key_fn* key acquisition routine of the **rpc_server_-register_auth_info** routine.

A value of NULL specifies that the default key file (**/krb/v5srvtab**) should be used. A key filename specifies that file should be used as the key file. You must prepend the file's absolute filename with **FILE:** and the file must have been created with the **rgy_edit ktadd** command or the **sec_key_mgmt_set_key** function.

Any other value specifies an argument for the *get_key_fn* key acquisition routine. See the **rpc_server_register_auth_info( )** reference page for more information.

principal_name
          A pointer to a character string indicating the name of the principal whose key is to be deleted.

key_vno   The version number of the desired key.

Output

status   A pointer to the completion status. On successful completion, the routine returns **error_status_ok**. Otherwise, it returns an error.

Description

The **sec_key_mgmt_delete_key( )** routine deletes the specified key from the local key store. If an administrator ever discovers or suspects that the security of a server's key has been compromised, the administrator should delete the key immediately with **sec_key_mgmt_delete_key( )**. This routine removes the key from the local key storage, which invalidates all extant tickets encoded with the key. If the compromised key is the current one, the principal should change the key with **sec_key_mgmt_change_key( )** before deleting it. It is not an error for a process to delete the current key (as long as it is done *after* the network context has been established), but it may seriously inconvenience legitimate clients of a service.

This routine deletes all key types that have the specified key version number. A key type identifies the data encryption algorithm being used (for example, DES). This routine differs from **sec_key_mgmt_delete_key_type( )** in that **sec_key_-mgmt_delete_key_type( )** deletes only the specified key version of the specified key type from the local key store.

Files   **/usr/include/dce/keymgmt.idl**

The **idl** file from which **dce/keymgmt.h** was derived.

Errors   Any error condition will leave the key state unchanged.

sec_key_mgmt_e_key_unavailable
The requested key is not present.

sec_key_mgmt_e_authn_invalid
The authentication protocol is not valid.

sec_key_mgmt_e_unauthorized
The caller is not authorized to perform the operation.

error_status_ok
The call was successful.

Related Information

Functions: **sec_intro(3sec)**, **sec_key_mgmt_delete_key_type(3sec)**, **sec_key_mgmt_garbage_collect(3sec)**.

sec_key_mgmt_delete_key_type

Purpose   Deletes a key version of a key type from the local key storage

Synopsis   **#include <dce/keymgmt.h>**

void sec_key_mgmt_delete_key_type(
　　　　sec_key_mgmt_authn_service *authn_service,*
　　　　void **arg,*
　　　　idl_char **principal_name,*
　　　　void **keytype,*
　　　　unsigned32 *key_vno,*
　　　　error_status_t **status);*

Parameters

Input

authn_service Identifies the authentication protocol using this key. The possible authentication protocols are as follows:

rpc_c_authn_dce_secret
　　　　DCE shared-secret key authentication.

rpc_c_authn_dce_public
　　　　DCE public key authentication (reserved for future use).

arg　　　This parameter can specify either the local key file or an argument to the *get_key_fn* key acquisition routine of the **rpc_server_-register_auth_info** routine.

A value of NULL specifies that the default key file (**/krb/v5srvtab**) should be used. A key filename specifies that file should be used as the key file. You must prepend the file's absolute filename with **FILE:** and the file must have been created with the **rgy_edit ktadd** command or the **sec_key_mgmt_set_key** routine.

Any other value specifies an argument for the *get_key_fn* key acquisition routine. See the **rpc_server_register_auth_info( )** reference page for more information.

principal_name
> A pointer to a character string indicating the name of the principal whose key type is to be deleted.

keytype
> A pointer to a value of type **sec_passwd_type_t**. The value identifies the data encryption algorithm that is being used (for example, DES).

key_vno
> The version number of the desired key.

Output

status
> A pointer to the completion status. On successful completion, the routine returns **error_status_ok**. Otherwise, it returns an error.

Description

The **sec_key_mgmt_delete_key_type( )** routine deletes the specified key version of the specified key type from the local key store. It differs from **sec_key_mgmt_delete_key( )** in that **sec_key_mgmt_delete_key( )** deletes all key types that have the same key version number.

This routine removes the key from the local key storage, which invalidates all extant tickets encoded with the key. If the key in question is the current one, the principal should change the key with **sec_key_mgmt_change_key( )** before deleting it. It is not an error for a process to delete the current key (as long as it is done *after* the network context has been established), but it may seriously inconvenience legitimate clients of a service.

Files

/usr/include/dce/keymgmt.idl
> The **idl** file from which **dce/keymgmt.h** was derived.

Errors

Any error condition will leave the key state unchanged.

sec_key_mgmt_e_key_unavailable
> The requested key is not present.

sec_key_mgmt_e_authn_invalid
> The authentication protocol is not valid.

sec_key_mgmt_e_unauthorized
> The caller is not authorized to perform the operation.

error_status_ok
> The call was successful.

sec_key_mgmt_delete_key_type(3sec)

Related Information

Functions: **sec_intro(3sec)**, **sec_key_mgmt_delete_key(3sec)**, **sec_key_mgmt_garbage_collect(3sec)**.

sec_key_mgmt_free_key

Purpose   Frees the memory used by a key value

Synopsis   **#include <dce/keymgmt.h>**

void sec_key_mgmt_free_key(
        void ***keydata,**
        error_status_t **status**);**

Parameters

Input

    keydata   A pointer to a structure of type **sec_passwd_rec_t**.

Output

    status   A pointer to the completion status. On successful completion, the routine returns **error_status_ok**.

Description

The **sec_key_mgmt_free_key( )** routine releases any storage allocated for the indicated key data by **sec_key_mgmt_get_key( )**. The storage for the key data returned by **sec_key_mgmt_get_key( )** is dynamically allocated.

Files

/usr/include/dce/keymgmt.idl
        The **idl** file from which **dce/keymgmt.h** was derived.

Errors

error_status_ok
        The call was successful.

Related Information

Functions: **sec_intro(3sec)**, **sec_key_mgmt_get_key(3sec)**.

sec_key_mgmt_garbage_collect

Purpose   Deletes obsolete keys

Synopsis   **#include <dce/keymgmt.h>**

void sec_key_mgmt_garbage_collect(
        sec_key_mgmt_authn_service *authn_service,*
        void **arg,*
        idl_char **principal_name,*
        error_status_t **status***);**

Parameters

Input

authn_service   Identifies the authentication protocol using this key. The possible
                  authentication protocols are as follows:

> **rpc_c_authn_dce_secret**
>   DCE shared-secret key authentication.
>
> **rpc_c_authn_dce_public**
>   DCE public key authentication (reserved for future
>   use).

arg   This parameter can specify either the local key file or an argument
                  to the *get_key_fn* key acquisition routine of the **rpc_server_-
                  register_auth_info** routine.

                  A value of NULL specifies that the default key file (**/krb/v5srvtab**)
                  should be used. A key filename specifies that file should be used as
                  the key file. You must prepend the file's absolute filename with
                  FILE: and the file must have been created with the **rgy_edit ktadd**
                  command or the **sec_key_mgmt_set_key** routine.

                  Any other value specifies an argument for the *get_key_fn* key
                  acquisition routine. See the **rpc_server_register_auth_info( )**
                  reference page for more information.

principal_name
                  A pointer to a character string indicating the name of the principal
                  whose key information is to be garbage collected.

Output

status   A pointer to the completion status. On successful completion, the routine returns **error_status_ok**. Otherwise, it returns an error.

Description

The **sec_key_mgmt_garbage_collect( )** routine discards any obsolete key information for this principal. An obsolete key is one that can only decode invalid tickets. As an example, consider a key that was in use on Monday, and was only used to encode tickets whose maximum lifetime was 1 day. If that key was changed at 8:00 a.m. Tuesday morning, then it would become obsolete by 8:00 a.m. Wednesday morning, at which time there could be no valid tickets outstanding.

Files

/usr/include/dce/keymgmt.idl
The **idl** file from which **dce/keymgmt.h** was derived.

Errors

sec_key_mgmt_e_authn_invalid
The authentication protocol is not valid.

sec_key_mgmt_e_unauthorized
The caller is not authorized to perform the operation.

sec_key_mgmt_e_key_unavailable
Requested key not present.

sec_rgy_server_unavailable
The DCE registry server is unavailable.

sec_rgy_object_not_found
No principal was found with the given name.

sec_login_s_no_memory
A memory allocation error occurred.

error_status_ok
The call was successful.

Related Information

Functions: **sec_intro(3sec)**, **sec_key_mgmt_delete_key(3sec)**.

sec_key_mgmt_gen_rand_key

Purpose   Generates a new random key of a specified key type

Synopsis   **#include <dce/keymgmt.h>**

void sec_key_mgmt_gen_rand_key(
> **sec_key_mgmt_authn_service** *authn_service,*
> **void** **arg,*
> **idl_char** **principal_name,*
> **void** **keytype,*
> **unsigned32** *key_vno,*
> **void** ***keydata,*
> **error_status_t** **status);*

Parameters

Input

> *authn_service* Identifies the authentication protocol using this key. The possible authentication protocols are as follows:
>
> > **rpc_c_authn_dce_secret**
> > > DCE shared-secret key authentication.
> >
> > **rpc_c_authn_dce_public**
> > > DCE public key authentication (reserved for future use).
>
> *arg*   This parameter can specify either the local key file or an argument to the *get_key_fn* key acquisition routine of the **rpc_server_register_auth_info** routine.
>
> > A value of NULL specifies that the default key file (**/krb/v5srvtab**) should be used. A key filename specifies that file should be used as the key file. You must prepend the file's absolute filename with **FILE:** and the file must have been created with the **rgy_edit ktadd** command or the **sec_key_mgmt_set_key** routine.
> >
> > Any other value specifies an argument for the *get_key_fn* key acquisition routine. See the **rpc_server_register_auth_info( )** reference page for more information.

principal_name
A pointer to a character string indicating the name of the principal for whom the key is to be generated.

keytype
A pointer to a value of type **sec_passwd_type_t**. The value identifies the data encryption algorithm to be used for the key (for example, DES).

key_vno
The version number of the new key.

Output

keydata
A pointer to a value of **sec_passwd_rec_t**. The storage for *keydata* is allocated dynamically, so the returned pointer actually indicates a pointer to the key value. The storage for this data may be freed with the **sec_key_mgmt_free_key( )** function.

status
A pointer to the completion status. On successful completion, the routine returns **error_status_ok**. Otherwise, it returns an error.

Description

The **sec_key_mgmt_gen_rand_key( )** routine generates a new random key for a specified principal and of a specified key type. The generated key can be used with the **sec_key_mgmt_change_key( )** and **sec_key_mgmt_set_key( )** routines.

Note that to initialize the random keyseed, the process must first make an authenticated call such as **sec_rgy_site_open( )**.

Files

/usr/include/dce/keymgmt.idl
The **idl** file from which **dce/keymgmt.h** was derived.

Errors

sec_key_mgmt_e_not_implemented
The specified key type is not supported.

sec_s_no_key_seed
No random key seed has been set.

sec_s_no_memory
Unable to allocate memory.

error_status_ok
The call was successful.

sec_key_mgmt_gen_rand_key(3sec)

Related Information

Functions: **sec_intro(3sec), sec_key_mgmt_change_key(3sec),
sec_key_mgmt_generate_key(3sec), sec_key_mgmt_set_key(3sec).**

sec_key_mgmt_get_key

Purpose   Retrieves a key from local storage

Synopsis   **#include <dce/keymgmt.h>**

    void sec_key_mgmt_get_key(
        sec_key_mgmt_authn_service *authn_service*,
        void *arg,
        idl_char *principal_name,
        unsigned32 *key_vno*,
        void **keydata,
        error_status_t **status***);**

Parameters

Input

authn_service Identifies the authentication protocol using this key. The possible authentication protocols are as follows:

> **rpc_c_authn_dce_secret**
> > DCE shared-secret key authentication.
>
> **rpc_c_authn_dce_public**
> > DCE public key authentication (reserved for future use).

arg   This parameter can specify either the local key file or an argument to the *get_key_fn* key acquisition routine of the **rpc_server_register_auth_info** routine.

A value of NULL specifies that the default key file (**/krb/v5srvtab**) should be used. A key filename specifies that file should be used as the key file. You must prepend the file's absolute filename with **FILE:** and the file must have been created with the **rgy_edit ktadd** command or the **sec_key_mgmt_set_key** routine.

Any other value specifies an argument for the *get_key_fn* key acquisition routine. See the **rpc_server_register_auth_info( )** reference page for more information.

principal_name
A pointer to a character string indicating the name of the principal to whom the key belongs.

key_vno
The version number of the desired key. To return the latest version of the key, set this parameter to **sec_c_key_version_none**.

Output

keydata
A pointer to a value of type **sec_passwd_rec_t**. The storage for *keydata* is allocated dynamically, so the returned pointer actually indicates a pointer to the key value. The storage for this data may be freed with the **sec_key_mgmt_free_key( )** routine.

status
A pointer to the completion status. On successful completion, the routine returns **error_status_ok**. Otherwise, it returns an error.

Description

The **sec_key_mgmt_get_key( )** routine extracts the specified key from the local key store.

Files

/usr/include/dce/keymgmt.idl
The **idl** file from which **dce/keymgmt.h** was derived.

Errors

sec_key_mgmt_e_key_unavailable
The requested key is not present.

sec_key_mgmt_e_authn_invalid
The authentication protocol is not valid.

sec_key_mgmt_e_unauthorized
The caller is not authorized to perform the operation.

sec_s_no_memory
Unable to allocate memory.

error_status_ok
The call was successful.

Related Information

Functions: **sec_intro(3sec)**.

sec_key_mgmt_get_next_key

Purpose   Retrieves successive keys from the local key storage

Synopsis   **#include <dce/keymgmt.h>**

void sec_key_mgmt_get_next_key(
      void **cursor***,**
      idl_char ***principal_name***,**
      unsigned32 **key_vno***,**
      void ***keydata***,**
      error_status_t **status***);**

Parameters

Input

    cursor   A pointer to the current cursor position in the local key storage. The cursor position is set via the routine **sec_key_mgmt_initialize_cursor( )**.

Output

    principal_name
        A pointer to a character string indicating the name of the principal associated with the extracted key. Free the storage for the principal name with the **free( )** function.

    key_vno   The version number of the extracted key.

    keydata   A pointer to a value of type **sec_passwd_rec_t**. The storage for *keydata* is allocated dynamically, so the returned pointer actually indicates a pointer to the key value. The storage for this data may be freed with the **sec_key_mgmt_free_key( )** function.

    status   A pointer to the completion status. On successful completion, the routine returns **error_status_ok**. Otherwise, it returns an error.

sec_key_mgmt_get_next_key(3sec)

Description

The **sec_key_mgmt_get_next_key**( ) routine extracts the key pointed to by the cursor in the local key store and updates the cursor to point to the next key. By repeatedly calling this routine you can scan all the keys in the local store.

Files

/usr/lib/dce/keymgmt.idl
The **idl** file from which **dce/keymgmt.h** was derived.

Errors

sec_key_mgmt_e_key_unavailable
The requested key is not present.

sec_key_mgmt_e_unauthorized
The caller is not authorized to perform the operation.

sec_s_no_memory
Unable to allocate memory.

error_status_ok
The call was successful.

Related Information

Functions: **sec_intro(3sec)**, **sec_key_mgmt_get_key(3sec)**, **sec_key_mgmt_initialize_cursor(3sec)**.

sec_key_mgmt_get_next_kvno

Purpose   Retrieves the next eligible key version number for a key

Synopsis   **#include <dce/keymgmt.h>**

void sec_key_mgmt_get_next_kvno(
        sec_key_mgmt_authn_service *authn_service*,
        void **arg*,
        idl_char **principal_name*,
        void **keytype*,
        unsigned32 **key_vno*,
        unsigned32 **next_key_vno*,
        error_status_t **status*);

Parameters

Input

authn_service Identifies the authentication protocol using this key. The possible authentication protocols are as follows:

    rpc_c_authn_dce_secret
        DCE shared-secret key authentication.

    rpc_c_authn_dce_public
        DCE public key authentication (reserved for future use).

arg   This parameter can specify either the local key file or an argument to the *get_key_fn* key acquisition routine of the **rpc_server_-register_auth_info** routine.

A value of NULL specifies that the default key file (**/krb/v5srvtab**) should be used. A key filename specifies that file should be used as the key file. You must prepend the file's absolute filename with **FILE:** and the file must have been created with the **rgy_edit ktadd** command or the **sec_key_mgmt_set_key** routine.

Any other value specifies an argument for the *get_key_fn* key acquisition routine. See the **rpc_server_register_auth_info( )** reference page for more information.

principal_name

A pointer to a character string indicating the name of the principal associated with the key.

keytype

A pointer to a value of type **sec_passwd_type_t**. The value identifies the data encryption algorithm (for example, DES) being used for the key.

Output

key_vno

The current version number of the key. Specify NULL if you do not need this value to be returned.

next_key_vno The next eligible version number for the key. Specify NULL if you do not need this value to be returned.

status

A pointer to the completion status. On successful completion, the routine returns **error_status_ok**. Otherwise, it returns an error.

Description

The **sec_key_mgmt_get_next_kvno( )** routine returns the current and next eligible version numbers for a key from the registry server (not from the local key table). The key is identified via its associated authentication protocol, principal name, and key type. The *arg* value associated with the key is also specified.

Files

/usr/include/dce/keymgmt.idl

The **idl** file from which **dce/keymgmt.h** was derived.

Errors

sec_key_mgmt_e_key_unavailable

The requested key is not present.

sec_key_mgmt_e_authn_invalid

The authentication protocol is not valid.

sec_key_mgmt_e_unauthorized

The caller is not authorized to perform the operation.

sec_rgy_server_unavailable

The DCE registry server is unavailable.

sec_rgy_object_not_found
>   No principal was found with the given name.

error_status_ok
>   The call was successful.

Related Information

Functions: **sec_intro(3sec)**.

sec_key_mgmt_initialize_cursor

Purpose   Repositions the cursor in the local key store

Synopsis   **#include <dce/keymgmt.h>**

void sec_key_mgmt_initialize_cursor(
          sec_key_mgmt_authn_service *authn_service,*
          void **arg,*
          idl_char **principal_name,*
          void **keytype,*
          void ***cursor,*
          error_status_t **status*);

Parameters

Input

authn_service Identifies the authentication protocol using this key. The possible authentication protocols are as follows:

> **rpc_c_authn_dce_secret**
> > DCE shared-secret key authentication.

> **rpc_c_authn_dce_public**
> > DCE public key authentication (reserved for future use).

arg   This parameter can specify either the local key file or an argument to the *get_key_fn* key acquisition routine of the **rpc_server_-register_auth_info** routine.

A value of NULL specifies that the default key file (**/krb/v5srvtab**) should be used. A key filename specifies that file should be used as the key file. You must prepend the file's absolute filename with **FILE:** and the file must have been created with the **rgy_edit ktadd** command or the **sec_key_mgmt_set_key** routine.

Any other value specifies an argument for the *get_key_fn* key acquisition routine. See the **rpc_server_register_auth_info( )** reference page for more information.

principal_name
A pointer to a character string indicating the name of the principal whose key is to be accessed. To access all keys in the local key store, supply NULL for this parameter.

keytype
A pointer to the data encryption algorithm (for example, DES) being used for the key.

Output

cursor
The returned cursor value. The storage for the cursor information is allocated dynamically, so the returned pointer actually indicates a pointer to the cursor value. The storage for this data may be freed with the **sec_key_mgmt_release_cursor( )** routine.

status
A pointer to the completion status. On successful completion, the routine returns **error_status_ok**. Otherwise, it returns an error.

Description

The **sec_key_mgmt_initialize_cursor( )** routine resets the cursor in the local key store.

Use this routine to reposition the cursor before performing a scan of the local store via **sec_key_mgmt_get_next_key( )**. The returned cursor value is supplied as input to **sec_key_mgmt_get_next_key( )**.

Files
/usr/include/dce/keymgmt.idl
The **idl** file from which **dce/keymgmt.h** was derived.

Errors
sec_s_no_memory
Unable to allocate memory.

sec_key_mgmt_e_authn_invalid
The authentication protocol is not valid.

sec_key_mgmt_e_unauthorized
The caller is not authorized to perform the operation.

error_status_ok
The call was successful.

Related Information

Functions: **sec_intro(3sec)**, **sec_key_mgmt_get_next_key(3sec)**, **sec_key_mgmt_release_cursor(3sec)**.

sec_key_mgmt_manage_key

Purpose   Automatically changes a principal's key before it expires

Synopsis   **#include <dce/keymgmt.h>**

void sec_key_mgmt_manage_key(
        sec_key_mgmt_authn_service *authn_service*,
        void **arg*,
        idl_char **principal_name*,
        error_status_t **status*);

Parameters

Input

authn_service Identifies the authentication protocol using this key. The possible authentication protocols are as follows:

rpc_c_authn_dce_secret
        DCE shared-secret key authentication.

rpc_c_authn_dce_public
        DCE public key authentication (reserved for future use).

arg   This parameter can specify either the local key file or an argument to the *get_key_fn* key acquisition routine of the **rpc_server_-register_auth_info** routine.

A value of NULL specifies that the default key file (**/krb/v5srvtab**) should be used. A key filename specifies that file should be used as the key file. You must prepend the file's absolute filename with **FILE:** and the file must have been created with the **rgy_edit ktadd** command or the **sec_key_mgmt_set_key** routine.

Any other value specifies an argument for the *get_key_fn* key acquisition routine. See the **rpc_server_register_auth_info( )** reference page for more information.

principal_name
        A pointer to a character string indicating the name of the principal whose key is to be managed.

Output

> *status*   A pointer to the completion status. On successful completion, the routine returns **error_status_ok**. Otherwise, it returns an error.

Description

The **sec_key_mgmt_manage_key( )** routine changes the specified principal's key on a regular basis, as determined by the local cell's policy. It will run indefinitely, never returning during normal operation, and therefore should be invoked only from a thread that has been devoted to managing keys.

This routine queries the DCE registry to determine the password expiration policy that applies to the named principal. It then idles until a short time before the current key is due to expire and then uses the **sec_key_mgmt_gen_rand_key( )** to produce a new random key, updating both the local key store and the DCE registry. This routine also invokes **sec_key_mgmt_garbage_collect( )** as needed.

Files

/usr/include/dce/keymgmt.idl
> The **idl** file from which **dce/keymgmt.h** was derived.

Errors

sec_key_mgmt_e_key_unavailable
> The old key is not present and therefore cannot be used to set a client side authentication context.

sec_key_mgmt_e_key_unsupported
> The key type is not supported.

sec_key_mgmt_e_authn_invalid
> The authentication protocol is not valid.

sec_key_mgmt_e_unauthorized
> The caller is not authorized to perform the operation.

sec_rgy_server_unavailable
> The DCE registry server is unavailable.

sec_rgy_object_not_found
> No principal was found with the given name.

error_status_ok
> The call was successful.

Related Information

Functions: **sec_intro(3sec)**, **sec_key_mgmt_gen_rand_key(3sec)**, **sec_key_mgmt_garbage_collect(3sec)**.

sec_key_mgmt_release_cursor

Purpose   Releases the memory used by an initialized cursor value

Synopsis   **#include <dce/keymgmt.h>**

void sec_key_mgmt_release_cursor(
        void ****cursor,**
        error_status_t **status**);**

Parameters

Input

cursor   A pointer to the cursor value for which the storage is to be released.

Output

status   A pointer to the completion status. On successful completion, the routine returns **error_status_ok**.

Description

The **sec_key_mgmt_release_cursor( )** routine releases any storage allocated for the indicated cursor value by **sec_key_mgmt_initialize_cursor( )**. The storage for the cursor value returned by **sec_key_mgmt_initialize_cursor( )** is dynamically allocated.

Files   **/usr/include/dce/keymgmt.idl**
        The **idl** file from which **dce/keymgmt.h** was derived.

Errors   **sec_key_mgmt_e_unauthorized**
        The caller is not authorized to perform the operation.

error_status_ok
        The call was successful.

Related Information

Functions: **sec_intro(3sec)**, **sec_key_mgmt_initialize_cursor(3sec)**.

sec_key_mgmt_set_key

Purpose   Inserts a key value into the local storage

Synopsis   **#include <dce/keymgmt.h>**

void sec_key_mgmt_set_key(
        sec_key_mgmt_authn_service *authn_service,*
        void **arg,*
        idl_char **principal_name,*
        unsigned32 *key_vno,*
        void **keydata,*
        error_status_t **status);*

Parameters

Input

authn_service Identifies the authentication protocol using this key. The possible authentication protocols are as follows:

> **rpc_c_authn_dce_secret**
>> DCE shared-secret key authentication.

> **rpc_c_authn_dce_public**
>> DCE public key authentication (reserved for future use).

arg   This parameter can specify either the local key file or an argument to the *get_key_fn* key acquisition routine of the **rpc_server_register_auth_info** routine.

A value of NULL specifies that the default key file (**/krb/v5srvtab**) should be used. A key filename specifies that file should be used as the key file. The filename must begin with **FILE:**. If the filename does not begin with **FILE:**, the code will add it.

Any other value specifies an argument for the *get_key_fn* key acquisition routine. See the **rpc_server_register_auth_info( )** reference page for more information.

principal_name
      A pointer to a character string indicating the name of the principal associated with the key to be set.

key_vno   The version number of the key to be set.

keydata   A pointer to the key value to be set.

Output

status   A pointer to the completion status. On successful completion, the routine returns **error_status_ok**. Otherwise, it returns an error.

Description

The **sec_key_mgmt_set_key( )** routine performs all local activities necessary to update a principal's key to the specified value. This routine will not update the authentication protocol's value for the principal's key.

In some circumstances, a server may only wish to change its key in the local key storage, and not in the DCE registry. For example, a database system may have several replicas of a master database, managed by servers running on independent machines. Since these servers together represent only one service, they should all share the same key. This way, a user with a ticket to use the database can choose whichever server is least busy. To change the database key, the master server would signal all the replica (slave) servers to change the current key in their local key storage. They would use the **sec_key_mgmt_set_key( )** routine, which does not communicate with the DCE registry. Once all the slaves have complied, the master server can then change the registry key and its own local storage.

Files

/usr/include/dce/keymgmt.idl
The **idl** file from which **dce/keymgmt.h** was derived.

Errors

sec_key_mgmt_e_key_unavailable
The old key is not present and therefore cannot be used to set a client side authentication context.

sec_key_mgmt_e_authn_invalid
The authentication protocol is not valid.

sec_key_mgmt_e_unauthorized
The caller is not authorized to perform the operation.

sec_key_mgmt_e_key_unsupported
The key type is not supported.

sec_key_mgmt_e_key_version_ex
> A key with this version number already exists.

error_status_ok
> The call was successful.

Related Information

Functions: **sec_intro(3sec)**, **sec_key_mgmt_change_key(3sec)**,
sec_key_mgmt_gen_rand_key(3sec).

sec_login_become_delegate

Purpose   Causes an intermediate server to become a delegate in traced delegation chain

Synopsis   **#include <dce/sec_login.h>**

sec_login_handle_t sec_login_become_delegate(
           rpc_authz_cred_handle_t *callers_identity*,
           sec_login_handle_t *my_login_context*,
           sec_id_delegation_type_t *delegation_type_permitted*,
           sec_id_restriction_set_t **delegate_restrictions*,
           sec_id_restriction_set_t **target_restrictions*,
           sec_id_opt_req_t **optional_restrictions*,
           sec_id_opt_req_t **required_restrictions*,
           sec_id_compatibility_mode_t *compatibility_mode*,
           error_status_t **status*);

Parameters

Input

callers_identity

> A handle of type **rpc_authz_cred_handle_t** to the authenticated identity of the previous delegate in the delegation chain. The handle is supplied by the **rpc_binding_inq_auth_caller( )** call.

my_login_context

> A value of **sec_login_handle_t** that provides an opaque handle to the identity of the client that is becoming the intermediate delegate. The **sec_login_handle_t** that specifies the client's identity is supplied as output of the following calls:

> - **sec_login_get_current_context( )**, if the client inherited the identity of the current context

> - The **sec_login_setup_identity( )** and the **sec_login_-validate_identity( )** pair that together establish an authenticated identity if a new identity was established

> Note that this identity specified by **sec_login_handle_t** must be a simple login context; it cannot be a compound identity created by a previous **sec_login_become_delegate( )** call.

delegation_type_permitted

A value of **sec_id_delegation_type_t** that specifies the type of delegation to be enabled. The types available are as follows:

sec_id_ deleg_type_none
No delegation.

sec_id_deleg_type_traced
Traced delegation.

sec_id_deleg_type_impersonation
Simple (impersonation) delegation.

Note that the initiating client sets the type of delegation. If it is set as traced, all delegates must also specify traced delegation; they cannot specify simple delegation. The same is true if the initiating client sets the delegation type as simple; all subsequent delegates must also specify simple delegation. The intermediate delegates can, however, specify no delegation to indicate that the delegation chain can proceed no further.

delegate_restrictions

A pointer to a **sec_id_restriction_set_t** that supplies a list of servers that can act as delegates for the intermediate client identified by *my_login_context*. These servers are added to delegates permitted by the *delegate_restrictions* parameter of the **sec_login_become_-initiator** call.

target_restrictions

A pointer to a **sec_id_restriction_set_t** that supplies a list of servers that can act as targets for the intermediate client identified by *my_login_context*. These servers are added to targets specified by the *target_restrictions* parameter of the **sec_login_become_-initiator** call.

optional_restrictions

A pointer to a **sec_id_opt_req_t** that supplies a list of application-defined optional restrictions that apply to the intermediate client identified by *my_login_context*. These restrictions are added to the restrictions identified by the *optional_restrictions* parameter of the **sec_login_become_initiator** call.

required_restrictions
> A pointer to a **sec_id_opt_req_t** that supplies a list of application-defined required restrictions that apply to the intermediate client identified by *my_login_context*. These restrictions are added to the restrictions identified *required_restrictions* parameter of the **sec_login_become_initiator** call.

compatibility_mode
> A value of **sec_id_compatibility_mode_t** that specifies the compatibility mode to be used when the intermediate client operates on pre-1.1 servers. The modes available are as follows:

sec_id_compat_mode_none
> Compatibility mode is off.

sec_id_compat_mode_initiator
> Compatibility mode is on. The pre-1.1 PAC data is extracted from the EPAC of the initiating client.

sec_id_compat_mode_caller
> Compatibility mode is on. The pre-1.1 PAC data extracted from the EPAC of the last client in the delegation chain.

Output

status
> A pointer to the completion status. On successful completion, *status* is assigned **error_status_ok**. Otherwise, it returns an error.

Description

The **sec_login_become_delegate( )** is used by intermediate servers to become a delegate for the client identified by *callers_identity*. The routine returns a new login context (of type **sec_login_handle_t**) that carries delegation information. This information includes the delegation type, delegate and target restrictions, and any application-defined optional and required restrictions.

The new login context created by this call can then used to to set up authenticated rpc with an intermediate or target server using the **rpc_binding_set_auth_info( )** call.

Any delegate, target, required, or optional restrictions specified in this call are added to the restrictions specified by the initiating client and any intermediate clients.

The **sec_login_become_delegate( )** call is run only if the initiating client enabled traced delegation by setting the *delegation_type_permitted* parameter in the **sec_login_become_initiator** call to **sec_id_deleg_type_traced**.

Files   **/usr/include/dce/sec_login.idl**

The **idl** file from which **dce/sec_login.h** was derived.

Errors   **err_sec_login_invalid_delegate_restriction**

err_sec_login_invalid_target_restriction

err_sec_login_invalid_opt_restriction

err_sec_login_invalid_req_restriction

sec_login_s_invalid_context

sec_login_s_compound_delegate

sec_login_s_invalid_deleg_type

sec_login_s_invalid_compat_mode

sec_login_s_deleg_not_enabled

error_status_ok

Related Information

Functions: **rpc_binding_inq_auth_caller(3rpc)**, **sec_intro(3sec)**, **sec_login_become_impersonator(3sec)**, **sec_login_become_initiator(3sec)**, **sec_login_get_current_context(3sec)**, **sec_login_setup_identity(3sec)**, **sec_login_validate_identity( )**.

sec_login_become_impersonator

Purpose   Causes an intermediate server to become a delegate in a simple delegation chain

Synopsis   **#include <dce/sec_login.h>**

sec_login_handle_t sec_login_become_impersonator(
        rpc_authz_cred_handle_t *callers_identity*,
        sec_id_delegation_type_t *delegation_type_permitted*,
        sec_id_restriction_set_t **delegate_restrictions*,
        sec_id_restriction_set_t **target_restrictions*,
        sec_id_opt_req_t **optional_restrictions*,
        sec_id_opt_req_t **required_restrictions*,
        error_status_t **status*);

Parameters

Input

callers_identity
          A handle of type **rpc_authz_cred_handle_t** to the authenticated
          identity of the previous delegate in the delegation chain. The handle
          is supplied by the **rpc_binding_inq_auth_caller( )** call.

delegation_type_permitted
          A value of **sec_id_delegation_type_t** that specifies the type of
          delegation to be enabled. The types available are as follows:

sec_id_deleg_type_none
          No delegation.

sec_id_deleg_type_traced
          Traced delegation.

sec_id_deleg_type_impersonation
          Simple (impersonation) delegation.

The initiating client sets the type of delegation. If it is set as traced,
all delegates must also specify traced delegation; they cannot
specify simple delegation. The same is true if the initiating client
sets the delegation type as simple; all subsequent delegates must
also specify simple delegation. The intermediate delegates can,
however, specify no delegation to indicate that the delegation chain
can proceed no further.

delegate_restrictions

A pointer to a **sec_id_restriction_set_t** that supplies a list of servers that can act as delegates for the client becoming the delegate. These servers are added to the delegates permitted by the *delegate_restrictions* parameter of the **sec_login_become_initiator** call

target_restrictions

A pointer to a **sec_id_restriction_set_t** that supplies a list of servers that can act as targets for the client becoming the delegate. These servers are added to targets specified by the *target_restrictions* parameter of the **sec_login_become_initiator** call.

optional_restrictions

A pointer to a **sec_id_opt_req_t** that supplies a list of application-defined optional restrictions that apply to the client becoming the delegate. These restrictions are added to the restrictions identified by the *optional_restrictions* parameter of the **sec_login_become_-initiator** call.

required_restrictions

A pointer to a **sec_id_opt_req_t** that supplies a list of application-defined required restrictions that apply to the client becoming the delegate. These restrictions are added to the restrictions identified *required_restrictions* parameter of the **sec_login_become_initiator** call.

Output

status

A pointer to the completion status. On successful completion, *status* is assigned **error_status_ok**. Otherwise, it returns an error.

Description

The **sec_login_become_impersonator( )** is used by intermediate servers to become a delegate for the client identified by *callers_identity*. The routine returns a new login context (of type **sec_login_handle_t**) that carries delegation information. This information includes the delegation type, delegate, and target restrictions, and any application-defined optional and required restrictions.

The new login context created by this call can then used to to set up authenticated rpc with an intermediate or target server using the **rpc_binding_set_auth_info( )** call.

sec_login_become_impersonator(3sec)

The effective optional and required restrictions are the union of the optional and required restrictions specified in this call and specified by the initiating client and any intermediate clients. The effective target and delegate restrictions are the intersection of the target and delegate restrictions specified in this call and specified by the initiating client and any intermediate clients.

The **sec_login_become_impersonator** call is call is run only if the initiating client enabled simple delegation by setting the *delegation_type_permitted* parameter in the **sec_login_become_initiator** call to **sec_id_deleg_type_simple**.

Files   **/usr/include/dce/sec_login.idl**
               The **idl** file from which **dce/sec_login.h** was derived.

Errors   **err_sec_login_invalid_delegate_restriction**

               err_sec_login_invalid_target_restriction

               err_sec_login_invalid_opt_restriction

               err_sec_login_invalid_req_restriction

               sec_login_s_invalid_deleg_type

               sec_login_s_invalid_compat_mode

               sec_login_s_deleg_not_enabled

               error_status_ok

Related Information

Functions: **rpc_binding_inq_auth_caller(3rpc)**, **sec_intro(3sec)**, **sec_login_become_initiator(3sec)**.

sec_login_become_initiator

Purpose   Constructs a new login context that enables delegation for the calling client

Synopsis   **#include <dce/sec_login.h>**

> **sec_login_handle_t sec_login_become_initiator(**
> **sec_login_handle_t** *my_login_context,*
> **sec_id_delegation_type_t** *delegation_type_permitted,*
> **sec_id_restriction_set_t** **delegate_restrictions,*
> **sec_id_restriction_set_t** **target_restrictions,*
> **sec_id_opt_req_t** **optional_restrictions,*
> **sec_id_opt_req_t** **required_restrictions,*
> **sec_id_compatibility_mode_t** *compatibility_mode,*
> **error_status_t** *status);

Parameters

Input

> *my_login_context*
>> A value of **sec_login_handle_t** that provides an opaque handle to
>> the identity of the client that is enabling delegation. The **sec_login_-
>> handle_t** that specifies the client's identity is supplied as output of
>> the following calls:
>>
>> - **sec_login_get_current_context( )** if the client inherited the
>>   identity of the current context
>>
>> - The **sec_login_setup_identity( )** and the **sec_login_-
>>   validate_identity( )** pair that together establish an
>>   authentiated identity if a new identity was established

> *delegation_type_permitted*
>> A value of **sec_id_delegation_type_t** that specifies the type of
>> delegation to be enabled. The types available are as follows:
>>
>> **sec_id_deleg_type_none**
>>> No delegation.
>>
>> **sec_id_deleg_type_traced**
>>> Traced delegation.

sec_id_deleg_type_impersonation
Simple (impersonation) delegation.

Note each subsequent intermediate delegate of the delegation chain started by the initiating client must set the delegation type to traced if the initiating client set it to traced or to simple if the initiating client set it to simple. Intermediate delegates, however, can set the delegation type to no delegation to indicate that the delegation chain can proceed no further.

delegate_restrictions
A pointer to a **sec_id_restriction_set_t** that supplies a list of servers that can act as delegates for the client initiating delegation.

target_restrictions
A pointer to a **sec_id_restriction_set_t** that supplies a list of servers that can act as targets for the client initiating delegation.

optional_restrictions
A pointer to a **sec_id_opt_req_t** that supplies a list of application-defined optional restrictions that apply to the client initiating delegation.

required_restrictions
A pointer to a **sec_id_opt_req_t** that supplies a list of application-defined required restrictions that apply to the client initiating delegation.

compatibility_mode
A value of **sec_id_compatibility_mode_t** that specifies the compatibility mode to be used when the initiating client interacts with pre-1.1 servers. The modes available are as follows:

sec_id_compat_mode_none
Compatibility mode is off.

sec_id_compat_mode_initiator
Compatibility mode is on. The pre-1.1 PAC data is extracted from the EPAC of the initiating client.

sec_id_compat_mode_caller
Compatibility mode is on. The pre-1.1 PAC data extracted from the EPAC of the last client in the delegation chain.

Output

status   A pointer to the completion status. On successful completion, *status* is assigned **error_status_ok**. Otherwise, it returns an error.

Description

The **sec_login_become_initiator( )** enables delegation for the calling client by constructing a new login context (in a **sec_login_handle_t**) that carries delegation information. This information includes the delegation type, delegate, and target restrictions, and any application-defined optional and required restrictions.

The new login context is then used to to set up authenticated rpc with an intermediate server using the **rpc_binding_set_auth_info( )** call. The intermediary can continue the delegation chain by calling **sec_login_become_delegate** (if the delegation type is **sec_id_deleg_type_traced**) or **sec_login_become_-impersonator** (if the delegation type is **sec_id_deleg_type_impersonation**).

Files

/usr/include/dce/sec_login.idl
        The **idl** file from which **dce/sec_login.h** was derived.

Errors

err_sec_login_invalid_delegate_restriction

err_sec_login_invalid_target_restriction

err_sec_login_invalid_opt_restriction

err_sec_login_invalid_req_restriction

error_status_ok

sec_login_s_invalid_compat_mode

sec_login_s_invalid_context

sec_login_s_invalid_deleg_type

Related Information

Functions: **sec_intro(3sec), sec_login_become_delegate(3sec), sec_login_become_impersonator(3sec), sec_login_get_current_context(3sec), sec_login_setup_identity(3sec), sec_login_validate_identity( ).**

sec_login_certify_identity

Purpose   Certifies the network authentication service

Synopsis   **#include <dce/sec_login.h>**

boolean32 sec_login_certify_identity(
    sec_login_handle_t *login_context*,
    error_status_t **status*);

Parameters

Input

login_context   An opaque handle to login context data. The login context contains, among other data, the account principal name and UUID, account restrictions, records of group membership, and the process home directory. (See **sec_intro(3sec)** for more details about the login context.)

Output

status   A pointer to the completion status. On successful completion, *status* is assigned **error_status_ok**. Otherwise, it returns an error.

Description

The **sec_login_certify_identity()** routine certifies that the security server used to set up and validate a login context is legitimate. A legitimate server is one that knows the host machine's secret key. On some systems, this may be a privileged operation.

Information may be retrieved via **sec_login_get_pwent()**, **sec_login_get_-groups()**, and **sec_login_get_expiration()** from an uncertified login context, but such information cannot be trusted. All system login programs that use the **sec_login** interface must call **sec_login_certify_identity()** to certify the security server. If they do not, they open the local file system to attacks by imposter Security servers returning suspect local process credentials (UUID and group IDs). This operation updates the local registry with the login context credentials if the certification check succeeds.

Files   **/usr/include/dce/sec_login.idl**
             The **idl** file from which **dce/sec_login.h** was derived.

Return Values

The routine returns a **boolean32** value that is TRUE if the certification was successful, and FALSE otherwise.

Errors   **sec_login_s_config**
             The DCE configuration (**dce_config**) information is not available.

             sec_login_s_context_invalid
                   The input context is invalid.

             sec_login_s_default_use
                   It is an error to try to certify the default context.

             error_status_ok
                   The call was successful.

Examples   Applications wishing to perform a straightforward login can use the **sec_login** package as follows:

```
if (sec_login_setup_identity(user_name, sec_login_no_flags, &login_context,
                             &st)) {
    ... get password from user...

    if (sec_login_validate_identity(login_context, password,
                                    &reset_passwd, &auth_src, &st)) {

        if (!sec_login_certify_identity(login_context, &st))
            exit(error_weird_auth_svc);

        sec_login_set_context(login_context, &st);

        if (auth_src != sec_login_auth_src_network)
            printf("no network credentials");

        if (reset_passwd) {
            ... get new password from user, reset registry record ...
        };

        sec_login_get_pwent(login_context, &pw_entry, &st);

        if (pw_entry.pw_expire < todays_date) {
            sec_login_purge_context(&login_context, &st);
            exit(0)
        }

        ... any other application specific login valid actions ...
    }

    } else {
        sec_login_purge_context(&login_context, &st);

        ... application specific login failure actions ...
    }
}
```

Related Information

Functions: **sec_intro(3sec)**, **sec_login_get_expiration(3sec)**,
sec_login_get_groups(3sec), **sec_login_get_pwent(3sec)**.

sec_login_cred_get_delegate

Purpose   Returns a handle to the privilege attributes of an intermediary in a delegation chain
Used by clients

Synopsis   **#include <dce/sec_login.h>**

sec_cred_pa_handle_t sec_login_cred_get_delegate(
    sec_login_handle_t *login_context,*
    sec_cred_cursor_t **cursor,*
    error_status_t **status*);

Parameters

Input

login_context   A value of **sec_login_handle_t** that provides an opaque handle to a login context for which delegation has been enabled. The **sec_login_handle_t** that specifies the identity is supplied as output of the **sec_login_become_delegate( )** call.

Input/Output

cursor   As input, a pointer to a cursor of type **sec_cred_cursor_t** that has been initialized by the **sec_login_cred_init_cursor( )** call. As an output parameter, *cursor* is a pointer to a cursor of type **sec_cred_cursor_t** that is positioned past the principal whose privilege attributes have been returned in this call.

Output

status   A pointer to the completion status. On successful completion, *status* is assigned **error_status_ok**. Otherwise, it returns an error.

Description

The **sec_login_cred_get_delegate( )** routine returns a handle of type **sec_login_handle_t** to the the privilege attributes of an intermediary in a delegation chain that performed an authenticated RPC operation.

This call is used by clients. Servers use the **sec_cred_get_delegate( )** routine to return the privilege attribute handle of an intermediary in a delegation chain.

The login context identified by *login_context* contains all members in the delegation chain. This call returns a handle (**sec_cred_pa_handle_t**) to the privilege attributes of one of the delegates in the login context. The **sec_cred_pa_handle_t** returned by this call is used in other **sec_cred_get_*** calls to obtain privilege attribute information for a single delegate.

To obtain the privilege attributes of each delegate in the credential handle identified by *callers_identity*, execute this call until the message **sec_cred_s_no_-more_entries** is returned.

Before you execute **sec_login_cred_get_delegate( )**, you must execute a **sec_-login_cred_init_cursor( )** call to initialize a cursor of type **sec_cred_cursor_t**.

Use the **sec_cred_free_pa_handle( ) sec_cred_free_cursor( )** calls to free the resources allocated to the **sec_cred_pa_handle_t** and *cursor*.

Files

/usr/include/dce/sec_login.idl
> The **idl** file from which **dce/sec_login.h** was derived.

Errors

sec_cred_s_invalid_cursor

sec_cred_s_no_more_entries

error_status_ok

Related Information

Functions: **sec_intro(3sec)**, **sec_cred_get_deleg_restrictions(3sec)**,
sec_cred_get_delegation_type(3sec), **sec_cred_get_extended_attrs(3sec)**,
sec_cred_get_opt_restrictions(3sec), **sec_cred_get_pa_date(3sec)**,
sec_cred_get_req_restrictions(3sec), **sec_cred_get_tgt_restrictions(3sec)**,
sec_cred_get_v1_pac(3sec), **sec_login_cred_init_cursor(3sec)**.

sec_login_cred_get_initiator

Purpose   Returns information about the delegation initiator in a specified login context

Synopsis   **#include <dce/sec_login.h>**

sec_cred_pa_handle_t sec_login_cred_get_initiator(
        sec_login_handle_t *login_context*,
        error_status_t **status*);

Parameters

Input

login_context A value of **sec_login_handle_t** that provides an opaque handle to a login context for which delegation has been enabled.

Output

status   A pointer to the completion status. On successful completion, *status* is assigned **error_status_ok**. Otherwise, it returns an error.

Description

The **sec_login_cred_get_initiator**( ) routine returns a handle of type **sec_cred_pa_handle_t** to the privilege attributes of the delegation initiator.

The login context identified by *login_context* contains all members in the delegation chain. This call returns a handle (**sec_cred_pa_handle_t**) to the privilege attributes of the initiator. The **sec_cred_pa_handle_t** returned by this call is used in other **sec_cred_get_*** calls to obtain privilege attribute information for the initiator single delegate.

Use the **sec_cred_free_pa_handle**( ) call to free the resources allocated to the **sec_cred_pa_handle_t** handle.

sec_login_cred_get_initiator(3sec)

Files　　/usr/include/dce/sec_login.idl

　　　　　　　　The **idl** file from which **dce/sec_login.h** was derived.

Errors　　sec_login_s_invalid_context

　　　　　　error_status_ok

Related Information

Functions: **sec_cred_get_deleg_restrictions(3sec)**,
sec_cred_get_delegation_type(3sec), **sec_cred_get_extended_attrs(3sec)**,
sec_cred_get_opt_restrictions(3sec), **sec_cred_get_pa_date(3sec)**,
sec_cred_get_req_restrictions(3sec), **sec_cred_get_tgt_restrictions(3sec)**,
sec_cred_get_v1_pac(3sec), **sec_intro(3sec)**.

sec_login_cred_init_cursor

Purpose   Initializes a **sec_cred_cursor_t**

Synopsis   **#include <dce/sec_cred.h>**

void sec_login_cred_init_cursor (
            sec_cred_cursor_t **cursor,**
            error_status_t **status);**

Parameters

Input/Output

cursor   As input, a pointer to a **sec_cred_cursor_t** to be initialized. As output, a pointer to an initialized **sec_cred_cursor_t**.

Output

status   A pointer to the completion status. On successful completion, the routine returns **error_status_ok**. Otherwise, it returns an error.

Description

The **sec_login_cred_init_cursor( )** routine allocates and initializes a cursor of type **sec_cursor_t** for use with the **sec_login_cred_get_delegate( )** call.

Use the **sec_cred_free_cursor( )** call to free the resources allocated to *cursor*.

Errors   **sec_cred_s_invalid_cursor**

            sec_login_s_no_memory

            error_status_ok

Related Information

Functions: **sec_intro(3sec)**, **sec_login_cred_get_delegate(3sec)**.

sec_login_disable_delegation

Purpose   Disables delegation for a specified login context

Synopsis   **#include <dce/sec_login.h>**

sec_logon_handle_t *sec_login_disable_delegation(
        sec_login_handle_t *login_context*,
        error_status_t * *status*);

Parameters

Input

login_context An opaque handle to login context for which delegation has been enabled.

Output

status   A pointer to the completion status. On successful completion, *status* is assigned **error_status_ok**. Otherwise, it returns an error.

Description

The **sec_login_disable_delegation( )** routine disables delegation for a specified login context. It returns a new login context of type **sec_login_handle_t** without any delegation information, thus preventing any further delegation.

Files   **/usr/include/dce/sec_login.idl**
        The **idl** file from which **dce/sec_login.h** was derived.

Errors   **sec_login_s_invalid_context**

        error_status_ok

Related Information

Functions: **sec_intro(3sec)**, **sec_login_become_delegate(3sec)**, **sec_login_become_impersonator(3sec)**, **sec_login_become_initiator(3sec)**.

sec_login_export_context

Purpose   Creates an exportable login context

Synopsis   **#include <dce/sec_login.h>**

void sec_login_export_context(
        sec_login_handle_t *login_context,*
        unsigned32 *buf_len,*
        idl_byte *buf*[ ],
        unsigned32 **len_used,*
        unsigned32 **len_needed,*
        error_status_t **status*);

Parameters

Input

login_context   An opaque handle to login context data. The login context contains, among other data, the account principal name and UUID, account restrictions, records of group membership, and the process home directory. (See **sec_intro(3sec)** for more details about the login context.)

buf_len   An unsigned 32-bit integer containing the allocated length (in bytes) of the buffer that is to contain the login context.

Output

buf[ ]   An idl_byte array that contains the exportable login context upon return.

len_used   A pointer to an unsigned 32-bit integer indicating the number of bytes needed for the entire login context, up to *buf_len*.

len_needed   If the allocated length of the buffer is too short, an error is issued (**sec_login_s_no_memory**), and on return this pointer indicates the number of bytes necessary to contain the login context.

status   A pointer to the completion status. On successful completion, the routine returns **error_status_ok**. Otherwise, it returns an error.

sec_login_export_context(3sec)

Description

The **sec_login_export_context( )** routine obtains an exportable version of the login context information. This information may be passed to another process running on the same machine.

Files   **/usr/include/dce/sec_login.idl**

The **idl** file from which **dce/sec_login.h** was derived.

Errors   **sec_login_s_no_memory**

Not enough space was allocated for the *buf*[ ] array. The *len_needed* parameter will point to the needed length.

sec_login_s_handle_invalid

The login context handle is invalid.

sec_login_s_context_invalid

The login context specified by the input handle is invalid.

Related Information

Functions: **sec_login_import_context(3sec)**, **sec_intro(3sec)**.

sec_login_free_net_info

Purpose   Frees storage allocated for a principal's network information

Synopsis   **#include <dce/sec_login.h>**

        void sec_login_free_net_info(
                sec_login_net_info_t **net_info***);**

Parameters

Input/Output

net_info   A pointer to the **sec_login_net_info_t** structure to be freed.

Description

The **sec_login_free_net_info( )** routine frees any memory allocated for a principal's network information. Network information is returned by a previous successful call to **sec_login_inquire_net_info( )**.

Cautions   This routine does not return any completion codes. Make sure that you supply a valid **sec_login_net_info_t** address. The routine simply frees a range of storage beginning at the supplied address, without regard to the actual contents of the storage.

Files   **/usr/include/dce/sec_login.idl**
        The **idl** file from which **dce/sec_login.h** was derived.

Related Information

Functions: **sec_intro(3sec)**, **sec_login_inquire_net_info(3sec)**.

sec_login_get_current_context

Purpose   Returns a handle to the current login context

Synopsis   **#include <dce/sec_login.h>**

void sec_login_get_current_context(
        sec_login_handle_t **login_context,*
        error_status_t **status*)**;**

Parameters

Output

login_context A pointer to an opaque handle to login context data. The login context contains, among other data, the account principal name and UUID, account restrictions, records of group membership, and the process home directory. (See **sec_intro(3sec)** for more details about the login context.)

status A pointer to the completion status. On successful completion, the routine returns **error_status_ok**. Otherwise, it returns an error.

Description

The **sec_login_get_current_context( )** routine retrieves a handle to the login context for the currently established network identity. The context returned is created from locally cached data so subsequent data extraction operations may return some NULL values.

Files   **/usr/include/dce/sec_login.idl**
        The **idl** file from which **dce/sec_login.h** was derived.

Errors   **sec_login_s_no_current_context**
        There was no current context to retrieve. (See **sec_login_setup_-identity(3sec)** for information about how to set up, validate, and implement a login context.)

    error_status_ok
        The call was successful.

Examples   The following example illustrates use of the **sec_login_get_current_context( )** routine as part of a process to change the groupset:

```
sec_login_get_current_context(&login_context, &st);

sec_login_get_groups(login_context, &num_groups, &groups, &st);

    ...the group IDs have to be converted from the returned UNIX
    numbers into UUIDs (use sec_rgy_pgo_unix_num_to_id(3sec)...

for (i=0; i < num_groups; i++) {
    ... query whether the user wants to discard any of the current
    group memberships.  Copy new groupset to the new_groups array ...
}

if ( !sec_login_newgroups(sec_login_no_flags, num_new_groups,
        new_groups, &login_context, &st)) {
    if (st == sec_login_s_groupset_invalid)
        printf("New groupset invalid0);

    ... application specific error handling ...
}
```

Related Information

Functions: **sec_intro(3sec)**, **sec_login_setup_identity(3sec)**.

sec_login_get_delegation_type

Purpose   Returns the type of delegation permitted by a given login context

Synopsis   **#include <dce/sec_login.h>**

void sec_login_get_delegation_type(
    sec_login_handle_t *my_login_context*,
    sec_id_delegation_type_t **deleg_permitted*,
    error_status_t **status*);

Parameters

Input

login_context A value of **sec_login_handle_t** that provides an opaque handle to a login context.

Output

deleg_permitted
        A pointer to a value of **sec_id_delegation_type_t** that contains the type of delegation used in *login_context*.

status   A pointer to the completion status. On successful completion, *status* is assigned **error_status_ok**. Otherwise, it returns an error.

Description

The **sec_login_get_delegation_type( )** routine returns the type of delegation permitted in the specified login context.

The routine works only on previously validated contexts.

Files   **/usr/include/dce/sec_login.idl**
        The **idl** file from which **dce/sec_login.h** was derived.

Errors   sec_login_s_invalid_context

error_status_ok

Related Information

Functions: **sec_intro(3sec)**, **sec_login_become_delegate(3sec)**,
sec_login_become_impersonator(3sec), **sec_login_become_initiator(3sec)**.

sec_login_get_expiration

Purpose   Returns the TGT lifetime for an authenticated identity

Synopsis   **#include <dce/sec_login.h>**

void sec_login_get_expiration(
        sec_login_handle_t *login_context,*
        signed32 **identity_expiration,*
        error_status_t *status);

Parameters

Input

login_context An opaque handle to login context data. The login context contains, among other data, the account principal name and UUID, account restrictions, records of group membership, and the process home directory. (See **sec_intro(3sec)** for more details about the login context.)

Output

identity_expiration
        The lifetime of the ticket-granting ticket (TGT) belonging to the authenticated identity identified by *login_context*. It can be used in the same ways as a UNIX **time_t**.

status   A pointer to the completion status.

Description

The **sec_login_get_expiration( )** routine extracts the lifetime for the TGT belonging to the authenticated identity contained in the login context. The lifetime value is filled in if available; otherwise, it is set to 0 (zero). This routine allows an application to tell an interactive user how long the user's network login (and authenticated identity) will last before having to be refreshed.

The routine works only on previously certified contexts.

Files   **/usr/include/dce/sec_login.idl**
        The **idl** file from which **dce/sec_login.h** was derived.

Errors   **sec_login_s_context_invalid**

The login context itself is invalid.

sec_login_s_default_use

There was illegal use of the default login handle.

sec_login_s_not_certified

The login context has not been certified.

sec_login_s_no_current_context

The calling process has no context of its own.

error_status_ok

The call was successful.

Examples   Since the authenticated network identity for a process has a finite lifetime, there is
a risk it will expire during some long network operation, preventing the operation
from completing. To avoid this situation, an application might, before initiating a
long operation, use the **sec_login** package to check the expiration time of its
identity and refresh it if there is not enough time remaining to complete the
operation. After refreshing the identity, the process must validate it again with
sec_login_validate_identity( ).

```
sec_login_get_expiration(login_context, &expire_time, &st);

if (expire_time < (current_time + operation_duration)) {

        if (!sec_login_refresh_identity(login_context, &st)) {
          if (st == sec_login_s_refresh_ident_bad) {
             ... identity has changed ...
          } else {
             ... login context cannot be renewed ...
             exit(error_context_not_renewable);
          }

        if (sec_login_validate_identity(login_context, password,
                          &reset_passwd, &auth_src, &st)) {
          ... identity validated ...
        } else {
          ... validation failed ...
          exit(error_validation_failure);
        }
     }
}

operation();
```

Related Information

Functions: **sec_intro(3sec)**, **sec_login_get_current_context(3sec)**.

sec_login_get_groups

Purpose   Returns the group set from a login context

Synopsis   **#include <dce/sec_login.h>**

void sec_login_get_groups(
        sec_login_handle_t *login_context,*
        unsigned32 **num_groups,*
        signed32 ***group_set,*
        error_status_t **status);*

Parameters

Input

login_context   An opaque handle to login context data. The login context contains, among other data, the account principal name and UUID, account restrictions, records of group membership, and the process home directory. (See **sec_intro(3sec)** for more details about the login context.)

Output

num_groups   An unsigned 32-bit integer indicating the total number of groups returned in the *group_set* array.

group_set   The list of groups to which the user belongs.

status   A pointer to the completion status.

Description

The **sec_login_get_groups( )** routine returns the groups contained in the supplied login context. Part of a network identity is a list of the various groups to which the principal belongs. The groups are used to determine a user's access to various objects and services. This routine extracts from the login context a list of the groups for which the user has established network privileges.

The routine works only on previously validated contexts.

sec_login_get_groups(3sec)

Files   **/usr/include/dce/sec_login.idl**
              The **idl** file from which **dce/sec_login.h** was derived.

Errors   **sec_login_s_context_invalid**
              The login context itself is not valid.

              sec_login_s_info_not_avail
              The login context has no UNIX information.

              sec_login_s_default_use
              Illegal use of the default login handle occurred.

              sec_login_s_not_certified
              The login context has not been certified.

              sec_login_s_not_certified
              The login context is not certified.

              sec_rgy_object_not_found
              The registry server could not find the specified login context data.

              sec_rgy_server_unavailable
              The DCE registry server is unavailable.

              error_status_ok
              The call was successful.

Examples   The following example illustrates use of the **sec_login_get_groups( )** routine as
part of a process to change the groupset:

```
sec_login_get_current_context(&login_context, &st);

sec_login_get_groups(login_context, &num_groups, &groups, &st);

    ...the group IDs have to be converted from the returned UNIX
    numbers into UUIDs (use sec_rgy_pgo_unix_num_to_id(3sec)...

for (i=0; i < num_groups; i++) {
    ... query whether the user wants to discard any of the current
    group memberships.  Copy new groupset to the new_groups array ...
}

if ( !sec_login_newgroups(sec_login_no_flags, num_new_groups,
        new_groups, &login_context, &st)) {
    if (st == sec_login_s_groupset_invalid)
        printf("New groupset invalid0);

    ... application specific error handling ...
}
```

Related Information

Functions: **sec_intro(3sec)**, **sec_rgy_acct_get_projlist(3sec)**.

sec_login_get_pwent

Purpose   Returns a **passwd**-style entry for a login context

Synopsis   #include <dce/sec_login.h>

void sec_login_get_pwent(
        sec_login_handle_t *login_context*,
        sec_login_passwd_t *pwent*,
        error_status_t *status*);

Parameters

Input

login_context An opaque handle to login context data. The login context contains, among other data, the account principal name and UUID, account restrictions, records of group membership, and the process home directory. (See **sec_intro(3sec)** for more details about the login context.)

Output

pwent   A pointer to a pointer to the returned **passwd**-style structure. The particular structure depends on the underlying system. For example, on a system with a **passwd** structure like that supported by 4.4BSD and OSF/1, the structure (found in **/usr/include/pwd.h**) is as follows:

```
struct passwd {
    char    *pw_name;    /* user name */
    char    *pw_passwd;  /* encrypted password */
    int     pw_uid;      /* user uid */
    int     pw_gid;      /* user gid */
    time_t  pw_change;   /* password change time */
    char    *pw_class;   /* user access class */
    char    *pw_gecos;   /* miscellaneous account info */
    char    *pw_dir;     /* home directory */
    char    *pw_shell;   /* default shell */
    time_t  pw_expire;   /* account expiration */
};
```

status   A pointer to the completion status.

Description

The **sec_login_get_pwent( )** routine creates a **passwd**-style structure for the current network login context. This is generally useful for establishing the local operating system context. Applications that require all of the data normally extracted via **getpwnam( )** should extract that data from the login context with this call.

This routine works only on explicitly created (not inherited or imported) contexts.

Cautions

The returned **sec_login_passwd_t** structure points to data stored in the structure indicated by the *login_context* pointer and must be treated as read-only data. Writing to these data objects may cause unexpected failures.

Files

/usr/include/dce/sec_login.idl
        The **idl** file from which **dce/sec_login.h** was derived.

Examples

The following example illustrates use of the **sec_login_get_pwent( )** routine:

```
#include <pwd.h>
struct passwd *pwd;
sec_login_get_pwent(login_context,&(sec_login_passwd_t*)pwd,&status);
printf ("%s",pwd->pw_name);
```

Errors

sec_login_s_context_invalid
        The login context itself is invalid.

sec_login_s_not_certified
        The login context has not been certified.

sec_login_s_default_use
        Illegal use of the default login handle occurred.

sec_login_s_info_not_avail
        The login context has no UNIX information.

sec_rgy_object_not_found
        The registry server could not find the specified login context data.

sec_login_get_pwent(3sec)

sec_rgy_server_unavailable
> The DCE registry server is unavailable.

error_status_ok
> The call was successful.

Related Information

Functions: **sec_intro(3sec)**.

sec_login_import_context

Purpose   Imports a login context

Synopsis   **#include <dce/sec_login.h>**

void sec_login_import_context(
   unsigned32 *buf_len*,
   idl_byte *buf*[ ],
   sec_login_handle_t **login_context*,
   error_status_t **status*);

Parameters

Input

 buf_len   The allocated length (in bytes) of the buffer containing the login context.

 buf[ ]   An idl_byte array containing the importable login context.

Output

 login_context An opaque handle to login context data. The login context contains, among other data, the account principal name and UUID, account restrictions, records of group membership, and the process home directory. (See **sec_intro(3sec)** for more details about the login context.)

 status   A pointer to the completion status. On successful completion, the routine returns **error_status_ok**. Otherwise, it returns an error.

Description

The **sec_login_import_context( )** routine imports a context obtained via a call to **sec_login_export_context( )** performed on the same machine. To import a login context, users must have the appropriate privileges. Non-privileged users can import only their own login context; privileged users can import the login contexts created by any users.

sec_login_import_context(3sec)

Files   **/usr/include/dce/sec_login.idl**
The **idl** file from which **dce/sec_login.h** was derived.

Errors   **sec_login_s_context_invalid**
The login context itself is not valid.

sec_login_s_default_use
Illegal use of the default login handle occurred.

error_status_ok
The call was successful.

Related Information

Functions: **sec_intro(3sec)**, **sec_login_export_context(3sec)**.

sec_login_init_first

Purpose   Initializes the default context

Synopsis   **#include <dce/sec_login.h>**

void sec_login_init_first(
            error_status_t *_status_**);**

Parameters

Output

status   A pointer to the completion status. On successful completion, the
            routine returns **error_status_ok**. Otherwise, it returns an error.

Description

The **sec_login_init_first( )** routine initializes the default context inheritance
mechanism. If the default inheritance mechanism is already initialized, the
operation fails. Typically, this routine is called by the initial process at machine
boot time to initialize the default context inheritance mechanism for the host
machine process hierarchy.

Files   **/usr/include/dce/sec_login.idl**
            The **idl** file from which **dce/sec_login.h** was derived.

Errors   **sec_login_s_default_use**
            The default context is already initialized.

          sec_login_s_privileged
            An unprivileged process was called in.

          error_status_ok
            The call was successful.

Related Information

Functions: **sec_intro(3sec)**, **sec_login_setup_first(3sec)**,
sec_login_validate_first(3sec).

sec_login_inquire_net_info

Purpose   Returns a principal's network information

Synopsis   **#include <dce/sec_login.h>**

void sec_login_inquire_net_info(
        sec_login_handle_t *login_context,*
        sec_login_net_info_t **net_info,*
        error_status_t *status);

Parameters

Input

login_context An opaque handle to the login context for the desired principal.
            (See **sec_intro(3sec)** for more details about the login context.)

Output

net_info   A pointer to the returned **sec_login_net_info_t** data structure that
            contains the principal's network information. The **sec_login_net_-
            info_t** structure is defined as follows:

            typedef struct {
              sec_id_pac_t pac;
              unsigned32   acct_expiration_date;
              unsigned32   passwd_expiration_date;
              unsigned32   identity_expiration_date;
            } sec_login_net_info_t;
            };

status   A pointer to the completion status.

Description

The **sec_login_inquire_net_info( )** routine returns network information for the
principal identified by the specified login context. The network information
consists of the following:

- The privilege attribute certificate (PAC) that describes the identity and
  group memberships of the principal.

- The expiration date for the principal's account in the DCE registry.

- The expiration date for the principal's password in the DCE registry.

- The lifetime for the principal's authenticated network identity. This is the lifetime of the principal's TGT (see the **sec_login_get_expiration( )** routine).

A value of 0 (zero) for an expiration date means there is no expiration date. In other words, the principal's account, password, or authenticated identity is good indefinitely.

To remove the returned **net_info** structure when it is no longer needed, use **sec_login_free_net_info( )**.

Files   **/usr/include/dce/sec_login.idl**

The **idl** file from which **dce/sec_login.h** was derived.

Errors   **sec_login_s_not_certified**

The login context is not certified.

sec_login_s_context_invalid

The login context is not valid.

sec_login_s_no_current_context

The default context was specified, but none exists.

sec_login_s_auth_local

Operation not valid on local context. The call's identity was not authenticated.

error_status_ok

The call was successful.

Related Information

Functions: **sec_intro(3sec)**, **sec_login_free_net_info(3sec)**, **sec_login_get_expiration(3sec)**.

sec_login_newgroups

Purpose   Changes the group list for a login context

Synopsis   **#include <dce/sec_login.h>**

boolean32 sec_login_newgroups(
　　　　sec_login_handle_t *login_context***,**
　　　　sec_login_flags_t *flags***,**
　　　　unsigned32 *num_local_groups***,**
　　　　sec_id_t *local_groups*[ ]**,**
　　　　sec_login_handle_t **restricted_context***,**
　　　　error_status_t **status***);**

Parameters

Input

login_context　An opaque handle to login context data. The login context contains, among other data, the account principal name and UUID, account restrictions, records of group membership, and the process home directory. (See **sec_intro(3sec)** for more details about the login context.)

flags　　　　A set of flags of type **sec_login_flags_t**. These contain information about how the new network credentials will be used. Currently, the only flag used is **sec_login_credentials_private**, that, when set, implies that the new context is only to be used by the calling process. If this flag is not set (*flags* = **sec_login_no_flags**), descendants of the calling process may also use the new network credentials.

num_local_groups
　　　　　　An unsigned 32-bit integer containing the number of local group identities to include in the new context.

local_groups[ ]
　　　　　　An array of **sec_id_t** elements. Each element contains the UUID of a local group identity to include in the new context. These identities are local to the cell. Optionally, each element may also contain a pointer to a character string containing the name of the local group.

Output

restricted_context
> An opaque handle to the login context containing the changed group list.

status
> A pointer to the completion status. On successful completion, the routine returns **error_status_ok**. Otherwise, it returns an error.

Description

The **sec_login_newgroups( )** routine changes the group list for the specified login context. Part of a network identity is a list of the various groups to which a principal belongs. The groups are used to determine a user's access to various objects and services. This routine returns a new login context that contains the changed group list. To remove the new login context when it is no longer needed, use **sec_login_purge_context( )**.

This operation does not need to be validated as the user identity does not change. Consequently, knowledge of the password is not needed.

Notes

Currently you can have only groups from the local cell.

Files

/usr/include/dce/sec_login.idl
> The **idl** file from which **dce/sec_login.h** was derived.

Return Values

This routine returns TRUE when the new login context is successfully established.

Errors

sec_login_s_auth_local
> Operation not valid on local context.

sec_login_s_default_use
> It is an error to try to certify the default context.

sec_login_s_groupset_invalid
> The input list of group names is invalid. There may be groups to which the caller does not belong, or the list may contain groups that do not exist.

error_status_ok
> The call was successful.

sec_login_newgroups(3sec)

Examples The following example illustrates use of the **sec_login_newgroups( )** routine as part of a process to change the groupset:

```
sec_login_get_current_context(&login_context, &st);

sec_login_get_groups(login_context, &num_groups, &groups, &st);

    ...the group IDs have to be converted from the returned UNIX
    numbers into UUIDs (use sec_rgy_pgo_unix_num_to_id(3sec)...

for (i=0; i < num_groups; i++) {
    ... query whether the user wants to discard any of the current
    group memberships.  Copy new groupset to the new_groups array ...
}

if ( !sec_login_newgroups(sec_login_no_flags, num_new_groups,
        new_groups, &login_context, &st)) {
    if (st == sec_login_s_groupset_invalid)
        printf("New groupset invalid0);

    ... application specific error handling ...
}
```

Related Information

Functions: **sec_intro(3sec)**, **sec_login_get_groups(3sec)**, **sec_login_purge_context(3sec)**.

sec_login_purge_context

Purpose   Destroys a login context and frees its storage

Synopsis   **#include <dce/sec_login.h>**

void sec_login_purge_context(
        sec_login_handle_t **login_context***,**
        error_status_t **status***);**

Parameters

Input

login_context   A pointer to an opaque handle to login context data. The login context contains, among other data, the account principal name and UUID, account restrictions, records of group membership, and the process home directory. (See **sec_intro(3sec)** for more details about the login context.) Note that a pointer to the handle is submitted, so the handle may be reset to NULL upon successful completion.

Output

status   A pointer to the completion status. On successful completion, the routine returns **error_status_ok**. Otherwise, it returns an error.

Description

The **sec_login_purge_context( )** routine frees any storage allocated for the specified login context and destroys the associated network credentials, if any exist.

Cautions

Applications must be cautious when purging the current context as this destroys network credentials for all processes that share the credentials.

Files   **/usr/include/dce/sec_login.idl**
                      The **idl** file from which **dce/sec_login.h** was derived.

Errors   **sec_login_s_default_use**
                      Illegal use of the default login handle occurred.

                   sec_login_s_context_invalid
                      The login context itself is not valid.

                   error_status_ok
                      The call was successful.

Examples   The following example illustrates use of the **sec_login_purge_context( )** routine as
part of a straightforward login process:

```
if (sec_login_setup_identity(user_name, sec_login_no_flags, &login_context,
                    &st)) {
... get password from user...

    if (sec login_validate_identity(login_context, password,
                        &reset_passwd, &auth_src, &st)) {

        if (!sec_login_certify_identity(login_context, &st))
            exit(error_wierd_auth_svc);

        sec_login_set_context(login_context, &st);

        if (auth_src != sec_login_auth_src_network)
            printf("no network credentials");

        if (reset_passwd) {
            ... get new password from user, reset registry record ...
        };

        sec_login_get_pwent(login_context, &pw_entry, &st);

        if (pw_entry.pw_expire < todays_date) {
            sec_login_purge_context(&login_context, &st);
            exit(0)
        }

        ... any other application specific login valid actions ...
        }

    } else {
        sec_login_purge_context(&login_context, &st);

        ... application specific login failure actions ...
    }
}
```

Related Information

Functions: **sec_intro(3sec), sec_login_set_context(3sec),
sec_login_setup_identity(3sec), sec_login_validate_identity(3sec)**.

sec_login_refresh_identity

Purpose   Refreshes an authenticated identity for a login context

Synopsis   **#include <dce/sec_login.h>**

boolean32 sec_login_refresh_identity(
      sec_login_handle_t *login_context***,**
      error_status_t **status***);**

Parameters

Input

login_context   An opaque handle to login context data. The login context contains, among other data, the account principal name and UUID, account restrictions, records of group membership, and the process home directory.

Output

status   A pointer to the completion status. On successful completion, the routine returns **error_status_ok**. Otherwise, it returns an error.

Description

The **sec_login_refresh_identity( )** routine refreshes a previously established identity. It operates on an existing valid context, and cannot be used to change credentials associated with that identity. The refreshed identity reflects changes that affect ticket lifetimes, but not other changes. For example, the identity will reflect a change to maximum ticket lifetime, but not the addition of the identity as a member to a group. Only a DCE login reflects all administrative changes made since the last login.

The refreshed identity must be validated with **sec_login_validate_identity( )** before it can be used.

It is an error to refresh a locally authenticated context.

Files   /usr/include/dce/sec_login.idl
                The **idl** file from which **dce/sec_login.h** was derived.

Errors   **sec_login_s_context_invalid**
                The login context itself is not valid.

                sec_login_s_default_use
                Illegal use of the default login handle occurred.

                sec_login_s_no_memory
                Not enough memory is available to complete the operation.

                error_status_ok
                The call was successful.

Examples Since the authenticated network identity for a process has a finite lifetime, there is
a risk it will expire during some long network operation, preventing the operation
from completing.

For a server application that must run with an authenticated network identity
because they themselves sometimes act as clients of another server, the **sec_login**
calls can be used to check the network identity expiration date, run **sec_login_-
refresh_identity** and **sec_login_validate_identity** before the expiration. This will
prevent interruptions in the server's operation due to the restrictions in network
access applied to an unauthenticated identity.

```
sec_login_get_expiration(login_context, &expire_time, &st);

if (expire_time < (current_time + operation_duration)) {

    if (!sec_login_refresh_identity(login_context, &st)) {
        ... login context cannot be renewed ...
        ... sleep and try again ....
    }

} else {

    if (sec_login_validate_identity(login_context, password,
                        &reset_passwd, &auth_src, &st)) {
        ... identity validated ...
    } else {
        ... validation failed ...
        exit(error_validation_failure);
    }
  }
}

operation();
```

Related Information

Functions: **sec_intro(3sec)**, **sec_login_validate_identity(3sec)**.

sec_login_release_context

Purpose   Frees storage allocated for a login context

Synopsis   **#include <dce/sec_login.h>**

void sec_login_release_context(
     sec_login_handle_t **login_context,*
     error_status_t **status***);**

Parameters

Input/Output

login_context A pointer to an opaque handle to login context data. The login context contains, among other data, the account principal name and UUID, account restrictions, records of group membership, and the process home directory. (See **sec_intro(3sec)** for more details about the login context.)

Output

status   A pointer to the completion status. On successful completion, the routine returns **error_status_ok**. Otherwise, it returns an error.

Description

The **sec_login_release_context( )** routine frees any memory allocated for a login context. Unlike **sec_login_purge_context( )**, it does not destroy the associated network credentials that still reside in the credential cache.

Files   **/usr/include/dce/sec_login.idl**
     The **idl** file from which **dce/sec_login.h** was derived.

sec_login_release_context(3sec)

Errors **sec_login_s_default_use**
        Illegal use of the default login handle occurred.

        sec_login_s_context_invalid
        The login context itself is invalid.

        error_status_ok
        The call was successful.

Related Information

Functions: **sec_intro(3sec)**, **sec_login_purge_context(3sec)**.

sec_login_set_context

Purpose Creates network credentials for a login context

Synopsis **#include <dce/sec_login.h>**

void sec_login_set_context(
        sec_login_handle_t *login_context,*
        error_status_t **status*);

Parameters

Input

login_context An opaque handle to login context data. The login context contains, among other data, the account principal name and UUID, account restrictions, records of group membership, and the process home directory. (See **sec_intro(3sec)** for more details about the login context.)

Output

status A pointer to the completion status. On successful completion, the routine returns **error_status_ok**. Otherwise, it returns an error.

Description

The **sec_login_set_context( )** routine sets the network credentials to those specified by the login context. This context must have been previously validated. Contexts acquired through **sec_login_get_current_context( )** or **sec_login_-newgroups( )** do not need to be validated since those routines return previously validated contexts.

Files **/usr/include/dce/sec_login.idl**
        The **idl** file from which **dce/sec_login.h** was derived.

Errors   **sec_login_s_context_invalid**
                     The login context itself is invalid.

              sec_login_s_default_use
                     Illegal use of the default login handle occurred.

              sec_login_s_auth_local
                     Operation not valid on local context.

              error_status_ok
                     The call was successful.

Examples   The following example illustrates use of the **sec_login_set_context( )** routine as
               part of a straightforward login process:

```
if (sec_login_setup_identity(user_name, sec_login_no_flags, &login_context,
                    &st)) {
  ... get password from user...

  if (sec_login_validate_identity(login_context, password,
                    &reset_passwd, &auth_src, &st)) {

    if (!sec_login_certify_identity(login_context, &st))
       exit(error_weird_auth_svc);

    sec_login_set_context(login_context, &st);

    if (auth_src != sec_login_auth_src_network)
       printf("no network credentials");

    if (reset_passwd) {
       ... get new password from user, reset registry record ...
    };

    sec_login_get_pwent(login_context, &pw_entry, &st);

    if (pw_entry.pw_expire < todays_date) {
       sec_login_purge_context(&login_context, &st);
       exit(0)
    }

    ... any other application specific login valid actions ...
    }

  } else {
    sec_login_purge_context(&login_context, &st);

    ... application specific login failure actions ...
  }
}
```

Related Information

Functions: **sec_intro(3sec)**, **sec_login_setup_identity(3sec)**,
sec_login_validate_identity(3sec).

sec_login_set_extended_attrs

Purpose   Constructs a new login context that contains extended registry attributes

Synopsis   **#include <dce/sec_login.h>**

sec_login_handle_t sec_login_set_extended_attrs(
sec_login_handle_t *my_login_context*,
unsigned32 *num_attributes*,
sec_attr_t *attributes*[ ]
error_status_t *status*);

Parameters

Input

my_login_context
A value of **sec_login_handle_t** that provides an opaque handle to the identity of the calling client.

num_attributes
An unsigned 32-bit integer that specifies the number of elements in the *attributes*[ ] array. The number must be greater than 0.

attributes[ ]   An array of values of type **sec_attr_t** that specifies the list of attributes to be set in the new login context.

Output

status   A pointer to the completion status. On successful completion, *status* is assigned **error_status_ok**. Otherwise, it returns an error.

Description

The **sec_login_set_extended_attrs( )** constructs a login context that contains extended registry attributes that have been established for the object identified by *my_login_context*. The attributes themselves must have been established and attached to the object using the extended registry attribute API.

The input *attributes*[ ] array of **sec_attr_t** values should specify the *attr_id* field for each requested attribute. Since the lookup is by attribute type ID only, set the *attribute.attr_value.attr_encoding* field to **sec_attr_enc_void** for each attribute. Note that **sec_attr_t** is an extended registry attribute data type. For more information on extended registry attributes, see the description of the **sec_attr** calls in this document and the *OSF DCE Application Development Guide—Core Components*.

You cannot use this call to add extended registry attributes to a delegation chain. If you pass in a login context that refers to a delegation chain, an invalid context error will be returned.

The routine returns a new login context of type **sec_login_handle_t** that includes the attributes specified in the *attributes*[ ] array.

Files   **/usr/include/dce/sec_login.idl**
                    The **idl** file from which **dce/sec_login.h** was derived.

Errors   **sec_login_s_invalid_context**

                    error_status_ok

Related Information

                    Functions: **sec_intro(3sec)**, **sec_login_become_impersonator(3sec)**,
                    sec_login_set_context(3sec), **sec_login_setup_identity(3sec)**,
                    sec_login_validate_identity(3sec), **sec_rgy_attr_*(3sec)** calls.

sec_login_setup_first

Purpose   Sets up the default network context

Synopsis   **#include <dce/sec_login.h>**

boolean32 sec_login_setup_first(
    sec_login_handle_t **init_context,*
    error_status_t **status);*

Parameters

Output

init_context   A pointer to an opaque handle to login context data. The login context contains, among other data, the account principal name and UUID, account restrictions, records of group membership, and the process home directory. In this call, the context will be that of the host machine initial process. (See **sec_intro(3sec)** for more details about the login context.)

status   A pointer to the completion status. On successful completion, *status* is assigned **error_status_ok**. Otherwise, it returns an error.

Description

The **sec_login_setup_first( )** routine sets up the default context network identity. If the default context already contains valid credentials, the routine fails. Typically, this routine is called from the security validation service of the **dced** process to breathe life into the default credentials for the host machine process hierarchy.

This routine uses the host name available via the local **dce_config** interface as the principal name for the setup, so it does need a principal name as input.

Return Values

The routine returns a **boolean32** value that is TRUE if the setup was successful, and FALSE otherwise.

Files   **/usr/include/dce/sec_login.idl**
The **idl** file from which **dce/sec_login.h** was derived.

Errors   **sec_login_s_default_use**
The default context is already in use and does not need to be set up again.

sec_login_s_no_current_context
The calling process has no context of its own.

sec_login_s_privileged
An unprivileged process was called in.

sec_login_s_config
The DCE configuration (**dce_config**) information is not available.

sec_rgy_object_not_found
The principal does not exist.

sec_rgy_server_unavailable
The network registry is not available.

sec_login_s_no_memory
A memory allocation error occurred.

error_status_ok
The call was successful.

Related Information

Functions: **sec_intro(3sec)**, **sec_login_init_first(3sec)**,
sec_login_validate_first(3sec).

sec_login_setup_identity

Purpose   Sets up the user's network identity

Synopsis   #include <dce/sec_login.h>

boolean32 sec_login_setup_identity(
       unsigned_char_p_t *principal*,
       sec_login_flags_t *flags*,
       sec_login_handle_t **login_context*,
       error_status_t **status*);

Parameters

Input

principal   A pointer (type **unsigned_char_p_t**) indicating a character string containing the principal name on the registry account corresponding to the calling process.

flags   A set of flags of type **sec_login_flags_t**. These contain information about how the new network credentials are to be used.

Output

login_context A pointer to an opaque handle to login context data. The login context contains, among other data, the account principal name and UUID, account restrictions, records of group membership, and the process home directory. (See **sec_intro(3sec)** for more details about the login context.)

status   A pointer to the completion status. On successful completion, *status* is assigned **error_status_ok**. Otherwise, it returns an error.

Description

The **sec_login_setup_identity( )** routine creates any local context necessary to perform authenticated network operations. It does not establish any local operating system context; that is the responsibility of the caller. It is the standard network login function. The network identity set up by this operation cannot be used until it is validated via **sec_login_validate_identity( )**.

The **sec_login_setup_identity( )** operation and the **sec_login_validate_identity( )** operation are two halves of a single logical operation. Together they collect the identity data needed to establish an authenticated identity.

Notes   Neither **sec_login_setup_identity( )** nor **sec_login_validate_identity( )** check for account or identity expiration. The application program using this interface is responsible for such checks.

Return Values

The routine returns TRUE if the identity has been successfully established.

Files   **/usr/include/dce/sec_login.idl**
The **idl** file from which **dce/sec_login.h** was derived.

Errors   **sec_rgy_object_not_found**
The principal does not exist.

sec_rgy_server_unavailable
The network registry is not available.

sec_login_s_no_memory
Not enough memory is available to complete the operation.

error_status_ok
The call was successful.

Examples   The following example illustrates use of the **sec_login_setup_identity( )** routine as part of a straightforward login process:

```
if (sec_login_setup_identity(user_name, sec_login_no_flags, &login_context,
                       &st)) {
 ... get password from user...

   if (sec_login_validate_identity(login_context, password,
                        &reset_passwd, &auth_src, &st)) {

      if (!sec_login_certify_identity(login_context, &st))
         exit(error_weird_auth_svc);

      sec_login_set_context(login_context, &st);

      if (auth_src != sec_login_auth_src_network)
         printf("no network credentials");

      if (reset_passwd) {
         ... get new password from user, reset registry record ...
      };
```

sec_login_setup_identity(3sec)

```
sec_login_get_pwent(login_context, &pw_entry, &st);

if (pw_entry.pw_expire < todays_date) {
    sec_login_purge_context(&login_context, &st);
    exit(0)
}

... any other application specific login valid actions ...
}

} else {
    sec_login_purge_context(&login_context, &st);

    ... application specific login failure actions ...
}
}
```

Related Information

Functions: **sec_intro(3sec)**, **sec_login_set_context(3sec)**, **sec_login_validate_identity(3sec)**.

sec_login_valid_and_cert_ident

Purpose   Validates and certifies a login context

Synopsis   **#include <dce/sec_login.h>**

boolean32 sec_login_valid_and_cert_ident(
    sec_login_handle_t *login_context,*
    sec_passwd_rec_t **passwd,*
    boolean32 **reset_passwd,*
    sec_login_auth_src_t **auth_src,*
    error_status_t **status);*

Parameters

Input

login_context An opaque handle to login context data. The login context contains, among other data, the account principal name and UUID, account restrictions, records of group membership, and the process home directory. (See **sec_intro(3sec)** for more details about the login context.)

passwd A password record to be checked against the password in the principal's registry account. The routine returns TRUE if the two match. The contents of the *passwd* parameter are erased after the call has finished processing it.

Output

reset_passwd A pointer to a 32-bit **boolean32** value. The routine returns TRUE if the account password has expired and must be reset.

auth_src A 32-bit set of flags identifying the source of the authentication. Upon return after successful authentication, the flags in *auth_src* indicate what authority was used to validate the login context. If the authentication was accomplished with the network authority, the **sec_login_auth_src_network** flag is set, and the process login context has credentials to use the network.

If the authentication was accomplished with local data only (either the principal's account is tailored for the local machine with overrides, or the network authority is unavailable), the **sec_login_auth_src_local** flag is set. Login contexts that are authenticated locally may not be used to establish network credentials because they have none.

status   A pointer to the completion status. On successful completion, *status* is assigned **error_status_ok**. Otherwise, it returns an error.

Description

The **sec_login_valid_and_cert_ident( )** routine validates and certifies a login context established with **sec_login_setup_identity( )**. The caller must supply the user's password as input with the *passwd* parameter.

This routine combines the operations of the **sec_login_validate_identity( )** and **sec_login_certify_identity( )** routines. It is intended for use by system login programs that need to extract trustworthy operating system credentials for use in setting the local identity for a process. This operation destroys the contents of the *passwd* input parameter.

If the network security service is unavailable or if the user's password has been overridden on the host, a locally authenticated context is created, and the *auth_src* parameter is set to **sec_login_auth_src_local**. Data extracted from a locally authenticated context may be used to set the local OS identity, but it cannot be used to establish network credentials.

This routine is a privileged operation.

Return Values

The routine returns TRUE if the login identity has been successfully validated.

Files

/usr/include/dce/sec_login.idl
    The **idl** file from which **dce/sec_login.h** was derived.

Errors

sec_rgy_passwd_invalid
    The input string does not match the account password.

sec_rgy_server_unavailable
    The DCE registry server is unavailable.

sec_login_s_acct_invalid
    The account is invalid or has expired.

sec_login_s_privileged
> This is a privileged operation and was invoked by an unprivileged process.

sec_login_s_null_password
> The input string is NULL.

sec_login_s_default_use
> The input context was the default context, which cannot be validated.

sec_login_s_already_valid
> The login context has already been validated.

sec_login_s_unsupp_passwd_type
> The password type is not supported.

sec_login_s_no_memory
> Not enough memory is available to complete the operation.

sec_login_s_preauth_failed
> Preauthentication failure.

error_status_ok
> The call was successful.

Examples The following example illustrates use of the **sec_login_valid_and_cert_ident()** routine as part of a system login process:

```
if (sec_login_setup_identity(<user>,
    sec_login_no_flags, &login_context, &st)) {
        ... get password ...
        if (sec_login_valid_and_cert_ident(login_context,
            password, &st)) {
            if (auth_src == sec_login_auth_src_network) {
                if (GOOD_STATUS(&st)
                sec_login_set_context(login_context);
                }
        }
        if (reset_passwd) {
            ... reset the user's password ...
            if (passwd_reset_fails) {
                sec_login_purge_context(login_context)
                ... application login failure actions ...
            }
            ... application specific login valid actions ...
        }
}
```

sec_login_valid_and_cert_ident(3sec)

Related Information

Functions: **sec_intro(3sec)**, **sec_login_certify_identity(3sec)**, **sec_login_setup_identity(3sec)**, **sec_login_validate_identity(3sec)**.

sec_login_valid_from_keytable

Purpose   Validates a login context's identity using input from a specified keytable file

Synopsis   **#include <dce/sec_login.h>**

boolean32 sec_login_valid_from_keytable(
>   **sec_login_handle_t** *login_context,*
>   **unsigned32** *authn_service,*
>   **void** **arg,*
>   **unsigned32** *try_kvno,*
>   **unsigned32** **used_kvno,*
>   **boolean32** **reset_passwd,*
>   **sec_login_auth_src_t** **auth_src,*
>   **error_status_t** **status*);

Parameters

Input

login_context   An opaque handle to login context data. The login context contains, among other data, the account principal's name and UUID, account restrictions, records of the account principal's group memberships, and the account's home directory. (See **sec_intro(3sec)** for more details about the login context.)

authn_service   Identifies the authentication protocol using the key. The possible authentication protocols are as follows:

rpc_c_authn_dce_secret
>   DCE shared-secret key authentication.

rpc_c_authn_dce_public
>   DCE public key authentication (reserved for future use).

arg   This parameter can specify either the local keytab file or an argument to the *get_key_fn* key acquisition routine of the **rpc_server_register_auth_info** routine.

A value of NULL specifies that the default keytab file should be used. A keytab filename specifies that that file should be used as the keytab file. You must prepend the file's absolute filename with **FILE:** and the file must have been created with the **rgy_edit** command or the **sec_key_mgmt_set_key** routine.

Any other value specifies an argument for the *get_key_fn* key acquisition routine. See the **rpc_server_register_auth_info( )** reference page for more information.

try_kvno The version number of the key in the keytab file to try first. Specify NULL to try the current version of the key.

Output

used_kvno A pointer to a 32-bit **boolean32** value that specifies the version number of the the key from the keytab file that was used to successfully validate the login context, if any.

reset_passwd A pointer to a 32-bit **boolean32** value. The routine returns TRUE if the account password has expired and should be reset.

auth_src How the the login context was authorized. The **sec_login_auth_-src_t** data type distinguishes the various ways the login context was authorized. There are three possible values:

sec_login_auth_src_network
Authentication accomplished through the normal network authority. A login context authenticated this way will have all the network credentials it ought to have.

sec_login_auth_src_local
Authentication accomplished via local data. Authentication occurs locally if a principal's account is tailored for the local machine, or if the network authority is unavailable. Since a login contexts authenticated locally has no network credentials, it can not be used for network operations.

sec_login_auth_src_overridden
Authentication accomplished via the override facility.

status A pointer to the completion status. On successful completion, *status* is assigned **error_status_ok**. Otherwise, it returns an error.

Description

The **sec_login_valid_from_keytable** () routine validates the login context established with **sec_login_setup_identity**(). The **sec_login_valid_from_keytable** () routine obtains the principal's password from the specified keytable.

If *try_kvno* specifies a key version number, that version number key is tried first, otherwise the current key version number is tried first. The function trys all keys in the keytable until it finds one that validates the login context. This operation must be invoked before the network credentials can be used.

Notes

A context is not secure and must not be set or exported until the authentication service is itself authenticated with the **sec_login_certify_identity**() call.

Return Values

The routine returns TRUE if the login context has been successfully validated.

Files

/usr/include/dce/sec_login.idl
> The **idl** file from which **dce/sec_login.h** was derived.

Errors

sec_rgy_passwd_invalid
> The input string does not match the account password.

sec_rgy_server_unavailable
> There is no data with which to compare the input string.

sec_login_s_acct_invalid
> The account is invalid or has expired.

sec_login_s_default_use
> The input context was the default context, which cannot be validated.

sec_login_s_already_valid
> The login context has already been validated.

sec_login_s_unsupp_passwd_type
> The password type is not supported.

sec_key_mgmt_e_key_unavailable
> The requested key is not present.

sec_key_mgmt_e_authn_invalid
> The authentication protocol is not valid.

sec_key_mgmt_e_unauthorized
> The caller is not authorized to perform the operation.

sec_s_no_memory
> Unable to allocate memory.

error_status_ok
> The call was successful.

Examples The following example illustrates use of the **sec_login_valid_from_keytable( )** routine as part of a straightforward login process:

```
if (sec_login_setup_identity(user_name, sec_login_no_flags, &login_context,
                             &st)) {
  ... get password from local keytable...

  if (sec_login_valid_from_keytable(login_context, authn_service, arg, try_kvno,
                     &used_kvno, &reset_passwd, &auth_src, &st)) {

    sec_login_set_context(login_context, &st);

    if (auth_src != sec_login_auth_src_network)
       printf("no network credentials");

    }

    ... any other application specific login valid actions ...
    }

  } else {
    sec_login_purge_context(&login_context, &st);

    ... application specific login failure actions ...
  }
}
```

Related Information

> Functions: **sec_intro(3sec), sec_login_certify_identity(3sec), sec_login_setup_identity(3sec), sec_login_valid_and_cert_ident(3sec), sec_login_validate_identity(3sec).**

sec_login_validate_first

Purpose   Validates the initial login context

Synopsis   **#include <dce/sec_login.h>**

boolean32 sec_login_validate_first(
            sec_login_handle_t *init_context*,
            boolean32 **reset_passwd*,
            sec_login_auth_src_t **auth_src*,
            error_status_t **status*);

Parameters

Input

init_context   An opaque handle to login context data. The login context contains, among other data, the account principal name and UUID, account restrictions, records of group membership, and the process home directory. In this call, the context will be that of the host machine initial process. (See **sec_intro(3sec)** for more details about the login context.)

Output

reset_passwd   A pointer to a 32-bit **boolean32** value. The routine returns TRUE if the account password has expired and must be reset.

auth_src   A 32-bit set of flags identifying the source of the authentication. Upon return after successful authentication, the flags in *auth_src* indicate what authority was used to validate the login context. If the authentication was accomplished with the network authority, the **sec_login_auth_src_network** flag is set, and the process login context has credentials to use the network. If the authentication was accomplished with local data only (either the principal's account is tailored for the local machine with overrides, or the network authority is unavailable), the **sec_login_auth_src_local** flag is set. Login contexts that are authenticated locally may not be used to establish network credentials because they have none.

status   A pointer to the completion status. On successful completion, *status* is assigned **error_status_ok**. Otherwise, it returns an error.

sec_login_validate_first(3sec)

Description

The **sec_login_validate_first( )** routine validates the default login context established via **sec_login_setup_first( )**. Typically, this operation is called from the security validation service of the **dced** process to validate the default credentials for the host machine process hierarchy. This operation uses the password for the local host, and therefore does not require a password parameter.

Return Values

The routine returns a **boolean32** value that is TRUE if the setup was successful, and FALSE otherwise.

Files

/usr/include/dce/sec_login.idl
> The **idl** file from which **dce/sec_login.h** was derived.

Errors

sec_login_s_privileged
> An unprivileged process was called in.

sec_rgy_server_unavailable
> The network authentication service was unavailable.

error_status_ok
> The call was successful.

Related Information

Functions: **sec_intro(3sec)**, **sec_login_init_first(3sec)**, **sec_login_setup_first(3sec)**.

sec_login_validate_identity

Purpose   Validates a login context's identity

Synopsis   **#include <dce/sec_login.h>**

boolean32 sec_login_validate_identity(
      sec_login_handle_t *login_context*,
      sec_passwd_rec_t **passwd*,
      boolean32 **reset_passwd*,
      sec_login_auth_src_t **auth_src*,
      error_status_t **status*);

Parameters

Input

login_context   An opaque handle to login context data. The login context contains, among other data, the account principal name and UUID, account restrictions, records of group membership, and the process home directory. (See **sec_intro(3sec)** for more details about the login context.)

passwd   A password record to be checked against the password in the principal's registry account. The routine returns TRUE if the two match. The contents of the *passwd* parameter are erased after the call has finished processing it.

Output

reset_passwd   A pointer to a 32-bit **boolean32** value. The routine returns TRUE if the account password has expired and must be reset.

auth_src   How the the login context was authorized. The **sec_login_auth_-src_t** data type distinguishes the various ways the login context was authorized. There are three possible values:

- **sec_login_auth_src_network**

- **sec_login_auth_src_local**

- **sec_login_auth_src_overridden**

status   A pointer to the completion status. On successful completion, *status* is assigned **error_status_ok**. Otherwise, it returns an error.

Description

The **sec_login_validate_identity( )** routine validates the login context established with **sec_login_setup_identity( )**. This operation must be invoked before the network credentials can be used. The caller must supply the user's password in a **sec_passwd_rec_t** as input with the *passwd* parameter. The following example sets up a plaintext password for the the *passwd* parameter:

```
sec_passwd_str_t        tmp_passwd;

passwd.version_number = sec_passwd_c_version_none;
passwd.pepper = NULL;
passwd.key.key_type = sec_passwd_plain;

strncpy((char *) tmp_passwd, (char *) my_passwd, sec_passwd_str_max_len);
tmp_passwd[sec_passwd_str_max_len] = ' ';
passwd_rec.key.tagged_union.plain = &(tmp_passwd[0]);
```

When a network identity is set, only state information for network operations has been established. The local operating system identity has not been modified. It is the responsibility of the caller to establish any local operating identity state.

The **sec_login_setup_identity( )** operation and the **sec_login_validate_identity( )** operation are two halves of a single logical operation. Together they collect the identity data needed to establish an authenticated identity. The operations are independent so the user's password need not be sent across the network. The identity validation performed by **sec_login_validate_identity( )** is a local operation.

Notes

A context is not secure and must not be set or exported until the authentication service is itself authenticated with the **sec_login_certify_identity( )** call.

System login programs that set local operating system identity using data extracted from a login context should use **sec_login_valid_and_cert_ident( )** instead of **sec_login_validate_identity( )**.

If the security server and client clocks are not synchronized to within 2 to 3 minutes of each other, this call can return a password validation error.

Return Values

The routine returns TRUE if the login identity has been successfully validated.

Files

/usr/include/dce/sec_login.idl
> The **idl** file from which **dce/sec_login.h** was derived.

Errors

sec_rgy_passwd_invalid
> The input string does not match the account password.

sec_rgy_server_unavailable
> There is no data with which to compare the input string.

sec_login_s_acct_invalid
> The account is invalid or has expired.

sec_login_s_null_password
> The input string is NULL.

sec_login_s_default_use
> The input context was the default context, which cannot be validated.

sec_login_s_already_valid
> The login context has already been validated.

sec_login_s_unsupp_passwd_type
> The password type is not supported.

sec_login_s_no_memory
> Not enough memory is available to complete the operation.

sec_login_s_preauth_failed
> Preauthentication failure.

error_status_ok
> The call was successful.

sec_login_validate_identity(3sec)

Examples   The following example illustrates use of the **sec_login_validate_identity**( ) routine as part of a straightforward login process:

```
if (sec_login_setup_identity(user_name, sec_login_no_flags, &login_context,
                             &st)) {
   ... get password from user...

   if (sec_login_validate_identity(login_context, password,
                             &reset_passwd, &auth_src, &st)) {

      if (!sec_login_certify_identity(login_context, &st))
         exit(error_weird_auth_svc);

      sec_login_set_context(login_context, &st);

      if (auth_src != sec_login_auth_src_network)
         printf("no network credentials");

      if (reset_passwd) {
         ... get new password from user, reset registry record ...
      };

      sec_login_get_pwent(login_context, &pw_entry, &st);

      if (pw_entry.pw_expire < todays_date) {
         sec_login_purge_context(&login_context, &st);
         exit(0)
      }

      ... any other application specific login valid actions ...
   }

   } else {
      sec_login_purge_context(&login_context, &st);

      ... application specific login failure actions ...
   }
}
```

Related Information

Functions: **sec_intro(3sec)**, **sec_login_certify_identity(3sec)**, **sec_login_setup_identity(3sec)**, **sec_login_valid_and_cert_ident(3sec)**.

sec_pwd_mgmt_free_handle

Purpose   Frees storage allocated for a password management handle

Synopsis   **#include <dce/sec_pwd_mgmt.h>**

void sec_pwd_mgmt_free_handle(
   sec_pwd_mgmt_handle_t **pwd_mgmt_h,*
   error_status_t **stp*
)

Parameters

Input/Output

pwd_mgmt_h A handle to the password management data which is to be freed.

Output

stp   A pointer to the completion status. On successful completion, the
                routine returns error_status_ok. Otherwise, it returns an error.

Description

The **sec_pwd_mgmt_free_handle**( ) routine frees any memory allocated for the
contents of a password management handle.

Files   **/usr/include/dce/sec_pwd_mgmt.idl**
                The idl file from which **dce/sec_pwd_mgmt.h** was derived.

Errors   **error_status_ok**
                The call was successful

Related Information

Functions: **sec_intro(3sec)**, **sec_pwd_mgmt_setup(3sec)**.

sec_pwd_mgmt_gen_pwd

Purpose   Generates a set of passwords

Synopsis   **#include <dce/sec_pwd_mgmt.h>**

   void sec_pwd_mgmt_gen_pwd(
      sec_pwd_mgmt_handle_t *pwd_mgmt_h*,
      unsigned32 *num_pwds*,
      unsigned32 **num_returned*,
      sec_passwd_rec_t *gen_pwds*[ ],
      error_status_t **stp*
)

Parameters

Input

   pwd_mgmt_h A handle to user's password management data.

   num_pwds   Number of generated passwords requested.

Output

   num_returned Number of generated passwords returned in the *gen_pwds*[ ] array.

   gen_pwds[ ] Array of generated passwords. Each generated password is stored in a **sec_passwd_rec_t** structure.

   stp   A pointer to the completion status. On successful completion, status is assigned **error_status_ok**. Otherwise, it returns an error.

Description

The **sec_pwd_mgmt_gen_pwd( )** routine retrieves a set of generated passwords from a password management server which is exporting the **rsec_pwd_mgmt_-gen_pwd( )** routine. It obtains the binding information to this server from the **pwd_mgmt_h** handle.

Files   **/usr/include/dce/sec_pwd_mgmt.idl**
               The idl file from which **dce/sec_pwd_mgmt.h** was derived.

Errors   **sec_rgy_era_pwd_mgmt_auth_type**
The pwd_mgmt_binding ERA must contain authentication information.

sec_pwd_mgmt_svr_unavail
The password management server is unavailable.

sec_pwd_mgmt_svr_error
Generic error returned from password management server. An administrator should check the password management server's log file for more information.

error_status_ok
The call was successful

Various RPC communication errors can be returned if there are failures when binding to the password management server.

Related Information

Functions: **pwd_strengthd(8sec)**, **sec_intro(3sec)**, **sec_pwd_mgmt_setup(3sec)**.

sec_pwd_mgmt_get_val_type

Purpose Gets users password validation type

Synopsis **#include <dce/sec_pwd_mgmt.h>**

void sec_pwd_mgmt_get_val_type(
   sec_pwd_mgmt_handle_t *pwd_mgmt_h***,**
   signed32 **pwd_val_type***,**
   error_status_t **stp*
)

Parameters

Input

pwd_mgmt_h A handle to a user's password management data.

Output

pwd_val_type The user's password validation type. This is retrieved from the **pwd_val_type** ERA. The possible values and their meaning are as follows:

0	(**none**): the user has no password policy.
1	(**user_select**): the user must choose his/her own password.
2	(**user_can_select**): the user can choose his/her own password or request a generated password.
3	(**generation_required**): the user must use a generated password.

stp A pointer to the completion status. On successful completion, stp is assigned **error_status_ok**. Otherwise, it returns an error.

Description

The **sec_pwd_mgmt_get_val_type( )** routine returns the value of the user's password validation type, as specified by the **pwd_val_type** ERA. If the ERA does not exist, **0** (**none**) is returned in *pwd_val_type*.

Files

/usr/include/dce/sec_pwd_mgmt.idl
>The idl file from which **dce/sec_pwd_mgmt.h** was derived.

Errors

error_status_ok
>The call was successful.

Various RPC communication errors can be returned if there are failures when binding to the password management server.

Related Information

Functions: **sec_intro(3sec)**, **sec_pwd_mgmt_setup(3sec)**.

sec_pwd_mgmt_setup

Purpose   Sets up the user's password policy information

Synopsis   **#include <dce/sec_pwd_mgmt.h>**

        void sec_pwd_mgmt_setup(
            sec_pwd_mgmt_handle_t **pwd_mgmt_h,*
            sec_rgy_handle_t *context,*
            sec_rgy_login_name_t *login_name,*
            sec_login_handle_t *your_lc,*
            rpc_binding_handle_t *pwd_mgmt_bind_h,*
            error_status_t **stp*
)

Parameters

Input

    context   A registry server handle indicating the desired registry site.

    login_name   The login name of the user.

    your_lc   The login context handle of the user currently logged in. If null is specified, the default login context will be used.

    pwd_mgmt_bind_h
            An RPC binding handle to the password management server. Use of this parameter is currently unsupported. The password management server binding handle will be retrieved from the **pwd_mgmt_-binding** ERA. Set this parameter to NULL.

Output

    pwd_mgmt_h A pointer to an opaque handle to password management/policy data. *pwd_mgmt_h* contains, among other data, the account name, values of password management ERAs, and a binding handle to the password management server.

    stp   A pointer to the completion status. On successful completion, *stp* is assigned **error_status_ok**. Otherwise, it returns an error.

Description

The **sec_pwd_mgmt_setup( )** routine collects the data required to perform remote password management calls to the password management server.

Files

/usr/include/dce/sec_pwd_mgmt.idl
> The idl file from which **dce/sec_pwd_mgmt.h** was derived.

Errors

sec_s_no_memory
> Not enough memory is available to complete the operation.

sec_rgy_server_unavailable
> The network registry is not available.

error_status_ok
> The call was successful.

Related Information

Functions: **pwd_strengthd(8sec)**, **sec_intro(3sec)**, **sec_pwd_mgmt_free_handle(3sec)**, **sec_pwd_mgmt_gen_pwd(3sec)**, **sec_pwd_mgmt_get_val_type(3sec)**.

sec_rgy_acct_add

Purpose   Adds an account for a login name

Synopsis   **#include <dce/acct.h>**

void sec_rgy_acct_add(
        sec_rgy_handle_t *context,*
        sec_rgy_login_name_t **login_name,*
        sec_rgy_acct_key_t **key_parts,*
        sec_rgy_acct_user_t **user_part,*
        sec_rgy_acct_admin_t **admin_part,*
        sec_passwd_rec_t **caller_key,*
        sec_passwd_rec_t **new_key,*
        sec_passwd_type_t *new_keytype,*
        sec_passwd_version_t **new_key_version,*
        error_status_t **status*);

Parameters

Input

context   An opaque handle bound to a registry server. Use **sec_rgy_site_-open( )** to acquire a bound handle.

login_name   A pointer to the account login name. A login name is composed of three character strings, containing the principal, group, and organization (PGO) names corresponding to the account. All three names must be completely specified.

key_parts   A pointer to the minimum abbreviation allowed when logging in to the account. Abbreviations are not currently implemented and the only legal value is **sec_rgy_acct_key_person**.

user_part   A pointer to the **sec_rgy_acct_user_t** structure containing the user part of the account data. This represents such information as the account password, home directory, and default shell.

admin_part   A pointer to the **sec_rgy_acct_admin_t** structure containing the administrative part of an account's data. This information includes the account creation and expiration dates and flags describing limits to the use of privilege attribute certificates, among other information.

caller_key　　A key to use to encrypt *new_key* for transmission to the registry server.

new_key　　The password for the new account. During transmission to the registry server, it is encrypted with *caller_key*.

new_keytype　　The type of the new key. The server uses this parameter to decide how to encode *new_key* if it is sent as plaintext.

Output

new_key_version

The key version number returned by the server. If the client requests a particular key version number (via the **version_number** field of the *new_key* input parameter), the server returns the requested version number back to the client.

status　　A pointer to the completion status. On successful completion, the routine returns **error_status_ok**. Otherwise, it returns an error.

Description

The **sec_rgy_acct_add( )** routine adds an account with the specified login name. The login name is given in three parts, corresponding to the principal, group, and organization names for the account.

The *key_parts* variable specifies the minimum login abbreviation for the account. If the requested abbreviation duplicates an existing abbreviation for another account, the routine supplies the next shortest unique abbreviation and returns this abbreviation in *key_parts*. Abbreviations are not currently implemented.

Permissions Required

The **sec_rgy_acct_add( )** routine requires the following permissions on the account (principal) that is to be added:

- The **m (mgmt_info)** permission to change management information.

- The **a (auth_info)** permission to change authentication information.

- The **u (user_info)** permission to change user information.

sec_rgy_acct_add(3sec)

Notes   The constituent principal, group, and organization (PGO) items for an account must be added before the account can be created. (See the **sec_rgy_pgo_add( )** routine). Also, the principal must have been added as a member of the specified group and organization. (See the **sec_rgy_pgo_add_member( )** routine).

Files   **/usr/include/dce/acct.idl**
              The **idl** file from which **dce/acct.h** was derived.

Errors   **sec_rgy_not_authorized**
              The client program is not authorized to add an account to the registry.

              sec_rgy_not_member_group
              The indicated principal is not a member of the indicated group.

              sec_rgy_not_member_org
              The indicated principal is not a member of the indicated organization.

              sec_rgy_not_member_group_org
              The indicated principal is not a member of the indicated group or organization.

              sec_rgy_object exists
              The account to be added already exists.

              sec_rgy_server_unavailable
              The DCE registry server is unavailable.

              error_status_ok
              The call was successful.

Related Information

Functions: **sec_intro(3sec)**, **sec_rgy_acct_delete(3sec)**,
sec_rgy_login_get_info(3sec), **sec_rgy_pgo_add(3sec)**,
sec_rgy_pgo_add_member(3sec), **sec_rgy_site_open(3sec)**.

sec_rgy_acct_admin_replace

Purpose   Replaces administrative account data

Synopsis   **#include <dce/acct.h>**

void sec_rgy_acct_admin_replace(
        sec_rgy_handle_t *context*,
        sec_rgy_login_name_t **login_name*,
        sec_rgy_acct_key_t **key_parts*,
        sec_rgy_acct_admin_t **admin_part*,
        error_status_t **status*);

Parameters

Input

context
An opaque handle bound to a registry server. Use **sec_rgy_site_-open( )** to acquire a bound handle.

login_name
A pointer to the account login name. A login name is composed of three character strings, containing the principal, group, and organization (PGO) names corresponding to the account. For the group and organization names, blank strings can serve as wildcards, matching any entry. The principal name must be input.

key_parts
A pointer to the minimum abbreviation allowed when logging in to the account. Abbreviations are not currently implemented and the only legal value is **sec_rgy_acct_key_person**.

admin_part
A pointer to the **sec_rgy_acct_admin_t** structure containing the administrative part of an account's data. This information includes the account creation and expiration dates and flags describing limits to the use of privilege attribute certificates, among other information, and can be modified only by an administrator. The **sec_rgy_acct_admin_t** structure contains the following fields:

      creator
      The identity of the principal who created this account in **sec_rgy_foreign_id_t** form. This field is set by the registry server.

creation_date

> The date (**sec_timeval_sec_t**) the account was created. This field is set by the registry server.

last_changer The identity of the principal who last modified any of the account information (user or administrative). This field is set by the registry server.

change_date The date (**sec_timeval_sec_t**) the account was last modified (either user or administrative data). This field is set by the registry server.

expiration_date

> The date (**sec_timeval_sec_t**) the account will cease to be valid.

good_since_date

> This date (**sec_timeval_sec_t**) is for Kerberos-style, ticket-granting ticket revocation. Ticket-granting tickets issued before this date will not be honored by authenticated network services.

flags

> Contains administration flags used as part of the administrator's information for any registry account. This field is in **sec_rgy_acct_admin_flags_t** form. (See **sec_intro(3sec)** for a complete description of these flags.)

authentication_flags

> Contains flags controlling use of authentication services. This field is in **sec_rgy_acct_auth_flags_t** form. (See **sec_intro(3sec)** for a complete description of these flags.)

Output

status A pointer to the completion status. On successful completion, the routine returns **error_status_ok**. Otherwise, it returns an error.

Description

The **sec_rgy_acct_admin_replace( )** routine replaces the administrative information in the account record specified by the input login name. The administrative information contains limitations on the account's use and privileges. It can be modified only by a registry administrator; that is, a user with the **admin_info** (abbreviated as **a**) privilege for an account.

The *key_parts* variable identifies how many of the *login_name* parts to use as the unique abbreviation for the account. If the requested abbreviation duplicates an existing abbreviation for another account, the routine supplies the next shortest unique abbreviation and returns this abbreviation using *key_parts*.

Permissions Required

The **sec_rgy_acct_admin_replace( )** routine requires the following permissions on the account principal:

- The **m** (**mgmt_info**) permission, if **flags** or **expiration_date** is to be changed.

- The **a** (**auth_info**) permission, if **authentication_flags** or **good_since_date** is to be changed.

Notes

All users need the **w** (**write**) privilege in the appropriate ACL entry to modify any account information.

Files

/usr/include/dce/acct.idl

The **idl** file from which **dce/acct.h** was derived.

Errors

sec_rgy_not_authorized

The client program is not authorized to change the administrative information for the specified account.

sec_rgy_object_not_found

The registry server could not find the specified name.

sec_rgy_server_unavailable

The DCE registry server is unavailable.

error_status_ok

The call was successful.

Related Information

Functions: **sec_intro(3sec)**, **sec_rgy_acct_lookup(3sec)**,
sec_rgy_acct_replace_all(3sec), **sec_rgy_acct_user_replace(3sec)**.

sec_rgy_acct_delete

Purpose   Deletes an account

Synopsis   **#include <dce/acct.h>**

void sec_rgy_acct_delete(
        sec_rgy_handle_t *context*,
        sec_rgy_login_name_t **login_name*,
        error_status_t **status*);

Parameters

Input

context   An opaque handle bound to a registry server. Use **sec_rgy_site_-open( )** to acquire a bound handle.

login_name   A pointer to the account login name. A login name is composed of three character strings, containing the principal, group, and organization (PGO) names corresponding to the account. Only the principal name is required to perform the deletion.

Output

status   A pointer to the completion status. On successful completion, the routine returns **error_status_ok**. Otherwise, it returns an error.

Description

The **sec_rgy_acct_delete( )** routine deletes from the registry the account corresponding to the specified login name.

Permissions Required

The **sec_rgy_acct_delete( )** routine requires the following permissions on the account principal:

- The **m** (**mgmt_info**) permission to remove management information.

- The **a** (**auth_info**) permission to remove authentication information.

- The **u** (**user_info**) permission to remove user information.

sec_rgy_acct_delete(3sec)

Notes   Even though the account is deleted, the PGO items corresponding to the account remain. These must be deleted with separate calls to **sec_rgy_pgo_delete( )**.

Files   **/usr/include/dce/acct.idl**
                        The **idl** file from which **dce/acct.h** was derived.

Errors   **sec_rgy_not_authorized**
                        The client program is not authorized to delete the specified account.

sec_rgy_object_not_found
                        No PGO item was found with the given name.

sec_rgy_server_unavailable
                        The DCE registry server is unavailable.

error_status_ok
                        The call was successful.

Related Information

Functions: **sec_intro(3sec)**, **sec_rgy_acct_add(3sec)**, **sec_rgy_pgo_delete(3sec)**.

sec_rgy_acct_get_projlist

Purpose   Returns the projects in an account's project list

Synopsis   **#include <dce/acct.h>**

> **void sec_rgy_acct_get_projlist(**
>   **sec_rgy_handle_t** *context*,
>   **sec_rgy_login_name_t** **login_name*,
>   **sec_rgy_cursor_t** **projlist_cursor*,
>   **signed32** *max_number*,
>   **signed32** **supplied_number*,
>   **uuid_t** *id_projlist*[ ],
>   **signed32** *unix_projlist*[ ],
>   **signed32** **num_projects*,
>   **error_status_t** **status*);

Parameters

Input

context
: An opaque handle bound to a registry server. Use **sec_rgy_site_-open( )** to acquire a bound handle.

login_name
: A pointer to the account login name. A login name is composed of three character strings, containing the principal, group, and organization (PGO) names corresponding to the account. For the group and organization names, blank strings can serve as wildcards, matching any entry. The principal name must be input.

max_number
: The maximum number of projects to be returned by the call. This must be no larger than the allocated size of the *projlist*[ ] arrays.

Input/Output

projlist_cursor
: An opaque pointer indicating a specific project in an account's project list. The **sec_rgy_acct_get_projlist( )** routine returns the project indicated by *projlist_cursor*, and advances the cursor to point to the next project in the list. When the end of the list is reached, the routine returns the value **sec_rgy_no_more_entries** in the *status* parameter. Use **sec_rgy_cursor_reset( )** to reset the cursor.

Output

supplied_number
A pointer to the actual number of projects returned. This will always be less than or equal to the *max_number* supplied on input. If there are more projects in the account list, **sec_rgy_acct_get_-projlist( )** sets *projlist_cursor* to point to the next entry after the last one in the returned list.

id_projlist[ ]
An array to receive the UUID of each project returned. The size allocated for the array is given by *max_number*. If this value is less than the total number of projects in the account project list, multiple calls must be made to return all of the projects.

unix_projlist[ ]
An array to receive the UNIX number of each project returned. The size allocated for the array is given by *max_number*. If this value is less than the total number of projects in the account project list, multiple calls must be made to return all of the projects.

num_projects
A pointer indicating the total number of projects in the specified account's project list.

status
A pointer to the completion status. On successful completion, the routine returns **error_status_ok**. Otherwise, it returns an error.

Description

The **sec_rgy_acct_get_projlist( )** routine returns members of the project list for the specified account. It returns the project information in two arrays. The *id_projlist*[ ] array contains the UUIDs for the returned projects. The *unix_projlist*[ ] array contains the UNIX numbers for the returned projects.

The project list cursor, *projlist_cursor*, provides an automatic place holder in the project list. The **sec_rgy_acct_get_projlist( )** routine automatically updates this variable to point to the next project in the project list. To return an entire project list, reset *projlist_cursor* with **sec_rgy_cursor_reset( )** on the initial call and then issue successive calls until all the projects are returned.

Permissions Required

The **sec_rgy_acct_get_projlist( )** routine requires the **r** (**read**) permission on the account principal for which the project list data is to be returned.

Cautions There are several different types of cursors used in the registry application programmer interface (API). Some cursors point to PGO items, others point to members in a membership list, and others point to account data. Do not use a cursor for one sort of object in a call expecting another sort of object. For example, you cannot use the same cursor on a call to **sec_rgy_acct_get_projlist( )** and **sec_rgy_pgo_get_next( )**. The behavior in this case is undefined.

Furthermore, cursors are specific to a server. A cursor pointing into one replica of the registry database is useless as a pointer into another replica.

Use **sec_rgy_cursor_reset( )** to refresh a cursor for use with another call or for another server.

Files **/usr/include/dce/acct.idl**
            The **idl** file from which **dce/acct.h** was derived.

Errors **sec_rgy_no_more_entries**
            The cursor is at the end of the list of projects.

sec_rgy_not_authorized
            The client program is not authorized to see a project list for this principal.

sec_rgy_object exists
            The account to be added already exists.

sec_rgy_server_unavailable
            The DCE registry server is unavailable.

error_status_ok
            The call was successful.

Related Information

Functions: **sec_intro(3sec)**, **sec_rgy_cursor_reset(3sec)**, **sec_rgy_pgo_get_next(3sec)**.

sec_rgy_acct_lookup

Purpose   Returns data for a specified account

Synopsis   **#include <dce/acct.h>**

void sec_rgy_acct_lookup(
    sec_rgy_handle_t *context,*
    sec_rgy_login_name_t **name_key,*
    sec_rgy_cursor_t **account_cursor,*
    sec_rgy_login_name_t **name_result,*
    sec_rgy_sid_t **id_sid,*
    sec_rgy_unix_sid_t **unix_sid,*
    sec_rgy_acct_key_t **key_parts,*
    sec_rgy_acct_user_t **user_part,*
    sec_rgy_acct_admin_t **admin_part,*
    error_status_t **status*);

Parameters

Input

context   An opaque handle bound to a registry server. Use **sec_rgy_site_-
                open( )** to acquire a bound handle.

name_key   A pointer to the account login name. A login name is composed of
                three character strings, containing the principal, group, and
                organization (PGO) names corresponding to the account. Blank
                strings serve as wildcards, matching any entry.

Input/Output

account_cursor
                An opaque pointer to a specific account in the registry database. If
                name_key is blank, **sec_rgy_acct_lookup( )** returns information
                about the account to which the cursor is pointing. On return, the
                cursor points to the next account in the database after the returned
                account. If *name_key* is blank and the *account_cursor* has been
                reset with **sec_rgy_cursor_reset( )**, **sec_rgy_acct_lookup( )** returns
                information about the first account in the database.

When the end of the list of accounts in the database is reached, the routine returns the value **sec_rgy_no_more_entries** in the *status* parameter. Use **sec_rgy_cursor_reset( )** to refresh the cursor.

Output

name_result   A pointer to the full login name of the account (including all three names) for which the information is returned. The remaining parameters contain the information belonging to the returned account.

id_sid   A structure containing the three UUIDs of the principal, group, and organization for the account.

unix_sid   A structure containing the three UNIX numbers of the principal, group, and organization for the account.

key_parts   A pointer to the minimum abbreviation allowed when logging in to the account. Abbreviations are not currently implemented and the only legal value is **sec_rgy_acct_key_person**.

user_part   A pointer to the **sec_rgy_acct_user_t** structure containing the user part of the account data. This represents such information as the account password, home directory, and default shell, all of which are accessible to, and may be modified by, the account owner.

admin_part   A pointer to the **sec_rgy_acct_admin_t** structure containing the administrative part of an account's data. This information includes the account creation and expiration dates and flags describing limits to the use of privilege attribute certificates, among other information, and can be modified only by an administrator.

status   A pointer to the completion status. On successful completion, the routine returns **error_status_ok**. Otherwise, it returns an error.

Description

The **sec_rgy_acct_lookup( )** routine returns all the information about an account in the registry database. The account can be specified either with *name_key* or *account_cursor*. If *name_key* is completely blank, the routine uses the *account_cursor* value instead.

For *name_key*, a zero-length principal, group, or organization key serves as a wildcard. For example, a login name key with the principal and organization fields blank returns the next (possibly first) account whose group matches the input group field. The full login name of the returned account is passed back in *name_result*.

sec_rgy_acct_lookup(3sec)

The *account_cursor* provides an automatic place holder in the registry database. The routine automatically updates this variable to point to the next account in the database, after the account for which the information was returned. If *name_key* is blank and the *account_cursor* has been reset with **sec_rgy_cursor_reset( )**, **sec_rgy_acct_lookup( )** returns information about the first account in the database.

Permissions Required

The **sec_rgy_acct_lookup( )** routine requires the **r** (**read**) permission on the account principal to be viewed.

Cautions   There are several different types of cursors used in the registry application programmer interface (API). Some cursors point to PGO items, others point to members in a membership list, and others point to account data. Do not use a cursor for one sort of object in a call expecting another sort of object. For example, you cannot use the same cursor on a call to **sec_rgy_acct_get_projlist( )** and **sec_rgy_pgo_get_next( )**. The behavior in this case is undefined.

Furthermore, cursors are specific to a server. A cursor pointing into one replica of the registry database is useless as a pointer into another replica.

Use **sec_rgy_cursor_reset( )** to renew a cursor for use with another call or for another server.

Files   **/usr/include/dce/acct.idl**
The **idl** file from which **dce/acct.h** was derived.

Errors   **sec_rgy_no_more_entries**
The cursor is at the end of the accounts in the registry.

sec_rgy_object_not_found
The input account could not be found by the registry server.

sec_rgy_server_unavailable
The DCE registry server is unavailable.

error_status_ok
The call was successful.

Related Information

Functions: **sec_intro(3sec)**, **sec_rgy_acct_admin_replace(3sec)**, **sec_rgy_acct_replace_all(3sec)**, **sec_rgy_acct_user_replace(3sec)**, **sec_rgy_cursor_reset(3sec)**.

sec_rgy_acct_passwd

Purpose   Changes the password for an account

Synopsis   **#include <dce/acct.h>**

    void sec_rgy_acct_passwd(
        sec_rgy_handle_t *context*,
        sec_rgy_login_name_t **login_name*,
        sec_passwd_rec_t **caller_key*,
        sec_passwd_rec_t **new_key*,
        sec_passwd_type_t *new_keytype*,
        sec_passwd_version_t **new_key_version*,
        error_status_t **status*);

Parameters

Input

context   An opaque handle bound to a registry server. Use **sec_rgy_site_-open( )** to acquire a bound handle.

login_name   A pointer to the account login name. A login name is composed of three character strings, containing the principal, group, and organization (PGO) names corresponding to the account. All three strings must be completely specified.

caller_key   A key to use to encrypt the key for transmission to the registry server. If communications secure to the **rpc_c_authn_level_pkt_-privacy** level are available on a system, then this parameter is not necessary, and the packet encryption is sufficient to ensure security.

new_key   The password for the new account. During transmission to the registry server, it is encrypted with *caller_key*.

new_keytype   The type of the new key. The server uses this parameter to decide how to encode *new_key* if it is sent as plaintext.

Output

new_key_version
> The key version number returned by the server. If the client requests a particular key version number (via the **version_number** field of the *new_key* input parameter), the server returns the requested version number back to the client.

status
> A pointer to the completion status. On successful completion, the routine returns **error_status_ok**. Otherwise, it returns an error.

Description

The **sec_rgy_acct_passwd( )** routine changes an account password to the input password character string. Wildcards (blank fields) are not permitted in the specified account name; the principal, group, and organization names of the account must be completely specified.

Permissions Required

The **sec_rgy_acct_passwd( )** routine requires the **u** (**user_info**) permission on the account principal whose password is to be changed.

Files

/usr/include/dce/acct.idl
> The **idl** file from which **dce/acct.h** was derived.

Errors

sec_rgy_not_authorized
> The client program is not authorized to change the password of this account.

sec_rgy_object_not_found
> The account to be modified was not found by the registry server.

sec_rgy_server_unavailable
> The DCE registry server is unavailable.

error_status_ok
> The call was successful.

Related Information

Functions: **sec_intro(3sec)**.

sec_rgy_acct_rename

Purpose   Changes an account login name

Synopsis   **#include <dce/acct.h>**

void sec_rgy_acct_rename(
      sec_rgy_handle_t *context*,
      sec_rgy_login_name_t *old_login_name,
      sec_rgy_login_name_t *new_login_name,
      sec_rgy_acct_key_t *new_key_parts,
      error_status_t *status);

Parameters

Input

context
    An opaque handle bound to a registry server. Use **sec_rgy_site_-open( )** to acquire a bound handle.

old_login_name
    A pointer to the current account login name. The login name is composed of three character strings, containing the principal, group, and organization (PGO) names corresponding to the account. All three strings must be completely specified.

new_login_name
    A pointer to the new account login name. Again, all three component names must be completely specified.

Input/Output

new_key_parts
    A pointer to the minimum abbreviation allowed when logging in to the account. Abbreviations are not currently implemented and the only legal value is **sec_rgy_acct_key_person**.

Output

status
    A pointer to the completion status. On successful completion, the routine returns **error_status_ok**. Otherwise, it returns an error.

Description

The **sec_rgy_acct_rename( )** routine changes an account login name from *old_login_name* to *new_login_name*. Wildcards (empty fields) are not permitted in either input name; both the old and new login names must completely specify their component principal, group, and organization names. Note, though, that the principal component in a login name cannot be changed.

The *new_key_parts* variable identifies how many of the *new_login_name* parts to use as the unique abbreviation for the account. If the requested abbreviation duplicates an existing abbreviation for another account, the routine identifies the next shortest unique abbreviation and returns this abbreviation using *new_key_parts*.

Permissions Required

The **sec_rgy_acct_rename( )** routine requires the **m** (**mgmt_info**) permission on the account principal to be renamed.

Notes   The **sec_rgy_acct_rename( )** routine does not affect any of the registry PGO data. The constituent principal, group, and organization items for an account must be added before the account can be created. (See the **sec_rgy_pgo_add( )** routine). Also, the principal must have been added as a member of the specified group and organization. (See the **sec_rgy_pgo_add_member( )** routine).

Files   **/usr/include/dce/acct.idl**
                The **idl** file from which **dce/acct.h** was derived.

Errors   **sec_rgy_not_authorized**
                The client program is not authorized to make the changes.

                sec_rgy_object_not_found
                The account to be modified was not found by the registry server.

                sec_rgy_name_exists
                The new account name is already in use by another account.

                sec_rgy_server_unavailable
                The DCE registry server is unavailable.

                error_status_ok
                The call was successful.

Related Information

Functions: **sec_intro(3sec)**, **sec_rgy_acct_add(3sec)**.

sec_rgy_acct_replace_all

Purpose   Replaces all account data for an account

Synopsis   **#include <dce/acct.h>**

> **void sec_rgy_acct_replace_all(**
> **sec_rgy_handle_t** *context,*
> **sec_rgy_login_name_t** **login_name,*
> **sec_rgy_acct_key_t** **key_parts,*
> **sec_rgy_acct_user_t** **user_part,*
> **sec_rgy_acct_admin_t** **admin_part,*
> **boolean32** *set_password,*
> **sec_passwd_rec_t** **caller_key,*
> **sec_passwd_rec_t** **new_key,*
> **sec_passwd_type_t** *new_keytype,*
> **sec_passwd_version_t** **new_key_version,*
> **error_status_t** **status);*

Parameters

Input

context   An opaque handle bound to a registry server. Use **sec_rgy_site_-
                   open( )** to acquire a bound handle.

login_name   A pointer to the account login name. A login name is composed of
                   three character strings, containing the principal, group, and
                   organization (PGO) names corresponding to the account. For the
                   group and organization names, blank strings can serve as wildcards,
                   matching any entry. The principal name must be input.

user_part   A pointer to the **sec_rgy_acct_user_t** structure containing the user
                   part of the account data. This represents such information as the
                   account password, home directory, and default shell, all of which
                   are accessible to, and may be modified by, the account owner.

admin_part   A pointer to the **sec_rgy_acct_admin_t** structure containing the
                   administrative part of an account's data. This information includes
                   the account creation and expiration dates and flags describing limits
                   to the use of privilege attribute certificates, among other
                   information, and can be modified only by an administrator.

set_passwd   The password reset flag. If you set this parameter to TRUE, the account's password will be changed to the value specified in *new_key*.

caller_key   A key to use to encrypt the key for transmission to the registry server. If communications secure to the **rpc_c_authn_level_pkt_-privacy** level are available on a system, then this parameter is not necessary, and the packet encryption is sufficient to ensure security.

new_key   The password for the new account. During transmission to the registry server, it is encrypted with *caller_key*.

new_keytype   The type of the new key. The server uses this parameter to decide how to encode the plaintext key.

Input/Output

key_parts   A pointer to the minimum abbreviation allowed when logging in to the account. Abbreviations are not currently implemented and the only legal value is **sec_rgy_acct_key_person**.

Output

new_key_version
    The key version number returned by the server. If the client requests a particular key version number (via the **version_number** field of the *new_key* input parameter), the server returns the requested version number back to the client.

status   A pointer to the completion status. On successful completion, the routine returns **error_status_ok**. Otherwise, it returns an error.

Description

The **sec_rgy_acct_replace_all( )** routine replaces both the user and administrative information in the account record specified by the input login name. The administrative information contains limitations on the account's use and privileges. The user information contains such information as the account home directory and default shell. Typically, the administrative information can only be modified by a registry administrator (users with **admin_info** (**a**) privileges for an account), while the user information can be modified by the account owner (users with **user_info** (**u**) privileges for an account).

sec_rgy_acct_replace_all(3sec)

Use the *set_passwd* parameter to reset the account password. If you set this parameter to TRUE, the account's pasword is changed to the value specified in *new_key*.

The *key_parts* variable identifies how many of the *login_name* parts to use as the unique abbreviation for the replaced account. If the requested abbreviation duplicates an existing abbreviation for another account, the routine identifies the next shortest unique abbreviation and returns this abbreviation using *key_parts*.

Permissions Required

The **sec_rgy_acct_replace_all( )** routine requires the following permissions on the account principal:

- The **m** (**mgmt_info**) permission, if **flags** or **expiration_date** is to be changed.

- The **a** (**auth_info**) permission, if **authentication_flags** or **good_since_date** is to be changed.

- The **u** (**user_info**) permission, if user **flags**, **gecos**, **homedir** (home directory), **shell**, or **passwd** (password) are to be changed.

Notes   All users need the **w** (**write**) privilege to modify any account information.

Files   **/usr/include/dce/acct.idl**
The **idl** file from which **dce/acct.h** was derived.

Errors   **sec_rgy_not_authorized**
The client program is not authorized to change account information.

sec_rgy_object_not_found
The specified account could not be found.

sec_rgy_server_unavailable
The DCE registry server is unavailable.

error_status_ok
The call was successful.

Related Information

Functions: **sec_intro(3sec), sec_rgy_acct_add(3sec),**
sec_rgy_acct_admin_replace(3sec), sec_rgy_acct_rename(3sec),
sec_rgy_acct_user_replace(3sec).

sec_rgy_acct_user_replace

Purpose   Replaces user account data

Synopsis   **#include <dce/acct.h>**

void sec_rgy_acct_user_replace(
        sec_rgy_handle_t *context,*
        sec_rgy_login_name_t **login_name,*
        sec_rgy_acct_user_t **user_part,*
        boolean32 *set_passwd,*
        sec_passwd_rec_t **caller_key,*
        sec_passwd_rec_t **new_key,*
        sec_passwd_type_t *new_keytype,*
        sec_passwd_version_t **new_key_version,*
        error_status_t **status);*

Parameters

Input

    context   An opaque handle bound to a registry server. Use **sec_rgy_site_-open( )** to acquire a bound handle.

    login_name   A pointer to the account login name. A login name is composed of three character strings, containing the principal, group, and organization (PGO) names corresponding to the account. For the group and organization names, blank strings can serve as wildcards, matching any entry. The principal name must be input.

    user_part   A pointer to the **sec_rgy_acct_user_t** structure containing the user part of the account data. This represents such information as the account password, home directory, and default shell, all of which are accessible to, and may be modified by, the account owner. The structure contains the following fields:

        gecos   A character string containing information about the account owner. This often includes such information as their name and telephone number.

        homedir   The default directory upon login for the account.

        shell   The default shell to use upon login.

passwd_version_number
The password version number, a 32-bit unsigned integer, set by the registry server.

passwd_dtm The date and time of the last password change (in **sec_timeval_sec_t** form), also set by the registry server.

flags A flag set of type **sec_rgy_acct_user_flags_t**.

passwd The account's encrypted password.

set_passwd The password reset flag. If you set this parameter to TRUE, the user's password will be changed to the value specified in *new_key*.

caller_key A key to use to encrypt the key for transmission to the registry server. If communications secure to the **rpc_c_authn_level_pkt_-privacy** level are available on a system, then this parameter is not necessary, and the packet encryption is sufficient to ensure security.

new_key The password for the new account. During transmission to the registry server, it is encrypted with *caller_key*.

new_keytype The type of the new key. The server uses this parameter to decide how to encode the plaintext key.

Output

new_key_version
The key version number returned by the server. If the client requests a particular key version number (via the **version_number** field of the *new_key* input parameter), the server returns the requested version number back to the client.

status A pointer to the completion status. On successful completion, the routine returns **error_status_ok**. Otherwise, it returns an error.

Description

The **sec_rgy_acct_user_replace( )** routine replaces the user information in the account record specified by the input login name. The user information contains such information as the account home directory and default shell. Typically, the the user information can be modified by the account owner (users with **user_info** (**u**) privileges for an account).

Use the *set_passwd* parameter to reset the user's password. If you set this parameter to TRUE, the user's pasword is changed to the value specified in *new_key*.

Permissions Required

The **sec_rgy_acct_user_replace( )** routine requires the **u** (**user_info**) permission on the account principal.

Notes   All users need the **w** (**write**) privilege to modify any account information.

Files   **/usr/include/dce/acct.idl**
                     The **idl** file from which **dce/acct.h** was derived.

Errors   **sec_rgy_not_authorized**
                       The client program is not authorized to modify the account data.

               sec_rgy_object_not_found
                       The specified account could not be found.

               sec_rgy_server_unavailable
                       The DCE registry server is unavailable.

               error_status_ok
                       The call was successful.

Related Information

Functions: **sec_intro(3sec)**, **sec_rgy_acct_add(3sec)**, **sec_rgy_acct_admin_replace(3sec)**, **sec_rgy_acct_rename(3sec)**, **sec_rgy_acct_replace_all(3sec)**.

sec_rgy_attr_cursor_alloc

Purpose   Allocates resources to a cursor used by **sec_rgy_attr_lookup_by_id**

Synopsis   #include <dce/sec_rgy_attr.h>

void sec_rgy_attr_cursor_alloc(
        sec_attr_cursor_t **cursor,*
        error_status_t **status*);

Parameters

Output

cursor   A pointer to a **sec_attr_cursor_t**.

status   A pointer to the completion status. On successful completion, the call returns **error_status_ok**. Otherwise, it returns an error.

Description

The **sec_rgy_attr_cursor_alloc( )** call allocates resources to a cursor used with the **sec_rgy_attr_lookup_by_id** call. This routine, which is a local operation, does not initialize *cursor.*

The **sec_rgy_attr_cursor_init( )** routine, which makes a remote call, allocates and initializes the cursor. In addition, **sec_rgy_attr_cursor_init( )** returns the total number of attributes attached to the object as an output parameter; **sec_rgy_attr_cursor_alloc( )** does not.

Permissions Required

None.

Files   **/usr/include/dce/sec_attr_base.idl**
            The **idl** file from which **dce/sec_attr_base.h** was derived.

Errors   **no such object**

       error_status_ok

Related Information

Functions: **sec_intro(3sec)**, **sec_rgy_attr_cursor_init(3sec)**, **sec_rgy_attr_cursor_release(3sec)**, **sec_rgy_attr_cursor_reset(3sec)**, **sec_rgy_attr_lookup_by_id(3sec)**.

sec_rgy_attr_cursor_init

Purpose   Initializes a cursor used by **sec_rgy_attr_lookup_by_id**

Synopsis   **#include <dce/sec_rgy_attr.h>**

        void sec_rgy_attr_cursor_init (
                sec_rgy_handle_t *context*,
                sec_rgy_domain_t *name_domain*,
                sec_rgy_name_t *name*,
                unsigned32 **cur_num_attrs*,
                sec_attr_cursor_t **cursor*,
                error_status_t **status*);

Parameters

Input

context   An opaque handle bound to a registry server. Use **sec_rgy_site_-open( )** to acquire a bound handle.

name_domain   A value of type **sec_rgy_domain_t** that identifies the registry domain in which the object specified by *name* resides. The valid values are as follows:

    sec_rgy_domain_person
        The name identifies a principal.

    sec_rgy_domain_group
        The name identifies a group.

    sec_rgy_domain_org
        The name identifies an organization.

    This parameter is ignored if *name* is **policy** or **replist**.

name   A pointer to a **sec_rgy_name_t** character string containing the name of the person, group, or organization to which the attribute to be scanned is attached.

Output

cur_num_attrs
A pointer to an unsigned 32-bit integer that specifies the number of attributes currently attached to the object.

cursor
A pointer to a **sec_rgy_cursor_t** positioned at the first attribute in the list of the object's attributes.

status
A pointer to the completion status. On successful completion, the routine returns **error_status_ok**. Otherwise, it returns an error.

Description

The **sec_rgy_attr_cursor_init( )** routine initializes a cursor of type **sec_attr_cursor_t** (used with the **sec_rgy_attr_lookup_by_id** call) and initializes the cursor to the first attribute in the specified object's list of attributes. This call also supplies the total number of attributes attached to the object as part of its output. The cursor allocation is a local operation. The cursor initialization is a remote operation and makes a remote call to the registry.

Use the **sec_rgy_attr_cursor_release( )** call to release all resources allocated to a **sec_attr_cursor_t** cursor.

Permissions Required

The **sec_rgy_attr_cursor_init( )** routine requires at least one permission (of any type) on the person, group, or organization to which the attribute to be scanned is attached.

Errors

no such object

error_status_ok

Related Information

Functions: **sec_intro(3sec)**, **sec_rgy_attr_cursor_release**, **sec_rgy_attr_lookup_by_id**.

sec_rgy_attr_cursor_release

Purpose   Releases a cursor

Synopsis   **#include <dce/sec_rgy_attr.h>**

void sec_rgy_attr_cursor_release (
        sec_attr_cursor_t **cursor*,
        error_status_t **status*);

Parameters

Input

context   An opaque handle bound to a registry server. Use **sec_rgy_site_-
            open(**) to acquire a bound handle.

Input/Output

cursor   As an input parameter, a pointer to an uninitialized cursor of type
          sec_attr_cursor_t. As an output parameter, a pointer to an
          uninitialized cursor of type **sec_attr_cursor_t** with all resources
          released.

Output

status   A pointer to the completion status. On successful completion, the
          routine returns **error_status_ok**. Otherwise, it returns an error.

Description

The **sec_rgy_attr_cursor_release(**) routine releases all resources allocated to a
sec_attr_cursor_t by the **sec_rgy_attr_cursor_init(**) or **sec_rgy_attr_cursor_-
alloc(**)** call.

This is a local-only operation and makes not remote calls.

Permissions Required

None.

Errors   No such object

error_status_ok

Related Information

Functions: **sec_intro(3sec)**, **sec_rgy_attr_cursor_alloc(3sec)**,
sec_rgy_attr_cursor_init(3sec), **sec_rgy_attr_lookup_by_id**.

sec_rgy_attr_cursor_reset

Purpose   Reinitializes a cursor

Synopsis   **#include <dce/sec_attr_base.h>**

void sec_attr_cursor_reset(
        sec_attr_cursor_t **cursor,*
        error_status_t **status***);**

Parameters

Input/Output

cursor   A pointer to a **sec_attr_cursor_t**. As an input parameter, an
             initialized *cursor*. As an output parameter, *cursor* is reset to the first
             attribute in the schema.

status   A pointer to the completion status. On successful completion, the
             routine returns **error_status_ok**. Otherwise, it returns an error.

Description

The **sec_rgy_attr_cursor_reset()** routine resets a **dce_attr_cursor_t** that has
been allocated by either a **sec_rgy_attr_cursor_init()** or **sec_rgy_attr_cursor_-
alloc()**. The reset cursor can then be used to process a new
sec_rgy_attr_lookup_by_id query by reusing the cursor instead of releasing and
reallocating it. This is a local operation and makes no remote calls.

Permissions Required

None.

Files   **/usr/include/dce/sec_rgy_attr.idl**
             The **idl** file from which **dce/sec_rgy_attr.h** was derived.

Errors   **error_status_ok**

Related Information

Functions: **sec_intro(3sec)**, **sec_rgy_attr_cursor_alloc(3sec)**,
sec_rgy_attr_cursor_init(3sec), sec_rgy_attr_lookup_by_ld(3sec).

sec_rgy_attr_delete

Purpose   Deletes specified attributes for a specified object

Synopsis   #include <dce/sec_rgy_attr.h>

void sec_rgy_attr_delete (
        sec_rgy_handle_t *context*,
        sec_rgy_domain_t *name_domain*,
        sec_rgy_name_t *name*,
        unsigned32 *num_to_delete*,
        sec_attr_t *attrs*[ ],
        signed32 **failure_index*,
        error_status_t **status*);

Parameters

Input

    context   An opaque handle bound to a registry server. Use **sec_rgy_site_- open**( ) to acquire a bound handle.

    name_domain A value of type **sec_rgy_domain_t** that identifies the registry domain in which the object identified by *name* resides. The valid values are as follows:

        sec_rgy_domain_person
            The name identifies a principal.

        sec_rgy_domain_group
            The name identifies a group.

        sec_rgy_domain_org
            The name identifies an organization.

    This parameter is ignored if *name* is **policy** or **replist**.

    name   A character string of type **sec_rgy_name_t** specifying the name of the person, group, or organization to which the attributes are attached.

    num_to_delete
        A 32-bit integer that specifies the number of elements in the *attrs*[ ] array. This integer must be greater than 0.

    attrs[ ]   An array of values of type **sec_attr_t** that specifies the attribute instances to be deleted. The size of the array is determined by *num_to_delete*.

Output

    failure_index In the event of an error, *failure_index* is a pointer to the element in the *in_attrs*[ ] array that caused the update to fail. If the failure cannot be attributed to a specific attribute, the value of *failure_index* is **-1**.

    status   A pointer to the completion status. On successful completion, the routine returns **error_status_ok**. Otherwise, it returns an error.

Description

The **sec_rgy_attr_delete**( ) routine deletes attributes. This is an atomic operation: if the deletion of any attribute in the *attrs*[ ] array fails, all deletions are aborted. The attribute causing the delete to fail is identified in *failure_index*. If the failure cannot be attributed to a given attribute, *failure_index* contains **-1**.

The *attrs* array, which specifies the attributes to be deleted, contains values of type **sec_attr_t** These values consist of

- **attr_id**, a UUID that identifies the attribute type

- **attr_value**, values of **sec_attr_value_t** that specify the attribute's encoding type and values.

To delete attributes that are not multivalued and to delete all instances of a multivalued attribute, an attribute UUID is all that is required. For these attribute instances, supply the attribute UUID in the input array and set the attribute encoding (in **sec_attr_encoding_t**) to **sec_attr_enc_void**.

To delete a specific instance of a multivalued attribute, supply the UUID and value that uniquely identify the multivalued attribute instance in the input array.

Note that if the deletion of any attribute instance in the array fails, all fail. However, to help pinpoint the cause of the failure, the call identifies the first attribute whose deletion failed in a failure index by array element number.

Permissions Required

The **sec_rgy_attr_delete**( ) routine requires the delete permission set for each attribute type identified in the *attrs*[ ] array. These permissions are defined as part of the ACL manager set in the schema entry for the attribute type.

sec_rgy_attr_delete(3sec)

Files   /usr/include/dce/sec_rgy_attr.idl

The **idl** file from which **dce/sec_rgy_attr.h** was derived.

Errors   database read only

invalid/unsupported attribute type

server unavailable

site read only

unauthorized

error_status_ok

Related Information

Functions: **sec_intro(3sec)**, **sec_rgy_attr_update(3sec)**.

sec_rgy_attr_get_effective

Purpose   Reads effective attributes by ID

Synopsis   **#include <dce/sec_rgy_attr.h>**

void sec_rgy_attr_get_effective(
        sec_rgy_handle_t *context*,
        sec_rgy_domain_t *name_domain*,
        sec_rgy_name_t *name*,
        unsigned32 *num_attr_keys*,
        sec_attr_t *attr_keys*[ ],
        sec_attr_vec_t **attr_list*,
        error_status_t *status*);

Parameters

Input

context   An opaque handle bound to a registry server. Use **sec_rgy_site_-open( )** to acquire a bound handle.

name_domain A value of type **sec_rgy_domain_t** that identifies the domain in which the named object resides. The valid values are as follows:

      sec_rgy_domain_principal
           The *name* identifies a principal.

      sec_rgy_domain_group
           The *name* identifies a group.

      sec_rgy_domain_org
           The *name* identifies an organization.

This parameter is ignored if *name* is **policy** or **replist**.

name   A pointer to a **sec_rgy_name_t** character string containing the name of the person, group, or organization to which the attribute is attached.

> *num_attr_keys*
>> An unsigned 32-bit integer that specifies the number of elements in the the *attr_keys*[ ] array. If *num_attr_keys* is set to 0 (zero), all of the effective attributes that the caller is authorized to see are returned.
>
> *attr_keys*[ ] An array of values of type **sec_attr_t** that specify the UUIDs of the attributes to be returned if they are effective. If the attribute type is associated with a query attribute trigger, the **sec_attr_t attr_value** field can be used to pass in optional information required by the attribute trigger query. If no information is to be passed in the **attr_value** field (whether the type indicates an attribute trigger query or not), set the attribute's encoding type to **sec_rgy_attr_enc_void**. The size of the *attr_keys*[ ] array is determined by the *num_attr_keys* parameter.

Output

> *attr_list* A pointer an attribute vector allocated by the server containing all of the effective attributes matching the search criteria (defined in *num_attr_keys* or *attr_keys*[ ]). The server allocates a buffer large enough to return all the requested attributes so that subsequent calls are not necessary.
>
> *status* A pointer to the completion status. On successful completion, the routine returns **error_status_ok**. Otherwise, it returns an error.

Description

The **sec_rgy_attr_get_effective**( ) routine returns the UUIDs of a specified object's effective attributes. Effective attributes are determined by setting of the schema entry **apply_defaults** flag:

- If the flag is set off, only the attributes directly attached to the object are effective.

- If the flag is set on, the effective attributes are obtained by performing the following steps for each attribute identified by UUID in the **attr_keys** array:

  — If the object named by *name* is a principal and if the a requested attribute exists on the principal, that attribute is effective and is returned. If it does not exist, the search continues.

— The next step in the search depends on the type of object:

For principals with accounts:

— The organization named in the principal's account is examined to see if an attribute of the requested type exists. If it does, it is effective and is returned; then the search for that attribute ends. If it does not exist, the search for that attribute continues to the **policy** object as described here.

— The registry **policy** object is examined to see if an attribute of the requested type exits. If it does, it is returned. If it does not, a message indicating the no attribute of the type exists for the object is returned.

For principals without accounts, for groups, and for organizations:

The registry **policy** object is examined to see if an attribute of the requested type exits. If it does, it is returned. If it does not, a message indicating the no attribute of the type exists for the object is returned.

For multivalued attributes, the call returns a **sec_attr_t** for each value as an individual attribute instance. For attribute sets, the call returns a **sec_attr_t** for each member of the set; it does not return the set instance.

If the attribute instance to be read is associated with a query attribute trigger that requires additional information before it can process the query request, use a **sec_attr_value_t** to supply the requested information. To do this

- Set the **sec_attr_encoding_t** to an encoding type that is compatible with the information required by the query attribute trigger.

- Set the **sec_attr_value_t** to hold the required information.

If the attribute instance to be read is not associated with a query trigger or no additional information is required by the query trigger, an attribute UUID is all that is required. For these attribute instances, supply the attribute UUID in the input array and set the attribute encoding (in **sec_attr_encoding_t**) to **sec_attr_enc_-void**.

sec_rgy_attr_get_effective(3sec)

If the requested attribute type is associated with a query trigger, the value returned for the attribute will be the binding (as set in the schema entry) of the trigger server. The caller must bind to the trigger server and pass the original input query attribute to the **sec_attr_trig_query** call in order to retrieve the attribute value.

Files   **/usr/include/dce/sec_rgy_attr.idl**
    The **idl** file from which **dce/sec_rgy_attr.h** was derived.

Errors   **error_status_ok**

Related Information

Functions: **sec_intro(3sec)**.

sec_rgy_attr_lookup_by_id

Purpose   Reads a specified object's attribute(s), expanding attribute sets into individual member attributes

Synopsis   **#include <dce/sec_rgy_attr.h>**

void sec_rgy_attr_lookup_by_id (
       sec_rgy_handle_t *context,*
       sec_rgy_domain_t *name_domain,*
       sec_rgy_name_t *name,*
       sec_attr_cursor_t **cursor,*
       unsigned32 *num_attr_keys,*
       unsigned32 *space_avail,*
       sec_attr_t *attr_keys*[ ],
       unsigned32 **num_returned,*
       sec_attr_t *attrs*[ ],
       unsigned32 **num_left,*
       error_status_t **status*);

Parameters

Input

context   An opaque handle bound to a registry server. Use **sec_rgy_site_-open( )** to acquire a bound handle.

name_domain A value of type **sec_rgy_domain_t** that identifies the registry domain in which the object specified by *name* resides. The valid values are as follows:

sec_rgy_domain_person
        The name identifies a principal.

sec_rgy_domain_group
        The name identifies a group.

sec_rgy_domain_org
        The name identifies an organization.

This parameter is ignored if *name* is **policy** or **replist**.

name
A pointer to a **sec_rgy_name_t** character string containing the name of the person, group, or organization to which the attribute is attached.

num_attr_keys
An unsigned 32-bit integer that specifies the number of elements in the *attr_keys* array. Set this parameter to 0 (zero) to return all of the object's attributes that the caller is authorized to see.

space_avail
An unsigned 32-bit integer that specifies the size of the *attr_keys* array.

attr_keys[ ]
An array of values of type **sec_attr_t** that identify the attribute type ID of the attribute instance(s) to be looked up. If the attribute type is associated with a query attribute trigger, the **sec_attr_t attr_value** field can be used to pass in optional information required by the attribute trigger query. If no information is to be passed in the **attr_value** field (whether the type indicates an attribute trigger query or not), set the attribute's encoding type to **sec_rgy_attr_-enc_void**.

The size of the *attr_keys*[ ] array is determined by the *num_attr_keys* parameter.

Input/Output

cursor
A pointer to a **sec_attr_cursor_t**. As an input parameter, *cursor* is a pointer to a **sec_attr_cursor_t** initialized by a **sec_rgy_attr_srch_-cursor_init** call. As an output parameter, *cursor* is a pointer to a **sec_attr_cursor_t** that is positioned past components returned in this call.

Output

num_returned A pointer to a 32-bit unsigned integer that specifies the number of attribute instances returned in the *attrs*[ ] array.

attrs
An array of values of type **sec_attr_t** that contains the attributes retrieved by UUID. The size of the array is determined by *space_avail* and the length by *num_returned*.

num_left
A pointer to a 32-bit unsigned integer that supplies the number of attributes that were found but could not be returned because of space constraints in the *attrs*[ ] buffer. To ensure that all the attributes will be returned, increase the size of the *attrs*[ ] array by increasing the size of *space_avail* and *num_returned*.

status   A pointer to the completion status. On successful completion, the routine returns **error_status_ok**, or, if the requested attributes were not available, it returns the message **not_all_available**. Otherwise, it returns an error.

Description

The **sec_rgy_attr_lookup_by_id( )** function reads those attributes specified by UUID for an object specified by name. This routine is similar to the **sec_rgy_attr_lookup_no_expand( )** routine with one exception: for attribute sets, the **sec_rgy_attr_lookup_no_expand( )** routine returns a **sec_attr_t** for the set instance only; it does not expand the set and return a **sec_attr_t** for each member in the set. This call expands attribute sets and returns a **sec_attr_t** for each member in the set.

If the *num_attr_keys* parameter is set to 0 (zero), all of the object's attributes that the caller is authorized to see are returned. This routine is useful for programmatic access.

For multivalued attributes, the call returns a **sec_attr_t** for each value as an individual attribute instance. For attribute sets, the call returns a **sec_attr_t** for each member of the set; it does not return the set instance.

The *attr_keys*[ ] array, which specifies the attributes to be returned, contains values of type **sec_attr_t**. These values consist of

- **attr_id**, a UUID that identifies the attribute type

- **attr_value**, values of **sec_attr_value_t** that specify the attribute's encoding type and values.

Use the **attr_id** field of each *attr_keys* array element, to specify the UUID that identifies the attribute type to be returned.

If the attribute instance to be read is not associated with a query trigger or no additional information is required by the query trigger, an attribute UUID is all that is required. For these attribute instances, supply the attribute UUID in the input array and set the attribute encoding (in **sec_attr_encoding_t**) to **sec_attr_enc_-void**.

If the attribute instance to be read is associated with a query attribute trigger that requires additional information before it can process the query request, use a **sec_attr_value_t** to supply the requested information:

- Set the **sec_attr_encoding_t** to an encoding type that is compatible with the information required by the query attribute trigger.

- Set the **sec_attr_value_t** to hold the required information.

Note that if you set *num_attr_keys* to zero to return all of the object's attributes and that attribute is associated with a query attribute trigger, the attribute trigger will be called with no input attribute information (that would normally have been passed in via the **attr_value** field).

The *cursor* parameter specifies a cursor of type **sec_attr_cursor_t** initialized to the point in the attribute list at which to start processing the query. Use the **sec_attr_cursor_init** function to initialize *cursor*. If *cursor* is uninitialized, the server begins processing the query at the first attribute that satisfies the search criteria.

The *num_left* parameter contains the number of attributes that were found but could not be returned because of space constraints of the *attrs*[ ] array. (Note that this number may be inaccurate if the target server allows updates between successive queries.) To obtain all of the remaining attributes, set the size of the *attrs*[ ] array so that it is large enough to hold the number of attributes listed in *num_left*.

Permissions Required

The **sec_rgy_attr_lookup_by_id**( ) routine requires the query permission set for each attribute type identified in the *attr_keys*[ ] array. These permissions are defined as part of the ACL manager set in the schema entry of each attribute type.

Files   **/usr/include/dce/sec_rgy_attr.idl**
                    The **idl** file from which **dce/sec_rgy_attr.h** was derived.

Errors   **registry server unavailable**

                trigger server unavailable

                unauthorized

                error_status_ok

Related Information

Functions: **sec_intro(3sec)**, **sec_rgy_attr_attr_lookup_by_name(3sec)**, **sec_rgy_attr_lookup_no_expand(3sec)**.

sec_rgy_attr_lookup_by_name

Purpose   Reads a single attribute instance for a specific object

Synopsis   **#include <dce/sec_rgy_attr.h>**

    void sec_rgy_attr_lookup_by_name(
        sec_rgy_handle_t *context*,
        sec_rgy_domain_t *name_domain*,
        sec_rgy_name_t *name*,
        char *attr_name,
        sec_attr_t *attr,
        error_status_t *status);

Parameters

Input

context   An opaque handle bound to a registry server. Use **sec_rgy_site_-open( )** to acquire a bound handle.

name_domain   A value of type **sec_rgy_domain_t** that identifies the domain in which the named object resides. The valid values are as follows:

sec_rgy_domain_principal
    The *name* identifies a principal.

sec_rgy_domain_group
    The *name* identifies a group.

sec_rgy_domain_org
    The *name* identifies an organization.

This parameter is ignored if *name* is **policy** or **replist**.

name   A pointer to a **sec_rgy_name_t** character string containing the name of the person, group, or organization to which the attribute is attached.

attr_name   An pointer to a character string that specifies the name of the attribute to be retrieved.

Output

attr   A pointer to a **sec_attr_t** that contains the first instance of the named attribute.

status   A pointer to the completion status. The completion status can be one of the following:

- **error_status_ok**, if all instances of the value are returned with no errors.

- **more_available**, if a multivalued attribute was specified as *name* and the routine completed successfully. For multivalued attributes, this routine returns the first instance of the attribute.

- **attribute_set_instance**, if an attribute set was specified as *name* and the routine completed successfully.

- An error message, if the routine did not complete successfully.

Description

The **sec_rgy_attr_lookup_by_name( )** routine returns the named attribute for a named object. This routine is useful for an interactive editor.

For multivalued attributes, this routine returns the first instance of the attribute. To retrieve every instance of the attribute, use the **sec_rgy_attr_lookup_by_id** call, supplying the attribute UUID returned in the *attr* parameter.

For attribute sets, the routine returns the attribute set instance, not the member instances. To retrieve all members of the set, use the **sec_rgy_attr_lookup_by_id** call, supplying the the attribute set UUID returned in the *attr* parameter.

Warning   This routine does not provide for input data to an attribute trigger query operation. If the named attribute is associated with a query attribute trigger, the attribute trigger will be called with no input attribute value information.

Permissions Required

The **sec_rgy_attr_lookup_by_name( )** routine requires the query permission set for the attribute type of the attribute instance identified by *attr_name*. These permissions are defined as part of the ACL manager set in the schema entry of each attribute type.

Errors   registry server unavailable

trigger server unavailable

unauthorized

error_status_ok

Related Information

Functions: **sec_intro(3sec)**, **sec_rgy_attr_lookup_by_id(3sec)**,
sec_rgy_attr_lookup_no_expand(3sec).

sec_rgy_attr_lookup_no_expand

Purpose   Reads a specified object's attribute(s), without expanding attribute sets into individual member attributes

Synopsis   **#include <dce/sec_rgy_attr.h>**

void sec_rgy_attr_lookup_no_expand(
        sec_rgy_handle_t *context*,
        sec_rgy_domain_t *name_domain*,
        sec_rgy_name_t *name*,
        sec_attr_cursor_t **cursor*,
        unsigned32 *num_attr_keys*,
        unsigned32 *space_avail*,
        uuid_t *attr_keys*[ ],
        unsigned32 **num_returned*,
        sec_attr_t *attr_sets*[ ],
        unsigned32 **num_left*,
        error_status_t *status*);

Parameters

Input

context   An opaque handle bound to a registry server. Use **sec_rgy_site_-open( )** to acquire a bound handle.

name_domain A value of type **sec_rgy_domain_t** that identifies the domain in which the named object resides. The valid values are as follows:

sec_rgy_domain_principal
        The *name* identifies a principal.

sec_rgy_domain_group
        The *name* identifies a group.

sec_rgy_domain_org
        The *name* identifies an organization.

This parameter is ignored if *name* is **policy** or **replist**.

name	A pointer to a **sec_rgy_name_t** character string containing the name of the person, group, or organization to which the attribute is attached.
num_attr_keys	An unsigned 32-bit integer that specifies the number of elements in the the *attr_keys*[ ] array. If *num_attr_keys* is set to 0 (zero), all attribute sets that the caller is authorized to see are returned.
space_avail	An unsigned 32-bit integer that specifies the size of the *attrs_sets*[ ] array.
attr_keys[ ]	An array of values of type **uuid_t** that specify the UUIDs of the attribute sets to be returned. The size of the *attr_keys*[ ] array is determined by the *num_attr_keys* parameter.

Input/Output

cursor	A pointer to a **sec_attr_cursor_t**. As an input parameter, *cursor* is a pointer to a **sec_attr_cursor_t** that is initialized by the **sec_rgy_attr_cursor_init**. As an output parameter, *cursor* is a pointer to a **sec_attr_cursor_t** that is positioned past the attribute sets returned in this call.

Output

num_returned	A pointer to a 32-bit integer that specifies the number of attribute sets returned in the *attrs*[ ] array.
attr_sets	An array of values of type **sec_attr_t** that contains the attribute sets retrieved by UUID. The size of the array is determined by *space_avail* and the length by *num_returned*.
num_left	A pointer to a 32-bit unsigned integer that supplies the number of attribute sets that were found but could not be returned because of space constraints in the *attr_sets*[ ] buffer. To ensure that all the attributes will be returned, increase the size of the *attr_sets*[ ] array by increasing the size of *space_avail* and *num_returned*.
status	A pointer to the completion status. On successful completion, the routine returns **error_status_ok**. Otherwise, it returns an error.

sec_rgy_attr_lookup_no_expand(3sec)

Description

The **sec_rgy_attr_lookup_no_expand**( ) routine reads attribute sets. This routine is similar to the **sec_rgy_attr_lookup_by_id**( ) routine with one exception: for attribute sets, the **sec_rgy_attr_lookup_by_id**( ) routine expands attribute sets and returns a **sec_attr_t** for each member in the set. This call does not. Instead it returns a **sec_attr_t** for the set instance only. The **sec_rgy_attr_lookup_no_-expand**( ) routine is useful for programmatic access.

cursor is a cursor of type **sec_attr_cursor_t** that establishes the point in the attribute set list from which the server should start processing the query. Use the **sec_rgy_attr_cursor_init** function to initialize *cursor*. If *cursor* is uninitialized, the server begins processing the query with the first attribute that satisfies the search criteria.

The *num_left* parameter contains the number of attribute sets that were found but could not be returned because of space constraints of the *attr_sets*[ ] array. (Note that this number may be inaccurate if the target server allows updates between successive queries.) To obtain all of the remaining attribute sets, set the size of the *attr_sets*[ ] array so that it is large enough to hold the number of attributes listed in *num_left*.

Permissions Required

The **sec_rgy_attr_lookup_no_expand**( ) routine requires the query permission set for each attribute type identified in the *attr_keys*[ ] array. These permissions are defined as part of the ACL manager set in the schema entry of each attribute type.

Files

/usr/include/dce/sec_rgy_attr.idl
> The **idl** file from which **dce/sec_rgy_attr.h** was derived.

Errors

invalid/unsupported attribute type

registry server unavailable

unauthorized

error_status_ok

Related Information

Functions: **sec_intro(3sec)**, **sec_rgy_attr_lookup_by_id(3sec)**, **sec_rgy_attr_lookup_by_name(3sec)**.

sec_rgy_attr_sch_aclmgr_strings

Purpose   Returns printable ACL strings associated with an ACL manager protecting a schema object

Synopsis   **#include <dce/dce_attr_base.h>**

void sec_rgy_attr_sch_aclmgr_strings(
        sec_rgy_handle_t *context*,
        sec_attr_component_name_t *schema_name*,
        uuid_t ***acl_mgr_type*,
        unsigned32 *size_avail*,
        uid_t ***acl_mgr_type_chain*,
        sec_acl_printstring_t ***acl_mgr_info*,
        boolean32 ***tokenize*,
        unsigned32 ***total_num_printstrings*,
        unsigned32 ***size_used*,
        sec_acl_printstring_t *permstrings*[ ],
        error_status_t ***status*);

Parameters

Input

context   An opaque handle bound to a registry server. Use **sec_rgy_site_-open( )** to acquire a bound handle.

schema_name Reserved for future use.

acl_manager_type
      A pointer to the UUID identifying the type of the ACL manager in question. There may be more than one type of ACL manager protecting the schema object whose ACL is bound to the input handle. Use this parameter to distinguish them. Use **sec_rgy_attr_-sch_get_acl_mgrs( )** to acquire a list of the manager types protecting a given schema object.

size_avail   An unsigned 32-bit integer containing the allocated length of the *permstrings*[ ] array.

Output

acl_mgr_type_chain

If the target object ACL contains more than 32 permission bits, chains of manager types are used: each manager type holds one 32-bit segment of permissions. The UUID returned in *acl_mgr_type_chain* refers to the next ACL manager in the chain. If there are no more ACL managers in the chain, **uuid_nil** is returned.

acl_mgr_info A pointer to a printstring that contains the ACL manager type's name, help information, and set of supported of permission bits.

tokenize A pointer to a variable that specifies whether or not printstrings will be passed separately:

- TRUE indicates that the printstrings must be printed or passed separately.

- FALSE indicates that the printstrings are unambiguous and can be concatenated when printed without confusion.

total_num_printstrings

A pointer to an unsigned 32-bit integer containing the total number of permission entries supported by this ACL manager type.

size_used A pointer to an unsigned 32-bit integer containing the number of permission entries returned in the *permstrings*[ ] array.

permstrings[ ] An array of printstrings of type **sec_acl_printstring_t**. Each entry of the array is a structure containing the following three components:

printstring A character string of maximum length **sec_acl_printstring_len** describing the printable representation of a specified permission.

helpstring A character string of maximum length **sec_acl_printstring_help_len** containing some text that can be used to describe the specified permission.

permissions A **sec_acl_permset_t** permission set describing the permissions that are represented with the companion printstring.

The array consists of one such entry for each permission supported by the ACL manager identified by *acl_mgr_type*.

status   A pointer to the completion status. On successful completion, the routine returns **error_status_ok**. Otherwise, it returns an error.

Description

The **sec_rgy_attr_sch_aclmgr_strings( )** routine returns an array of printable representations (called *printstrings*) for each permission bit or combination of permission bits the specified ACL manager supports. The ACL manager type specified by **acl_mgr_type** must be one of the types protecting the schema object bound to by *h*.

In addition to returning the printstrings, this routine also returns instructions about how to print the strings in the *tokenize* variable. If this variable is set to FALSE, the printstrings can be concatenated. If it is set to TRUE, the printstrings cannot be concatenated. For example a printstrings of **r** or **w** could be concatenated as **rw** without any confusion. However, printstrings in a form of **read** or **write**, should not be concatenated.

ACL managers often define aliases for common permission combinations. By convention, simple entries appear at the beginning of the *printstrings*[ ] array, and combinations appear at the end.

Permissions Required

The **sec_rgy_attr_sch_scl_mgr_strings( )** routine requires the **r** permission on the **attr_schema** object.

Files

/usr/include/dce/sec_rgy_attr_sch.idl
           The **idl** file from which **dce/sec_rgy_attr_sch.h** was derived.

Errors

sec_attr_no_memory

sec_attr_svr_unavailable

sec_attr_unauthorized

error_status_ok

Related Information

Functions: **sec_intro(3sec)**, **sec_rgy_attr_sch_get_acl_mgrs(3sec)**.

sec_rgy_attr_sch_create_entry

Purpose   Creates a schema entry

Synopsis   **#include <dce/sec_rgy_attr_sch.h>**

void sec_rgy_attr_sch_create_entry(
> **sec_rgy_handle_t** *context*,
> **sec_attr_component_name_t** *schema_name*,
> **sec_attr_schema_entry_t** **schema_entry*,
> **error_status_t** **status*);

Parameters

Input

> *context*   An opaque handle bound to a registry server. Use **sec_rgy_site_-open( )** to acquire a bound handle.
>
> *schema_name* Reserved for future use.
>
> *schema_entry* A pointer to a **sec_attr_schema_entry_t** that contains the schema entry values for the schema in which the entry is to be created.

Output

> *status*   A pointer to the completion status. On successful completion, the routine returns **error_status_ok**. Otherwise, it returns an error.

Description

The **sec_rgy_attr_sch_create_entry( )** routine creates schema entries that define attribute types.

Permissions Required

The **sec_rgy_attr_sch_create_entry( )** routine requires **i** permission on the **attr_schema** object.

Files   **/usr/include/dce/sec_rgy_attr_sch.idl**
> The **idl** file from which **dce/sec_rgy_attr_sch.h** was derived.

Errors   sec_attr_bad_acl_mgr_set

sec_attr_bad_acl_mgr_type

sec_attr_bad_bind_authn_svc

sec_attr_bad_bind_authz_svc

sec_attr_bad_bind_info

sec_attr_bad_bind_prot_level

sec_attr_bad_bind_svr_name

sec_attr_bad_comment

sec_attr_bad_encoding_type

sec_attr_bad_intercell_action

sec_attr_bad_name

sec_attr_bad_permset

sec_attr_bad_scope

sec_attr_bad_uniq_query_accept

sec_attr_name_exists

sec_attr_no_memory

sec_attr_svr_read_only

sec_attr_svr_unavailable

sec_attr_trig_bind_info_missing

sec_attr_type_id_exists

sec_attr_unauthorized

Related Information

Functions: **sec_intro(3sec), sec_rgy_attr_sch_delete_entry(3sec), sec_rgy_attr_sch_update(3sec)**.

sec_rgy_attr_sch_cursor_alloc

Purpose   Allocates resources to a cursor used with **sec_rgy_attr_sch_scan**

Synopsis   **void sec_rgy_att_sch_cursor_alloc(**
        dce_attr_cursor_t **cursor*,
        error_status_t **status*);

Parameters

Output

cursor   A pointer to a **sec_attr_cursor_t**.

status   A pointer to the completion status. On successful completion, the call returns **error_status_ok**. Otherwise, it returns an error.

Description

The **sec_rgy_attr_sch_cursor_alloc( )** call allocates resources to a cursor used with the **sec_rgy_attr_sch_scan( )** call. This routine, which is a local operation, does not initialize *cursor*.

The **sec_rgy_attr_sch_cursor_init( )** routine, which makes a remote call, allocates and initializes the cursor. In addition, **sec_rgy_attr_sch_cursor_init( ) returns the total number of entries found in the schema as an output parameter;** **sec_rgy_attr_sch_cursor_alloc( )** does not.

Permissions Required

None.

Files   **/usr/include/dce/sec_rgy_attr_sch.idl**
        The **idl** file from which **dce/sec_rgy_attr_sch.id** was derived.

Errors   **sec_attr_no_memory**

       error_status_ok

Related Information

Functions: **sec_intro(3sec)**, **sec_rgy_attr_sch_cursor_init(3sec)**, **sec_rgy_attr_sch_cursor_release(3sec)**, **sec_rgy_attr_sch_scan(3sec)**.

sec_rgy_attr_sch_cursor_init

Purpose   Initializes and allocates a cursor used with **sec_rgy_attr_sch_scan**

Synopsis   #include <dce/sec_rgy_attr_sch.h>

                void sec_rgy_attr_cursor_init(
                        sec_rgy_handle_t *context*,
                        sec_attr_component_name_t *schema_name*,
                        unsigned32 **cur_num_entries*,
                        sec_attr_cursor_t **cursor*,
                        error_status_t *status*);

Parameters

Input

    context   An opaque handle bound to a registry server. Use **sec_rgy_site_-open( )** to acquire a bound handle.

    schema_name Reserved for future use.

Output

    cur_num_entries
              A pointer to an unsigned 32-bit integer that specifies the total number of entries contained in the schema at the time of this call.

    cursor   A pointer to a **sec_attr_cursor_t** that is initialized to the first entry in the the schema.

    status   A pointer to the completion status. On successful completion, the call returns **error_status_ok**. Otherwise, it returns an error.

Description

The **sec_rgy_attr_sch_cursor_init( )** call initializes and allocates resources to a cursor used with the **sec_rgy_attr_sch_scan** call. This call makes remote calls to initialize the cursor.

To limit the number of remote calls, use the **sec_rgy_attr_sch_cursor_alloc( )** call to allocate *cursor*, but not initialize it. Be aware, however, that the the **sec_rgy_attr_sch_cursor_init( )** call supplies the total number of entries found in the schema as an output parameter; the **sec_rgy_attr_sch_cursor_alloc( )** call does not.

If the cursor iunput to **sec_rgy_attr_sch_scan** has not been initialized, the **sec_rgy_attr_sch_scan** call will initialize it; if it has been initialized, **sec_rgy_attr_sch_scan** advances it.

Permissions Required

None.

Files

/usr/include/dce/sec_rgy_attr_sch.idl
    The **idl** file from which **dce/sec_rgy_attr_sch.h** was derived.

Errors

sec_attr_no_memory

sec_attr_svr_unavailable

sec_attr_unauthorized

error_status_ok

Related Information

Functions: **sec_intro(3sec), sec_rgy_attr_sch_cursor_alloc(3sec), sec_rgy_attr_sch_cursor_release(3sec), sec_rgy_attr_sch_scan(3sec).**

sec_rgy_attr_sch_cursor_release

Purpose   Releases states associated with a cursor used by **sec_rgy_attr_sch_scan**

Synopsis   #include <dce/sec_rgy_attr_sch.h>

void sec_rgy_attr_cursor_release(
        sec_attr_cursor_t *cursor,
        error_status_t *status);

Parameters

Input/Output

cursor   A pointer to a **sec_attr_cursor_t**. As an input parameter, *cursor* must have been initialized to the first entry in a schema. As an output parameter, *cursor* is uninitialized with all resources releases.

Output

status   A pointer to the completion status. On successful completion, the routine returns **error_status_ok**. Otherwise, it returns an error.

Description

The **sec_rgy_attr_sch_cursor_init**( ) routine releases the resources allocated to the cursor used by the **sec_rgy_attr_sch_scan** routine. This call is a local operation and makes no remote calls.

Permissions Required

None.

Files   **/usr/include/dce/sec_rgy_attr_sch.idl**
                The **idl** file from which **dce/sec_rgy_attr_sch.h** was derived.

Errors   **error_status_ok**

Related Information

Functions: **sec_intro(3sec)**, **sec_rgy_attr_sch_cursor_allocate(3sec)**, **sec_rgy_attr_sch_cursor_init(3sec)**, **sec_rgy_attr_sch_scan(3sec)**.

sec_rgy_attr_sch_cursor_reset

Purpose   Resets a cursor that has been allocated

Synopsis   **#include <dce/sec_rgy_attr_sch.h>**

void dce_attr_cursor_reset(
        sec_attr_cursor_t **cursor*,
        error_status_t **status*);

Parameters

Input/Output

cursor   A pointer to a **sec_attr_cursor_t**. As an input parameter, an
            initialized *cursor*. As an output parameter, *cursor* is reset to the first
            attribute in the schema.

status   A pointer to the completion status. On successful completion, the
            routine returns **error_status_ok**. Otherwise, it returns an error.

Description

The **sec_rgy_attr_sch_cursor_reset( )** routine resets a **dce_attr_cursor_t** that has
been allocated by either a **sec_rgy_attr_sch_cursor_init( )** or **sec_rgy_attr_sch_-
cursor_alloc( )**. The reset cursor can then be used to process a new
sec_rgy_attr_sch_scan query by reusing the cursor instead of releasing and
reallocating it. This is a local operation and makes no remote calls.

Permissions Required

None.

Files   **/usr/include/dce/sec_rgy_attr_sch.idl**
                The **idl** file from which **dce/sec_rgy_attr_sch.h** was derived.

Errors   **sec_attr_bad_cursor**

error_status_ok

Related Information

Functions: **sec_intro**(3sec), **sec_rgy_attr_sch_cursor_alloc**(3sec),
sec_rgy_attr_sch_cursor_init(3sec), **sec_rgy_attr_sch_scan**(3sec).

sec_rgy_attr_sch_delete_entry

Purpose   Deletes a schema entry

Synopsis   #include <dce/sec_rgy_attr_sch.h>

void sec_rgy_attr_sch_delete_entry(
        sec_rgy_handle_t *context*,
        sec_attr_component_name_t *schema_name*,
        uuid_t *attr_id*,
        error_status_t *status*);

Parameters

Input

context   An opaque handle bound to a registry server. Use **sec_rgy_site_-open**( ) to acquire a bound handle.

schema_name Reserved for future use.

attr_id   A pointer to a **uuid_t** that identifies the schema entry to be deleted.

Output

status   A pointer to the completion status. On successful completion, the routine returns **error_status_ok**. Otherwise, it returns an error.

Description

The **sec_rgy_attr_sch_delete_entry**( ) routine deletes a schema entry. Because this is a radical operation that invalidates any existing attributes of this type on objects dominated by the schema, access to this operation should be severely limited.

Permissions Required

The **sec_rgy_attr_sch_delete_entry**( ) routine requires the **d** permission on the **attr_schema** object.

Files   **/usr/include/dce/sec_rgy_attr_sch.idl**
            The **idl** file from which **dce/sec_rgy_attr_sch.h** was derived.

Errors   sec_attr_no_memory

sec_attr_sch_entry_not_found

sec_attr_svr_read_only

sec_attr_svr_unavailable

sec_attr_unauthorized

error_status_ok

Related Information

Functions: **sec_intro(3sec)**, **sec_rgy_attr_sch_create_entry(3sec)**, **sec_rgy_attr_sch_update_entry(3sec)**.

sec_rgy_attr_sch_get_acl_mgrs

Purpose   Retrieves the manager types of the ACLs protecting the objects dominated by a named schema

Synopsis   #include <dce/sec_rgy_attr_sch.h>

void sec_rgy_attr_sch_get_acl_mgrs(
        sec_rgy_handle_t *context*,
        sec_attr_component_name_t *schema_name*,
        unsigned32 *size_avail*,
        unsigned32 **size_used*,
        unsigned32 **num_acl_mgr_types*,
        uuid_t *acl_mgr_types*[ ],
        error_status_t **status*);

Parameters

Input

context   An opaque handle bound to a registry server. Use **sec_rgy_site_-open**( ) to acquire a bound handle.

schema_name Reserved for future use.

size_avail   An unsigned 32-bit integer containing the allocated length of the *acl_manager_types*[ ] array.

Output

size_used   An unsigned 32-bit integer containing the number of output entries returned in the *acl_mgr_types*[ ] array.

num_acl_mgr_types
               An unsigned 32-bit integer containing the number of types returned in the *acl_mgr_types*[ ] array. This may be greater than *size_used* if there was not enough space allocated by *size_avail* for all the manager types in the *acl_manager_types*[ ] array.

acl_mgr_types[ ]
               An array of the length specified in *size_avail* to contain UUIDs (of type **uuid_t**) identifying the types of ACL managers protecting the target object.

status   A pointer to the completion status. On successful completion, the routine returns **error_status_ok**. Otherwise, it returns an error.

Description

The **sec_rgy_attr_sch_get_acl_mgrs**( ) routine returns a list of the manager types protecting the schema object identified by *context*.

ACL editors and browsers can use this operation to determine the ACL manager types protecting a selected schema object. Then, using the **sec_rgy_attr_sch_-aclmgr_strings**( ) routine, they can determine how to format for display the permissions supported by that ACL manager type.

Permissions Required

The **sec_rgy_attr_sch_get_acl_mgrs**( ) routine requires the **r** permission on the **attr_schema** object.

Files   **/usr/include/dce/sec_rgy_attr_sch.idl**
The **idl** file from which **dce/sec_rgy_attr_sch.h** was derived.

Errors   **sec_attr_no_memory**

sec_attr_svr_unavailable

sec_attr_unauthorized

error_status_ok

Related Information

Functions: **sec_intro(3sec), sec_rgy_attr_sch_aclmgr_strings(3sec)**.

sec_rgy_attr_sch_lookup_by_id

Purpose   Reads a schema entry identified by UUID

Synopsis   #include <dce/sec_rgy_attr_sch.h>

void sec_rgy_attr_sch_lookup_by_id(
        sec_rgy_handle_t *context*,
        sec_attr_component_name_t *schema_name*,
        uuid_t **attr_id*,
        sec_attr_schema_entry_t **schema_entry*,
        error_status_t **status*);

Parameters

Input

context   An opaque handle bound to a registry server. Use **sec_rgy_site_-
              open**( ) to acquire a bound handle.

schema_name Reserved for future use.

attr_id   A pointer to a **uuid_t** that identifies a schema entry.

Output

schema_entry A **sec_attr_schema_entry_t** that contains an entry identified by
              attr_id.

status   A pointer to the completion status. On successful completion, the
              routine returns **error_status_ok**. Otherwise, it returns an error.

Description

The **sec_rgy_attr_sch_lookup_by_id**( ) routine reads a schema entry identified by
attr_id. This routine is useful for programmatic access.

Permissions Required

The **sec_rgy_attr_sch_lookup_by_id**( ) routine requires the **r** permission on the
attr_schema object.

Files   **/usr/include/dce/sec_rgy_attr_sch.idl**
          The **idl** file from which **dce/sec_rgy_attr_sch.h** was derived.

Errors   **sec_attr_no_memory**

          sec_attr_sch_entry_not_found

          sec_attr_svr_unavailable

          sec_attr_unauthorized

          error_status_ok

Related Information

Functions: **sec_intro(3sec)**, **sec_rgy_attr_sch_lookup_by_name(3sec)**,
sec_rgy_attr_sch_scan(3sec).

sec_rgy_attr_sch_lookup_by_name

Purpose   Reads a schema entry identified by name

Synopsis   **#include <dce/sec_rgy_attr_sch.h>**

   void sec_rgy_attr_sch_lookup_by_name(
      sec_rgy_handle_t *context*,
      sec_attr_component_name_t *schema_name*,
      char **attr_name*,
      sec_attr_schema_entry_t **schema_entry*,
      error_status_t **status*);

Parameters

Input

   context   An opaque handle bound to a registry server. Use **sec_rgy_site_-open( )** to acquire a bound handle.

   schema_name Reserved for future use.

   attr_name   A pointer to a character string that identifies the schema entry.

Output

   schema_entry A **sec_attr_schema_entry_t** that contains the schema entry identified by *attr_name*.

   status   A pointer to the completion status. On successful completion, the routine returns **error_status_ok**. Otherwise, it returns an error.

Description

   The **sec_rgy_attr_sch_lookup_by_name( )** routine reads a schema entry identified by name. This routine is useful for use with an interactive editor.

Permissions Required

   The **sec_rgy_attr_sch_lookup_by_name( )** routine requires the **r** permission on the **attr_schema** object.

Files   **/usr/include/dce/sec_rgy_attr_sch.idl**

The **idl** file from which **dce/sec_rgy_attr_sch.h** was derived.

Errors   **sec_attr_bad_name**

sec_attr_no_memory

sec_attr_sch_entry_not_found

sec_attr_svr_unavailable

sec_attr_unauthorized

error_status_ok

Related Information

Functions: **sec_intro(3sec)**, **sec_rgy_attr_sch_lookup_by_id(3sec)**, **sec_rgy_attr_sch_scan(3sec)**.

sec_rgy_attr_sch_scan

Purpose   Reads a specified number of schema entries

Synopsis   **#include <dce/sec_rgy_attr_sch.h>**

      void sec_rgy_attr_sch_scan(
            sec_rgy_handle_t *context*,
            sec_attr_component_name_t *schema_name*,
            sec_attr_cursor_t **cursor*,
            unsigned32 *num_to_read*,
            unsigned32 **num_read*,
            sec_attr_schema_entry_t *schema_entries*[ ],
            error_status_t **status*);

Parameters

Input

    context   An opaque handle bound to a registry server. Use **sec_rgy_site_-open**( ) to acquire a bound handle.

    schema_name Reserved for future use.

    num_to_read An unsigned 32-bit integer specifying the size of the *schema_entries*[ ] array and the maximum number of entries to be returned.

Input/Output

    cursor   A pointer to a **sec_attr_cursor_t**. As input *cursor* must be allocated and can be initialized. If *cursor* is not initialized, **sec_rgy_attr_sch_scan** will initialized. As output, *cursor* is positioned at the first schema entry after the returned entries.

Output

    num_read   A pointer an unsigned 32-bit integer specifying the number of entries returned in *schema_entries*[ ].

    schema_entrieso[ ]
            A **sec_attr_schema_entry_t** that contains an array of the returned schema entries.

status   A pointer to the completion status. On successful completion, the routine returns **error_status_ok**. Otherwise, it returns an error.

Description

The **sec_rgy_attr_sch_scan( )** routine reads schema entries. The read begins at the entry at which the input *cursor* is positioned and ends after the number of entries specified in *num_to_read*.

The input *cursor* must have been allocated by either the **sec_rgy_attr_sch_-cursor_init( )** or the **sec_rgy_attr_sch_cursor_alloc( )** call. If the input *cursor* is not initialzed, **sec_rgy_attr_sch_scan( )** initializes it; if cursor is initialized, **sec_-rgy_attr_sch_scan( )** simply advances it.

To read all entries in a schema, make successive **sec_rgy_attr_sch_scan( )** calls. When all entries have been read, the call returns the message **no_more_entries**.

This routine is useful as a browser.

Permissions Required

The **sec_rgy_attr_sch_scan( )** routine requires **r** permission on the **attr_schema** object.

Files   **/usr/include/dce/sec_rgy_attr_sch.idl**
                  The **idl** file from which **dce/sec_rgy_attr_sch.h** was derived.

Errors   sec_attr_bad_cursor

                  sec_attr_no_memory

                  sec_attr_svr_unavailable

                  sec_attr_unauthorized

                  error_status_ok

Related Information

Functions: **sec_intro(3sec)**, **sec_rgy_attr_sch_cursor_alloc(3sec)**, **sec_rgy_attr_sch_cursor_init(3sec)**, **sec_rgy_attr_sch_cursor_release(3sec)**.

sec_rgy_attr_sch_update_entry

Purpose   Updates a schema entry

Synopsis   #include <dce/sec_rgy_attr_sch.h>

void sec_rgy_attr_sch_update_entry(
        sec_rgy_handle_t *context*,
        sec_attr_component_name_t *schema_name*,
        sec_attr_schema_entry_parts_t *modify_parts*,
        sec_attr_schema_entry_t *schema_entry,
        error_status_t *status);

Parameters

Input

context   An opaque handle bound to a registry server. Use **sec_rgy_site_-
                open**( ) to acquire a bound handle.

schema_name Reserved for future use.

modify_parts A value of type **sec_attr_schema_entry_parts_t** that identifies the
                fields in *schema_entry* that can be modified.

schema_entry A pointer to a **sec_attr_schema_entry_t** that contains the schema
                entry values for the schema entry to be updated.

Output

status   A pointer to the completion status. On successful completion, the
                routine returns **error_status_ok**. Otherwise, it returns an error.

Description

The **sec_rgy_attr_sch_update_entry**( ) routine modifies schema entries. Only
those schema entry fields set to be modified in the **sec_attr_schema_entry_-
parts_t** data type can be modified.

Some schema entry components can never be modified. Instead to make any
changes to these components, the schema entry must be deleted (which deletes all
attribute instances of that type) and recreated.

The schema entry components that can never be modified are as follows:

- Attribute name

- Reserved flag

- Apply defaults flag

- Intercell action flag

- Trigger binding

- Comment

Fields that are arrays of structures (such as **acl_mgr_set** and **trig_binding**) are completely replaced by the new input array. This operation cannot be used to add a new element to the existing array.

Permissions Required

The **sec_rgy_attr_sch_update_entry( )** routine requires the **M** permission on the **attr_schema** object.

Files

/usr/include/dce/sec_rgy_attr_sch.idl
> The **idl** file from which **dce/sec_rgy_attr_sch.h** was derived.

Errors

sec_attr_bad_acl_mgr_set

sec_attr_bad_acl_mgr_type

sec_attr_bad_bind_authn_svc

sec_attr_bad_bind_authz_svc

sec_attr_bad_bind_info

sec_attr_bad_bind_prot_level

sec_attr_bad_bind_svr_name

sec_attr_bad_comment

sec_attr_bad_intercell_action

sec_attr_bad_name

sec_attr_bad_permset

sec_attr_bad_uniq_query_accept

sec_rgy_attr_sch_update_entry(3sec)

sec_attr_field_no_update

sec_attr_name_exists

sec_attr_no_memory

sec_attr_sch_entry_not_found

sec_attr_svr_read_only

sec_attr_svr_unavailable

sec_attr_trig_bind_info_missing

sec_attr_unauthorized

error_status_ok

Related Information

Functions: **sec_intro(3sec)**, **sec_rgy_attr_sch_create_entry(3sec)**, **sec_rgy_attr_sch_delete_entry(3sec)**.

sec_rgy_attr_test_and_update

Purpose   Updates specified attribute instances for a specified object only if a set of control attribute instances match the object's existing attribute instances

Synopsis   **#include <dce/sec_rgy_attr.h>**

void sec_rgy_attr_test_and_update (
        sec_rgy_handle_t *context,*
        sec_rgy_domain_t *name_domain,*
        sec_rgy_name_t *name,*
        unsigned32 *num_to_test,*
        sec_attr_t *test_attrs*[ ],
        unsigned32 *num_to_write,*
        sec_attr_t *update_attrs*[ ],
        signed32 **failure_index,*
        error_status_t **status***);**

Parameters

Input

    context   An opaque handle bound to a registry server. Use **sec_rgy_site_-open( )** to acquire a bound handle.

    name_domain A value of type **sec_rgy_domain_t** that identifies the registry domain in which the object specified by *name* resides. The valid values are as follows:

        sec_rgy_domain_person
                The name identifies a principal.

        sec_rgy_domain_group
                The name identifies a group.

        sec_rgy_domain_org
                The name identifies an organization.

        This parameter is ignored if *name* is **policy** or **replist**.

    name   A character string of type **sec_rgy_name_t** specifying the name of the person, group, or organization to which the attribute is attached.

    num_to_test   An unsigned 32-bit integer that specifies the number of elements in the *test_attrs*[ ] array. This integer must be greater than 0 (zero).

    test_attrs[ ]   An array of values of type **sec_attr_t** that specifies the control attributes. The update takes place only if the types and values of the control attributes exactly match those of the attribute instances on the named registry object. The size of the array is determined by *num_to_test*.

    num_to_write A 32-bit integer that specifies the number of attribute instances returned in the *update_attrs*[ ] array.

    update_attrs An array of values of type **sec_attr_t** that specifies the attribute instances to be updated. The size of the array is determined by *num_to_write*.

Output

    failure_index In the event of an error, *failure_index* is a pointer to the element in the **update_attrs**[ ] array that caused the update to fail. If the failure cannot be attributed to a specific attribute, the value of *failure_index* is **-1**.

    status   A pointer to the completion status. On successful completion, the routine returns **error_status_ok**. Otherwise, it returns an error.

Description

The **sec_rgy_attr_test_and_update( )** routine updates an attribute only if the set of control attributes specified in the *test_attrs*[ ] match attributes that already exist for the object.

This update is an atomic operation: if any of the control attributes do not match existing attributes, none of the updates are performed, and if an update should be performed, but the write cannot occur for whatever reason to any member of the *update_attrs*[ ] array, all updates are aborted. The attribute causing the update to fail is identified in *failure_index*. If the failure cannot be attributed to a given attribute, *failure_index* contains **-1**.

If an attribute instance already exists which is identical in both **attr_id** and **attr_value** to an attribute specified in *in_attrs*[ ], the existing attribute information is overwritten by the new information. For multivalued attributes, every instance with the same **attr_id** is overwritten with the supplied values.

If an attribute instance does not exist, it is created.

If you specify an attribute set for updating, the update applies to the set instance, the set itself, not the members of the set. To update a member of an attribute set, supply the UUID of the set member.

If an input attribute is associated with an update attribute trigger server, the attribute trigger server is invoked (by the **sec_attr_trig_update( )** function) and the *in_attr*[ ] array is supplied as input. The output attributes from the update attribute trigger server are stored in the registry database and returned in the *out_attrs*[ ] array. Note that the update attribute trigger server may modify the values before they are used to update the registry database. This is the only circumstance under which the values in the *out_attrs*[ ] array differ from the values in the *in_attrs*[ ] array.

Permissions Required

The **sec_rgy_attr_test_and_update( )** routine routine requires the test permission and the update permission set set for each attribute type identified in the *test_attrs*[ ] array. These permissions are defined as part of the ACL manager set in the schema entry of each attribute type.

Files

/usr/include/dce/sec_rgy_attr.idl
    The **idl** file from which **dce/sec_rgy_attr.h** was derived.

Errors

control attribute has changed

database read only

invalid encoding type

invalid/unsupported attribute type

server unavailable

site read only

trigger server unavailable

unauthorized

value not unique

error_status_ok

Related Information

Functions: **sec_intro(3sec)**, **sec_rgy_attr_delete(3sec)**,
sec_rgy_attr_update(3sec).

sec_rgy_attr_update

Purpose   Creates and updates attribute instances for a specified object

Synopsis   **#include <dce/sec_rgy_attr.h>**

void sec_rgy_attr_update (
            sec_rgy_handle_t *context***,**
            sec_rgy_domain_t *name_domain***,**
            sec_rgy_name_t *name***,**
            unsigned32 *num_to_write***,**
            unsigned32 *space_avail***,**
            sec_attr_t *in_attrs*[ ]**,**
            unsigned32 **num_returned***,**
            sec_attr_t *out_attrs*[ ]**,**
            unsigned32 **num_left***,**
            signed32 **failure_index***,**
            error_status_t **status***);**

Parameters

Input

            context   An opaque handle bound to a registry server. Use **sec_rgy_site_-
                            open( )** to acquire a bound handle.

            name_domain A value of type **sec_rgy_domain_t** that identifies the registry
                            domain in which the object specified by *name* resides. The valid
                            values are as follows:

                            sec_rgy_domain_person
                                    The name identifies a principal.

                            sec_rgy_domain_group
                                    The name identifies a group.

                            sec_rgy_domain_org
                                    The name identifies an organization.

                            This parameter is ignored if *name* is **policy** or **replist**.

            name   A character string of type **sec_rgy_name_t** specifying the name of
                            the person, group, or organization to which the attribute is attached.

    num_to_write A 32-bit unsigned integer that specifies the number of elements in the *in_attrs* array. This integer must be greater than 0 (zero).

    space_avail A 32-bit unsigned integer that specifies the size of the *out_attrs* array. This integer must be greater than 0 (zero).

    in_attrs[ ] An array of values of type **sec_attr_t** that specifies the attribute instances to be updated. The size of the array is determined by *num_to_write*.

Output

    num_returned A pointer to an unsigned 32-bit integer that specifies the number of attribute instances returned in the *out_attrs*[ ] array.

    out_attrs An array of values of type **sec_attr_t** that specifies the updated attribute instances. Not that only if these attributes were processed by an update attribute trigger server will they differ from the attributes in the *in_attrs*[ ] array. The size of the array is determined by *space_avail* and the length by *num_returned*.

    num_left A pointer to an unsigned 32-bit integer that supplies the number of attributes that could not be returned because of space constraints in the *out_attrs*[ ] buffer. To ensure that all the attributes will be returned, increase the size of the *out_attrs*[ ] array by increasing the size of *space_avail* and *num_returned*.

    failure_index In the event of an error, *failure_index* is a pointer to the element in the *in_attrs*[ ] array that caused the update to fail. If the failure cannot be attributed to a specific attribute, the value of *failure_index* is **-1**.

    status A pointer to the completion status. On successful completion, the routine returns **error_status_ok**. Otherwise, it returns an error.

Description

The **sec_rgy_attr_update**( ) routine creates new attribute instances and updates existing attribute instances attached to a object specified by name and registry domain. The instances to be created or updated are passed as an array of **sec_attr_t** data types. This is an atomic operation: if the creation of any attribute in the *in_attrs*[ ] array fails, all updates are aborted. The attribute causing the update to fail is identified in *failure_index*. If the failure cannot be attributed to a given attribute, *failure_index* contains **-1**.

The *in_attrs* array, which specifies the attributes to be created, contains values of type **sec_attr_t**. These values are as follows:

- **attr_id**, a UUID that identifies the attribute type

- **attr_value**, values of **sec_attr_value_t** that specify the attribute's encoding type and values.

If an attribute instance already exists which is identical in both **attr_id** and **attr_value** to an attribute specified in *in_attrs*, the existing attribute information is overwritten by the new information. For multivalued attributes, every instance with the same **attr_id** is overwritten with the supplied values.

If an attribute instance does not exist, it is created.

For multivalued attributes, because every instance of the multivalued attribute is identified by the same UUID, every instance is overwritten with the supplied value. To change only one of the values, you must supply the values that should be unchanged as well as the new value.

To create instances of multivalued attributes, create individual **sec_attr_t** data types to define each multivalued attribute instance and then pass all of them in in the input array.

If an input attribute is associated with an update attribute trigger server, the attribute trigger server is invoked (by the **sec_attr_trig_update( )** function) and the *in_attr*[ ] array is supplied as input. The output attributes from the update attribute trigger server are stored in the registry database and returned in the *out_attrs*[ ] array. Note that the update attribute trigger server may modify the values before they are used to update the registry database. This is the only circumstance under which the values in the *out_attrs*[ ] array differ from the values in the *in_attrs*[ ] array.

Permissions Required

The **sec_rgy_attr_update( )** routine requires the update permission set for each attribute type identified in the *in_attrs*[ ] array. These permissions are defined as part of the ACL manager set in the schema entry of each attribute type.

Files   **/usr/include/dce/sec_rgy_attr.idl**
                 The **idl** file from which **dce/sec_rgy_attr.h** was derived.

Errors   **attribute instance already exists**

              database read only

              invalid encoding type

              invalid/unsupported attribute type

server unavailable

site read only

trigger server unavailable

unauthorized

value not unique

error_status_ok

Related Information

Functions: **sec_intro(3sec)**, **sec_rgy_attr_delete(3sec)**,
sec_rgy_attr_test_and_update(3sec).

sec_rgy_auth_plcy_get_effective

Purpose   Returns the effective authentication policy for an account

Synopsis   **#include <dce/policy.h>**

void sec_rgy_auth_plcy_get_effective(
          sec_rgy_handle_t *context*,
          sec_rgy_login_name_t **account*,
          sec_rgy_plcy_auth_t **auth_policy*,
          error_status_t **status*);

Parameters

Input

context   An opaque handle bound to a registry server. Use **sec_rgy_site_-open( )** to acquire a bound handle.

account   A pointer to the account login name (type **sec_rgy_login_name_t**). A login name is composed of three character strings, containing the principal, group, and organization (PGO) names corresponding to the account. If all three fields contain empty strings, the authentication policy returned is that of the registry.

Output

auth_policy   A pointer to the **sec_rgy_plcy_auth_t** structure to receive the authentication policy. The authentication policy structure contains the maximum lifetime for an authentication ticket, and the maximum amount of time for which one can be renewed.

status   A pointer to the completion status. On successful completion, the routine returns **error_status_ok**. Otherwise, it returns an error.

Description

The **sec_rgy_auth_plcy_get_effective( )** routine returns the effective authentication policy for the specified account. The authentication policy in effect is the more restrictive of the registry and the account policies for each policy category. If no account is specified, the registry's authentication policy is returned.

Permissions Required

The **sec_rgy_auth_plcy_get_effective( )** routine requires the **r** (**read**) permission on the policy object from which the data is to be returned. If an account is specified and an account policy exists, the routine also requires the **r** (**read**) permission on the account principal.

Files

/usr/include/dce/policy.idl
> The **idl** file from which **dce/policy.h** was derived.

Errors

sec_rgy_object_not_found
> The specified account could not be found.

sec_rgy_server_unavailable
> The DCE registry server is unavailable.

error_status_ok
> The call was successful.

Related Information

Functions: **sec_intro(3sec)**, **sec_rgy_auth_plcy_get_info(3sec)**, **sec_rgy_auth_plcy_set_info(3sec)**.

sec_rgy_auth_plcy_get_info

Purpose   Returns the authentication policy for an account

Synopsis   **#include <dce/policy.h>**

void sec_rgy_auth_plcy_get_info(
        sec_rgy_handle_t *context,*
        sec_rgy_login_name_t **account,*
        sec_rgy_plcy_auth_t **auth_policy,*
        error_status_t **status*);

Parameters

Input

context   An opaque handle bound to a registry server. Use **sec_rgy_site_-open( )** to acquire a bound handle.

account   A pointer to the account login name (type **sec_rgy_login_name_t**). A login name is composed of three character strings, containing the principal, group, and organization (PGO) names corresponding to the account.

Output

auth_policy   A pointer to the **sec_rgy_plcy_auth_t** structure to receive the authentication policy. The authentication policy structure contains the maximum lifetime for an authentication ticket, and the maximum amount of time for which one can be renewed.

status   A pointer to the completion status. On successful completion, the routine returns **error_status_ok**. Otherwise, it returns an error.

Description

The **sec_rgy_auth_plcy_get_info( )** routine returns the authentication policy for the specified account. If no account is specified, the registry's authentication policy is returned.

Permissions Required

The **sec_rgy_auth_plcy_get_info( )** routine requires the **r** (**read**) permission on the policy object or account principal from which the data is to be returned.

Notes　　The actual policy in effect will not correspond precisely to what is returned by this call if the overriding registry authentication policy is more restrictive than the policy for the specified account. Use **sec_rgy_auth_plcy_get_effective( )** to return the policy currently in effect for the given account.

Files　　**/usr/include/dce/policy.idl**

The **idl** file from which **dce/policy.h** was derived.

Errors　　**sec_rgy_object_not_found**

No account with the given login name could be found.

sec_rgy_server_unavailable

The DCE registry server is unavailable.

error_status_ok

The call was successful.

Related Information

Functions: **sec_intro(3sec)**, **sec_rgy_auth_plcy_get_effective(3sec)**, **sec_rgy_auth_plcy_set_info(3sec)**.

sec_rgy_auth_plcy_set_info

Purpose   Sets the authentication policy for an account

Synopsis   #include <dce/policy.h>

void sec_rgy_auth_plcy_set_info(
          sec_rgy_handle_t *context*,
          sec_rgy_login_name_t **account*,
          sec_rgy_plcy_auth_t **auth_policy*,
          error_status_t **status*);

Parameters

Input

context   An opaque handle bound to a registry server. Use **sec_rgy_site_-open( )** to acquire a bound handle.

account   A pointer to the account login name (type **sec_rgy_login_name_t**). A login name is composed of three character strings, containing the principal, group, and organization (PGO) names corresponding to the account. All three names must be completely specified.

auth_policy   A pointer to the **sec_rgy_plcy_auth_t** structure containing the authentication policy. The authentication policy structure contains the maximum lifetime for an authentication ticket, and the maximum amount of time for which one can be renewed.

Output

status   A pointer to the completion status. On successful completion, the routine returns **error_status_ok**. Otherwise, it returns an error.

Description

The **sec_rgy_auth_plcy_set_info( )** routine sets the indicated authentication policy for the specified account. If no account is specified, the authentication policy is set for the registry as a whole.

Permissions Required

The **sec_rgy_auth_plcy_set_info( )** routine requires the **a** (**auth_info**) permission on the policy object or account principal for which the data is to be set.

Notes

The policy set on an account may be less restrictive than the policy set for the registry as a whole. In this case, the change in policy has no effect, since the effective policy is the most restrictive combination of the principal and registry authentication policies. (See the **sec_rgy_auth_plcy_get_effective( )** routine).

Files

/usr/include/dce/policy.idl
> The **idl** file from which **dce/policy.h** was derived.

Errors

sec_rgy_object_not_found
> No account with the given login name could be found.

sec_rgy_not_authorized
> The user is not authorized to update the specified record.

sec_rgy_server_unavailable
> The DCE registry server is unavailable.

error_status_ok
> The call was successful.

Related Information

Functions: **sec_intro(3sec)**, **sec_rgy_auth_plcy_get_effective(3sec)**, **sec_rgy_auth_plcy_get_info(3sec)**.

sec_rgy_cell_bind

Purpose   Binds to a registry in a cell

Synopsis   **#include <dce/binding.h>**

void sec_rgy_cell_bind(
        unsigned_char_t *cell_name**,**
        sec_rgy_bind_auth_info_t *auth_info**,**
        sec_rgy_handle_t *context**,**
        error_status_t *status**);**

Parameters

Input

cell_name   A character string (type **unsigned_char_t**) containing the name of the cell in question. Upon return, a security server for that cell is associated with *context*, the registry server handle. The cell must be specified completely and precisely. This routine offers none of the pathname resolving services of **sec_rgy_site_bind( )**.

auth_info   A pointer to the **sec_rgy_bind_auth_info_t** structure that identifies the authentication protocol, protection level, and authorization protocol to use in establishing the binding. (See the **rpc_binding_- set_auth_info( )** routine).

Output

context   A pointer to a **sec_rgy_handle_t** variable. Upon return, this contains a registry server handle indicating (bound to) the desired registry site.

status   A pointer to the completion status. On successful completion, the routine returns **error_status_ok**. Otherwise, it returns an error.

Description

The **sec_rgy_cell_bind( )** routine establishes a relationship with a registry site at an arbitrary level of security. The *cell_name* parameter identifies the target cell.

Files

/usr/include/dce/binding.idl
> The **idl** file from which **dce/binding.h** was derived.

Errors

sec_rgy_server_unavailable
> The DCE registry server is unavailable.

error_status_ok
> The call was successful.

Related Information

Functions: **sec_intro(3sec)**, **sec_rgy_site_bind(3sec)**.

sec_rgy_cursor_reset

Purpose   Resets the registry database cursor

Synopsis   #include <dce/misc.h>

void sec_rgy_cursor_reset(
        sec_rgy_cursor_t *cursor);

Parameters

Input/Output

cursor   A pointer into the registry database.

Description

The **sec_rgy_cursor_reset( )** routine resets the database cursor to return the first suitable entry. A cursor is a pointer into the registry. It serves as a place holder when returning successive items from the registry.

A cursor is bound to a particular server. In other words, a cursor that is in use with one replica of the registry has no meaning for any other replica. If a calling program attempts to use a cursor from one replica with another, the cursor is reset and the routine for which the cursor was specified returns the first item in the database.

A cursor that is in use with one call cannot be used with another. For example, you cannot use the same cursor on a call to **sec_rgy_acct_get_projlist( )** and **sec_rgy_pgo_get_next( )**. The behavior in this case is undefined.

Files   **/usr/include/dce/misc.idl**
        The **idl** file from which **dce/misc.h** was derived.

Examples   The following example illustrates use of the cursor within a loop. The initial **sec_rgy_cursor_reset( )** call resets the cursor to point to the first item in the registry. Successive calls to **sec_rgy_pgo_get_next( )** return the next PGO item and update the cursor to reflect the last item returned. When the end of the list of PGO items is reached, the routine returns the value **sec_rgy_no_more_entries** in the *status* parameter.

```
sec_rgy_cursor_reset(&cursor);
do {
    sec_rgy_pgo_get_next(context, domain, scope, &cursor,
                    &item, name &status);
    if (status == error_status_ok) {
        /* Print formatted PGO item info */
    }
}while (status == error_status_ok);
```

Related Information

Functions: **sec_intro(3sec)**, **sec_rgy_acct_get_projlist(3sec)**,
sec_rgy_acct_lookup(3sec), **sec_rgy_pgo_get_by_id(3sec)**,
sec_rgy_pgo_get_by_name(3sec), **sec_rgy_pgo_get_by_unix_num(3sec)**,
sec_rgy_pgo_get_members(3sec), **sec_rgy_pgo_get_next(3sec)**.

sec_rgy_login_get_effective

Purpose   Returns the effective login data for an account

Synopsis   **#include <dce/misc.h>**

void sec_rgy_login_get_effective(
      sec_rgy_handle_t *context,*
      sec_rgy_login_name_t **login_name,*
      sec_rgy_acct_key_t **key_parts,*
      sec_rgy_sid_t **sid,*
      sec_rgy_unix_sid_t **unix_sid,*
      sec_rgy_acct_user_t **user_part,*
      sec_rgy_acct_admin_t **admin_part,*
      sec_rgy_plcy_t **policy_data,*
      signed32 *max_number,*
      signed32 **supplied_number,*
      uuid_t *id_projlist[ ],*
      signed32 *unix_projlist[ ],*
      signed32 **num_projects,*
      sec_rgy_name_t *cell_name,*
      uuid_t **cell_uuid,*
      sec_override_fields_t **overridden,*
      error_status_t **status);*

Parameters

Input

    context   The registry server handle.

    max_number The maximum number of projects to be returned by the call. This must be no larger than the allocated size of the *projlist*[ ] arrays.

Input/Output

    login_name A pointer to the account login name. A login name is composed of the names for the account's principal, group, and organization (PGO) items.

Output

key_parts A pointer to the minimum abbreviation allowed when logging in to the account. Abbreviations are not currently implemented and the only legal value is **sec_rgy_acct_key_person**.

sid A pointer to a **sec_rgy_sid_t** structure to receive the returned subject identifier (SID) for the account. This structure consists of the UUIDs for the account's PGO items.

unix_sid A pointer to a **sec_rgy_unix_sid_t** structure to receive the returned UNIX subject identifier (SID) for the account. This structure consists of the UNIX numbers for the account's PGO items.

user_part A pointer to a **sec_rgy_acct_user_t** structure to receive the returned user data for the account.

admin_part A pointer to a **sec_rgy_acct_admin_t** structure to receive the returned administrative data for the account.

policy_data A pointer to a **sec_rgy_policy_t** structure to receive the policy data for the account. The policy data is associated with the account's organization, as identified in the login name.

supplied_number
A pointer to the actual number of projects returned. This will always be less than or equal to the *max_number* supplied on input.

id_projlist[ ] An array to receive the UUID of each project returned. The size allocated for the array is given by *max_number*. If this value is less than the total number of projects in the account project list, multiple calls must be made to return all of the projects.

unix_projlist[ ]
An array to receive the UNIX number of each project returned. The size allocated for the array is given by *max_number*. If this value is less than the total number of projects in the account project list, multiple calls must be made to return all of the projects.

num_projects A pointer indicating the total number of projects in the specified account's project list.

cell_name The name of the account's cell.

cell_uuid The UUID for the account's cell.

overridden A pointer to a 32-bit set of flags identifying the local overrides, if any, for the account login information.

status   A pointer to the completion status. On successful completion, the routine returns **error_status_ok**. Otherwise, it returns an error.

Description

The **sec_rgy_login_get_effective( )** routine returns effective login information for the specified account. Login information is extracted from the account's entry in the registry database. Effective login information is a combination of the login information from the registry database and any login overrides defined for the account on the local machine.

The *overridden* parameter indicates which, if any, of the following local overrides have been defined for the account:

- The UNIX user ID

- The group ID

- The encrypted password

- The account's miscellaneous information (**gecos**) field

- The account's home directory

- The account's login shell

Local overrides for account login information are defined in the **/etc/passwd_override** file and apply only to the local machine.

Files   **/usr/include/dce/misc.idl**
                 The **idl** file from which **dce/misc.h** was derived.

                 /etc/passwd_override
                 The file that defines local overrides for account login information.

Errors   **sec_rgy__object_not_found**
                 The specified account could not be found.

                 sec_rgy_server_unavailable
                 The DCE registry server is unavailable.

                 error_status_ok
                 The call was successful.

Related Information

Functions: **sec_intro(3sec)**, **sec_rgy_acct_add(3sec)**, **sec_rgy_login_get_info(3sec)**.

Files: **passwd_override(5sec)**.

sec_rgy_login_get_info

Purpose   Returns login information for an account

Synopsis   **#include <dce/misc.h>**

void sec_rgy_login_get_info(
            sec_rgy_handle_t *context*,
            sec_rgy_login_name_t **login_name*,
            sec_rgy_acct_key_t **key_parts*,
            sec_rgy_sid_t **sid*,
            sec_rgy_unix_sid_t **unix_sid*,
            sec_rgy_acct_user_t **user_part*,
            sec_rgy_acct_admin_t **admin_part*,
            sec_rgy_plcy_t **policy_data*,
            signed32 *max_number*,
            signed32 **supplied_number*,
            uuid_t *id_projlist*[ ],
            signed32 *unix_projlist*[ ],
            signed32 **num_projects*,
            sec_rgy_name_t *cell_name*,
            uuid_t **cell_uuid*,
            error_status_t **status*);

Parameters

Input

context   The registry server handle.

max_number The maximum number of projects to be returned by the call. This
              must be no larger than the allocated size of the *projlist*[ ] arrays.

Input/Output

login_name A pointer to the account login name. A login name is composed of
              the names for the account's principal, group, and organization
              (PGO) items.

Output

key_parts
: A pointer to the minimum abbreviation allowed when logging in to the account. Abbreviations arc not currently implemented and the only legal value is **sec_rgy_acct_key_person**.

sid
: A pointer to a **sec_rgy_sid_t** structure to receive the UUID's representing the account's PGO items.

unix_sid
: A pointer to a **sec_rgy_unix_sid_t** structure to receive the UNIX numbers for the account's PGO items.

user_part
: A pointer to a **sec_rgy_acct_user_t** structure to receive the returned user data for the account.

admin_part
: A pointer to a **sec_rgy_acct_admin_t** structure to receive the returned administrative data for the account.

policy_data
: A pointer to a **sec_rgy_policy_t** structure to receive the policy data for the account. The policy data is associated with the account's organization, as identified in the login name.

supplied_number
: A pointer to the actual number of projects returned. This will always be less than or equal to the *max_number* supplied on input.

id_projlist[ ]
: An array to receive the UUID of each project returned. The size allocated for the array is given by *max_number*. If this value is less than the total number of projects in the account project list, multiple calls must be made to return all of the projects.

unix_projlist[ ]
: An array to receive the UNIX number of each project returned. The size allocated for the array is given by *max_number*. If this value is less than the total number of projects in the account project list, multiple calls must be made to return all of the projects.

num_projects
: A pointer indicating the total number of projects in the specified account's project list.

cell_name
: The name of the account's cell.

cell_uuid
: The UUID for the account's cell.

status
: A pointer to the completion status. On successful completion, the routine returns **error_status_ok**. Otherwise, it returns an error.

sec_rgy_login_get_info(3sec)

Description

The **sec_rgy_login_get_info( )** routine returns login information for the specified account. This information is extracted from the account's entry in the registry database. To return any local overrides for the account's login data, use **sec_rgy_login_get_effective( )**.

Permissions Required

The **sec_rgy_login_get_info( )** routine requires the **r** (**read**) permission on the account principal from which the data is to be returned.

Files   **/usr/lib/dce/misc.idl**

The **idl** file from which **dce/misc.h** was derived.

Errors   **sec_rgy_object_not_found**

The specified account could not be found.

sec_rgy_server_unavailable

The DCE registry server is unavailable.

error_status_ok

The call was successful.

Related Information

Functions: **sec_intro(3sec), sec_rgy_acct_add(3sec), sec_rgy_login_get_effective(3sec)**.

sec_rgy_pgo_add

Purpose   Adds a PGO item to the registry database

Synopsis   **#include <dce/pgo.h>**

void sec_rgy_pgo_add(
        sec_rgy_handle_t *context*,
        sec_rgy_domain_t *name_domain*,
        sec_rgy_name_t *name*,
        sec_rgy_pgo_item_t **pgo_item*,
        error_status_t **status*);

Parameters

Input

context   An opaque handle bound to a registry server. Use **sec_rgy_site_-open( )** to acquire a bound handle.

name_domain This variable identifies the type of the principal, group, or organization (PGO) item identified by the given name. The valid values are as follows:

    sec_rgy_domain_person
        The name identifies a principal.

    sec_rgy_domain_group
        The name identifies a group.

    sec_rgy_domain_org
        The name identifies an organization.

name   A pointer to a **sec_rgy_name_t** character string containing the name of the new PGO item.

pgo_item   A pointer to a **sec_rgy_pgo_item_t** structure containing the data for the new PGO item. The data in this structure includes the PGO item's name, UUID, UNIX number (if any), and administrative data, such as whether the item may have (or belong to) a concurrent group set.

Output

status   A pointer to the completion status. On successful completion, the routine returns **error_status_ok**. Otherwise, it returns an error.

Description

The **sec_rgy_pgo_add( )** routine adds a PGO item to the registry database.

The PGO data consists of the following:

- The universal unique identifier (UUID) of the PGO item. Specify NULL to have the registry server create a new UUID for an item.

- The UNIX number for the PGO item. If the registry uses embedded UNIX IDs (where a subset of the UUID bits represent the UNIX ID), then the specified ID must match the UUID, if both are specified. Use a value of -1 for the UNIX number to match any value.

- The quota for subaccounts allowed for this item entry.

- The full name of the PGO item.

- Flags (in the **sec_rgy_pgo_flags_t** format) indicating whether

    — A principal item is an alias.

    — The PGO item can be deleted from the registry.

    — A principal item can have a concurrent group set.

    — A group item can appear in a concurrent group set.

Permissions Required

The **sec_rgy_pgo_add( )** routine requires the **i** (**insert**) permission on the parent directory in which the the PGO item is to be created.

Notes   An account can be added to the registry database only when all its constituent PGO items are already in the database, and the appropriate membership relationships between them are established. For example, to establish an account with principal name **tom**, group name **writers**, and organization name **hp**, all three names must exist as independent PGO items in the database. Furthermore, **tom** must be a member of **writers**, which must be a member of **hp**. (See **sec_rgy_acct_add( )** to add an account to the registry.)

Files   **/usr/include/dce/pgo.idl**

   The **idl** file from which **dce/pgo.h** was derived.

Errors   **sec_rgy_not_authorized**

   The client program is not authorized to add the specified PGO item.

sec_rgy_object_exists

   A PGO item already exists with the name given in *name*.

sec_rgy_server_unavailable

   The DCE registry server is unavailable.

error_status_ok

   The call was successful.

Related Information

Functions: **sec_intro(3sec)**, **sec_rgy_acct_add(3sec)**, **sec_rgy_pgo_delete(3sec)**, **sec_rgy_pgo_rename(3sec)**, **sec_rgy_pgo_replace(3sec)**.

sec_rgy_pgo_add_member

Purpose   Adds a person to a group or organization

Synopsis   **#include <dce/pgo.h>**

void sec_rgy_pgo_add_member(
          sec_rgy_handle_t *context,*
          sec_rgy_domain_t *name_domain,*
          sec_rgy_name_t *go_name,*
          sec_rgy_name_t *person_name,*
          error_status_t *status);

Parameters

Input

context   An opaque handle bound to a registry server. Use **sec_rgy_site_-open( )** to acquire a bound handle.

name_domain This variable identifies the type of the person, group, or organization (PGO) item identified by the given name. The valid values are as follows:

          sec_rgy_domain_group
                    The *go_name* parameter identifies a group.

          sec_rgy_domain_org
                    The *go_name* parameter identifies an organization.

go_name   A character string (type **sec_rgy_name_t**) containing the name of the group or organization to which the specified person will be added.

person_name A character string (type **sec_rgy_name_t**) containing the name of the person to be added to the membership list of the group or organization specified by *go_name*.

Output

status   A pointer to the completion status. On successful completion, the routine returns **error_status_ok**. Otherwise, it returns an error.

Description

The **sec_rgy_pgo_add_member( )** routine adds a member to the membership list of a group or organization in the registry database.

Permissions Required

The **sec_rgy_pgo_add_member( )** routine requires the **M** (**Member_list**) permission on the group or organization item specified by *go_name*. If *go_name* specifies a group, the routine also requires the **g** (**groups**) permission on the principal *person_name*.

Notes

An account can be added to the registry database only when all its constituent PGO items are already in the database, and the appropriate membership relationships between them are established. For example, to establish an account with person name **tom**, group name **writers**, and organization name **hp**, all three names must exist as independent PGO items in the database. Furthermore, **tom** must be a member of **writers**, which must be a member of **hp**. (See the **sec_rgy_acct_add( )** routine to add an account to the registry.)

Files

/usr/include/dce/pgo.idl
The **idl** file from which **dce/pgo.h** was derived.

Errors

sec_rgy_not_authorized
The client program is not authorized to add members to the specified group or organization.

sec_rgy_bad_domain
An invalid domain was specified. A member can be added only to a group or organization, not a person.

sec_rgy_object_not_found
The registry server could not find the specified name.

sec_rgy_server_unavailable
The DCE registry server is unavailable.

error_status_ok
The call was successful.

Related Information

Functions: **sec_intro(3sec)**, **sec_rgy_pgo_add(3sec)**,
sec_rgy_pgo_delete_member(3sec), **sec_rgy_pgo_get_members(3sec)**,
sec_rgy_pgo_is_member(3sec).

sec_rgy_pgo_delete

Purpose   Deletes a PGO item from the registry database

Synopsis   **#include <dce/pgo.h>**

void sec_rgy_pgo_delete(
> **sec_rgy_handle_t** *context*,
> **sec_rgy_domain_t** *name_domain*,
> **sec_rgy_name_t** *name*,
> **error_status_t** **status*);

Parameters

Input

context   An opaque handle bound to a registry server. Use **sec_rgy_site_-open( )** to acquire a bound handle.

name_domain This variable identifies the type of principal, group, or organization (PGO) item identified by the given name. The valid values are as follows:

> **sec_rgy_domain_person**
> > The name identifies a principal.

> **sec_rgy_domain_group**
> > The name identifies a group.

> **sec_rgy_domain_org**
> > The name identifies an organization.

name   A pointer to a **sec_rgy_name_t** character string containing the name of the PGO item to be deleted.

Output

status   A pointer to the completion status. On successful completion, the routine returns **error_status_ok**. Otherwise, it returns an error.

sec_rgy_pgo_delete(3sec)

Description

The **sec_rgy_pgo_delete**( ) routine deletes a PGO item from the registry database. Any account depending on the deleted PGO item is also deleted.

Permissions Required

The **sec_rgy_pgo_delete**( ) routine requires the following permissions:

- The **d** (**delete**) permission on the parent directory that contains the the PGO item to be deleted.

- The **D** (**Delete_object**) permission on the PGO item itself.

Files   **/usr/include/dce/pgo.idl**
                The **idl** file from which **dce/pgo.h** was derived.

Errors   **sec_rgy_not_authorized**
                The client program is not authorized to delete the specified item.

                sec_rgy_object_not_found
                The registry server could not find the specified item.

                sec_rgy_server_unavailable
                The DCE registry server is unavailable.

                error_status_ok
                The call was successful.

Related Information

Functions: **sec_intro(3sec)**, **sec_rgy_pgo_add(3sec)**.

sec_rgy_pgo_delete_member

Purpose   Deletes a member of a group or organization

Synopsis   **#include <dce/pgo.h>**

void sec_rgy_pgo_delete_member(
  sec_rgy_handle_t *context,*
  sec_rgy_domain_t *name_domain,*
  sec_rgy_name_t *go_name,*
  sec_rgy_name_t *person_name,*
  error_status_t **status);*

Parameters

Input

context An opaque handle bound to a registry server. Use **sec_rgy_site_-open( )** to acquire a bound handle.

name_domain This variable identifies the type of the person, group, or organization (PGO) item identified by the given name. The valid values are as follows:

  sec_rgy_domain_group
    The *go_name* parameter identifies a group.

  sec_rgy_domain_org
    The *go_name* parameter identifies an organization.

go_name A character string (type **sec_rgy_name_t**) containing the name of the group or organization from which the specified person will be deleted.

person_name A character string (type **sec_rgy_name_t**) containing the name of the person to be deleted from the membership list of the group or organization specified by *go_name*.

Output

status A pointer to the completion status. On successful completion, the routine returns **error_status_ok**. Otherwise, it returns an error.

sec_rgy_pgo_delete_member(3sec)

Description

The **sec_rgy_pgo_delete_member( )** routine deletes a member from the membership list of a group or organization. Any accounts in which the person holds the deleted group or organization membership are also deleted.

Permissions Required

The **sec_rgy_pgo_delete_member( )** routine requires the **M** (**Member_list**) permission on the group or organization item specified by *go_name*.

Files   **/usr/include/dce/pgo.idl**

The **idl** file from which **dce/pgo.h** was derived.

Errors   **sec_rgy_not_authorized**

The client program is not authorized to delete the specified member.

sec_rgy_bad_domain

An invalid domain was specified. Members can exist only for groups and organizations, not for persons.

sec_rgy_object_not_found

The specified group or organization was not found.

sec_rgy_server_unavailable

The DCE registry server is unavailable.

error_status_ok

The call was successful.

Related Information

Functions: **sec_intro(3sec)**, **sec_rgy_pgo_add(3sec)**, **sec_rgy_pgo_add_member**.

sec_rgy_pgo_get_by_eff_unix_num

Purpose   Returns the name and data for a PGO item identified by its effective UNIX number

Synopsis   **#include <dce/pgo.h>**

> **void sec_rgy_pgo_get_by_eff_unix_num(**
>   **sec_rgy_handle_t** *context***,**
>   **sec_rgy_domain_t** *name_domain***,**
>   **sec_rgy_name_t** *scope***,**
>   **signed32** *unix_id***,**
>   **boolean32** *allow_aliases***,**
>   **sec_rgy_cursor_t** **item_cursor***,**
>   **sec_rgy_pgo_item_t** **pgo_item***,**
>   **sec_rgy_name_t** *name***,**
>   **boolean32** **overridden***,**
>   **error_status_t** **status***);**

Parameters

Input

context   An opaque handle bound to a registry server. Use **sec_rgy_site_-open( )** to acquire a bound handle.

name_domain   This variable identifies the type of the principal, group, or organization (PGO) item identified by the given name. The valid values are as follows:

sec_rgy_domain_person
    The UNIX number identifies a principal.

sec_rgy_domain_group
    The UNIX number identifies a group.

Note that this function does *not* support the value **sec_rgy_domain_org**.

scope   A character string (type **sec_rgy_name_t**) containing the scope of the desired search. The registry database is designed to accommodate a tree-structured name hierarchy. The scope of a search is the name of the branch under which the search takes place. For example, all names in a registry might start with **/alpha**, and be divided further into **/beta** or **/gamma**. To search only the part of the database under **/beta**, the scope of the search would be **/alpha/beta**, and any resulting PGO items would have names beginning with this string. Note that these naming conventions need not have anything to do with group or organization PGO item membership lists.

unix_id   The UNIX number of the desired registry PGO item.

allow_aliases A **boolean32** value indicating whether to search for a primary PGO item, or whether the search can be satisfied with an alias. If TRUE, the routine returns the next entry found for the PGO item. If FALSE, the routine returns only the primary entry.

Input/Output

item_cursor   An opaque pointer indicating a specific PGO item entry in the registry database. The **sec_rgy_pgo_get_next( )** routine returns the PGO item indicated by *item_cursor*, and advances the cursor to point to the next item in the database. When the end of the list of entries is reached, the routine returns the value **sec_rgy_no_more_entries** in the *status* parameter. Use **sec_rgy_cursor_reset( )** to reset the cursor.

Output

pgo_item   A pointer to a **sec_rgy_pgo_item_t** structure to receive the data for the returned PGO item. The data in this structure includes the PGO item's name, UUID, UNIX number (if any), and administrative data, such as whether the item, if a principal, may have a concurrent group set. The data is as it appears in the registry, for that UNIX number, even though some of the fields may have been overridden locally.

name   A pointer to a **sec_rgy_name_t** character string containing the returned name for the PGO item. This string might contain a local override value if the supplied UNIX number is found in the **passwd_override** or **group_override** file.

overridden   A pointer to a **boolean32** value indicating whether or not the supplied UNIX number has an entry in the local override file (**passwd_override** or **group_override**).

status   A pointer to the completion status. On successful completion, the routine returns **error_status_ok**. Otherwise, it returns an error.

Description

The **sec_rgy_pgo_get_by_eff_unix_num( )** routine returns the name and data for a PGO item. The desired item is identified by its type (domain) and its UNIX number.

This routine is similar to the **sec_rgy_pgo_get_by_unix_num( )** routine. The difference between the routines is that **sec_rgy_pgo_get_by_eff_unix_num( )** first searches the local override files for the respective *name_domain* for a match with the supplied UNIX number. If an override match is found, and an account or group name is found in that entry, then that name is used to obtain PGO data from the registry and the value of the *overridden* parameter is set to TRUE.

The *item_cursor* parameter specifies the starting point for the search through the registry database. It provides an automatic place holder in the database. The routine automatically updates this variable to point to the next PGO item after the returned item. The returned cursor location can be supplied on a subsequent database access call that also uses a PGO item cursor.

Permissions Required

The **sec_rgy_pgo_get_by_eff_unix_num( )** routine requires the **r** (**read**) permission on the PGO item to be viewed.

Cautions

There are several different types of cursors used in the registry application programmer interface (API). Some cursors point to PGO items, others point to members in a membership list, and others point to account data. Do not use a cursor for one sort of object in a call expecting another sort of object. For example, you cannot use the same cursor on a call to **sec_rgy_acct_get_projlist( )** and **sec_rgy_pgo_get_next( )**. The behavior in this case is undefined.

Furthermore, cursors are specific to a server. A cursor pointing into one replica of the registry database is useless as a pointer into another replica.

Use **sec_rgy_cursor_reset( )** to renew a cursor for use with another call or for another server.

sec_rgy_pgo_get_by_eff_unix_num(3sec)

Files /usr/include/dce/pgo.idl
> The **idl** file from which **dce/pgo.h** was derived.

group_override
> The local group override file.

passwd_override
> The local password override file.

Errors **sec_rgy_no_more_entries**
> The cursor is at the end of the list of PGO items.

sec_rgy_object_not_found
> The specified PGO item was not found.

sec_rgy_server_unavailable
> The DCE registry server is unavailable.

error_status_ok
> The call was successful.

Related Information

Functions: **sec_intro(3sec)**, **sec_rgy_cursor_reset(3sec)**,
sec_rgy_pgo_add(3sec), **sec_rgy_pgo_get_by_id(3sec)**,
sec_rgy_pgo_get_by_name(3sec), **sec_rgy_pgo_get_by_unix_num(3sec)**,
sec_rgy_pgo_get_next(3sec), **sec_rgy_pgo_id_to_name(3sec)**,
sec_rgy_pgo_id_to_unix_num(3sec), **sec_rgy_pgo_name_to_id(3sec)**,
sec_rgy_pgo_unix_num_to_id(3sec).

sec_rgy_pgo_get_by_id

Purpose   Returns the name and data for a PGO item identified by its UUID

Synopsis   #include <dce/pgo.h>

void sec_rgy_pgo_get_by_id(
        sec_rgy_handle_t *context*,
        sec_rgy_domain_t *name_domain*,
        sec_rgy_name_t *scope*,
        uuid_t **item_id*,
        boolean32 *allow_aliases*,
        sec_rgy_cursor_t **item_cursor*,
        sec_rgy_pgo_item_t **pgo_item*,
        sec_rgy_name_t *name*,
        error_status_t **status*);

Parameters

Input

context   An opaque handle bound to a registry server. Use **sec_rgy_site_-open( )** to acquire a bound handle.

name_domain This variable identifies the type of the principal, group, or organization (PGO) item identified by the given name. The valid values are as follows:

sec_rgy_domain_person
        The UUID identifies a principal.

sec_rgy_domain_group
        The UUID identifies a group.

sec_rgy_domain_org
        The UUID identifies an organization.

scope   A character string (type **sec_rgy_name_t**) containing the scope of
the desired search. The registry database is designed to
accommodate a tree-structured name hierarchy. The scope of a
search is the name of the branch under which the search takes place.
For example, all names in a registry might start with **/alpha**, and be
divided further into **/beta** or **/gamma**. To search only the part of the
database under **/beta**, the scope of the search would be **/alpha/beta**,
and any resulting PGO items would have names beginning with this
string. Note that these naming conventions need not have anything
to do with group or organization PGO item membership lists.

item_id   A pointer to the **uuid_t** variable containing the UUID (Unique
Universal Identifier) of the desired PGO item.

allow_aliases   A **boolean32** value indicating whether to search for a primary PGO
item, or whether the search can be satisfied with an alias. If TRUE,
the routine returns the next entry found for the PGO item. If
FALSE, the routine returns only the primary entry.

Input/Output

item_cursor   An opaque pointer indicating a specific PGO item entry in the
registry database. The **sec_rgy_pgo_get_by_id( )** routine returns
the PGO item indicated by *item_cursor*, and advances the cursor to
point to the next item in the database. When the end of the list of
entries is reached, the routine returns **sec_rgy_no_more_entries** in
the *status* parameter. Use **sec_rgy_cursor_reset( )** to reset the
cursor.

Output

pgo_item   A pointer to a **sec_rgy_pgo_item_t** structure to receive the data for
the returned PGO item. The data in this structure includes the PGO
item's name, UUID, UNIX number (if any), and administrative data,
such as whether the item, if a principal, may have a concurrent
group set.

name   A pointer to a **sec_rgy_name_t** character string containing the
returned name for the PGO item.

status   A pointer to the completion status. On successful completion, the
routine returns **error_status_ok**. Otherwise, it returns an error.

Description

The **sec_rgy_pgo_get_by_id( )** routine returns the name and data for a PGO item. The desired item is identified by its type (domain) and its UUID.

The *item_cursor* parameter specifies the starting point for the search through the registry database. It provides an automatic place holder in the database. The routine automatically updates this variable to point to the next PGO item after the returned item. The returned cursor location can be supplied on a subsequent database access call that also uses a PGO item cursor.

Permissions Required

The **sec_rgy_pgo_get_by_id( )** routine requires the **r** (**read**) permission on the PGO item to be viewed.

Cautions

There are several different types of cursors used in the registry application programmer interface (API). Some cursors point to PGO items, others point to members in a membership list, and others point to account data. Do not use a cursor for one sort of object in a call expecting another sort of object. For example, you cannot use the same cursor on a call to **sec_rgy_acct_get_projlist( )** and **sec_rgy_pgo_get_next( )**. The behavior in this case is undefined.

Furthermore, cursors are specific to a server. A cursor pointing into one replica of the registry database is useless as a pointer into another replica.

Use **sec_rgy_cursor_reset( )** to renew a cursor for use with another call or for another server.

Files

/usr/include/dce/pgo.idl
    The **idl** file from which **dce/pgo.h** was derived.

Errors

sec_rgy_no_more_entries
    The cursor is at the end of the list of PGO items.

sec_rgy_object_not_found
    The specified PGO item was not found.

sec_rgy_server_unavailable
    The DCE registry server is unavailable.

error_status_ok
    The call was successful.

sec_rgy_pgo_get_by_id(3sec)

Related Information

Functions: **sec_intro(3sec)**, **sec_rgy_cursor_reset(3sec)**,
sec_rgy_pgo_add(3sec), **sec_rgy_pgo_get_by_name(3sec)**,
sec_rgy_pgo_get_by_unix_num(3sec), **sec_rgy_pgo_get_next(3sec)**,
sec_rgy_pgo_id_to_name(3sec), **sec_rgy_pgo_id_to_unix_num(3sec)**,
sec_rgy_pgo_name_to_id(3sec), **sec_rgy_pgo_unix_num_to_id(3sec)**.

sec_rgy_pgo_get_by_name

Purpose   Returns the data for a named PGO item

Synopsis   #include <dce/pgo.h>

void sec_rgy_pgo_get_by_name(
        sec_rgy_handle_t *context*,
        sec_rgy_domain_t *name_domain*,
        sec_rgy_name_t *pgo_name*,
        sec_rgy_cursor_t **item_cursor*,
        sec_rgy_pgo_item_t **pgo_item*,
        error_status_t **status*);

Parameters

Input

context   An opaque handle bound to a registry server. Use **sec_rgy_site_-open**( ) to acquire a bound handle.

name_domain This variable identifies the type of the principal, group, or organization (PGO) item identified by the given name. The valid values are as follows:

sec_rgy_domain_person
                The name identifies a principal.

sec_rgy_domain_group
                The name identifies a group.

sec_rgy_domain_org
                The name identifies an organization.

pgo_name   A character string (type **sec_rgy_name_t**) containing the name of the principal, group, or organization to search for.

Input/Output

item_cursor   An opaque pointer indicating a specific PGO item entry in the registry database. The **sec_rgy_pgo_get_by_name( )** routine returns the PGO item indicated by *item_cursor*, and advances the cursor to point to the next item in the database. When the end of the list of entries is reached, the routine returns the value **sec_rgy_no_more_entries** in the *status* parameter. Use **sec_rgy_cursor_reset( )** to reset the cursor.

Output

pgo_item   A pointer to a **sec_rgy_pgo_item_t** structure to receive the data for the returned PGO item. The data in this structure includes the PGO item's name, UUID, UNIX number (if any), and administrative data, such as whether the item, if a principal, may have a concurrent group set.

status   A pointer to the completion status. On successful completion, the routine returns **error_status_ok**. Otherwise, it returns an error.

Description

The **sec_rgy_pgo_get_by_name( )** routine returns the data for a named PGO item from the registry database. The desired item is identified by its type (*name_domain*) and name.

The *item_cursor* parameter specifies the starting point for the search through the registry database. It provides an automatic place holder in the database. The routine automatically updates this variable to point to the next PGO item after the returned item. The returned cursor location can be supplied on a subsequent database access call that also uses a PGO item cursor.

Permissions Required

The **sec_rgy_pgo_get_by_name( )** routine requires the **r** (**read**) permission on the PGO item to be viewed.

Cautions

There are several different types of cursors used in the registry application programmer interface (API). Some cursors point to PGO items, others point to members in a membership list, and others point to account data. Do not use a cursor for one sort of object in a call expecting another sort of object. For example, you cannot use the same cursor on a call to **sec_rgy_acct_get_projlist( )** and **sec_rgy_pgo_get_next( )**. The behavior in this case is undefined.

Furthermore, cursors are specific to a server. A cursor pointing into one replica of the registry database is useless as a pointer into another replica.

Use **sec_rgy_cursor_reset( )** to renew a cursor for use with another call or for another server.

Files   **/usr/include/dce/pgo.idl**
> The **idl** file from which **dce/pgo.h** was derived.

Errors   **sec_rgy_no_more_entries**
> The cursor is at the end of the list of PGO items.

sec_rgy_object_not_found
> The specified PGO item was not found.

sec_rgy_server_unavailable
> The DCE registry server is unavailable.

error_status_ok
> The call was successful.

Related Information

Functions: **sec_intro(3sec)**, **sec_rgy_cursor_reset(3sec)**, **sec_rgy_pgo_add(3sec)**, **sec_rgy_pgo_get_by_id(3sec)**, **sec_rgy_pgo_get_by_unix_num(3sec)**, **sec_rgy_pgo_get_next(3sec)**, **sec_rgy_pgo_id_to_name(3sec)**, **sec_rgy_pgo_id_to_unix_num(3sec)**, **sec_rgy_pgo_name_to_id(3sec)**, **sec_rgy_pgo_unix_num_to_id(3sec)**.

sec_rgy_pgo_get_by_unix_num

Purpose   Returns the name and data for a PGO item identified by its UNIX ID

Synopsis   **#include <dce/pgo.h>**

    void sec_rgy_pgo_get_by_unix_num(
        sec_rgy_handle_t *context,*
        sec_rgy_domain_t *name_domain,*
        sec_rgy_name_t *scope,*
        signed32 *unix_id,*
        boolean32 *allow_aliases,*
        sec_rgy_cursor_t **item_cursor,*
        sec_rgy_pgo_item_t **pgo_item,*
        sec_rgy_name_t *name,*
        error_status_t **status);*

Parameters

Input

    context   An opaque handle bound to a registry server. Use **sec_rgy_site_-open( )** to acquire a bound handle.

    name_domain This variable identifies the type of the principal, group, or organization (PGO) item identified by the given name. The valid values are as follows:

        sec_rgy_domain_person
            The UNIX number identifies a principal.

        sec_rgy_domain_group
            The UNIX number identifies a group.

        sec_rgy_domain_org
            The UNIX number identifies an organization.

scope   A character string (type **sec_rgy_name_t**) containing the scope of the desired search. The registry database is designed to accommodate a tree-structured name hierarchy. The scope of a search is the name of the branch under which the search takes place. For example, all names in a registry might start with **/alpha**, and be divided further into **/beta** or **/gamma**. To search only the part of the database under **/beta**, the scope of the search would be **/alpha/beta**, and any resulting PGO items would have names beginning with this string. Note that these naming conventions need not have anything to do with group or organization PGO item membership lists.

unix_id   The UNIX number of the desired registry PGO item.

allow_aliases   A **boolean32** value indicating whether to search for a primary PGO item, or whether the search can be satisfied with an alias. If TRUE, the routine returns the next entry found for the PGO item. If FALSE, the routine returns only the primary entry.

Input/Output

item_cursor   An opaque pointer indicating a specific PGO item entry in the registry database. The **sec_rgy_pgo_get_by_unix_num**( ) routine returns the PGO item indicated by *item_cursor*, and advances the cursor to point to the next item in the database. When the end of the list of entries is reached, the routine returns the value **sec_rgy_no_more_entries** in the *status* parameter. Use **sec_rgy_cursor_reset**( ) to reset the cursor.

Output

pgo_item   A pointer to a **sec_rgy_pgo_item_t** structure to receive the data for the returned PGO item. The data in this structure includes the PGO item's name, UUID, UNIX number (if any), and administrative data, such as whether the item, if a principal, may have a concurrent group set.

name   A pointer to a **sec_rgy_name_t** character string containing the returned name for the PGO item.

status   A pointer to the completion status. On successful completion, the routine returns **error_status_ok**. Otherwise, it returns an error.

Description

The **sec_rgy_pgo_get_by_unix_num**( ) routine returns the name and data for a PGO item. The desired item is identified by its type (domain) and its UNIX number.

The *item_cursor* parameter specifies the starting point for the search through the registry database. It provides an automatic place holder in the database. The routine automatically updates this variable to point to the next PGO item after the returned item. The returned cursor location can be supplied on a subsequent database access call that also uses a PGO item cursor.

Permissions Required

The **sec_rgy_pgo_get_by_unix_num**( ) routine requires the **r** (**read**) permission on the PGO item to be viewed.

Cautions

There are several different types of cursors used in the registry application programmer interface (API). Some cursors point to PGO items, others point to members in a membership list, and others point to account data. Do not use a cursor for one sort of object in a call expecting another sort of object. For example, you cannot use the same cursor on a call to **sec_rgy_acct_get_projlist**( ) and **sec_rgy_pgo_get_next**( ). The behavior in this case is undefined.

Furthermore, cursors are specific to a server. A cursor pointing into one replica of the registry database is useless as a pointer into another replica.

Use **sec_rgy_cursor_reset**( ) to renew a cursor for use with another call or for another server.

Files

/usr/include/dce/pgo.idl
The **idl** file from which **dce/pgo.h** was derived.

Errors

sec_rgy_no_more_entries
The cursor is at the end of the list of PGO items.

sec_rgy_object_not_found
The specified PGO item was not found.

sec_rgy_server_unavailable
The DCE registry server is unavailable.

error_status_ok
The call was successful.

Related Information

Functions: **sec_intro(3sec)**, **sec_rgy_cursor_reset(3sec)**,
sec_rgy_pgo_add(3sec), **sec_rgy_pgo_get_by_id(3sec)**,
sec_rgy_pgo_get_by_name(3sec), **sec_rgy_pgo_get_next(3sec)**,
sec_rgy_pgo_id_to_name(3sec), **sec_rgy_pgo_id_to_unix_num(3sec)**,
sec_rgy_pgo_name_to_id(3sec), **sec_rgy_pgo_unix_num_to_id(3sec)**.

sec_rgy_pgo_get_members

Purpose   Returns the membership list for a specified group or organization or returns the set of groups in which the specified principal is a member

Synopsis   **#include <dce/pgo.h>**

void sec_rgy_pgo_get_members(
         sec_rgy_handle_t *context,*
         sec_rgy_domain_t *name_domain,*
         sec_rgy_name_t *go_name,*
         sec_rgy_cursor_t **member_cursor,*
         signed32 *max_members,*
         sec_rgy_member_t *member_list*[ ],
         signed32 **number_supplied,*
         signed32 **number_members,*
         error_status_t *status);

Parameters

Input

context   An opaque handle bound to a **secd** server. Use **sec_rgy_site_-open( )** to acquire a bound handle.

name_domain This variable specifies whether *go_name* identifies a principal, group, or organization. The valid values are as follows:

sec_rgy_domain_group
         The *go_name* parameter identifies a group.

sec_rgy_domain_org
         The *go_name* parameter identifies an organization.

sec_rgy_domain_person
         The *go_name* parameter identifies an principal.

go_name　　　　　A character string (type **sec_rgy_name_t**) that contains the name of a group, organization, or principal. If *go_name* is the name of a group or organization, the call returns the group's or organization's member list. If *go_name* is the name of a principal, the call returns a list of all groups in which the principal is a member. (Contrast this with the **sec_rgy_acct_get_proj** call, which returns only those groups in which the principal is a member and that have been marked to be included in the principal's project list.)

max_members

A **signed32** variable containing the allocated dimension of the *member_list*[ ] array. This is the maximum number of members or groups that can be returned by a single call.

Input/Output

member_cursor

An opaque pointer to a specific entry in the membership list or list of groups. The returned list begins with the entry specified by *member_cursor*. Upon return, the cursor points to the next entry after the last one returned. If there are no more entries, the routine returns the value **sec_rgy_no_more_entries** in the *status* parameter. Use **sec_rgy_cursor_reset( )** to reset the cursor to the beginning of the list.

Output

member_list[ ]

An array of character strings to receive the returned member or group names. The size allocated for the array is given by *max_number*. If this value is less than the total number of members or group names, multiple calls must be made to return all of the members or groups.

number_supplied

A pointer to a **signed32** variable to receive the number of members or groups actually returned in *member_list*[ ].

number_members

A pointer to a **signed32** variable to receive the total number of members or groups. If this number is greater than *number_supplied*, multiple calls to **sec_rgy_pgo_get_members( )** are necessary. Use the *member_cursor* parameter to coordinate successive calls.

status   A pointer to the completion status. On successful completion, *status* is assigned **error_status_ok**. Otherwise, it returns an error.

Description

The **sec_rgy_pgo_get_members( )** routine returns a list of the members in the specified group or organization, or a list of groups in which a specified principal is a member.

The *member_cursor* parameter specifies the starting point for the search through the registry database. It provides an automatic place holder in the database. The routine automatically updates *member_cursor* to point to the next member or group (if any) after the returned list. If not all of the members or groups are returned, the updated cursor can be supplied on successive calls to return the remainder of the list.

Permissions Required

The **sec_rgy_pgo_get_members( )** routine requires the **r** (**read**) permission on the group, organization, or principal object specified by *go_name*.

Cautions

There are several different types of cursors used in the registry application programmer interface (API). Some cursors point to PGO items, others point to members in a membership list, and others point to account data. Do not use a cursor for one sort of object in a call expecting another sort of object. For example, you cannot use the same cursor on a call to **sec_rgy_acct_get_projlist( )** and **sec_rgy_pgo_get_next( )**. The behavior in this case is undefined.

Furthermore, cursors are specific to a server. A cursor pointing into one replica of the registry database is useless as a pointer into another replica.

Use **sec_rgy_cursor_reset( )** to renew a cursor for use with another call or for another server.

Return Values

The routine returns

- The names of the groups or members in *member_list*[ ]

- The number of members or groups returned by the call in *number_supplied*

- The total number of members in the group or organization, or the total number of groups in which the principal is a member in *number_members*

Files   **/usr/include/dce/pgo.idl**

The **idl** file from which **dce/pgo.h** was derived.

Errors   **sec_rgy_no_more_entries**

The cursor points to the end of the membership list for a group or organization or to the end of the list of groups for a principal.

sec_rgy_object_not_found

The specified group, organization, or principal could not be found.

sec_rgy_server_unavailable

The DCE registry server is unavailable.

error_status_ok

The call was successful.

Related Information

Functions: **sec_intro(3sec), sec_rgy_acct_get_proj(3sec), sec_rgy_cursor_reset(3sec), sec_rgy_pgo_add_member(3sec), sec_rgy_pgo_is_member(3sec)**.

sec_rgy_pgo_get_next

Purpose   Returns the next PGO item in the registry database

Synopsis   **#include <dce/pgo.h>**

void sec_rgy_pgo_get_next(
        sec_rgy_handle_t *context*,
        sec_rgy_domain_t *name_domain*,
        sec_rgy_name_t *scope*,
        sec_rgy_cursor_t **item_cursor*,
        sec_rgy_pgo_item_t **pgo_item*,
        sec_rgy_name_t *name*,
        error_status_t **status*);

Parameters

Input

context   An opaque handle bound to a registry server. Use **sec_rgy_site_-
open( )** to acquire a bound handle.

name_domain This variable identifies the type of the principal, group, or
organization (PGO) item identified by the given name. The valid
values are as follows:

    sec_rgy_domain_person
        Returns the next principal item.

    sec_rgy_domain_group
        Returns the next group item.

    sec_rgy_domain_org
        Returns the next organization item.

    scope   A character string (type **sec_rgy_name_t**) containing the scope of the desired search. The registry database is designed to accommodate a tree-structured name hierarchy. The scope of a search is the name of the branch under which the search takes place. For example, all names in a registry might start with **/alpha**, and be divided further into **/beta** or **/gamma**. To search only the part of the database under **/beta**, the scope of the search would be **/alpha/beta**, and any resulting PGO items would have names beginning with this string. Note that these naming conventions need not have anything to do with group or organization PGO item membership lists.

Input/Output

    item_cursor   An opaque pointer indicating a specific PGO item entry in the registry database. The **sec_rgy_pgo_get_next( )** routine returns the PGO item indicated by *item_cursor*, and advances the cursor to point to the next item in the database. When the end of the list of entries is reached, the routine returns the value **sec_rgy_no_more_-entries** in the *status* parameter. Use **sec_rgy_cursor_reset( )** to reset the cursor.

Output

    pgo_item   A pointer to a **sec_rgy_pgo_item_t** structure to receive the data for the returned PGO item. The data in this structure includes the PGO item's name, UUID, UNIX number (if any), and administrative data, such as whether the item, if a principal, may have a concurrent group set.

    name   A pointer to a **sec_rgy_name_t** character string containing the name of the returned PGO item.

    status   A pointer to the completion status. On successful completion, the routine returns **error_status_ok**. Otherwise, it returns an error.

Description

The **sec_rgy_pgo_get_next( )** routine returns the data and name for the PGO in the registry database indicated by *item_cursor*. It also advances the cursor to point to the next PGO item in the database. Successive calls to this routine return all the PGO items in the database of the specified type (given by *name_domain*), in storage order.

The PGO data consists of the following:

- The universal unique identifier (UUID) of the PGO item.

- The UNIX number for the PGO item.

- The quota for subaccounts.

- The full name of the PGO item.

- Flags indicating whether

    — A principal item is an alias.

    — The PGO item can be deleted.

    — A principal item can have a concurrent group set.

    — A group item can appear on a concurrent group set.

Permissions Required

The **sec_rgy_pgo_get_next( )** routine requires the **r** (**read**) permission on the PGO item to be viewed.

Cautions   There are several different types of cursors used in the registry application programmer interface (API). Some cursors point to PGO items, others point to members in a membership list, and others point to account data. Do not use a cursor for one sort of object in a call expecting another sort of object. For example, you cannot use the same cursor on a call to **sec_rgy_acct_get_projlist( )** and **sec_rgy_pgo_get_next( )**. The behavior in this case is undefined.

Furthermore, cursors are specific to a server. A cursor pointing into one replica of the registry database is useless as a pointer into another replica.

Use **sec_rgy_cursor_reset( )** to renew a cursor for use with another call or for another server.

Return Values

The routine returns the data for the returned PGO item in *pgo_item* and the name in *name*.

Files   **/usr/include/dce/pgo.idl**
              The **idl** file from which **dce/pgo.h** was derived.

Errors   **sec_rgy_no_more_entries**
              The cursor is at the end of the list of PGO items.

              sec_rgy_server_unavailable
              The DCE registry server is unavailable.

              error_status_ok
              The call was successful.

Related Information

Functions: **sec_intro(3sec)**, **sec_rgy_cursor_reset(3sec)**,
sec_rgy_pgo_add(3sec), **sec_rgy_pgo_get_by_id(3sec)**,
sec_rgy_pgo_get_by_name(3sec), **sec_rgy_pgo_get_by_unix_num(3sec)**,
sec_rgy_pgo_id_to_unix_num(3sec), **sec_rgy_pgo_unix_num_to_id(3sec)**.

sec_rgy_pgo_id_to_name

Purpose   Returns the name for a PGO item identified by its UUID

Synopsis   **#include <dce/pgo.h>**

void sec_rgy_pgo_id_to_name(
        sec_rgy_handle_t *context,*
        sec_rgy_domain_t *name_domain,*
        uuid_t **item_id,*
        sec_rgy_name_t *pgo_name,*
        error_status_t **status*);

Parameters

Input

context   An opaque handle bound to a registry server. Use **sec_rgy_site_-open**( ) to acquire a bound handle.

name_domain This variable identifies the type of the principal, group, or organization (PGO) item identified by the given name. The valid values are as follows:

    sec_rgy_domain_person
        The *item_id* parameter identifies a principal.

    sec_rgy_domain_group
        The *item_id* parameter identifies a group.

    sec_rgy_domain_org
        The *item_id* parameter identifies an organization.

item_id   A pointer to the **uuid_t** variable containing the input UUID (unique universal identifier).

Output

pgo_name   A character string (type **sec_rgy_name_t**) containing the name of the principal, group, or organization with the input UUID.

status   A pointer to the completion status. On successful completion, the routine returns **error_status_ok**. Otherwise, it returns an error.

Description

The **sec_rgy_pgo_id_to_name( )** routine returns the name of the PGO item having the specified UUID.

Permissions Required

The **sec_rgy_pgo_id_to_name( )** routine requires at least one permission of any kind on the PGO item to be viewed.

Files /usr/include/dce/pgo.idl
The **idl** file from which **dce/pgo.h** was derived.

Errors sec_rgy_object_not_found
No item with the specified UUID could be found.

sec_rgy_server_unavailable
The DCE registry server is unavailable.

error_status_ok
The call was successful.

Related Information

Functions: **sec_intro(3sec)**, **sec_rgy_pgo_add(3sec)**,
sec_rgy_pgo_get_by_id(3sec), **sec_rgy_pgo_get_by_name(3sec)**,
sec_rgy_pgo_get_by_unix_num(3sec), **sec_rgy_pgo_id_to_unix_num(3sec)**,
sec_rgy_pgo_name_to_id(3sec), **sec_rgy_pgo_unix_num_to_id(3sec)**.

sec_rgy_pgo_id_to_unix_num

Purpose   Returns the UNIX number for a PGO item identified by its UUID

Synopsis   **#include <dce/pgo.h>**

void sec_rgy_pgo_id_to_unix_num(
        sec_rgy_handle_t *context,*
        sec_rgy_domain_t *name_domain,*
        uuid_t **item_id,*
        signed32 **item_unix_id,*
        error_status_t **status);*

Parameters

Input

context   An opaque handle bound to a registry server. Use **sec_rgy_site_-
                 open( )** to acquire a bound handle.

name_domain This variable identifies the type of the principal, group, or
                 organization (PGO) item identified by the given name. The valid
                 values are as follows:

sec_rgy_domain_person
                 The *item_id* parameter identifies a principal.

sec_rgy_domain_group
                 The *item_id* parameter identifies a group.

sec_rgy_domain_org
                 The *item_id* parameter identifies an organization.

item_id   A pointer to the **uuid_t** variable containing the input UUID (unique
                 universal identifier).

Output

item_unix_id A pointer to the **signed32** variable to receive the returned UNIX
                 number for the PGO item.

status   A pointer to the completion status. On successful completion, the
                 routine returns **error_status_ok**. Otherwise, it returns an error.

Description

The **sec_rgy_pgo_id_to_unix_num**( ) routine returns the UNIX number for the PGO item having the specified UUID.

Files

/usr/include/dce/pgo.idl
> The **idl** file from which **dce/pgo.h** was derived.

Errors

sec_rgy_object_not_found
> No item with the specified UUID could be found.

sec_rgy_server_unavailable
> The DCE registry server is unavailable.

error_status_ok
> The call was successful.

Related Information

Functions: **sec_intro(3sec), sec_rgy_pgo_add(3sec),
sec_rgy_pgo_get_by_id(3sec), sec_rgy_pgo_get_by_name(3sec),
sec_rgy_pgo_get_by_unix_num(3sec), sec_rgy_pgo_id_to_name(3sec),
sec_rgy_pgo_name_to_id(3sec), sec_rgy_pgo_unix_num_to_id(3sec).**

sec_rgy_pgo_is_member

Purpose   Checks group or organization membership

Synopsis   **#include <dce/pgo.h>**

boolean32 sec_rgy_pgo_is_member(
      sec_rgy_handle_t *context*,
      sec_rgy_domain_t *name_domain*,
      sec_rgy_name_t *go_name*,
      sec_rgy_name_t *person_name*,
      error_status_t **status*);

Parameters

Input

context   An opaque handle bound to a registry server. Use **sec_rgy_site_-
open( )** to acquire a bound handle.

name_domain   This variable identifies the type of the principal, group, or
organization (PGO) item identified by the given name. The valid
values are as follows:

    sec_rgy_domain_group
        The *go_name* parameter identifies a group.

    sec_rgy_domain_org
        The *go_name* parameter identifies an organization.

go_name   A character string (type **sec_rgy_name_t**) containing the name of
the group or organization whose membership list is in question.

person_name   A character string (type **sec_rgy_name_t**) containing the name of
the principal whose membership in the group or organization
specified by *go_name* is in question.

Output

status   A pointer to the completion status. On successful completion, *status*
is assigned **error_status_ok**. Otherwise, it returns an error.

Description

The **sec_rgy_pgo_is_member**( ) routine tests whether the specified principal is a member of the named group or organization.

Permissions Required

The **sec_rgy_pgo_is_member**( ) routine requires the **t** (**test**) permission on the group or organization item specified by *go_name*.

Return Values

The routine returns TRUE if the principal is a member of the named group or organization. If the principal is not a member, the routine returns FALSE.

Files   /usr/include/dce/pgo.idl

The **idl** file from which **dce/pgo.h** was derived.

Errors   sec_rgy_object_not_found

The named group or organization was not found.

sec_rgy_server_unavailable

The DCE registry server is unavailable.

error_status_ok

The call was successful.

Related Information

Functions: **sec_intro(3sec)**, **sec_rgy_pgo_add_member(3sec)**, **sec_rgy_pgo_get_members(3sec)**.

sec_rgy_pgo_name_to_id

Purpose   Returns the UUID for a named PGO item

Synopsis   **#include <dce/pgo.h>**

void sec_rgy_pgo_name_to_id(
        sec_rgy_handle_t *context*,
        sec_rgy_domain_t *name_domain*,
        sec_rgy_name_t *pgo_name*,
        uuid_t **item_id*,
        error_status_t **status*);

Parameters

Input

context   An opaque handle bound to a registry server. Use **sec_rgy_site_-open( )** to acquire a bound handle.

name_domain This variable identifies the type of the principal, group, or organization (PGO) item identified by the given name. The valid values are as follows:

    sec_rgy_domain_person
        The name identifies a principal.

    sec_rgy_domain_group
        The name identifies a group.

    sec_rgy_domain_org
        The name identifies an organization.

pgo_name   A character string (type **sec_rgy_name_t**) containing the name of the principal, group, or organization whose UUID is desired.

Output

item_id   A pointer to the **uuid_t** variable containing the UUID (unique universal identifier) of the resulting PGO item.

status   A pointer to the completion status. On successful completion, the routine returns **error_status_ok**. Otherwise, it returns an error.

Description

The **sec_rgy_pgo_name_to_id**( ) routine returns the UUID associated with the named PGO item.

Files

/usr/include/dce/pgo.idl
> The **idl** file from which **dce/pgo.h** was derived.

Errors

sec_rgy_object_not_found
> The specified PGO item could not be found.

sec_rgy_server_unavailable
> The DCE registry server is unavailable.

error_status_ok
> The call was successful.

Related Information

Functions: **sec_intro(3sec)**, **sec_rgy_pgo_add(3sec)**,
sec_rgy_pgo_get_by_id(3sec), **sec_rgy_pgo_get_by_name(3sec)**,
sec_rgy_pgo_get_by_unix_num(3sec), **sec_rgy_pgo_id_to_name(3sec)**,
sec_rgy_pgo_id_to_unix_num(3sec), **sec_rgy_pgo_unix_num_to_id(3sec)**.

sec_rgy_pgo_name_to_unix_num

Purpose   Returns the UNIX number for a PGO item identified by its name

Synopsis   **#include <dce/pgo.h>**

void sec_rgy_pgo_name_to_unix_num(
        sec_rgy_handle_t *context,*
        sec_rgy_domain_t *name_domain,*
        sec_rgy_name_t *pgo_name,*
        signed32 **item_unix_id,*
        error_status_t **status*);

Parameters

Input

context   An opaque handle bound to a registry server. Use **sec_rgy_site_-open( )** to acquire a bound handle.

name_domain This variable identifies the type of the principal, group, or organization (PGO) item identified by the given name. The valid values are as follows:

    sec_rgy_domain_person
        The name identifies a principal.

    sec_rgy_domain_group
        The name identifies a group.

    sec_rgy_domain_org
        The name identifies an organization.

pgo_name   A character string containing the name of the PGO item in question.

Output

item_unix_id A pointer to the **signed32** variable to receive the returned UNIX number for the PGO item.

status   A pointer to the completion status. On successful completion, the routine returns **error_status_ok**. Otherwise, it returns an error.

Description

The **sec_rgy_pgo_name_to_unix_num( )** routine returns the UNIX number for the PGO item having the specified name.

Files

/usr/include/dce/pgo.idl

The **idl** file from which **dce/pgo.h** was derived.

Errors

sec_rgy_object_not_found

No item with the specified UUID could be found.

sec_rgy_server_unavailable

The DCE registry server is unavailable.

error_status_ok

The call was successful.

Related Information

Functions: **sec_intro(3sec)**, **sec_rgy_pgo_add(3sec)**, **sec_rgy_pgo_get_by_id(3sec)**, **sec_rgy_pgo_get_by_name(3sec)**, **sec_rgy_pgo_get_by_unix_num(3sec)**, **sec_rgy_pgo_id_to_name(3sec)**, **sec_rgy_pgo_name_to_id(3sec)**, **sec_rgy_pgo_unix_num_to_id(3sec)**.

sec_rgy_pgo_rename

Purpose   Changes the name of a PGO item in the registry database

Synopsis   **#include <dce/pgo.h>**

void sec_rgy_pgo_rename(
            sec_rgy_handle_t *context*,
            sec_rgy_domain_t *name_domain*,
            sec_rgy_name_t *old_name*,
            sec_rgy_name_t *new_name*,
            error_status_t **status*);

Parameters

Input

context   An opaque handle bound to a registry server. Use **sec_rgy_site_-open( )** to acquire a bound handle.

name_domain   This variable identifies the type of the principal, group, or organization (PGO) item identified by the given name. The valid values are as follows:

> **sec_rgy_domain_person**
>   The name identifies a principal.
>
> **sec_rgy_domain_group**
>   The name identifies a group.
>
> **sec_rgy_domain_org**
>   The name identifies an organization.

old_name   A pointer to a **sec_rgy_name_t** character string containing the existing name of the PGO item.

new_name   A pointer to a **sec_rgy_name_t** character string containing the new name for the PGO item.

Output

status   A pointer to the completion status. On successful completion, the routine returns **error_status_ok**. Otherwise, it returns an error.

Description

The **sec_rgy_pgo_rename( )** routine renames a PGO item in the registry database.

Permissions Required

If the **sec_rgy_pgo_rename( )** routine is performing a rename within a directory, it requires the **n** (**name**) permission on the old name of the PGO item. If the routine is performing a move between directories, it requires the following permissions:

- The **d** (**delete**) permission on the parent directory that contains the PGO item.

- The **n** (**name**) permission on the old name of the PGO item.

- The **i** (**insert**) permission on the parent directory in which the PGO item is to be added under the new name.

Files

/usr/include/dce/pgo.idl
The **idl** file from which **dce/pgo.h** was derived.

Errors

sec_rgy_not_authorized
The client program is not authorized to change the name of the specified PGO item.

sec_rgy_object_not_found
The registry server could not find the specified PGO item.

sec_rgy_server_unavailable
The DCE registry server is unavailable.

error_status_ok
The call was successful.

Related Information

Functions: **sec_intro(3sec)**, **sec_rgy_pgo_add(3sec)**, **sec_rgy_pgo_replace(3sec)**.

sec_rgy_pgo_replace

Purpose   Replaces the data in an existing PGO item

Synopsis   **#include <dce/pgo.h>**

void sec_rgy_pgo_replace(
sec_rgy_handle_t *context*,
sec_rgy_domain_t *name_domain*,
sec_rgy_name_t *pgo_name*,
sec_rgy_pgo_item_t **pgo_item*,
error_status_t **status*);

Parameters

Input

context   An opaque handle bound to a registry server. Use **sec_rgy_site_-open**( ) to acquire a bound handle.

name_domain This variable identifies the type of the principal, group, or organization (PGO) item identified by the given name. The valid values are as follows:

sec_rgy_domain_person
The name identifies a principal.

sec_rgy_domain_group
The name identifies a group.

sec_rgy_domain_org
The name identifies an organization.

pgo_name   A character string (type **sec_rgy_name_t**) containing the name of the principal, group, or organization whose data is to be replaced.

pgo_item   A pointer to a **sec_rgy_pgo_item_t** structure containing the new data for the PGO item. The data in this structure includes the PGO item's name, UUID, UNIX number (if any), and administrative data, such as whether the item, if a principal, may have a concurrent group set.

Output

status   A pointer to the completion status. On successful completion, the routine returns **error_status_ok**. Otherwise, it returns an error.

Description

The **sec_rgy_pgo_replace( )** routine replaces the data associated with a PGO item in the registry database.

The UNIX ID and UUID of a PGO item cannot be replaced. To change the UNIX ID or UUID, the existing PGO item must be deleted and a new PGO item added in its place. The one exception to this rule is that the UNIX ID can be replaced in the PGO item for a cell principal. The reason for this exception is that the UUID for a cell principal does not contain an embedded UNIX ID.

Permissions Required

The **sec_rgy_pgo_replace( )** routine requires at least one of the following permissions:

- The **m** (**mgmt_info**) permission on the PGO item, if **quota** or **flags** is being set.

- The **f** (**fullname**) permission on the PGO item, if **fullname** is being set.

Files   **/usr/include/dce/pgo.idl**
The **idl** file from which **dce/pgo.h** was derived.

Errors   **sec_rgy_not_authorized**
The client program is not authorized to replace the specified PGO item.

sec_rgy_object_not_found
No PGO item was found with the given name.

sec_rgy_unix_id_changed
The UNIX number of the PGO item was changed.

sec_rgy_server_unavailable
The DCE registry server is unavailable.

error_status_ok
The call was successful.

sec_rgy_pgo_replace(3sec)

Related Information

Functions: **sec_intro(3sec)**, **sec_rgy_pgo_add(3sec)**, **sec_rgy_pgo_delete(3sec)**, **sec_rgy_pgo_rename(3sec)**.

sec_rgy_pgo_unix_num_to_id

Purpose   Returns the UUID for a PGO item identified by its UNIX number

Synopsis   **#include <dce/pgo.h>**

void sec_rgy_pgo_unix_num_to_id(
        sec_rgy_handle_t *context*,
        sec_rgy_domain_t *name_domain*,
        signed32 *item_unix_id*,
        uuid_t *item_id,
        error_status_t *status);

Parameters

Input

context   An opaque handle bound to a registry server. Use **sec_rgy_site_-open( )** to acquire a bound handle.

name_domain This variable identifies the type of the principal, group, or organization (PGO) item identified by the given name. The valid values are as follows:

    sec_rgy_domain_person
        The *item_unix_id* parameter identifies a principal.

    sec_rgy_domain_group
        The *item_unix_id* parameter identifies a group.

    sec_rgy_domain_org
        The *item_unix_id* parameter identifies an organization.

item_unix_id The **signed32** variable containing the UNIX number for the PGO item.

Output

item_id   A pointer to the **uuid_t** variable containing the UUID (unique universal identifier) of the resulting PGO item.

sec_rgy_pgo_unix_num_to_id(3sec)

status   A pointer to the completion status. On successful completion, the routine returns **error_status_ok**. Otherwise, it returns an error.

Description

The **sec_rgy_pgo_unix_num_to_id**( ) routine returns the universal unique identifier (UUID) for a PGO item that has the specified UNIX number.

Files

/usr/include/dce/pgo.idl
The **idl** file from which **dce/pgo.h** was derived.

Errors

sec_rgy_object_not_found
No item with the specified UNIX number could be found.

sec_rgy_server_unavailable
The DCE registry server is unavailable.

error_status_ok
The call was successful.

Related Information

Functions: **sec_intro(3sec)**, **sec_rgy_pgo_add(3sec)**,
sec_rgy_pgo_get_by_id(3sec), **sec_rgy_pgo_get_by_name(3sec)**,
sec_rgy_pgo_get_by_unix_num(3sec), **sec_rgy_pgo_id_to_name(3sec)**,
sec_rgy_pgo_id_to_unix_num(3sec), **sec_rgy_pgo_name_to_id(3sec)**.

sec_rgy_pgo_unix_num_to_name

Purpose   Returns the name for a PGO item identified by its UNIX number

Synopsis   **#include <dce/pgo.h>**

void sec_rgy_pgo_unix_num_to_name(
sec_rgy_handle_t *context*,
sec_rgy_domain_t *name_domain*,
signed32 *item_unix_id*,
sec_rgy_name_t *pgo_name*,
error_status_t **status*);

Parameters

Input

context   An opaque handle bound to a registry server. Use **sec_rgy_site_-
open( )** to acquire a bound handle.

name_domain The type of the principal, group, or organization (PGO) item
identified by *item_unix_id*. Valid values are as follows:

sec_rgy_domain_person
The *item_unix_id* parameter identifies a principal.

sec_rgy_domain_group
The *item_unix_id* parameter identifies a group.

sec_rgy_domain_org
The *item_unix_id* parameter identifies an
organization.

item_unix_id The **signed32** variable containing the UNIX number for the PGO
item.

Output

pgo_name   A character string containing the name of the PGO item in question.

status   A pointer to the completion status. On successful completion, the
routine returns **error_status_ok**. Otherwise, it returns an error.

sec_rgy_pgo_unix_num_to_name(3sec)

Description

The **sec_rgy_pgo_unix_num_to_name( )** routine returns the name for a PGO item that has the specified UNIX number.

Permissions Required

The **sec_rgy_pgo_unix_num_to_name( )** routine requires at least one permission of any kind on the PGO item identified by *item_unix_id*.

Files

/usr/include/dce/pgo.idl
The **idl** file from which **dce/pgo.h** was derived.

Errors

sec_rgy_object_not_found
No item with the specified UNIX number could be found.

sec_rgy_server_unavailable
The DCE registry server is unavailable.

error_status_ok
The call was successful.

Related Information

Functions: **sec_intro(3sec)**, **sec_rgy_pgo_add(3sec)**,
sec_rgy_pgo_get_by_id(3sec), **sec_rgy_pgo_get_by_name(3sec)**,
sec_rgy_pgo_get_by_unix_num(3sec), **sec_rgy_pgo_id_to_name(3sec)**,
sec_rgy_pgo_id_to_unix_num(3sec), **sec_rgy_pgo_name_to_id(3sec)**.

sec_rgy_plcy_get_effective

Purpose   Returns the effective policy for an organization

Synopsis   **#include <dce/policy.h>**

> **void sec_rgy_plcy_get_effective(**
> **sec_rgy_handle_t** *context,*
> **sec_rgy_name_t** *organization,*
> **sec_rgy_plcy_t** **policy_data,*
> **error_status_t** **status);*

Parameters

Input

context   An opaque handle bound to a registry server. Use **sec_rgy_site_-open( )** to acquire a bound handle.

organization   A character string (type **sec_rgy_name_t**) containing the name of the organization for which the policy data is to be returned. If this string is empty, the routine returns the registry's policy data.

Output

policy_data   A pointer to the **sec_rgy_plcy_t** structure to receive the authentication policy. This structure contains the minimum length of a user's password, the lifetime of a password, the expiration date of a password, the lifetime of the entire account, and some flags describing limitations on the password spelling.

status   A pointer to the completion status. On successful completion, the routine returns **error_status_ok**. Otherwise, it returns an error.

Description

The **sec_rgy_plcy_get_effective( )** routine returns the effective policy for the specified organization.

The effective policy data is the most restrictive combination of the registry and the organization policies.

sec_rgy_plcy_get_effective(3sec)

The policy data consists of the following:

- The password expiration date. This is the date on which account passwords will expire.

- The minimum length allowed for account passwords.

- The period of time (life span) for which account passwords will be valid.

- The period of time (life span) for which accounts will be valid.

- Flags indicating whether account passwords can consist entirely of spaces or entirely of alphanumeric characters.

Permissions Required

The **sec_rgy_plcy_get_effective( )** routine requires the **r** (**read**) permission on the policy object from which the data is to be returned. If an organization is specified, the routine also requires the **r** (**read**) permission on the organization.

Notes

If no organization is specified, the routine returns the registry's policy data. To return the effective policy, an organization must be specified. This is because the routine compares the registry's policy data with that of the organization to determine which is more restrictive.

Files

/usr/include/dce/policy.idl
The **idl** file from which **dce/policy.h** was derived.

Errors

sec_rgy_object_not_found
The registry server could not find the specified organization.

sec_rgy_server_unavailable
The DCE registry server is unavailable.

error_status_ok
The call was successful.

Related Information

Functions: **sec_intro(3sec)**, **sec_rgy_plcy_get_info(3sec)**, **sec_rgy_plcy_set_info(3sec)**.

sec_rgy_plcy_get_info

Purpose   Returns the policy for an organization

Synopsis   **#include <dce/policy.h>**

void sec_rgy_plcy_get_info(
        sec_rgy_handle_t *context,*
        sec_rgy_name_t *organization,*
        sec_rgy_plcy_t **policy_data,*
        error_status_t **status*);

Parameters

Input

> *context*   An opaque handle bound to a registry server. Use **sec_rgy_site_-open( )** to acquire a bound handle.
>
> *organization*   A character string (type **sec_rgy_name_t**) containing the name of the organization for which the policy data is to be returned. If this string is empty, the routine returns the registry's policy data.

Output

> *policy_data*   A pointer to the **sec_rgy_plcy_t** structure to receive the authentication policy. This structure contains the minimum length of a user's password, the lifetime of a password, the expiration date of a password, the lifetime of the entire account, and some flags describing limitations on the password spelling.
>
> *status*   A pointer to the completion status. On successful completion, the routine returns **error_status_ok**. Otherwise, it returns an error.

Description

The **sec_rgy_plcy_get_info( )** routine returns the policy data for the specified organization. If no organization is specified, the registry's policy data is returned.

sec_rgy_plcy_get_info(3sec)

The policy data consists of the following:

- The password expiration date. This is the date on which account passwords will expire.

- The minimum length allowed for account passwords.

- The period of time (life span) for which account passwords will be valid.

- The period of time (life span) for which accounts will be valid.

- Flags indicating whether account passwords can consist entirely of spaces or entirely of alphanumeric characters.

Permissions Required

The **sec_rgy_plcy_get_info( )** routine requires the **r** (**read**) permission on the policy object or organization from which the data is to be returned.

Notes The returned policy may not be in effect if the overriding registry authorization policy is more restrictive. (See the **sec_rgy_auth_plcy_get_effective( )** routine.)

Files **/usr/include/dce/policy.idl**
The **idl** file from which **dce/policy.h** was derived.

Errors **sec_rgy_object_not_found**
The registry server could not find the specified organization.

sec_rgy_server_unavailable
The DCE registry server is unavailable.

error_status_ok
The call was successful.

Related Information

Functions: **sec_intro(3sec)**, **sec_rgy_plcy_get_effective_info(3sec)**, **sec_rgy_plcy_set_info(3sec)**.

sec_rgy_plcy_set_info

Purpose   Sets the policy for an organization

Synopsis   **#include <dce/policy.h>**

void sec_rgy_plcy_set_info(
          sec_rgy_handle_t *context*,
          sec_rgy_name_t *organization*,
          sec_rgy_plcy_t **policy_data*,
          error_status_t **status*);

Parameters

Input

context   An opaque handle bound to a registry server. Use **sec_rgy_site_-open( )** to acquire a bound handle.

organization   A character string (type **sec_rgy_name_t**) containing the name of the organization for which the policy data is to be returned. If this string is empty, the routine sets the registry's policy data.

policy_data   A pointer to the **sec_rgy_plcy_t** structure containing the authentication policy. This structure contains the minimum length of a user's password, the lifetime of a password, the expiration date of a password, the lifetime of the entire account, and some flags describing limitations on the password spelling.

Output

status   A pointer to the completion status. On successful completion, the routine returns **error_status_ok**. Otherwise, it returns an error.

Description

The **sec_rgy_plcy_set_info( )** routine sets the authentication policy for a specified organization. If no organization is specified, the registry's policy data is set.

Policy data can be returned or set for individual organizations and for the registry as a whole.

sec_rgy_plcy_set_info(3sec)

Permissions Required

The **sec_rgy_plcy_set_info( )** routine requires the **m** (**mgmt_info**) permission on the policy object or organization for which the data is to be set.

Notes

The policy set on an account may be less restrictive than the policy set for the registry as a whole. In this case, the changes in policy have no effect, since the effective policy is the most restrictive combination of the organization and registry authentication policies. (See the **sec_rgy_auth_plcy_get_effective( )** routine.)

Files

/usr/include/dce/policy.idl

The **idl** file from which **dce/policy.h** was derived.

Errors

sec_rgy_not_authorized

The user is not authorized to perform this operation.

sec_rgy_object_not_found

The registry server could not find the specified organization.

sec_rgy_server_unavailable

The DCE registry server is unavailable.

error_status_ok

The call was successful.

Related Information

Functions: **sec_intro(3sec)**, **sec_rgy_plcy_get_effective(3sec)**, **sec_rgy_plcy_get_info(3sec)**.

sec_rgy_properties_get_info

Purpose   Returns registry properties

Synopsis   **#include <dce/policy.h>**

            void sec_rgy_properties_get_info(
                sec_rgy_handle_t *context,*
                sec_rgy_properties_t **properties,*
                error_status_t **status*)**;**

Parameters

Input

    context   An opaque handle bound to a registry server. Use **sec_rgy_site_-
open( )** to acquire a bound handle.

Output

    properties   A pointer to a **sec_rgy_properties_t** structure to receive the
returned property information. A registry's property information
contains information such as the default and minimum lifetime and
other restrictions on privilege attribute certificates, the realm
authentication name, and whether or not this replica of the registry
supports updates.

    status   A pointer to the completion status. On successful completion, the
routine returns **error_status_ok**. Otherwise, it returns an error.

Description

The **sec_rgy_properties_get_info( )** routine returns a list of the registry properties.

The property information consists of the following:

read_version A stamp specifying the earliest version of the registry server
software that can read from this registry.

write_version

                A stamp specifying the earliest version of the registry server
software that can write to this registry.

minimum_ticket_lifetime

The minimum period of time for which an authentication ticket remains valid.

default_certificate_lifetime

The default period of time for which an authentication certificate (ticket-granting ticket) remains valid. A process can request an authentication certificate with a longer lifetime. Note that the maximum lifetime for an authentication certificate cannot exceed the lifetime established by the effective policy for the requesting account.

low_unix_id_person

The lowest UNIX ID that can be assigned to a principal in the registry.

low_unix_id_group

The lowest UNIX ID that can be assigned to a group in the registry.

low_unix_id_org

The lowest UNIX ID that can be assigned to an organization in the registry.

max_unix_id The maximum UNIX ID that can be used for any item in the registry.

realm A character string naming the cell controlled by this registry.

realm_uuid The UUID of the cell controlled by this registry.

flags Flags include the following:

sec_rgy_prop_readonly

If TRUE, the registry database is read-only.

sec_rgy_prop_auth_cert_unbound

If TRUE, privilege attribute certificates can be generated for use at any site.

sec_rgy_prop_shadow_password

If FALSE, passwords can be distributed over the network. If this flag is TRUE, passwords will be stripped from the returned data to the **sec_rgy_acct_lookup( )**, and other calls that return an account's encoded password.

sec_rgy_prop_embedded_unix_id
All registry UUIDs contain embedded UNIX IDs. This implies that the UNIX ID of any registry object cannot be changed, since UUIDs are immutable.

Permissions Required

The **sec_rgy_properties_get_info( )** routine requires the **r** (**read**) permission on the policy object from which the property information is to be returned.

Files **/usr/include/dce/policy.idl**
The **idl** file from which **dce/policy.h** was derived.

Errors **sec_rgy_server_unavailable**
The DCE registry server is unavailable.

error_status_ok
The call was successful.

Related Information

Functions: **sec_intro(3sec)**, **sec_rgy_properties_set_info(3sec)**.

sec_rgy_properties_set_info

Purpose   Sets registry properties

Synopsis   **#include <dce/policy.h>**

        void sec_rgy_properties_set_info(
            sec_rgy_handle_t *context*,
            sec_rgy_properties_t *properties,
            error_status_t *status);

Parameters

Input

    context   The registry server handle. An opaque handle bound to a registry server. Use **sec_rgy_site_open( )** to acquire a bound handle.

    properties   A pointer to a **sec_rgy_properties_t** structure containing the registry property information to be set. A registry's property information contains information such as the default and minimum lifetime and other restrictions on privilege attribute certificates, the realm authentication name, and whether or not this replica of the registry supports updates.

Output

    status   A pointer to the completion status. On successful completion, the routine returns **error_status_ok**. Otherwise, it returns an error.

Description

The **sec_rgy_properties_set_info( )** routine sets the registry properties.

The property information consists of the following:

read_version A stamp specifying the earliest version of the registry server software that can read from this registry.

write_version

    A stamp specifying the earliest version of the registry server software that can write to this registry.

minimum_ticket_lifetime
> The minimum period of time for which an authentication ticket remains valid.

default_certificate_lifetime
> The default period of time for which an authentication certificate (ticket-granting ticket) remains valid. A process can request an authentication certificate with a longer lifetime. Note that the maximum lifetime for an authentication certificate cannot exceed the lifetime established by the effective policy for the requesting account.

low_unix_id_person
> The lowest UNIX ID that can be assigned to a principal in the registry.

low_unix_id_group
> The lowest UNIX ID that can be assigned to a group in the registry.

low_unix_id_org
> The lowest UNIX ID that can be assigned to an organization in the registry.

max_unix_id The maximum UNIX ID that can be used for any item in the registry.

realm A character string naming the cell controlled by this registry.

realm_uuid The UUID of the cell controlled by this registry.

flags Flags include the following:

> **sec_rgy_prop_readonly**
>> If TRUE, the registry database is read-only.

> **sec_rgy_prop_auth_cert_unbound**
>> If TRUE, privilege attribute certificates can be generated for use at any site.

> **sec_rgy_prop_shadow_password**
>> If FALSE, passwords can be distributed over the network. If this flag is TRUE, passwords will be stripped from the returned data to the **sec_rgy_acct_lookup( )**, and other calls that return an account's encoded password.

sec_rgy_properties_set_info(3sec)

> **sec_rgy_prop_embedded_unix_id**
>> All registry UUIDs contain embedded UNIX IDs. This implies that the UNIX ID of any registry object cannot be changed, since UUIDs are immutable.

Permissions Required

The **sec_rgy_properties_set_info( )** routine requires the **m** (**mgmt_info**) permission on the policy object for which the property information is to be set.

Files

/usr/include/dce/policy.idl
>> The **idl** file from which **dce/policy.h** was derived.

Errors

sec_rgy_not_authorized
>> The user is not authorized to change the registry properties.

sec_rgy_server_unavailable
>> The DCE registry server is unavailable.

error_status_ok
>> The call was successful.

Related Information

Functions: **sec_intro(3sec)**, **sec_rgy_properties_get_info(3sec)**.

sec_rgy_site_bind

Purpose   Binds to a registry site

Synopsis   **#include <dce/binding.h>**

void sec_rgy_site_bind(
        unsigned_char_t **site_name,*
        sec_rgy_bind_auth_info_t **auth_info,*
        sec_rgy_handle_t **context,*
        error_status_t **status*);

Parameters

Input

> *site_name*   A character string (type **unsigned_char_t**) containing the name of the registry site to bind to. Supply this name in any of the following forms:
>
> > • To randomly choose a site to bind to in the named cell, specify a cell name (for example, **/.../r_d.com** or **/.:** for the local cell)
> >
> > • To bind to a specific site in a specific cell, specify either the site's global name or the site's network address.
>
> *auth_info*   A pointer to the **sec_rgy_bind_auth_info_t** structure that identifies the authentication protocol, protection level, and authorization protocol to use in establishing the binding. (See the **rpc_binding_-set_auth_info( )** routine). If the **sec_rgy_bind_auth_info_t** structure specifies authenticated rpc, the caller must have established a valid network identity for this call to succeed.

Output

> *context*   A pointer to a **sec_rgy_handle_t** variable. Upon return, this contains a registry server handle indicating (bound to) the desired registry site.

status   A pointer to the completion status. On successful completion, the
                  routine returns **error_status_ok**. Otherwise, it returns an error.

Description

The **sec_rgy_site_bind( )** call binds to a registry site at the security level specified
by the *auth_info* parameter. The *site_name* parameter identifies the registry to use.
If *site_name* is NULL, or a zero-length string, a registry site in the local cell is
selected by the client agent.

Notes

Like the **sec_rgy_site_bind_query( )** routine, this routine binds arbitrarily to either
an update or query site. Although update sites can accept queries, query sites
cannot accept updates. To specifically select an update site, use **sec_rgy_site_-
bind_update( )**.

Files

/usr/include/dce/binding.idl
          The **idl** file from which **dce/binding.h** was derived.

Errors

sec_login_s_no_current_context
          The caller does not have a valid network login context.

sec_rgy_server_unavailable
          The DCE registry server is unavailable.

error_status_ok
          The call was successful.

Related Information

Functions: **sec_intro(3sec)**, **sec_rgy_cell_bind(3sec)**, **sec_rgy_site_open(3sec)**.

sec_rgy_site_bind_query

Purpose　　Binds to a registry query site

Synopsis　　**#include <dce/binding.h>**

void sec_rgy_site_bind_query(
　　　　unsigned_char_t **site_name***,**
　　　　sec_rgy_bind_auth_info_t **auth_info***,**
　　　　sec_rgy_handle_t **context***,**
　　　　error_status_t **status***);**

Parameters

Input

site_name　　A character string (type **unsigned_char_t**) containing the name of the registry site to bind to. Supply this name in any of the following forms:

- To randomly choose a site to bind to in the named cell, specify a cell name (for example, **/.../r_d.com** or **/.:** for the local cell)

- To bind to a specific site in a specific cell, specify either the site's global name or the site's network address

auth_info　　A pointer to the **sec_rgy_bind_auth_info_t** structure that identifies the authentication protocol, protection level, and authorization protocol to use in establishing the binding. (See the **rpc_binding_-set_auth_info( )** routine). If the **sec_rgy_bind_auth_info_t** structure specifies authenticated rpc, the caller must have established a valid network identity for this call to succeed.

Output

context　　A pointer to a **sec_rgy_handle_t** variable. Upon return, this contains a registry server handle indicating (bound to) the desired registry site.

sec_rgy_site_bind_query(3sec)

      status   A pointer to the completion status. On successful completion, the routine returns **error_status_ok**. Otherwise, it returns an error.

Description

The **sec_rgy_site_bind_query**( ) routine binds to a registry query site at an arbitrary level of security. A registry query site is a satellite server that operates on a periodically updated copy of the main registry database. To change the registry database, it is necessary to change a registry update site, which then automatically updates its associated query sites. No changes can be made directly to a registry query database.

The *site_name* parameter identifies the query site to use. If *site_name* is NULL, or a zero-length string, a query site in the local cell is selected by the client agent.

The handle for the associated registry server is returned in *context*.

Notes

Like **sec_rgy_bind_open**( ) routine, this routine binds arbitrarily to either an update or query site. Although update sites can accept queries, query sites cannot accept updates. To specifically select an update site, use **sec_rgy_site_bind_-update**( ).

Files

/usr/include/dce/binding.idl
      The **idl** file from which **dce/binding.h** was derived.

Errors

sec_login_s_no_current_context
      The caller does not have a valid network login context.

sec_rgy_server_unavailable
      The DCE registry server is unavailable.

error_status_ok
      The call was successful.

Related Information

Functions: **sec_intro(3sec)**, **sec_rgy_site_bind(3sec)**, **sec_rgy_site_open(3sec)**.

sec_rgy_site_bind_update

Purpose   Binds to a registry update site

Synopsis   **#include <dce/binding.h>**

void sec_rgy_site_bind_update(
> **unsigned_char_t ****site_name**,*
> **sec_rgy_bind_auth_info_t ****auth_info**,*
> **sec_rgy_handle_t ****context**,*
> **error_status_t ****status**);*

Parameters

Input

site_name   A character string (type **unsigned_char_t**) containing the name of the registry site to bind to. Supply this name in any of the following forms:

- To choose the update site to bind to in the named cell, specify a cell name (for example, **/.../r_d.com** or **/.:** for the local cell)

- To start the search for the update site at a specific replica in the replica's cell, specify either the replica's global name or the replica's network address

auth_info   A pointer to the **sec_rgy_bind_auth_info_t** structure that identifies the authentication protocol, protection level, and authorization protocol to use in establishing the binding. (See the **rpc_binding_-set_auth_info( )** routine). If the **sec_rgy_bind_auth_info_t** structure specifies authenticated rpc, the caller must have established a valid network identity for this call to succeed.

Output

context   A pointer to a **sec_rgy_handle_t** variable. Upon return, this contains a registry server handle indicating (bound to) the desired registry site.

status   A pointer to the completion status. On successful completion, the routine returns **error_status_ok**. Otherwise, it returns an error.

Description

The **sec_rgy_site_bind_update()** routine binds to a registry update site. A registry update site is a master server that may control several satellite (query) servers. To change the registry database, it is necessary to change a registry update site, which then automatically updates its associated query sites. No changes can be made directly to a registry query database.

The *site_name* parameter identifies either the cell in which to find the update site or the replica at which to start the search for the update site. If *site_name* is NULL, or a zero-length string, an update site in the local cell is selected by the client agent.

The handle for the associated registry server is returned in *context*. The handle is to an update site. Use this registry context handle in subsequent calls that update or query the the registry database (for example, the **sec_rgy_pgo_add()** or **sec_rgy_acct_lookup()** call).

Files

/usr/include/dce/binding.idl
> The **idl** file from which **dce/binding.h** was derived.

Errors

sec_login_s_no_current_context
> The caller does not have a valid network login context.

sec_rgy_server_unavailable
> The DCE registry server is unavailable.

error_status_ok
> The call was successful.

Related Information

Functions: **sec_intro(3sec)**, **sec_rgy_site_bind(3sec)**, **sec_rgy_site_open(3sec)**.

sec_rgy_site_binding_get_info

Purpose   Returns information from the registry binding handle

Synopsis   #include <dce/binding.h>

void sec_rgy_site_binding_get_info(
        sec_rgy_handle_t *context*,
        unsigned_char_t **cell_name*,
        unsigned_char_t **server_name*,
        unsigned_char_t **string_binding*,
        sec_rgy_bind_auth_info_t *auth_info*,
        error_status_t *status*);

Parameters

Input

context
A **sec_rgy_handle_t** variable that contains a registry server handle indicating (bound to) the desired registry site. To obtain information on the default binding handle, initialize *context* to **sec_rgy_default_handle**. A valid login context must be set for the process if *context* is set to **sec_rgy_default_handle**; otherwise the error **sec_under_login_s_no_current_context** is returned.

Output

cell_name
The name of the home cell for this registry.

server_name
The name of the node on which the server is resident. This name is either a global name or a network address, depending on the form in which the name was input to the call that bound to the site.

string_binding
A string containing binding information from **sec_rgy_handle_t**.

auth_info
A pointer to the **sec_rgy_bind_auth_info_t** structure that identifies the authentication protocol, protection level, and authorization protocol to use in establishing the binding. (See the **rpc_binding_-set_auth_info**( ) routine).

status
A pointer to the completion status. On successful completion, the routine returns **error_status_ok**. Otherwise, it returns an error.

sec_rgy_site_binding_get_info(3sec)

Description

The **sec_rgy_site_binding_get_info**( ) routine returns the site name and authentication information associated with the *context* parameter. If the context is the default context, the information for the default binding is returned. Passing in a NULL value for any of the output values (except for *status*) will prevent that value from being returned. Memory is allocated for the string returned in the *cell_name*, *server_name*, and *string_binding* parameters. The application calls the **rpc_string_free**( ) routine to deallocate that memory.

Files

/usr/include/dce/binding.idl
The **idl** file from which **dce/binding.h** was derived.

Errors

sec_under_login_s_no_current_context

sec_rgy_server_unavailable
The DCE registry server is unavailable.

error_status_ok
The call was successful.

Related Information

Functions: **sec_intro(3sec)**, **sec_rgy_site_bind(3sec)**, **sec_rgy_site_open(3sec)**.

sec_rgy_site_close

Purpose   Frees the binding handle for a registry server

Synopsis   **#include <dce/binding.h>**

void sec_rgy_site_close(
          sec_rgy_handle_t *context*,
          error_status_t *status);

Parameters

Input

> *context*   An opaque handle indicating (bound to) a registry server. Use **sec_-rgy_site_open( )** to acquire a bound handle.

Output

> *status*   A pointer to the completion status. On successful completion, the routine returns **error_status_ok**. Otherwise, it returns an error.

Description

The **sec_rgy_site_close( )** routine frees the memory occupied by the specified handle and destroys its binding with the registry server.

Notes   A handle cannot be used after it is freed.

Files   **/usr/include/dce/binding.idl**
          The **idl** file from which **dce/binding.h** was derived.

Errors   error_status_ok
          The call was successful.

Related Information

Functions: **sec_intro(3sec)**, **sec_rgy_site_get(3sec)**,
sec_rgy_site_is_readonly(3sec), **sec_rgy_site_open(3sec)**,
sec_rgy_site_open_query(3sec), **sec_rgy_site_open_update(3sec)**.

sec_rgy_site_get

Purpose   Returns the string representation for a bound registry site

Synopsis   **#include <dce/binding.h>**

void sec_rgy_site_get(
    sec_rgy_handle_t *context*,
    **unsigned_char_t ***site_name*,
    **error_status_t ***status*);

Parameters

Input

context   An opaque handle indicating (bound to) a registry server. Use **sec_-rgy_site_open( )** to acquire a bound handle. To obtain information on the default binding handle, initialize *context* to **sec_rgy_default_handle**. A valid login context must be set for the process if *context* is set to **sec_rgy_default_handle**; otherwise the error **sec_under_login_s_no_current_context** is returned.

Output

site_name   A pointer to a character string (type **unsigned_char_t**) containing the returned name of the registry site associated with *context*, the given registry server handle.

The name is either a global name or a network address, depending on the form in which the name was input to the call that bound to the site.

status   A pointer to the completion status. On successful completion, the routine returns **error_status_ok**. Otherwise, it returns an error.

Description

The **sec_rgy_site_get( )** routine returns the name of the registry site associated with the specified handle. If the handle is the default context, the routine returns the name of the default context's site. Memory is allocated for the string returned in the *site_name* parameter. The application calls the **rpc_string_free( )** routine to deallocate that memory.

Notes   To obtain binding information, the use of the **sec_rgy_site_binding_get_info( )** call is recommended in place of this call.

Files   **/usr/include/dce/binding.idl**
                   The **idl** file from which **dce/binding.h** was derived.

Errors   **sec_under_login_s_no_current_context**

              sec_rgy_server_unavailable
                   The requested registry server is not available.

              error_status_ok
                   The call was successful.

Related Information

              Functions: **sec_intro(3sec)**, **sec_rgy_site_open(3sec)**.

sec_rgy_site_is_readonly

Purpose   Checks whether a registry site is read-only

Synopsis   **#include <dce/binding.h>**

boolean32 sec_rgy_site_is_readonly(
          sec_rgy_handle_t *context***);**

Parameters

Input

context   An opaque handle indicating (bound to) a registry server. Use **sec_-rgy_site_open**( ) to acquire a bound handle.

Description

The **sec_rgy_site_is_readonly**( ) routine checks whether the registry site associated with the specified handle is a query site or an update site. A query site is a read-only replica of a master registry database. The update site accepts changes to the registry database, and duplicates the changes in its associated query sites.

Return Values

The routine returns

- TRUE, if the registry site is read-only or if there was an error using the specified handle

- FALSE, if the registry site is an update site

Files   **/usr/include/dce/binding.idl**
          The **idl** file from which **dce/binding.h** was derived.

Related Information

Functions: **sec_intro(3sec), sec_rgy_site_open(3sec),
sec_rgy_site_open_query(3sec).**

sec_rgy_site_open

Purpose   Binds to a registry site

Synopsis   **#include <dce/binding.h>**

        void sec_rgy_site_open(
                unsigned_char_t **site_name*,
                sec_rgy_handle_t **context*,
                error_status_t **status*);

Parameters

Input

site_name   A pointer to a character string (type **unsigned_char_t**) containing the name of the registry site to bind to. Supply this name in any of the following forms:

- To randomly choose a site to bind to in the named cell, specify a cell name (for example, **/.../r_d.com** or **/.:** for the local cell)

- To bind to a specific site in a specific cell, specify either the site's global name or the site's network address

Note that if you specify the name of a specific **secd** to bind to and the name is not valid, the call will bind to a random site in the cell if the specified cell name is valid.

Output

context   A pointer to a **sec_rgy_handle_t** variable. Upon return, this contains a registry server handle indicating (bound to) the desired registry site.

status   A pointer to the completion status. On successful completion, the routine returns **error_status_ok**. Otherwise, it returns an error.

sec_rgy_site_open(3sec)

Description

The **sec_rgy_site_open( )** routine binds to a registry site at the level of security specified in the **rpc_binding_set_auth_info( )** call. The *site_name* parameter identifies the registry to use. If *site_name* is NULL, or a zero-length string, a registry site in the local cell is selected by the client agent. The caller must have established a valid network identity for this call to succeed.

Notes

To bind to a registry site, the use of the **sec_rgy_site_bind( )** call is recommended in place of this call.

Like **sec_rgy_site_open_query( )** routine, this routine binds arbitrarily to either an update or query site. Although update sites can accept queries, query sites cannot accept updates. To specifically select an update site, use **sec_rgy_site_open_-update( )**.

Files
/usr/include/dce/binding.idl
The **idl** file from which **dce/binding.h** was derived.

Errors
sec_login_s_no_current_context
The caller does not have a valid network login context.

sec_rgy_server_unavailable
The requested registry server is not available.

error_status_ok
The call was successful.

Related Information

Functions: **sec_intro(3sec)**, **sec_rgy_site_close(3sec)**, **sec_rgy_site_is_readonly(3sec)**, **sec_rgy_site_open_query(3sec)**, **sec_rgy_site_open_update(3sec)**.

sec_rgy_site_open_query

Purpose   Binds to a registry query site

Synopsis   **#include <dce/binding.h>**

void sec_rgy_site_open_query(
          unsigned_char_t **site_name*,
          sec_rgy_handle_t **context*,
          error_status_t **status*);

Parameters

Input

site_name   A character string (type **unsigned_char_t**) containing the name of
               the registry query site to bind to. Supply this name in any of the
               following forms:

- To randomly choose a site to bind to in the named cell,
  specify a cell name (for example, **/.../r_d.com** or **/.:** for the
  local cell)

- To bind to a specific site in a specific cell, specify either the
  site's global name or the site's network address

Output

context   A pointer to a **sec_rgy_handle_t** variable. Upon return, this
               contains a registry server handle indicating (bound to) the desired
               registry site.

status   A pointer to the completion status. On successful completion, the
               routine returns **error_status_ok**. Otherwise, it returns an error.

Description

The **sec_rgy_site_open_query( )** routine binds to a registry query site. A registry
query site is a satellite server that operates on a periodically updated copy of the
main registry database. To change the registry database, it is necessary to change a
registry update site, which then automatically updates its associated query sites.
No changes can be made directly to a registry query database.

The *site_name* parameter identifies the query site to use. If *site_name* is NULL, or a zero-length string, a query site in the local cell is selected by the client agent.

The handle for the associated registry server is returned in *context*.

The caller must have established a valid network identity for this call to succeed.

Notes   To bind to a registry query site, the use of the **sec_rgy_site_bind_query( )** call is recommended in place of this call.

Like **sec_rgy_site_open( )** routine, this routine binds arbitrarily to either an update or query site. Although update sites can accept queries, query sites cannot accept updates. To specifically select an update site, use **sec_rgy_site_open_update( )**.

Files   **/usr/include/dce/binding.idl**
    The **idl** file from which **dce/binding.h** was derived.

Errors   **sec_login_s_no_current_context**
    The caller does not have a valid network login context.

sec_rgy_server_unavailable
    The DCE registry server is unavailable.

error_status_ok
    The call was successful.

Related Information

Functions: **sec_intro(3sec)**, **sec_rgy_site_close(3sec)**, **sec_rgy_site_get(3sec)**, **sec_rgy_site_is_readonly(3sec)**, **sec_rgy_site_open(3sec)**, **sec_rgy_site_open_update(3sec)**.

sec_rgy_site_open_update

Purpose   Binds to a registry update site

Synopsis   **#include <dce/binding.h>**

void sec_rgy_site_open_update(
        unsigned_char_t **site_name*,
        sec_rgy_handle_t **context*,
        error_status_t **status*);

Parameters

Input

site_name   A character string (type **unsigned_char_t**) containing the name of an update registry site to bind to. Supply this name in any of the following forms:

- To choose the update site to bind to in the named cell, specify a cell name (for example, **/.../r_d.com** or **/.:** for the local cell)

- To start the search for the update site at a specific replica in the replica's cell, specify either the site's global name or the site's network address

Output

context   A pointer to a **sec_rgy_handle_t** variable. Upon return, this contains a registry server handle indicating (bound to) the desired registry site.

status   A pointer to the completion status. On successful completion, the routine returns **error_status_ok**. Otherwise, it returns an error.

sec_rgy_site_open_update(3sec)

Description

The **sec_rgy_site_open_update( )** routine binds to a registry update site. A registry update site is a master server that may control several satellite (query) servers. To change the registry database, it is necessary to change a registry update site, which then automatically updates its associated query sites. No changes can be made directly to a registry query database.

The *site_name* parameter identifies either the cell in which to find the update site or the replica at which to start the search for the update site. If *site_name* is NULL, or a zero-length string, an update site in the local cell is selected by the client agent.

The handle for the associated registry server is returned in *context*. The handle is to an update site. Use this registry context handle in subsequent calls that update or query the the registry database (for example, the **sec_rgy_pgo_add( )** or **sec_rgy_acct_lookup( )** call). The caller must have established a valid network identity for this call to succeed.

Notes

To bind to a registry update site, the use of the **sec_rgy_site_bind_update( )** call is recommended in place of this call.

Files

/usr/include/dce/binding.idl
> The **idl** file from which **dce/binding.h** was derived.

Errors

sec_login_s_no_current_context
> The caller does not have a valid network login context.

sec_rgy_server_unavailable
> The DCE registry server is unavailable.

error_status_ok
> The call was successful.

Related Information

Functions: **sec_intro(3sec), sec_rgy_site_close(3sec), sec_rgy_site_get(3sec), sec_rgy_site_is_readonly(3sec), sec_rgy_site_open(3sec), sec_rgy_site_open_query(3sec)**.

sec_rgy_unix_getgrgid

Purpose   Returns a UNIX style group entry for the account matching the specified group ID

Synopsis   **#include <dce/rgynbase.h>**

void sec_rgy_unix_getgrgid(
        sec_rgy_handle_t *context*,
        signed32 *gid*,
        signed32 *max_number*,
        sec_rgy_cursor_t **item_cursor*,
        sec_rgy_unix_group_t **group_entry*,
        signed32 **number_members*,
        sec_rgy_member_t *member_list*[ ],
        error_status_t **status*);

Parameters

Input

    context   An opaque handle bound to a registry server. Use **sec_rgy_site_-open( )** to acquire a bound handle.

    gid   A 32-bit integer specifying the group ID to match.

    max_number   The maximum number of members to be returned by the call. This must be no larger than the allocated size of the *member_list*[ ] array.

Input/Output

    item_cursor   An opaque pointer indicating a specific PGO item entry in the registry database. The **sec_rgy_unix_getgrgid( )** routine returns the PGO item indicated by *item_cursor*, and advances the cursor to point to the next item in the database. When the end of the list of entries is reached, the routine returns **sec_rgy_no_more_entries**. Use **sec_rgy_cursor_reset( )** to refresh the cursor.

Output

    group_entry   A UNIX style group entry structure returned with information about the account matching *gid*.

number_members
An signed 32-bit integer containing the total number of member names returned in the *member_list*[ ] array.

member_list[ ]
An array of character strings to receive the returned member names. The size allocated for the array is given by *max_number*. If this value is less than the total number of members in the membership list, multiple calls must be made to return all of the members.

status
On successful completion, the routine returns **error_status_ok**. Otherwise, it returns an error.

Description

The **sec_rgy_unix_getgrgid**( ) routine returns the next UNIX group structure that matches the input UNIX group ID. The structure is in the following form:

typedef struct {
  sec_rgy_name_t name;
  signed32 gid;
  sec_rgy_member_buf_t members;
}   sec_rgy_unix_group_t;

The structure includes the following:

- The name of the group.

- The group's UNIX ID.

- A string containing the names of the group members. This string is limited in size by the size of the **sec_rgy_member_buf_t** type defined in **rgynbase.idl**.

The routine also returns an array of member names, limited in size by the *number_members* parameter.

This call is supplied in source code form.

Files
/usr/include/dce/rgynbase.idl
The **idl** file from which **dce/rgybase.h** was derived.

Errors   **sec_rgy_nomore_entries**

The end of the list of entries has been reached.

scc_rgy_server_unavailable

The DCE registry server is unavailable.

error_status_ok

The call was successful.

Related Information

Functions: **sec_intro(3sec)**.

sec_rgy_unix_getgrnam

Purpose   Returns a UNIX style group entry for the account matching the specified group name

Synopsis   **#include <dce/rgynbase.h>**

void sec_rgy_unix_getgrnam(
        sec_rgy_handle_t *context,*
        sec_rgy_name_t *name,*
        signed32 *name_length,*
        signed32 *max_num_members,*
        sec_rgy_cursor_t *item_cursor,*
        sec_rgy_unix_group_t *group_entry,*
        signed32 *number_members,*
        sec_rgy_member_t *member_list*[ ],
        error_status_t **status*);

Parameters

Input

    context   An opaque handle bound to a registry server. Use **sec_rgy_site_-open( )** to acquire a bound handle.

    name   A character string (of type **sec_rgy_name_t**) specifying the group name to be matched.

    name_length   An signed 32-bit integer specifying the length of *name* in characters.

    max_num_members
        The maximum number of members to be returned by the call. This must be no larger than the allocated size of the *member_list*[ ] array.

Input/Output

    item_cursor   An opaque pointer indicating a specific PGO item entry in the registry database. The **sec_rgy_unix_getgrnam( )** routine returns the PGO item indicated by *item_cursor*, and advances the cursor to point to the next item in the database. When the end of the list of entries is reached, the routine returns **sec_rgy_no_more_entries**. Use **sec_rgy_cursor_reset( )** to refresh the cursor.

Output

group_entry   A UNIX style group entry structure returned with information about the account matching *name*.

number_members

An signed 32-bit integer containing the total number of member names returned in the *member_list*[ ] array.

member_list[ ]

An array of character strings to receive the returned member names. The size allocated for the array is given by *max_number*. If this value is less than the total number of members in the membership list, multiple calls must be made to return all of the members.

status   On successful completion, the routine returns **error_status_ok**. Otherwise, it returns an error.

Description

The **sec_rgy_unix_getgrnam( )** routine looks up the next group entry in the registry that matches the input group name and returns the corresponding UNIX style group structure. The structure is in the following form:

typedef struct {
  sec_rgy_name_t name;
  signed32 gid;
  sec_rgy_member_buf_t members;
}   **sec_rgy_unix_group_t;**

The structure includes the following:

- The name of the group.

- The group's UNIX ID.

- A string containing the names of the group members. This string is limited in size by the size of the **sec_rgy_member_buf_t** type defined in **rgynbase.idl**.

The routine also returns an array of member names, limited in size by the *number_members* parameter. Note that the array contains only the names explicitly specified as members of the group. A principal that was made a member of the group because that group was assigned as the principal's primary group will not appear in the array.

sec_rgy_unix_getgrnam(3sec)

This call is provided in source code form.

Files **/usr/include/dce/rgynbase.idl**
The **idl** file from which **dce/rgybase.h** was derived.

Errors **sec_rgy_no_more_entries**
The end of the list of entries has been reached.

sec_rgy bad_data
The name supplied as input was too long.

error_status_ok
The call was successful.

sec_rgy_server_unavailable
The DCE registry server is unavailable.

Related Information

Functions: **sec_intro(3sec)**.

sec_rgy_unix_getpwnam

Purpose   Returns a UNIX style passwd entry for account matching the specified name

Synopsis   **#include <dce/rgynbase.h>**

void sec_rgy_unix_getpwnam (
sec_rgy_handle_t *context,*
sec_rgy_name_t *name,*
unsigned32 *name_len,*
sec_rgy_cursor_t **item_cursor,*
sec_rgy_unix_passwd_t **passwd_entry,*
error_status_t **status);*

Parameters

Input

context   An opaque handle bound to a registry server. Use **sec_rgy_site_-**
open to acquire a bound handle.

name   A character string (of type **sec_rgy_name_t**) containing the name
of the person, group, or organization whose name entry is desired.

name_len   A 32-bit integer representing the length of the *name* in characters.

Input/Output

item_cursor   An opaque pointer indicating a specific PGO item entry in the
registry database. The **sec_rgy_unix_getpwnam** routine returns the
PGO item indicated by *item_cursor*, and advances the cursor to
point to the next item in the database. When the end of the list of
entries is reached, the routine returns **sec_rgy_no_more_entries**.
Use **sec_rgy_cursor_reset** to refresh the cursor.

Output

passwd_entry   A UNIX style passwd structure returned with information about the
account matching *name*.

status   On successful completion, the routine returns **error_status_ok**.
Otherwise, it returns an error.

Description

The **sec_rgy_unix_getpwnam** routine returns the next UNIX passwd structure that matches the input name. The structure is in the following form:

typedef struct {
    sec_rgy_unix_login_name_t name;
    sec_rgy_unix_passwd_buf_t passwd;
    signed32 uid;
    signed32 gid;
    signed32 oid;
    sec_rgy_unix_gecos_t gecos;
    sec_rgy_pname_t homedir;
    sec_rgy_pname_t shell;
  }   **sec_rgy_unix_passwd_t;**

The structure includes the following:

- The account's login name.

- The account's password.

- The account's UNIX ID.

- The UNIX ID of group and organization associated with the account.

- The account's GECOS information.

- The account's home directory.

- The account's login shell

This call is provided in source code form.

Files

/usr/include/dce/rgynbase.idl
      The **idl** file from which **rgynbase.h** was derived.

Errors

sec_rgy bad_data
      The name supplied as input was too long.

error_status_ok
      The call was successful.

sec_rgy_no_more_entries
      The end of the list of entries has been reached.

Related Information

Functions: **sec_intro(3sec)**.

sec_rgy_unix_getpwuid

Purpose   Returns a UNIX style **passwd** entry for the account matching the specified UID

Synopsis   **#include <dce/rgynbase.h>**

> **void sec_rgy_unix_getpwuid(**
>   **sec_rgy_handle_t** *context,*
>   **signed32** *uid,*
>   **sec_rgy_cursor_t** **item_cursor,*
>   **sec_rgy_unix_passwd_t** **passwd_entry,*
>   **error_status_t** **status);*

Parameters

Input

> *context*   An opaque handle bound to a registry server. Use **sec_rgy_site_-open( )** to acquire a bound handle.
>
> *uid*   A 32-bit integer UNIX ID.

Input/Output

> *item_cursor*   An opaque pointer indicating a specific PGO item entry in the registry database. The **sec_rgy_unix_getpwuid( )** routine returns the PGO item indicated by *item_cursor*, and advances the cursor to point to the next item in the database. When the end of the list of entries is reached, the routine returns **sec_rgy_no_more_entries**. Use **sec_rgy_cursor_reset( )** to refresh the cursor.

Output

> *passwd_entry*   A UNIX style password structure returned with information about the account matching *uid*.
>
> *status*   On successful completion, the routine returns **error_status_ok**. Otherwise, it returns an error.

Description

The **sec_rgy_unix_getpwuid( )** routine looks up the next **passwd** entry in the registry that matches the input UNIX ID and returns the corresponding **sec_rgy_passwd** structure. The structure is in the following form:

typedef struct {
 sec_rgy_unix_login_name_t name;
 sec_rgy_unix_passwd_buf_t passwd;
 signed32 Vuid;
 signed32 Vgid;
 signed32 oid;
 sec_rgy_unix_gecos_t gecos;
 sec_rgy_pname_t homedir;
 sec_rgy_pname_t shell;
}   sec_rgy_unix_passwd_t;

The structure includes the following:

- The account's login name.

- The account's password.

- The account's UNIX ID.

- The UNIX ID of group and organization associated with the account.

- The account's GECOS information.

- The account's home directory.

- The account's login shell

Files

/usr/include/dce/rgynbase.idl
 The **idl** file from which **dce/rgynbase.h** was derived.

This call is provided in source code form.

Errors

sec_rgy_no_more_entries
 The end of the list of entries has been reached.

sec_rgy_server_unavailable
 The DCE registry server is unavailable.

error_status_ok
 The call was successful.

Related Information

Functions: **sec_intro(3sec)**.

sec_rgy_wait_until_consistent

Purpose   Blocks the caller while prior updates are propagated to the registry replicas

Synopsis   **#include <dce/misc.h>**

boolean32 sec_rgy_wait_until_consistent(
     sec_rgy_handle_t *context,*
     error_status_t ***status*);

Parameters

Input

context   The registry server handle associated with the master registry.

Output

status   A pointer to the completion status. On successful completion, *status* is assigned **error_status_ok**. Otherwise, it returns an error.

Description

The **sec_rgy_wait_until_consistent( )** routine blocks callers until all prior updates to the master registry have been propagated to all active registry replicas.

Return Values

The routine returns TRUE when all active replicas have received the prior updates. It returns FALSE if at least one replica did not receive the updates.

Files   **/usr/include/dce/misc.idl**
     The **idl** file from which **dce/misc.h** was derived.

Errors   **sec_rgy_server_unavailable**
     The server for the master registry is not available.

sec_rgy_read_only
> Either the master site is in maintenance mode or the site associated with the handle is a read-only (query) site.

error_status_ok
> The call was successful.

Related Information

Functions: **sec_intro(3sec)**.